Incommensurability, Incomparability, and Practical Reason

Incommensurability, Incomparability, and Practical Reason

Edited by Ruth Chang

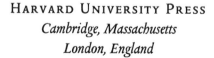

HARVARD UNIVERSITY PRESS
Cambridge, Massachusetts
London, England

Library of Congress Cataloging-in-Publication Data
Incommensurability, incomparability, and practical reason / edited by Ruth Chang.
p. cm.
Includes bibliographical references and index.
ISBN 0-674-44755-7 (cloth)
ISBN 0-674-44756-5 (pbk.)
1. Comparison (Philosophy)   I. Chang, Ruth.
BD236.I53 1997
121'.4—dc21   97-19161

This book has been digitally reprinted.
The content remains identical to that of previous printings.

TO THE MEMORY OF ISAIAH BERLIN

Contents

Acknowledgments

Many people helped in one way or another in the completion of this book. Without the support of Derek Parfit, Joseph Raz, and Bernard Williams, this volume would not exist. I thank them wholeheartedly for their belief that the project was a worthy one. Kit Fine was an endless source of wisdom, encouragement, and good humor. Lindsay Waters of Harvard University Press gave valuable guidance. Glenn Branch efficiently standardized thirteen wildly divergent sets of endnotes and compiled the index. Thanks are also due to Brad Hooker, Lewis Kornhauser, and Seana Shiffrin for helpful suggestions on various matters, to Henry Hardy for learned bibliographical advice, and to Kimberly Steere and Jane Judge Bonassar for unerring patience in helping to put the whole thing together. I also owe a debt of gratitude to Balliol College, Oxford, for providing me with a stimulating environment conducive to the genesis of this volume.

The authors of this volume had the opportunity to exchange their ideas with a group of distinguished economists and psychologists at a conference held at the Château du Baffy in Normandy in April 1994. Thanks go to my co-organizers, John Broome and Maurice Salles, who provided the inspiration and wherewithal for the event. Some of the economists' papers from that conference can be found in *Social Choice and Welfare* 13 (1996).

As originally conceived, the collection was to include an essay by Ronald Dworkin; however, Professor Dworkin published his essay earlier elsewhere, and it therefore could not be published here. Dworkin argues that there can be no successful skepticism about moral, ethical, or aesthetic judgments based on general philosophical considerations rather than on substantive, positive judgments within those domains. His essay appears as "Objectivity and Truth: You'd Better Believe It," *Philosophy and Public Affairs* 25 (1996): 87–139.

Incommensurability, Incomparability, and Practical Reason

1

Introduction

RUTH CHANG

There is a growing interest among moral, political, and legal philosophers in what is called 'the incommensurability of values'. Typically, however, the interest is not in values per se but in bearers of value that are alternatives for choice. How are we to choose between incommensurables? If two alternatives are incommensurable, does it follow that there can be no justified choice between them? What it is for bearers of value to be incommensurable, whether they are, and what significance incommensurability has for practical reason are the main topics of this volume.

Philosophical investigation of 'incommensurability' is as yet in an early stage. Perhaps as a symptom of this, there is even disagreement over what 'incommensurability' means. We can reject one notion straight off as inapplicable for our purposes. This is the idea, spawned by the writings of Thomas Kuhn, that evaluation across different conceptual schemata, ways of life, or cultures is impossible. Incommensurabilists about bearers of value are worried about the possibility of evaluation for us—that is, within a conceptual scheme, way of life, or culture. The Kuhnian notion aside, there are two main ideas that pass under the 'incommensurability' label. One is that incommensurable items cannot be precisely measured by a single 'scale' of units of value. This idea has historical roots. The Pythagoreans first determined as incommensurable the diameter and side of a regular pentagon: the proportional lengths could not be expressed in terms of integers, and thus it was thought that there was no single scale in terms of which their lengths could be measured.[1] Other writers have moved away from the Pythagorean idea and have focused instead on *incomparability*, the idea that items cannot be compared. Joseph Raz, for example, has used 'incommensurability' as synonymous with 'incomparability'.[2]

It is sometimes thought that the first idea entails the second—that if there is no common unit of value in terms of which two items can be measured, they are incomparable.[3] But it is a platitude of economic and measurement theory that the lack of a single scale of units of value does not entail incomparability.

Comparison does not require any single scale of units of value according to which items can be precisely measured; one alternative can be morally better than another without being better by 2.34 units. Comparable items can be ordinally ranked—ranked on a list—and need not be cardinally ranked—precisely ranked by some unit of value. Given that the two ideas are distinct, let us henceforth reserve the term 'incommensurable' for items that cannot be precisely measured by some common scale of units of value and the term 'incomparable' for items that cannot be compared.[4] In our proposed terminology, then, the topics of this volume are incommensurability and incomparability.

Recent discussions of incommensurability have revolved around its putative significance for the valuation of goods,[5] consequentialism and utilitarianism,[6] practical deliberation,[7] akrasia,[8] and even the very subject matter of ethics.[9] In this volume, Cass Sunstein urges that certain items, like pristine beaches, love relationships, and civil rights, cannot be precisely measured by any monetary scale, and so economic approaches to valuation such as cost-benefit analysis are inappropriate for these goods. John Finnis argues that the conditions for commensuration of goods do not hold in the moral realm, and therefore utilitarianism and expected utility theory, which presuppose commensurability among moral options, must fail. Finnis, David Wiggins, and Michael Stocker argue that if there is no common unit of value in terms of which items can be precisely measured, then maximization, which requires an agent to pursue the greatest amount of value, must be rejected. Each thinks that incommensurability points the way to (different) nonmaximizing accounts of practical rationality. Indeed, Stocker thinks that hard on the heels of the recognition of incommensurability comes a 'concrete' conception of value according to which traditional abstract, action-guiding ethics is wrongheaded.

Interesting as these claims are, in this Introduction I am going to set aside the first idea—incommensurability—and focus on the second—incomparability. I do so for two reasons. Despite recent interest in incomparability, philosophical investigation of the notion is almost nonexistent. More importantly, though, incomparability is, I think, ultimately the more significant notion. It is unclear, for example, whether incommensurability has the significance that incommensurabilists attribute to it. The various views usually under attack—cost-benefit valuation, consequentialism, utilitarianism, maximization, and so on—seem to have available to them ways of circumventing the problems that incommensurability poses, for precise measurement of items by a single unit of value does not seem to be essential to any of these views. Comparability, however, is essential. How could things be valued in terms of trade-offs between costs and benefits if costs and benefits are incomparable? How could utility or good consequences or value be maximized if their instances cannot be compared? How could practical reason guide choices at all if alternatives are incomparable? Indeed, the purported significance of incommensurability is less controversial if claimed for incomparability instead.

Although the issues I consider in this Introduction are in part a reflection of the contents of this volume, it is not my intention to provide a systematic survey of the articles which follow. The Introduction has two aims: to provide a general conceptual backdrop to the subject of incomparability and to suggest a focus for future debate. Thus, it should be understood primarily as an attempt to clear some ground rather than to argue for a substantive position. However, with some important distinctions in hand and common confusions banished, two large-scale conclusions emerge. First, there is almost certainly no easy argument for incomparability. Many of the existing arguments are *fatally* flawed, and those that are not either force us to take a stand on some general, controversial position like verificationism or are more plausibly understood as arguments not for incomparability but for a more capacious view of comparability than received wisdom would allow. Second, and following on the first, any argument for incomparability, if it is to succeed, must confront the question of how comparability is to be understood. As I shall suggest, there is more to comparability than meets the eye. The ways in which things *can* be compared is a question that should be settled before the question of whether comparison ever fails is tackled.

 The Introduction is in four parts. The first provides a definition of incomparability that highlights a critical but often overlooked structural feature of comparison. Neglect of this feature, I suggest, is the error behind certain claims of incomparability. The second part examines the significance of incomparability for practical reason. There is good reason to think that the justification of choice, whatever one's substantive view of reasons, depends on the comparability of the alternatives. The third surveys the leading seven types of incomparabilist argument. I argue that none is compelling: four are nonstarters and the remaining three, as so far developed, have other difficulties. In the final part, the phenomenon of 'noncomparability' and, more generally, of formal failures of comparison is introduced. If, as I suggest, the distinction between formal and substantive failures of comparison tracks the scope of practical reason, then practical reason never presents agents with choices between items whose comparison formally fails. A common type of practical predicament often appealed to by incomparabilists is then defused.

If my claims in this Introduction are correct, common arguments for and putative examples of incomparability rest on mistakes. The view that there are incomparable bearers of value is then cast into doubt. My own view, which I do not defend here, is that there is no bearer incomparability. I hope that at the conclusion of this Introduction the reader will be able to see why the denial of incomparability is less implausible than it might at first seem.

I. The Basic Notion

We start with a rough definition of incomparability: two items are incomparable if no positive value relation holds between them. For our purposes, what it is for a relation to be positive can be given an intuitive gloss: in saying that a positive relation holds between two items, one is saying something affirmative about what their relation is. So, for example, the claim that x is 'better than'—or 'less kind than' or 'as cruel as'—y says something affirmative about how x and y relate, while the claim that x is 'not better than'—or 'if kind, not much kinder than' or 'neither crueler than nor kinder than'—does not. Call the former claims relating items by positive value relations 'positive comparisons', or just 'comparisons', and the latter claims 'negative comparisons'. If items are incomparable, nothing affirmative can be said about what value relation holds between them. Negative comparisons may be true of them as may be positive comparisons of each of them to some other item, but there can be no positive comparison of them to one another.

It is almost universally assumed that the logical space of positive value relations for any two items is exhausted by the trichotomy of relations *better than, worse than,* and *equally good.* Call this assumption the *Trichotomy Thesis.* According to this thesis, if one item is neither better nor worse than another and yet the items are not equally good, nothing affirmative can be said about what relation holds between them: they are incomparable. Some philosophers have thought that incomparability is to be defined in these terms. But the Trichotomy Thesis is a substantive thesis that requires defense, and we should be careful not to build it into the intuitive notion of incomparability. Much of rational choice theory can be seen as making just this mistake, taking as definitional of the notion what is in fact substantive.

Several authors in this volume define the notion of incomparability as the failure of the trichotomy to hold, and many implicitly take the Trichotomy Thesis as true, whether definitionally or not. Donald Regan, for instance, provides a tenacious defense of the view that there is no incomparability by arguing that one of the standard trichotomy of relations always holds between two items. In my view, the Trichotomy Thesis is false; there is a fourth positive value relation—'on a par'—that, together with the traditional three, exhausts the logical space of comparability. Parity is, I believe, central to the argument against incomparability. Kindred notions of 'imprecise equality' and 'rough equality' have been suggested by Derek Parfit, James Griffin, and Thomas Hurka.[10] In this volume, James Griffin briefly discusses his notion of 'rough equality', and Regan takes issue with it. We will return to the question of whether there is a fourth relation in the final part of this Introduction. Let us here simply note that our discussion should be understood as leaving open the possibility that there is such a relation.

We know that incomparability involves some failure of comparability, but what sort of failure? A given positive value relation may fail to hold between items determinately (it may be false of them) or indeterminately (it may be neither true nor false of them). It is usually assumed that the failure of comparability is determinate. In this volume, John Broome provides a striking argument for the opposite conclusion: incomparability may be the result of the vagueness of comparative predicates.[11] Since the disagreement is substantive, our definition should be neutral between the two types of failure: two items are incomparable if, for each particular positive value relation, it is not true—that is, false or neither true nor false—that it holds between them.

There is a further, crucial refinement we must make to the definition. Every comparison must proceed in terms of a value. A 'value' is any consideration with respect to which a meaningful evaluative comparison can be made. Call such a consideration the *covering value* of that comparison. Covering values can be oriented toward the good, like generosity and kindness; toward the bad, like dishonor and cruelty; general, like prudence and moral goodness; specific, like tawdriness and pleasingness-to-my-grandmother; intrinsic, like pleasurableness and happiness; instrumental, like efficiency; consequentialist, like pleasurableness of outcome; deontological, like fulfillment of one's obligations; moral, like courage; prudential, like foresight; aesthetic, like beauty; and so on.[12] Most covering values have multiple contributory values—that is, values that contribute to the content of the covering value. The contributory values of philosophical talent include originality, clarity of thought, insightfulness, and so on. How well an item does with respect to a value is its *merit*.

Value relations are either generic or specific. Generic relations, like 'better than', 'as valuable as', and 'worse than', presuppose a covering value. They are strictly three-place; x is better than y with respect to V, where V ranges over values. When V is specified, the generic relation is thereby relativized. Specific value relations, like 'kinder than', 'as cruel as', and 'tawdrier than', have their covering values built in. It is plausible to suppose (as implied by the Trichotomy Thesis) that every specific value relation has a relativized generic equivalent;

'kinder than', for example, is equivalent to 'better than with respect to kindness'. Thus, we can dispense with talk of specific value relations in favor of their relativized generic counterparts. 'Comparison' and 'value relation' shall refer to their generic, positive varieties.

That all comparisons necessarily proceed in terms of a value becomes evident once we attempt to understand a comparative claim that flouts the requirement. A bald claim that philosophy is better than pushpin, for example, cannot be fully understood without reference to some respect in terms of which the claim is made. Philosophy may be better in terms of gaining a kind of understanding or intrinsic worthwhileness but worse in terms of providing relaxation or developing hand-eye coordination. Although the respect in terms of which a comparison is made is not always explicit, some value must always be implicit for there to be any comparison to be understood.

To deny that comparisons must be relative to a value is to assert that there is a sensible notion of comparable simpliciter. But there is no such notion. Consider the nonevaluative relation 'greater than'. This rod may be greater than that one with respect to length or mass or conductivity, but it cannot be greater, period. Just as it makes no sense to say that one thing is simply greater than another, it makes no sense to say that one thing is simply better than another; things can be better only in a respect. This is not to deny that a certain value might somehow be privileged. It might be thought, for example, that what it is for something to be simply better is for it to maximize happiness for the greatest number. Still, the bald claim that something is better than something else must be understood as relativized to some value, privileged or not.[13] So it goes for all value relations. For convenience, I will often omit explicit mention of a covering value, but one should always be understood.

Just as a comparison must be relativized to a covering value, so must its failure. Our definition of incomparability, then, is this: *two items are incomparable with respect to a covering value if, for every positive value relation relativized to that covering value, it is not true that it holds between them.* Those who think the Trichotomy Thesis is true would say that two items are incomparable with respect to a covering value just in case it is not true that the first is better than the second, that it is worse, or that they are equally good with respect to that covering value.

Failure to appreciate the relativization of incomparability to a covering value is responsible for certain mistaken claims of incomparability. These involve items as different as 'apples and oranges' or 'chalk and cheese'. How can the samurai code of honor be compared with the Protestant work ethic? An act of patriotism and one of filial love? A novel and a war film? Once these questions are relativized to a covering value, comparison is no longer elusive: cheese is better

than chalk with respect to goodness as a housewarming gift, and oranges are
better than apples with respect to preventing scurvy.

But perhaps those who cite these examples do not mean to claim that *no*
comparison can be made. Perhaps their claim is only that the *intrinsic* merits of
these items cannot be compared. For example, the samurai code of honor might
be comparable with the Protestant work ethic with respect to some instrumental
value, like 'efficiency in reducing the trade deficit', but there is no covering value
in terms of which their intrinsic merits can be compared. This is what Elizabeth
Anderson has in mind when she says that attempts to compare the genius of a
scientist and the honor of a gentleman must fail.[14] The claim that there is no
covering value in these cases is, however, ambiguous between two claims: (1)
that there is no covering value with respect to which the intrinsic merits of the
items can be compared and (2) that there is such a covering value but the intrinsic merits are incomparable with respect to it. The first is not a claim of incomparability but rather the claim that a certain sort of covering value does not exist.
It is not a claim of incomparability because incomparability must proceed relative to a covering value, and if there is no covering value with respect to which
the intrinsic merits can be compared, then there can be neither comparability nor
incomparability with respect to it. (We shall have more to say about this possibility in the final part.) The second, however, is a claim of incomparability.
'Goodness as a moral code' might be a covering value that pits the intrinsic value
of the code of honor against that of the work ethic. And perhaps the honor
code and work ethic cannot be compared with respect to goodness as a moral
code. But this is not obvious. Indeed, we will see below that providing grounds
for such a claim is no easy task.

II. Significance

We should ask why any of this matters. Why should we care whether there is
any positive value relation that holds between two items with respect to a given
covering value? Although incomparability has, I believe, interesting implications
for certain metaphysical questions about value, here I want to focus on its implications for practical reason and, in particular, for the possibility of justified
choice.

Every choice situation is governed by some value. Call this the *choice value.*
The choice value is, roughly, 'what matters' in the choice situation. In choosing between two philosophers, for example, the choice value might be philosophical talent if the situation involves choosing someone to fill a philosophy
post or sartorial elegance if it involves choosing someone to fill the title of

'Nattiest Philosopher'. The choice value helps to determine what justifies choice in that situation. 'Because one wears polyester and the other does not' may justify choice in the one case but not in the other. This is so whether the justification is objective or subjective.[15]

All choice situations are either comparative or noncomparative. In comparative choice situations, a comparison of the alternatives with respect to an appropriate covering value is necessary to the justification of choice. In noncomparative choice situations, this is not the case. That there are comparative choice situations is intuitively obvious. The clearest cases are ones in which alternatives 'compete' against one another with respect to the covering value. Suppose, for instance, that as the judge of a piano competition, you must award the first-place prize to Anastice or Beatrice. The choice value governing the situation is, say, 'musical talent'. Surely any justification for choosing one over the other must depend on how the two pianists compare with respect to musical talent. If the candidates cannot be compared with respect to musical talent, then any choice between them in that choice situation cannot be justified. Suppose you award the prize to Anastice. Beatrice, convinced that she belongs in Carnegie Hall, demands justification for what she takes to be an outrageous decision. If you attempt to justify your decision on the grounds that Anastice played your favorite Chopin or that she was very becoming in appearance or that she had a better reputation, Beatrice will be rightly incensed, for these considerations provide no grounds at all in the situation as described. What matters to the choice situation, Beatrice reminds you, is musical talent. So you point out that Anastice's phrasing was simply delightful. But that will not do, either; although 'delightfulness of phrasing' is a contributory value of musical talent, what if Beatrice's phrasing was even more delightful? So you point out that Anastice's phrasing was more delightful than Beatrice's. But that too will fail to justify your choice if Beatrice is better with respect to musical talent. For although Anastice may be better with respect to some contributory values, if Beatrice is better overall, there can be no justification for your choice.

Suppose Anastice and Beatrice are incomparable with respect to musical talent. You, as judge, must nevertheless render a decision. We should not be fooled into thinking that the fact that a decision is made—even if it is justified—shows that Anastice and Beatrice were comparable with respect to musical talent all along. For a decision—even a justified one—can be made, but only if the choice situation is reconceived as one in which what matters is not (only) musical talent but, say, delightfulness of phrasing or effort or pleasing the underwriter of the event—Anastice's uncle. This switching of choice values is a common deliberative ploy. We often switch from one choice situation to another when we lack the facts we need to make the relevant comparison. You may, for instance, have to choose between a Hitchcock thriller and a Bach concert for the weekend's entertainment. What matters is pleasurableness, but since you do not know how you will like the Bach Inventions tinkled out on wine glasses, you may shift the choice value to novelty to ease your decision making. The choice situation has changed, and your choice will be justified or not relative to that new choice situation.

Call *comparativism* the view that all choice situations are comparative. Even if a choice situation changes because there is a shift in choice value, the new choice situation will require the comparability of the alternatives with respect to the new choice value. There is, according to comparativism, no avoiding the comparability of alternatives with respect to the choice value if there is to be justified choice. Thus, if comparativism is correct, the significance of incomparability among alternatives is very great indeed. For if alternatives are incomparable, justified choice is precluded, and the role of practical reason in guiding choice is thereby restricted.

The very serious threat to practical reason posed by incomparability if comparativism is correct motivates the search for alternatives to comparativism. Perhaps widespread incomparability and the universal success of practical reason can coexist. We do not have space to give a full accounting of all the possible alternative accounts here, but it is worth mentioning those that appear in this volume.

Some authors argue that although comparisons seem to be required for justified choice in some situations, when those comparisons fail, there are nevertheless noncomparative considerations that can justify choice. So, for example, Elizabeth Anderson thinks that norms of rationality can provide grounds for choice among incomparables.[16] James Griffin maintains that prudence as well as legal or moral consensus may help to shape and extend the moral norms that provide the standards according to which choice between morally incomparable alternatives may be justified.[17] Charles Taylor urges that "articulation" of goods and a keen sense of the "shape" of our lives and the different goods fit within it provide some of the many resources available for justified choice among incomparables. Each of these authors seems to recognize that incomparability poses a threat to justified choice, though not one that their accounts cannot ultimately handle.

Others maintain that comparisons of certain alternatives cannot be required because a comparison does violence to their nature or the norms of rationality governing choice among them. Steven Lukes points out that a monk's choice of celibacy is not justified by a comparison of the alternatives but is instead a "sacrifice" demanded of him. Elizabeth Anderson thinks that some goods have a higher "status" than others and that any comparison of goods of different status is a mistake. Since money and friendship are goods of different status, the choice between them cannot depend on a comparison of their merits. Cass Sunstein holds a similar view about incommensurability; something properly valued in one way cannot be commensurated with something properly valued in another way.

Still others suggest that comparisons of alternatives are never, or rarely, required for justified choice. Michael Stocker presents a view of practical rationality in which comparisons seem to play no part. He argues that choices may be justified if they meet some "absolute"—that is, noncomparative—evaluative standard; a choice of this over that can be justified simply on the ground that this is good—it need not be better than or even comparable with that. David Wiggins thinks that justified choice is determined by "standards of evaluation and normative ends and ideals that is the substantive work of evidential, axiological, moral, and whatever other reflection to determine" and that these standards derive from "lived experience" and an overall practical conception of how to be and how to live.[18] Elijah Millgram thinks that a practical deliberator may ground her choice on things learned incrementally through experience.[19] The suggestion seems to be that specifying the values at stake or applying insight gained through experience need not rely on any comparison of the merits of the given alternatives.

Joseph Raz offers a quasi-existentialist view of justified choice in the face of incomparability. Reasons determine the rational *eligibility* of options, and the "will," that is, "the ability to choose and perform intentional actions," steps in to determine the choice among them. An exercise of the "will" is not an exercise of reason; willing is *just choosing.* Thus, reason provides us with a menu of rationally eligible options, and we are simply to plump among them. Whatever we choose will be justified, however, for the reason that it is sanctioned by rationality. Incomparable options, Raz assumes, are rationally eligible, and therefore justified choice is always possible in the face of incomparability.[20] The comparability of *some* options is required for justified choice since it is through comparison that alternatives are whittled down to the rationally eligible set. Once eligibility is determined, however, comparisons between those alternatives is not necessary—or even possible—for justified choice.

Rather than examine these and other views on their merits, I want to pose two general challenges any alternative to comparativism must meet: a pragmatic *reductio* and a theoretical reduction. Start with the *reductio,* familiar in decision and rational choice theory. On any alternative view, choice between incomparables can be justified; perhaps either alternative is justified or only one of them is. But if choice among incomparables can be justified, practical reason or the "will" could, in principle, justify a series of choices analogous to cyclical preferences with disastrous 'money pump' consequences.

Suppose I am about to enjoy a steaming cup of freshly brewed tea. You intervene, offering your cup of coffee for my tea. Suppose too that the tea and coffee are incomparable with respect to goodness of taste. According to alternative views, choice between incomparables can be justified. Suppose my trading the tea for the coffee may be justified. Just as I am about to sip the coffee, you again intervene, this time offering me a cup of not-quite-so-hot-or-fresh tea. The warm tea is incomparable with the coffee, and again I make what could be a justified trade. I am thus left with a cup of warm tea, but I began with a cup of hot tea, which by my lights is definitely tastier. Through a series of choices sanctioned by practical reason or the "will", I have moved from something I consider better to something I consider worse. Iterated across alternatives and covering values, such a pattern of choice would leave us with lives barely worth living; in this way merit can be 'pumped' from an agent's life. Thus, a pragmatic challenge to those who would oppose comparativism is to provide a well-motivated, non-ad-hoc account of how practical reason prohibits agents from becoming 'merit pumps'.[21]

The more serious challenge to alternatives to comparativism, though, is theoretical. Take any justification of a choice that putatively does not depend on a comparison of the alternatives. Such an account will hold that the reason justifying choice is not a comparison of the alternatives. So, for example, a choice might be justified because it is sanctioned by some norm of rationality or morality, or is eligible, or meets some evaluative standard, or is favored by a deliberative understanding achieved by a keen sense of the shape of one's life or by a specification of the values at stake or by reflection on one's past experiences. There are, of course, other putative noncomparative justifications besides these: a whim for the chosen alternative, a duty to choose it, the fact that the chosen alternative satisfies a desire, that it is what an agent with good character would choose, and so on. We can ask of each of these accounts, 'Is the proffered justification properly understood as a comparison of the alternatives?' Why aren't these candidate justifications of choice properly understood as comparisons of the alternatives with respect to, for instance, 'satisfying the norm', or 'eligibility', or 'expressing my deliberative understanding', or 'gratifying my desire', or 'fulfilling my duty' or 'expressing a virtuous character', and so on? Some justifications that appear to be noncomparisons might turn out to be comparisons after all.

I doubt, however, that all, or even many, of the putatively noncomparative justifications of choice turn out, when properly understood, to be comparisons (though I think an interesting range of them do). A duty to one's family, for instance, when properly understood, is not plausibly a comparison of the alternatives, and yet such a duty can be a justification for choice. The same goes, it seems to me, for each of the views on offer by the authors of this volume. But the comparativist need not give up here, for there is still the question of whether these noncomparisons depend on comparisons of the alternatives, though they are not themselves comparisons.

We are now heading toward very dense territory of which we will have only an aerial glimpse here. At its center is a distinction between the justifying reason for choice and *that in virtue* of which the reason justifies. Every reason has normative force; a justifying reason has the normative force required to justify a choice. For any given justifying reason, we can ask, 'In virtue of what does it have the justifying force that it has?' A reason's justifying force is more or less analogous to a premise's logical force, a cause's causal force, and a motivation's motivational force. Take the inference to 'q' from the premises 'p' and 'if p then q'. The premises logically support the conclusion, but that in virtue of which they support it is the rule of inference, *modus ponens*. The rule is no part of the support for the conclusion but is instead what gives the premises their logical force. Or take the cause of a window's breaking. The ball caused the window to break. The ball has the causal force to break the window in virtue of certain nomological laws that relate things together as cause and effect. These nomological laws are no part of the cause; they are rather that in virtue of which a cause has the causal powers that it has. The same goes for motivational force. As Thomas Nagel has argued, a motivation may motivate in virtue of a disposition to be so motivated, but that disposition need not itself be understood as part of the motivation. It is rather that in virtue of which the motivation motivates.[22] Similarly, I believe, a reason is one thing, its justifying force another. A reason can justify in virtue of something that is no part of the justification but is what gives the reason its justifying force.

Every justifying reason, I wish to claim, has its justifying force in virtue of a comparison of the alternatives. To see why this is so, suppose the opposite. If a choice can be justified without depending on a comparison of the alternatives, then the putative justifying reason will justify the choice no matter what the comparative merits of the alternatives. Suppose that the fact that going out to dinner will be fun can justify my choosing to go out to dinner rather than stay home to grade papers. But can that fact justify the choice if the dinner is only mildly amusing and grading the papers a riot? Or take the choice between two careers. I may be justified in choosing a legal career over a philosophical one because that choice expresses my understanding of what matters in life. But how can that justify my choice if the choosing the philosophical career *better* expresses that understanding?[23] Or take my duty to keep my promises. How can such a duty justify attending, as promised, my friend's wedding if attending, as promised, my uncle's funeral better fulfills that duty? (This, of course, assumes that a duty can be more or less well fulfilled. I believe that the special 'non-weighing' nature of duties can be maintained in the face of the claim that duties can be fulfilled better or worse. But I defer this discussion for another time.) Even the eligibility of an option cannot justify choosing it unless it is true that the option is as good as all the others with respect to eligibility. Of course, in this case, the comparison of equality is entailed by the eligibility, but it is the positive fact of being as rationally sanctioned as all other alternatives that renders the choice of the chosen alternative justified. In general, insofar as what matters to the choice situation is something with respect to which meaningful evaluative comparisons can be made, there can be no justification of choice in that situation unless there is such an evaluative comparison.[24]

The theoretical attack on alternatives to comparativism, then, is two-pronged. Either the justification of a choice is itself, properly understood, a comparison of the alternatives with respect to an appropriate value, or the justification depends on such a comparison. If, as I have suggested, we have good reason to think this is correct, then any putative alternative to comparativism will fail. A comparison of the alternatives is necessary to the justification of choice. The incomparability of alternatives, then, poses an ineliminable threat to practical justification.

III. Incomparabilist Arguments

If two alternatives are incomparable with respect to an appropriate covering value, justified choice between them is precluded. But are alternatives ever incomparable?

In this part, I examine what I take to be the leading arguments for incomparability that exist in the literature. These can be divided into seven types. Each type appeals to one of seven putatively sufficient grounds for incomparability: (1) the 'diversity' of values; (2) the 'bidirectionality' of comparative merits, that is, the condition that one item is better in some contributory respects of the covering value but worse in others; (3) the 'noncalculative' practical deliberation required in some choice situations; (4) constitutive features of certain goods or the norms governing appropriate attitudes toward them; (5) the rational irresolvability of conflicts between items; (6) the multiplicity of legitimate rankings of the alternatives; and (7) the rationality of judging in some choice situations that neither alternative is better than the other and yet a slightly improved version of one is not better than the other. Although arguments of the first four types have currency and influence, I shall argue that they are fatally flawed. The debate about incomparability should, I think, be focused on the last three types of argument. Arguments of the last three types, however, also prove to be not without difficulty. They either rely on controversial general philosophical positions or are better understood as arguments not for incomparability but for the existence of a fourth relation of comparability beyond the traditional trichotomy of 'better than', 'worse than', and 'equally good'. I end by attempting to motivate further the existence of a fourth relation by briefly sketching some of its essential features.

1. Arguments from the Diversity of Values

The most commonly cited ground for incomparability among alternatives is the diversity of values they respectively bear. This diversity is understood in myriad ways. Some understand it as a plurality of ontologically irreducible values.[25] Others understand diverse values to be of different ' types' or the goods that bear them of different 'genres', whether ontologically reducible or not. Nagel, for instance, thinks that values come in six types—obligations, rights, utility, perfectionist ends, private commitments, and self-interest—and that this fragmentation explains the existence of genuine dilemmas between alternatives bearing one type of value and those bearing another type.[26] Joseph Raz claims that some goods, like novels and war movies, cannot be compared because they belong to different "genres".[27] Still others explain the diversity of values in terms of their occupying different "dimensions" or "scales".[28] The underlying idea of diversity arguments is that some items are 'so different' that there is no 'common basis' on which a comparison can proceed. Assuming that incomparability must be relative to a covering value, diversity arguments should be understood as turning on the diversity of the contributory values of the covering value borne. So, for example, Mozart and Michelangelo are incomparable with respect to creativity if the contributory values of creativity borne by Mozart are so different—that is, irreducibly distinct, or of a different type or genre, or occupying a different scale or dimension—from those borne by Michelangelo that comparison is impossible.

Diversity arguments, regardless of their substantive differences, are subject to a compelling objection. The objection turns on what we might call 'nominal-notable' comparisons. Call a bearer 'notable' with respect to a value if it is an exceptionally fine exemplar of that value and 'nominal' if it is an exceptionally poor one. Mozart and Michelangelo, for instance, are notable bearers of creativity and Talentlessi, a very bad painter, a nominal one. Nominal-notable comparisons succeed by definition; notable bearers are always better than nominal ones with respect to the value in terms of which they are respectively nominal or notable. Now suppose that Talentlessi bears the same contributory values of creativity as Michelangelo—only in a nominal way. Both, for example, bear the value of technical skill, but Talentlessi bears it in a markedly nominal way. If Mozart and Michelangelo are incomparable in virtue of the diverse contributory values of creativity they bear, then so too are Mozart and Talentlessi. But we know that Mozart is better than Talentlessi with respect to creativity. If Mozart and Michelangelo are incomparable with respect to creativity, it cannot be for the reason that they bear diverse contributory values. For any two items putatively incomparable in virtue of the diversity of contributory values they respectively bear, it is plausible to suppose that there are notable and nominal bearers of the same values that are *ipso facto* comparable. Therefore, it cannot be the diversity of the values borne *per se* that accounts for bearer incomparability.

Arguments from the diversity of values fail because they are not sufficiently fine-grained to differentiate cases of putative incomparability from ones of certain comparability. To meet the nominal-notable objection, proponents of these arguments must either explain why nominal-notable comparisons are exceptions or give a more nuanced account of diversity that relies not on values borne but on something more specific, like the way in which a value is borne.[29] But the first response will probably be *ad hoc,* and the second, insofar as it no longer relies on the diversity of values *per se,* will amount to a different account of what makes bearers incomparable.

In any case, there is good reason to think that Mozart and Michelangelo are comparable with respect to creativity, given that Mozart and Talentlessi are. We start with the idea that Talentlessi and Michelangelo differ in creativity only in the way they bear creativity; they bear the same contributory values of creativity, but one bears them in a notable way and the other in a nominal way. Consider, now, Talentlessi+, just a bit better than Talentlessi with respect to creativity and bearing exactly the same contributory values, but a bit more notably. This small improvement in creativity surely cannot trigger incomparability; if something is comparable with Talentlessi, it is also comparable with Talentlessi+. Thus we can construct a 'continuum' of painters including Talentlessi and Michelangelo, each bearing the same contributory values of creativity but with increasing notability. No difference in creativity between any contiguous painters can plausibly be grounds for incomparability; if Mozart is comparable with one item on the continuum, he is comparable with all items on the continuum. Therefore, given that Mozart is comparable with Talentlessi, he is comparable with Michelangelo, who differs from Talentlessi only by some notches on the continuum. How can Mozart be incomparable with Michelangelo if Mozart is comparable with something that differs from Michelangelo only by successive increments of notability in the way in which the covering value is borne? The argument has a striking conclusion. Whenever a continuum of the above sort can be constructed and a comparison made between any items on the continuum and some other item, every item on that continuum is comparable with that other item.[30]

A digression here is useful before turning to the other incomparabilist grounds. We have seen that value pluralism does not entail incomparability. It turns out that there is also good reason to think that value monism does not entail comparability. According to monism, all values ultimately reduce to a supervalue. Comparability follows, it is thought, because if there is in the end only one value, evaluative differences between items must always reduce to differences in amount of the supervalue, and quantities of the same thing can always be compared. Thus if monism is correct, complete comparability follows. Many philosophers who assume the soundness of this argument have, as a consequence, thought that incomparability defeats classical forms of utilitarianism. Insofar as utilitarianism is committed to the idea that all goods are a matter of amounts of utility, it is committed to complete comparability.

The inference from monism to comparability, however, is mistaken on two counts. First, monism need not be this crude. As J. S. Mill pointed out long ago, values have qualitative as well as quantitative dimensions. Although pleasure is one value, there is the luxurious, wallowing pleasure of lying in the sun and the intense, sharp pleasure of hearing much-anticipated good news.[31] Thus, there may ultimately be one supervalue, but like all other values, it may have qualitative dimensions that could, in principle, give rise to incomparability among its bearers. Accordingly, there could be sophisticated, monistic forms of utilitarianism that allow for incomparability.[32]

Second, even the crude form of monism does not entail complete bearer comparability, for it is a mistake to assume that all quantities of a single value are comparable. The mistake probably derives from an ambiguity in the phrase 'more valuable'. Something can be 'more *V*', where *V* ranges over values, in an *evaluative* or a *nonevaluative* sense.

The nonevaluative sense is quantitative and is the same sense in which one item can be 'more *N*', where *N* ranges over nonevaluative considerations like length or weight. This stick is longer than that one if it has a greater quantity of length. Items that bear quantities of a value like friendliness are thereby nonevaluatively comparable with respect to that value; the one with a greater quantity of friendliness is more friendly. But a greater quantity of a value is not necessarily equivalent to betterness with respect to that value; a greater quantity of friendship may be worse with respect to friendship—one can be too friendly. Thus, while a greater amount of a value makes something 'more valuable' in a nonevaluative sense, it need not make it 'more valuable' in an evaluative sense.

Some values are essentially quantitative, that is, the nonevaluative sense of 'more *V*' is equivalent to the evaluative sense. A greater quantity of 'the number of lives saved' is always better with respect to the number of lives saved. And a particular increase in the amount of a value may turn out to be better with respect to that value, but there is no general equivalence between evaluative and nonevaluative notions of 'more *V*' for all *V*. Let us refer to the nonevaluative, quantitative notion of 'more *V*' as '*q*more *V*'. Since *q*more is not always better, it is possible that different quantities of a single value are incomparable. Thus value pluralism/monism cuts across bearer incomparability/comparability.

2. *Arguments from 'Bidirectionality'*

A common thought among incomparabilists is that if one item is better in some respects of the covering value but worse in others, the items must be incomparable with respect to the covering value. Commuting to work by car is more relaxing than going by train in that it is more reliable, but going by train is more relaxing in that one need not worry about negotiating freeway traffic.

'Bidirectionality', however, cannot be grounds for bearer incomparability. Suppose that, because the tracks are rickety and the switches rusty, the arrival and departure times of the trains are thoroughly unreliable. While it is true that commuting by train is more relaxing in one respect—one need not worry about negotiating freeway traffic—and less relaxing in another—the train is very unreliable—it is clearly the less relaxing option. In general, bidirectionality cannot be a ground for incomparability since there are nominal-notable comparisons in which the nominal bearer is better than the notable one in some respect but worse in another.

3. *Arguments from Calculation*

Confusion over the locution ' more valuable' may be responsible for another set of incomparabilist arguments. According to these, the fact that practical deliberation is not always a matter of 'calculation'—that is, adding and subtracting quantities of a unit of value—gives us grounds for thinking that items are incomparable. Arguments from calculation have the following form: (1) comparison is simply a matter of adding and subtracting quantities of a unit of value; (2) if comparison is quantitative in this way, then proper deliberation about which to choose must take the form of 'calculation', 'balancing', 'weighing', or 'trading off'; (3) in some situations, proper deliberation cannot take this form; (4) therefore, some items are incomparable. These arguments confuse comparability with commensurability.

In their contributions to this volume, Elizabeth Anderson and Steven Lukes offer arguments of this type. Anderson argues that those who believe that rational choice depends on comparisons of the alternatives must believe that "the sole practical role of the concept of value is to assign *weights* to goods [and] . . . that all values are scalar" (emphasis original). To ask whether a value is "scalar" is to ask "whether it is a magnitude, whether various mathematical relations and operations apply to it." Moreover "[d]eterminations of weight are continuous, require a common unit of measurement for the goods being compared, and place those goods on the same plane." But, she argues persuasively, intrinsic values are not scalar and yield the assignment of a "status", not a "weight", to goods. So, for example, she thinks that a friendship and the life of one's mother are intrinsic goods with different status, and therefore cannot be compared; the choice between them must proceed instead on principles of obligation.

Steven Lukes also seems to assume a similar view of comparability. He confronts the issue of comparability and calculability squarely in an endnote: "It may be claimed that comparison need not involve calculation. But I find this claim hard to accept for normal cases. To the extent that it is claimed that if X is better than Y, there is some answer, however imprecise, to the question 'how much better?' I assume that comparison implies calculation."[33] Like Anderson, Lukes seems to think that comparison can proceed only in terms of a common quantitative unit of value. According to Lukes, 'sacred' goods cannot be assessed by calculation. Since comparison entails calculability, if goods cannot be assessed by calculation, they must be incomparable. Lukes concludes that the sacred is incomparable with the secular.

We have already seen that comparison is not a matter of qmore of some value; *a fortiori*, it is not a matter of quantities of some *unit* of the value. Once we recognize that the evaluative sense of 'more *V*' is not in general equivalent to the quantitative sense, we have no reason to think that comparison is a matter of arithmetic operations on amounts of value. Put another way, an answer to Luke's quantitative question, 'How much better?', is not required by comparison. Perhaps the questions 'In what way better?' or 'To what extent better?' are, but the answers to these questions need not be quantitative. Although there is no general equivalence between betterness with respect to a value and a greater quantity of it, there are some values for which the greater the quantity of units, the better with respect to the value. For instance, the greater quantity of the number of lives saved, the better something is with respect to number of lives saved, and an option saving four lives is twice as good as an option saving two, with respect to number of lives saved. But in these cases, when comparison *is* a matter of adding and subtracting quantities of a value, deliberation *is* properly calculative in form. If confronted with a choice in which what matters is number of lives saved, surely the right way to deliberate, assuming deliberation is appropriate, is to calculate which alternative saves the greater number of lives.

This type of incomparabilist argument misconceives comparability as presupposing that value is scalar and, thus, that deliberation is calculative. Comparability does not require that comparison be a matter of quantities of a value, let alone quantities of some unit of a value. To think that comparability requires a single quantitative unit of value according to which items can be measured is to mistake commensurability with comparability.

4. Arguments from Constitution or Norms

A related line of argument locates grounds for incomparability in either constitutive features of certain goods or the norms determining the attitudes appropriate toward them. Joseph Raz, for example, argues that it is a conceptual truth that friends judge that friendships are incomparable with cash. Judging that they are incomparable is part of what it is to be a friend. There is no irrationality, however, in judging that friendships and money are comparable; making such a judgment shows only that one is incapable of being a friend. Thus, the incomparability of friendships and money is a constitutive feature of friendship.

This is a curious argument in several ways.[34] It derives a supposed truth about the incomparability of items from a claim that one must judge that they are—on pain not of being irrational but of being incapable of realizing a good. Moreover, the conclusion that items are incomparable is relativized to an agent's capacity to realize certain goods. So friendships and money may be incomparable for you but comparable for me.

It is hard to believe, however, that as a conceptual matter, one's capacity for being a friend depends on judging that friendships are incomparable with money. Suppose I am faced with a choice between a friendship and a dollar. If I judge that the friendship is worth more than a dollar, have I thereby lost all of my friends? Even assuming that this judgment renders me unfit for friendship, a judgment of incomparability in the context of choosing does not imply the same judgment detached from a practical context. It might, for instance, be a constitutive obligation owed to one's friends that when confronted with a choice between a friendship and a sum of cash, one judge that they are incomparable. This judgment, made with an eye toward deciding what to do, is, however, consistent with the recognition that there is a different theoretical judgment about whether they are incomparable—regardless of one's capacity to realize certain goods or special obligations to others. How one answers the question, 'Are they comparable?' when confronted with the choice may be very different from how one answers the question in philosophical discussion. I take it that it is the theoretical judgment—a judgment true 'for' everyone—that the incomparabilist needs to establish.

Of course, it might be insisted by way of reply that the judgment constitutive of friendship is the theoretical one. Taking the philosophical position that friendships and money are incomparable is constitutive of being a friend. This is highly implausible, but let us grant the claim for the sake of argument. There is still the question of whether the theoretical claim of incomparability is true. To see that there is this further question, consider an analogy from Moore. It is conceptually impossible for one to believe that one falsely believes, but there nevertheless is a real question as to whether one does falsely believe; it may be true that one does. Similarly, it may be conceptually impossible for one to be a friend and to judge—theoretically or practically—that friendships and money are comparable, but there is nevertheless a real question as to whether they are, and it may be true they are.

This distinction between practical or theoretical evaluative judgments on the one hand and what is really true on the other loses its bite if one thinks, as do pragmatists like Elizabeth Anderson, that value is a construction of practical reason. According to Anderson, norms governing the appropriate attitudes toward goods like friendship give us no good reason to compare friendships and money, and the lack of any good practical reason is all there is to the fact that they are incomparable.[35] The pragmatist argument is not without difficulty, however. It cannot be denied that there are norms governing appropriate attitudes toward friendships. There does seem to be a norm, for example, against being prepared to sell one's friends for the right price. But closer examination of the norms governing attitudes toward goods like friendships shows that, far from giving us reason to think that items are incomparable, such norms give us reason to think just the opposite. For the norms entail (or at the very least are compatible with) an asymmetry in merit while incomparability entails that there is no such asymmetry.

Note that friendship is largely an intrinsic good and money is largely instrumental. The most persuasive examples the pragmatist cites have this feature. Norms governing attitudes appropriate toward certain intrinsic goods seem to block comparison with certain instrumental goods because these norms have as part of their content the thought that the comparison somehow sullies the intrinsic good, but not vice versa. Thus, these norms depend on the judgment that the intrinsic good is, in some sense, more valuable or of a higher status than the instrumental good—that the one is, we might say, 'emphatically' better than the other.[36] That is why it seems odd to insist that someone with an appropriate attitude toward friendship must refuse to judge that a friendship is better than a dollar. How can making that judgment display an inappropriate attitude toward friendship? The norms governing appropriate attitudes toward friendship entail not that there is no good reason to compare friendships and money but rather that there is good reason to think that friendships are worth more. Incomparability, however, entails the opposite: if two items are incomparable, neither is better than the other. Therefore, norms of friendship cannot determine the incomparability of friendships and money since they are inconsistent with it.[37]

None of the above arguments is convincing. Any attempt to develop these lines of argument, however interesting they are in their own right, will not yield a successful argument for incomparability. Each makes a fundamental error: diversity and bidirectionality arguments run afoul of nominal-notable comparisons; calculation arguments wrongly presuppose that comparison must be cardinal; constitution and norm arguments misunderstand emphatic betterness as incomparability. I now want to turn to arguments that I think hold greater promise.

5. Arguments from the Rational Irresolvability of Conflict

An incomparabilist argument often appealed to but left unexplained holds that rationally irresolvable conflict between alternatives is sufficient for their incomparability. A 'rational resolution' of conflict might be understood as the determination of what comparative relation holds between them.[38] The argument then becomes: If we cannot in principle know how two items compare, then they are incomparable. Such an argument, however, presupposes verificationism, which is, to say the least, highly dubious as a general account of truth. Even if verificationism is correct, there is the problem of how we can know we are not in principle capable of knowing how two items compare. If the argument is to get us to the conclusion that there are incomparable items, it will have to tell us when we cannot in principle know how items compare. This is a notoriously difficult problem,

In any case, the argument may not yield incomparability. For if it presupposes that a conflict cannot be rationally resolved unless one alternative is better than the other or the two are equally good, then it presupposes the substantive Trichotomy Thesis, which requires defense. Perhaps the alternatives are related by a fourth relation beyond the traditional trichotomy. If, on the other hand, it understands rational resolvability to encompass every possible value relation, then irresolvability does force us to conclude that the items are incomparable. But in this case, the plausibility of judging that conflicts are rationally irresolvable is greatly diminished. For we now have the possibility that the items are comparable by a fourth relation. Thus, it is far from clear that the argument gives us grounds for concluding that there is incomparability.

6. Arguments from Multiple Rankings

Perhaps items are incomparable if there are multiple legitimate rankings of them and none is privileged. Take, for example, a comparison between Eunice and Janice with respect to philosophical talent. There are multiple contributory values of philosophical talent: originality, insightfulness, clarity of thought, and so on. But perhaps there is no single correct way to 'weigh' these aspects of philosophical talent; each contributory value contributes to the covering value in multiple, alternative ways. Put differently, there are different ways we can 'sharpen' our understanding of the covering value. On one sharpening, for example, originality may be extremely important, insightfulness rather important, clarity of thought relatively unimportant. On another sharpening, something different may be true. Different sharpenings may yield different comparisons. On one sharpening, Eunice may be better than Janice. On another sharpening, she might be worse. On yet another, the two might be equally good. Each of these comparisons of Eunice and Janice is legitimate since each sharpening is. Since there is no one correct comparison of Eunice and Janice, they must, the argument goes, be incomparable. Arguments from multiple rankings are, I think, most powerfully understood as arguments from the vagueness of covering value concepts. Philosophical talent is a vague concept, and so there are multiple ways in which it can be sharpened. John Broome's essay in this volume provides an important discussion of this type of argument.[39]

But this is peculiar as an argument for *incomparability*. It holds that incomparability obtains when there are conflicting comparisons, not when there are no comparisons to be found. Why should we think that Eunice and Janice are incomparable with respect to philosophical talent just because there are multiple legitimate ways to compare them?

To see why the thought is unwarranted, consider Eunice and Eunice*. These philosophers differ only in that Eunice* is slightly more technically proficient and slightly less clear in expression than Eunice. On some sharpenings—those in which technical proficiency makes a significant contribution to philosophical talent—Eunice* will be better than Eunice. On other sharpenings, Eunice* will be worse than Eunice. On all others, they will be equally good. Thus, there are multiple legitimate rankings of these philosophers. But clearly Eunice and Eunice* are not incomparable with respect to philosophical talent. How could two things so nearly equal in merit be incomparable? Therefore, if Eunice and Eunice* are not incomparable on the grounds that they can be multiply ranked, then neither are Eunice and Janice on those grounds.

Arguments from multiple rankings do not establish that items are incomparable. They do, however, give us reason to think that none of the trichotomy of better than, worse than, and equally good holds between such items. Since there is no privileged sharpening, there are no grounds for thinking that any particular one of the trichotomy holds. But this is puzzling. How can a reason to think that the trichotomy fails to hold not be a reason to think that the items are incomparable? The puzzle disappears once we recognize the possibility of a fourth value relation. If Eunice and Janice are related by a fourth relation, they are not incomparable and yet not related by one of the traditional trichotomy. Of course, the puzzle might be solved in another way. It might be thought, for instance, that some comparisons are vague. In any case, arguments from multiple rankings do not establish incomparability; instead, they give us good reason to believe that there is more to comparability than one might think.

7. *Arguments from Small Improvements*

The final type of incomparabilist argument is, I think, the most powerful. It has as its ground the putative rationality of judging that neither of two items is better than the other and yet an improvement in one of them does not make it better than the other. Incomparabilists who have employed arguments of this type include Joseph Raz, Walter Sinnott-Armstrong, and Ronald de Sousa.[41]

Consider the following example modified from Raz.[42] Suppose we rationally judge that a particular career as a clarinetist is neither better nor worse than a particular career as a lawyer, say, with respect to goodness of careers. (Fill in whatever detail makes the judgment most plausible.) We can improve the clarinetist career a little with respect to goodness of careers, perhaps by increasing the salary by ten dollars. Are we thereby rationally compelled to judge that the improved music career is better than the legal one? It seems rational to resist this conclusion. If it is rational, then the original careers cannot be equally good, since if they were, a small improvement in one must make it better than the other. Therefore they must be incomparable. In general, if (1) *A* is neither better nor worse than *B*, (2) *A*+ is better than *A*, and (3) *A*+ is not better than *B*, then (4) *A* and *B* are incomparable. A small improvement in one of two items, neither of which is better than the other, does not always warrant the conclusion that the improved item is better. Where it does not, the argument goes, the two original items are incomparable.

Donald Regan has presented an epistemic objection to this argument that looks fatal. Regan is what we might call a 'strict trichotomist', that is, someone who believes that between any two items one of 'better than', 'worse than', and 'equally good' holds.[43] In short, he argues that there is no warrant for premise 1 when there is warrant for premises 2 and 3. Note that the sorts of cases in which the pattern of judgment 1 through 3 seems rational involve very different items and a complex covering value. Judgments about comparative merit in these cases are hard to get right. Thus, the objection goes, we are not justified in judging, for example, that the clarinetist career is neither better nor worse than the legal one with respect to goodness of careers; such a case is inherently too difficult for us justifiably to rule out the 'better than' and 'worse than' relations (although of course *some* clarinetist careers will clearly be better while others will clearly be worse). In these cases it is rational to judge only that we are *uncertain* as to which, if any, value relation holds between them. And if our judgment that neither career is better is unwarranted, the conclusion that they are incomparable does not follow.

It does, however, seem in the abstract perfectly rational to make judgments 1 through 3. It seems possible, for instance, that if God put all comparable pairs of careers (say, with respect to goodness as a career) in a black box, there would be at least one pair for which judgments 1 through 3 would be true. One might, for instance, think that values are lumpy or imprecise so that a small improvement in an item that is neither better nor worse than another does not thereby make it better. If lumpy or imprecise value is a conceptual possibility, the strict trichotomist must allow that there *could* be some warrant for judgments 1 through 3.

The phenomenology in particular cases also lends support to the idea that judgments 1 through 3 may be rational. Suppose you are a member of a philosophy appointments committee whose task is to compare Eunice, a metaphysician, and Janice, a moral philosopher, with respect to philosophical talent. You and your colleagues have agreed that the candidate with the greater philosophical talent will be offered the vacant chair in your department. Imagine that, in conjunction with your fellow committee members, you have researched both candidates thoroughly, discussed and examined at great length their written work, canvassed considered opinions from across the country, evaluated letters of recommendation, and so forth. It is possible surely that after careful, cool-headed deliberation you, and people whose judgment you respect, rationally conclude that Janice is not more philosophically talented than Eunice and that Eunice is not more philosophically talented than Janice. The judgment made is not one of uncertainty; it is not that you do not know which is better. Rather, the care and length of deliberation and the authority of expert opinion provide the positive evidence needed rationally to conclude that neither is better. At the very least, the judgment that neither is better has some warrant. And yet it is plausible in such a case to think that a small improvement in one of the candidates will not decide the case.

The strict trichotomist must, by way of response, simply dig in his heels and insist that the phenomenology is misleading; it may seem rational to judge that Eunice is neither better nor worse than Janice, but in fact she is either better or worse. Perhaps a fact about her has been overlooked or underappreciated, or, less plausibly, where the evaluative facts look indeterminate, there is really a truth of the matter. The strict trichotomist commits us to an error theory about our judgments. But the phenomenology is in tension with the theory; the greater occurrence of such judgments and the more widespread the thought that they are rational, the less reason there is to think that the judgments are in error.[44] And it cannot be denied that the phenomenology is very common. Moreover, the stronger the putative modality by which one of the trichotomy of relations holds, the less plausible it is that we make such an error. It is hard to believe, for instance, that we overlook a *conceptual* necessity. If, on the other hand, the trichotomy holds by a weaker modality, the failure of the trichotomy to hold is conceptually possible. Why, then, should the strict trichotomist be so certain that there are no such cases?

Although the epistemic objection is not decisive, we have other grounds for thinking that small improvement arguments fail. Recall our argument concerning Eunice and Eunice*. Eunice* differs from Eunice only by being a bit more technically proficient and a bit less clear as a writer. Now take Eunice+, just a touch less philosophically talented than Eunice* but a touch more philosophically talented than Eunice. Neither Eunice nor Eunice* is better than one another. But Eunice+ is a bit better than Eunice. Does it follow that Eunice+ is better than Eunice*? It seems perfectly rational to deny that it follows, yet it is highly implausible to think that Eunice* and Eunice are incomparable, for they are very nearly equally good. How could they be incomparable? Therefore, if the small improvement arguments fail to show that Eunice and Eunice* are incomparable, they fail to show that Eunice and Janice are.

In these cases, I believe, the alternatives are on a par. If items are neither better nor worse than one another, and yet a small improvement in one does not make it better than the other, the items are on a par. We can take as true the premises of small improvement arguments but deny that incomparability follows. In short, the Trichotomy Thesis, crucial to the incomparabilist's conclusion, is false. Small improvement arguments give us reason to think not that there is incomparability, but rather that there is a fourth relation of comparability.[45]

What is this fourth relation? Let me give a brief intuitive sketch of what I believe are its essential features. The core idea of parity can be approached by focusing on the idea of an *evaluative difference* with respect to a covering value. Where there *is* some evaluative difference between items, that difference is (1) *zero* or *nonzero,* and (2) *biased* or *unbiased.* A difference is zero if it does not have extent. A difference is biased if it favors one item and, correspondingly, disfavors the other. A zero difference, then, must be unbiased. The traditional trichotomy of value relations can be explained in these terms. If a difference is nonzero and biased, one of the items is better than the other. If it is biased in favor of x and against y, x is better than y. And if the difference is very great, then x is very much better than y. If instead, a difference is zero and therefore unbiased, the items are equally good.

If we take the idea of evaluative differences as explanatory of value relations, the question naturally arises, Why should we think nonzero, biased differences (better than and worse than) and zero (unbiased) differences (equally good) are the only kind of differences there are? In particular, why should we rule out the possibility of nonzero, *unbiased* differences?

The notion of a nonzero, unbiased difference is familiar. We might want to know the unbiased difference in the time it takes to get to London by two different routes. Is the difference between going via Oxford and going via Cambridge greater than an hour? Or we might want to know the nonzero, unbiased difference in length between two novels or in price between two kitchen appliances or in mass between two heavenly bodies. In mathematics, the unbiased— 'absolute'—difference between 3 and 5, and 5 and 3, is 2. Of course, these examples of unbiased differences correlate with an underlying biased difference. I want to suggest that in the evaluative realm there can be unbiased differences without there being underlying biased differences. If we analogize evaluative differences between items to distances between points, an unbiased evaluative difference between two items is like the absolute distance between two points. The absolute distance between London and Glasgow is 345 air miles—not 345 *northerly* air miles. Like biased differences, unbiased differences can be lesser or greater. The unbiased difference with respect to philosophical talent of Eunice and Janice may be greater than the unbiased difference between Eunice and

Eunice*. Items that differ evaluatively but in an unbiased way cannot be incomparable, for if two items are incomparable, there is no evaluative difference—zero or nonzero—between them. There may be differences with respect to contributory values but no difference with respect to the covering value. *A fortiori,* incomparable items cannot differ by more or less with respect to the covering value.

The distinction between biased and unbiased differences is nicely captured by modifying a model of incomparability proposed by Adam Morton.[46] Imagine four points configured so that if we connected them we would have the shape of a diamond. Call the point at the top A, the point at the bottom C, and the points horizontally across from one another B_1 and B_2. A, connected to and above C, is better than C, and C is worse than A. Similarly, A is better than B_1 and B_2, and C is worse than them. How far apart two connected items are from one another on the vertical axis *may*, though it need not, reflect the extent to which one item is better than another. B_1 and B_2, however, are unconnected, and the distance between them is therefore irrelevant. Although they can each be compared with A and C, they cannot be compared with one another.

Now, departing from Morton's model, we draw a horizontal line connecting B_1 and B_2. The distance between B_1 and B_2 is reflective of the difference between them, just as the distance between A and B_1 is reflective of the extent to which A is better. B_1 and B_2 are connected, and thus comparable with one another, but their difference is measured on the horizontal, not vertical, axis. Differences measured on the vertical axis are biased, differences measured on the horizontal axis are unbiased. B_1 and B_2 are not incomparable, they are not equally good, since the difference between equally good items is not nonzero to begin with, and one is not better than the other, since their difference is not measured along the vertical axis. Any two points connected on a horizontal axis are related by a fourth value relation.

If the evaluative difference between two items is nonzero and unbiased, then the items are *on a par*. I cannot give a full defense of parity here, but its possibility, as described, is, I hope, intuitive and suggestive.

IV. Noncomparability and Covering Values

In the first part I claimed that incomparability must proceed with respect to a covering value; unless there is some value stated or implied, no comparison can be understood. But the covering value requirement also requires that the relevant value 'cover' the items at stake. 'Gustatory pleasure' does not cover chalk and cheddar, but it does cover cheesecake and cheddar. In this part, I argue that the failure of a putative covering value to cover gives rise not to incomparability but to a different phenomenon: *noncomparability*. Noncomparability is distinct from incomparability in that it is a formal failure of comparison, while incomparability is a substantive failure.

We start with the idea that every predicate has a domain of application. Since comparability is always relative to a covering value, we can take the third place of the argument as fixed and focus on two-place predicates like 'comparable with respect to beauty/prudence/moral goodness, etc.' For each two-place comparability predicate, there is a domain of pairs of items to which the predicate can apply.

The distinction between comparability and incomparability on the one hand and noncomparability on the other can be regarded as an instance of the distinction between the applicability and nonapplicability of a predicate. Two items are comparable or incomparable if the pair belongs to the domain of application of the comparability predicate; they are noncomparable if it does not. A pair of items, it is plausible to suppose, falls within the domain of a comparability predicate if both members of the pair belong to the domain of the associated covering value predicate. Take, for instance, the comparability predicate, 'comparable with respect to aural beauty'. The pair <fried eggs, the number nine> does not belong within the domain of the comparability predicate because fried eggs and the number nine do not belong within the domain of 'aurally beautiful'. Similarly, the pair falls outside the domain of application of the incomparability predicate. We shall say that the value of aural beauty does not 'cover' fried eggs.

Although I shall take the distinction between applicability and nonapplicability of a predicate for granted, two points of clarification are in order. First, nonapplicability may derive from either essential or contingent features of the item. We know, for example, that the number nine, in virtue of being an abstract object, cannot be aurally beautiful. But there are also contingent features of objects in virtue of which application is ruled out; Michelangelo, who never happened to give a musical performance in his life, is not within the domain of 'success in musical performance'. (Of course, some contingent features do not rule out application but only make the application false; an ugly building, contingently ugly, falls within the domain of 'beautiful', though it is false that it is.) Second, it is plausible to suppose that if items belong to the domain of application, then, as a rule, the predicate will be true or false of the items, while if they do not belong—since it is natural to think truth and falsity presuppose application—there will be indeterminacy in truth value. I say that there will be truth or falsity where there is application 'as a rule' since vagueness in the predicate (or in the value to which it refers) may give rise to indeterminacy in truth value even though the predicate applies. ('Phil Collins is bald' may be neither true nor false, but Phil Collins falls within the domain of 'bald'.) And there may be other sources of indeterminacy in truth value where there is application.

We can thus distinguish *formal* from *substantive* failures of comparability. The failure is formal if some condition necessary for both the possibility of comparability and the possibility of incomparability fails to hold. The formal condition on which we have focused is that there be a covering value with respect to which the comparison could proceed. We have already seen one way in which this formal requirement might not be met: if no value is stated or implied. We now see another way in which there can fail to be a covering value: if the value stated or implied does not cover the items. In both cases, we cannot understand what is being said. Without some value with respect to which the comparison proceeds, no comparison can be understood. And unless the comparability or incomparability predicate applies to the items at stake, we cannot understand that anything is being said about them. A substantive failure of comparability, in contrast, presupposes that the conditions for the possibility of comparability and of incomparability hold but maintains, as a matter of substance, that the items cannot be compared with respect to the covering value.

The requirement that the putative covering value cover the items is, I suspect, what incomparabilists have in mind when they insist that comparison can succeed only if there is some 'common basis' for comparison. The covering value predicate must apply to the items at stake; if the items are 'so different' that the relevant value does not cover them, they cannot be compared. But this failure of a value to cover is formal, and so it cannot entail incomparability. Noncomparability is neutral between comparability and incomparability.

This distinction between formal and substantive failures of comparability is basic to the scope of practical reason. Practical reason never confronts agents with comparisons that could formally fail. It is evident that practical reason does not require us to compare noncomparables; as rational agents, we will never be confronted, for example, with a choice between french toast and the city of Chicago for breakfast or between a lamp and a window for prime minister. Indeed, no choice could ever have as its justification or its justifying force a comparison of the alternatives with respect to a value that does not cover them. Noncomparability, for this reason, cannot threaten practical reason, but incomparability, as we have seen, can.

That practical reason never requires agents to compare noncomparables provides a response to two possible objections to our account of noncomparability. First, there are those who deny the distinction between applicability and nonapplicability; every predicate applies to every item (but may apply falsely), and, thus, there will be no room for noncomparability as we have described it. Second, assuming there is nonapplicability, it might be denied that both items need be in the domain of the covering value predicate in order for there to be either comparability or incomparability; french toast might be better than Chicago with respect to gustatory value, or perhaps the two are incomparable. To both objections we can make the same response. Even if there is never a failure of applicability, we would still want to make a distinction between cases that practical reason might present to us and ones beyond its scope. So we have an equivalent distinction, not made in terms of applicability and nonapplicability. Similarly, even if, assuming now there is nonapplication, only one item need be in the domain of the covering value predicate for there to be either comparability or incomparability, the fact that none of those cases ever arises in practical deliberation is worth marking in some way. Given each denial, we nevertheless have reason to make the distinction we have between noncomparability and incomparability.

Practical reason never asks us to compare where there is noncomparability. But what of the other way in which the covering value requirement can fail? Does practical reason ever require us to compare items where there is no value stated or implied in terms of which the comparison can proceed? There are two cases here. The straightforward case is the largely theoretical one in which there is no restriction on the content of the covering value; any value, so long as it covers the items, will satisfy the requirement that there be some value. But there is another more complicated case. A choice situation will put restrictions on the content of the covering value. If we are comparing philosophers for a job, for instance, intelligence, insightfulness, clarity of thought, and so on will be relevant, while sartorial elegance will be irrelevant. In some choice situations, what is relevant to choice are intrinsic values; in other situations, it is instrumental values; in still others, it is the values of utility and of duty. In a given choice situation, we are not looking to make any comparison whatever, but a comparison of the alternatives with respect to a value that reflects what matters in the choice situation.

Sometimes, however, it seems that there is no such covering value. Suppose we know that both the enjoyment to be gained and the duty owed to others are relevant to a choice. There seems to be no value in terms of which the merits of alternatives with respect to both of those values can be compared—no value with respect to which we can say that, given enjoyment and duty, one of the alternatives is better 'overall'. Thus, it seems that practical reason sometimes asks us to compare alternatives where there is no covering value, and comparison must fail on formal grounds. The claim that practical reason tracks the distinction between formal and substantive failures of comparability would then be mistaken.

We have already seen why the lack of a covering value with respect to which the relevant merits of alternatives can be compared cannot give rise to incomparability. If there is no covering value with respect to which the relevant merits of the alternatives can be compared, there can be neither comparability nor incomparability with respect to it. But there is another way in which we can defuse the incomparabilist intuition: by showing that practical reason never confronts us with such cases.

Consider, as a typical example, the following simplified case. Suppose you must decide between two ways of spending your Christmas bonus: either donate the money to feed starving children in a faraway land or invest the funds as a nest egg for your retirement. The donation option has great moral merit, and the nest egg option has great prudential merit. Perhaps, as well, the donation option has nominal prudential merit and the investment option nominal moral merit. Practical reason seems to require an answer to the question, 'Given that the values relevant to choice are morality and prudence, which alternative is better overall?' We can say which is better with respect to morality and which is better with respect to prudence,[47] but there does not seem to be any way to say which is better with respect to both morality and prudence. Put another way, there seems to be no covering value that has both moral and prudential value as parts. And yet it seems that practical reason might require us to compare with respect to this nonexistent value.

The response to the challenge has two steps. First, there is often reason to think that, despite appearances, there is such a covering value. And second, in cases where there is no such covering value, it is plausible to think that the choice situation has been misconceived; practical reason requires not *that* comparison but a different one—one that is not, as a formal matter, guaranteed to fail.

What reason might there be for thinking that there is an appropriate covering value in the present case? One suggestion might be that there are always very general considerations like 'what there is most reason to do, all things considered' or 'betterness, all things considered', in terms of which a comparison of any two alternatives can proceed. Such considerations, however, have no content apart from that given to them by the choice situations in which they figure. They are *schematic*. A schematic consideration, like 'whether there is most reason to do, all things considered' amounts to intrinsic moral values in some cases, instrumental aesthetic values in others, and consequentialist economic values in still others. Schematic considerations cover the same ground as what Bernard Williams has called 'the deliberative ought'.[48] They are placeholders for any value whatever. Since they are mere placeholders, they are not themselves values, for it is only in virtue of the values they stand for that there is any meaningful evaluative comparison with respect to them. We are left with the same question with which we began: Is there a covering value with respect to which the moral and prudential merits of alternatives can be compared?

There is good reason to suppose there is such a covering value. Consider the following case. You can either save yourself a small inconvenience, or you can save a remote stranger severe physical and emotional trauma. Suppose that the one act bears only nominal prudential (and perhaps nominal moral) value, while the other bears notable moral value (and perhaps nominal prudential value). We can say more than that the one act is better morally and the other is better prudentially. We can also say that, with respect to both prudential and moral value, the latter act is better: given *both* values, saving the stranger is better *overall*. In general, a notable moral act is better with respect to both morality and prudence than a nominal prudential one. There must therefore be a covering value in terms of which comparisons of moral and prudential merits proceed, one that has both moral and prudential values as components. We know it exists because we know something about its structure: certain moral merits are more important than certain prudential ones. We cannot make a judgment about the relative importance of these considerations without there being some value, however indefinite, in terms of which the judgment proceeds. In general, nominal-notable comparisons help us to find covering values where they seem elusive.

What makes recognition that there is a covering value difficult in these cases is that, unlike other values, these values are typically *nameless*. (Put differently, the only names for such values are the names of schematic considerations; as placeholders for any value, their names provide alternative names for every value.) It is through the 'nominal-notable test' that we can see there are such values. Some varieties of intuitionism and specificationism might be understood as devoted to determining the contours of nameless values. And talk of 'what is really important', 'self-ideals', 'integral human fulfillment', and the like by Charles Taylor, Elizabeth Anderson, John Finnis, James Griffin, David Wiggins, and others, might be illuminatingly understood as attempts to work out the content of some of these nameless values. If my suggestion that the structure of a value is constituted by comparisons of bearers of that value, then this project will require further examination of comparisons among bearers of those values.[49]

This is not to say that in all instances in which it appears there is no appropriate covering value, a nameless value can be revealed. But it is plausible that the cases in which the nominal-notable test fails are ones in which the agent has misconceived what practical reason requires. Suppose I am contemplating two possible birthday gifts for a friend: a handsome copy of *Pride and Prejudice* and an elegant chiffon scarf. I assume that the choice turns on the answer to the question, 'Which is intrinsically better?' The book has, among other intrinsic merits, literary merits and the scarf, among others, sartorial merits. But there is no nominal-notable comparison of a literary masterpiece and a sartorial banality. It makes no sense to say, given that literary and sartorial values are the only relevant ones, *War and Peace* is better than a pair of seersucker bell-bottoms overall. Therefore, there is no covering value with respect to which all the respective intrinsic merits of the book and scarf can be compared.[50]

In light of this, it is natural to conclude that I have misconceived the choice situation as requiring such a comparison. I might, for instance, have fixed on an inappropriate choice value. On reflection, I might realize that the choice between the gifts is not governed by intrinsic value but by my friend's tastes, or intrinsic beauty, or any number of choice values with respect to which comparison is formally possible. Just as we need never compare candy bars with pencils with respect to moral goodness, we need never compare with respect to a value that does not exist. How can practical reason, as a part of rationality in general, require an exercise of deliberation that cannot, on formal grounds, succeed?

The practical predicament we started with is this: We determine which values are relevant to choice, but there does not seem to be any covering value with respect to which the merits of the alternatives with respect to those values can be compared. We can now diagnose the predicament as follows. Either there is a covering value, or there is not. If there is a covering value, its existence can presumably be discovered by the nominal-notable test. If it exists, it will likely be nameless. Whether the items are incomparable with respect to it is, then, a further question. If there is no covering value, the covering value requirement has not been satisfied, and we have therefore misunderstood the choice situation as one requiring that comparison. The items are not incomparable since there is no covering value with respect to which they could be incomparable. In either case, it is a mistake to think that the difficulty in finding an appropriate covering value is grounds for concluding that items are incomparable.

Of course, we have not shown that where there is a covering value, there is comparability with respect to it. Perhaps the donating and investing options are incomparable with respect to an appropriate nameless value. It is hard to see, however, what grounds there might be for such a conclusion.

We have, in this Introduction, surveyed three categories of incomparabilist arguments. There are those that make a fatal substantive error: by neglecting the existence of nominal-notable comparisons, by overooking the possibility of ordinal comparison, or by mistaking an emphatic claim of betterness for incomparability. There are those that make a fatal formal error: by neglecting to relativize incomparability to a value, by relativizing it to a value that does not cover, or by claiming that incomparability holds when there is no covering value that captures the values putatively relevant to a choice situation. And finally, there are those that make no fatal error but have difficulties of their own. Either they rely on controversial substantive positions like verificationism, or they are better understood as arguments not for incomparability but for a fourth value relation beyond 'better than', 'worse than', and 'equally good'.

❦2❧

Incommensurability: What's the Problem?

JAMES GRIFFIN

I ask, What's the problem?, not to suggest, as colloquially that question can, that there is really no problem about incommensurable values at all or that it is not as hard as it is being made out to be. There is surely a problem, and its difficulty is, if anything, underestimated. We do not even know quite what the problem is. There are too many different interpretations of 'incommensurable' in play, unacknowledged and perhaps unnoticed; we treat 'values' as being more homogeneous than in fact they are; and, in any case, the issue finally turns on the nature and extent of practical rationality, about which we are abysmally ignorant.[1]

1. 'Incommensurability'

What nearly all of us, on reflection, mean by the 'incommensurability' of values is their 'incomparability'—that there are values that cannot be got on *any* scale, that they cannot even be compared as to 'greater', 'less', or 'equal'. Sometimes, though, we use the word in considerably looser ways. We use it to mean that two values cannot be got on some particular scale, say, a cardinal scale allowing addition. We meet a certain heavyweight value that, we think, cannot be equaled by any amount of some lightweight value—the first, we might say, is 'incommensurably higher' than the second. But this is not incomparability; on the contrary, it is a particularly emphatic form of comparison. And when many of us insist, for instance, that complex decisions about the environment cannot be reduced to cost-benefit analysis because some of the clashing values are incommensurable, we do not just mean that those values cannot be got on to additive cardinal scales, but that they cannot be got even on to the ordinal scales that economists are by and large content to work with. What is more, we are right to take 'incommensurability' as 'incomparability'. The serious threat to practical rationality comes not from, say, a mere breakdown in addition or from the appearance of a lexicographical ordering, but from a breakdown in ranking. That threat is the most important one to confront.[2]

Although 'incomparability' is what we accept, and should accept, 'incommensurability' strictly to mean, we philosophers provide examples that, almost without exception, do not fit the definition or, at least, turn out in the end to be better explained some other way.

We tend to think that incommensurable values are not at all rare because a certain sort of conflict between them is quite common. Happiness can conflict with knowledge, mercy with justice, liberty with fraternity, and so on.[3] And they can conflict in a way that allows no resolution without often wrenching loss of value. It is a fact of life that some values, by their nature, exclude others. We can choose between them because the demands of living often mean that we must, but the choice is not a matter of deciding which, if either, has compensatingly more of some deep value than the other. Our choices can leave us with uncompensated loss.

That seems to me undeniable but not a matter of strict incommensurability. If all values were reducible to a single substantive supervalue (take, for illustration, the rather crude example of money, but it could be the most subtle intrinsic supervalue that monism might come up with), then choice is eased. The choice between £100 and £200 is hardly painful; what one forgoes (£100) is just the same as what one acquires, only inferior to it.[4] There is a good point and a bad point here. The bad point is that commensurability requires value monism, that we cannot compare values unless there is one substantive supervalue in terms of which the comparison can be made.[5] But this is a mistake. All that is needed for comparison is that the notion of 'value' itself be quantitative, that it be capable of appearing in basic judgments of 'more', 'less', and 'equal', which it can.[6] The issue of monism and pluralism about values has little to do with the issue of their commensurability and incommensurability.[7] The good point, however, is that values, being irreducibly plural, can, and often do, exclude one another; life sometimes forces us to sacrifice one value for another. But this is the incompatibility of values (they cannot both be realized together), not their incomparability.

Although the explanation in terms of pluralism that accompanies those examples is flawed, the examples themselves might nonetheless be quite sound. Can we really rank liberty and fraternity? Or liberty and prosperity? Liberty, after all, has a very special place among values. It is part of an Enlightenment picture of human dignity, and we value our human standing especially highly—often more highly than our happiness or even our life. And we see our human standing as consisting centrally in our choosing for ourselves a path through life (autonomy) and our not then being blocked from going down it (liberty). While some values have substitutes (that is, the loss of some values can be made up for by the gain of others), the elements of our human dignity have no substitutes. Still, unsubstitutability is not incomparability. And we are willing to give up a small liberty for a great, broadly life-enhancing material gain—not just choose the gain but do so precisely because we regard it as more valuable. We accept trade-offs between liberty and all sorts of other elements of a good life (for instance, sacrificing some political liberty to live in a country with someone one loves). The most that can be found, I think, are certain major liberties that, once we are at a certain level of prosperity, no further material gain can outrank. But that, as we saw earlier, is the impossibility of addition, not the impossibility of ranking.[8]

Comparing liberty with fraternity is more difficult, mainly because of the tangle of considerations that go to make up our notion of 'fraternity'. Still, we do seem able to judge that some major liberty—say, our being able to carry out the most central parts of our conception of a worthwhile life—is more important than some minor social divisiveness that might result. It is true that if the liberty were less major and the divisiveness greater, we might be stumped to know how to rank them. But we have uncovered incommensurability not when we cannot decide how to rank values but when we can decide that they are unrankable.[9]

Perhaps liberty is not quite different enough from other values to provide the sort of example we need. A human life, though, is uniquely valuable, beyond substitution or compensation. Nothing could replace a lost spouse or child, no matter how favorably life subsequently goes.[10] But, again, that is not a case of incomparability. To think that it is, I believe, is to succumb once more to the money model. Nothing can replace the loss of someone one loves, because that individual cannot be replaced. But that is not to say that nothing can compare in value with an individual human life. The irreplaceability of individuals is not the incomparability of values. Governments regularly decide when to stop putting resources into lifesaving medical procedures in order to support education or the arts. They decide when to divert funds from saving life into relieving pain. Of course, these decisions are so opaque and difficult that one may well be skeptical that they are based on anything as rational as comparison of the values involved. That governments decide does not show that they, or we, are capable of comparing those values. But although these decisions are extremely rough, they are not entirely arbitrary. True, life is not a value of the same kind as the various elements of a good life, such as enjoyment, personal relations, understanding, and so on. Life is, instead, a necessary condition for their realization and, as such, valuable. Anyway, mere life itself is not valuable; good life is. And it is on such grounds that it is unreasonable to pour resources endlessly into saving life, at the expense of such things as education and the arts, or as relief of pain, that supply or preserve its value. What goes on in these comparisons is indeed dark. But if it is not clear that they are examples of comparability, it is not clear, for the same reason, that they are examples of incomparability either.

So what we must look for is not the incompatibility or unsubstitutability or nonadditivity or irreplaceability of values, but their incomparability. And 'look for' does not mean merely 'observe'. Debate about the incommensurability of values has been hampered by our assuming that incommensurability is the sort of thing that appears on the surface, that it is easy to detect, whereas it is a matter of the quite deep structure of value judgments.

2. 'Values' (Prudential)

Let me turn now to the other key term, 'value', and first of all to the values that make up a good individual life.

My own view, which is widely shared, is that there are irreducibly many ends of life: enjoyment, deep personal relations, understanding, the elements of human dignity (such as autonomy and liberty), and so on. I also think that there are many ideal forms of life, very different from one another but all worthy of pursuit. So I am a pluralist about both individual values and forms of life. Certain things follow from these pluralist beliefs. One form of good life (say, a life of contemplation) can be incompatible with another (say, a life of action). A choice between them can mean uncompensated loss of value. But none of this amounts to incomparability. Still, are there incomparable values nonetheless? If there are (as I think there are) certain specifiable elements of a good life, then they supply the background for our judgments about ideal forms of life. They are the ingredients out of which these various ideal forms of life are made up—in very different proportions, some values perhaps not even appearing at all in certain lives and being virtually the sole component in others. The different ideal forms of life—forms all of which strike us as a way for human life to flourish—will then be worthy of pursuit because, unlike the many competitors that we meet and reject as inferior, they are all of a high quality—all in the same league, as it were. But, of course, they are not incomparable; we have just compared them: they are roughly equal.[11]

That conclusion may look too easy. If these various forms of life were indeed roughly equal, would we not, if rational, be indifferent between them? Is not indifference the sign of equality? But we clearly are not indifferent. If I were faced with a choice between a career in law and a career as a clarinetist and were equally suited to both, I should hardly be indifferent: this would be one of the major decisions of my life; I would have a lot to lose either way.[12] It seems that we can therefore accept that 'incommensurability' should be understood as 'incomparability', yet hold that forms of life can be incommensurable: we are agreed that one is not better than the other, and as we are not indifferent between them, they are not equal. But that we are not indifferent between them should not, I think, be taken to show that they are not roughly equal. The decision between them is fateful (we have a lot to lose either way), and that is motive enough not to be indifferent between them in this sense at least: we should, if wise, delve deeply into the content and the consequences of each way of life to see what is at stake. The lack of that sort of indifference is appropriate to any decision that is both important to one's life and difficult. But none of this shows that the options are not roughly equal. It shows only that we do not easily accept that verdict. If, in the end, we do understand what each life is like, and we do decide that they are roughly equal, we might, in effect, toss a coin—say, take whichever job came along first—and so be indifferent in that quite different sense.

Just now I have been able to argue for comparability between different forms of life because I have been assuming a single background list of values. It is precisely that comfortable assumption that is often challenged.[13] My list is very much out of a particular tradition: modern, Western, and atheist. But take someone with a radically different list: instead of enjoyment, the mortification of the flesh; instead of deep personal relations, cloistered solitude; instead of autonomy, submission to the will of God. How can two radically clashing conceptions of life, out of very different metaphysical beliefs or vastly different cultures, be made comparable?

Of course, if I believed in a certain sort of God, I might have a different list of the ends of life. But faced with incompatible metaphysical views, we must decide, as best we can, which is true. There is the extreme position that some radically different worldviews are themselves incommensurable in the strong sense that T. S. Kuhn sometimes seems to have had in mind: that they cannot be compared in terms of truth or rational support.[14] Besides being implausibly strong, this position also delivers a much stronger form of incommensurability of values than we have so far been talking about. If this extreme position were right, each of us would have simply to opt, in an arbitrary way, for one or another worldview. If you and I plumped for different ones, your values might indeed turn out to be incommensurable with mine. But this is incommensurability between two persons' values, not incommensurability within one person's values. I do not want to deny what is obvious, that sometimes a single person can feel the tug of radically different ways of life—say, a life of gentleness and oneness with nature against a life of competition, risk, and the productive exploitation of nature.[15] But one feels the tug of these two ways of life for the good reason that they are both, in their own ways, valuable. Any sensible person would want both, though would also have to face up to the fact that they often cannot be combined. But this is just incompatibility again, not incomparability. These two values will fit on the same scale: the scale of contribution to quality of life (where the notion of 'quality of life' is formal, not the name of a further, though especially large-scale substantive value). And the notion 'quality of life' seems capable of supplying a broad framework within which comparisons can take place. It is true of many prudential values that to identify them as valuable is to have a sense of what they contribute to the quality of life and so roughly how valuable they are. In looking for possible incommensurable values in the prudential sphere, we seem to shift between dubious and extreme clashes between worldviews beyond rational resolution, which may indeed supply a particularly strong form of interpersonal incomparability, and entirely plausible clashes of different ways of life, which come within the scope of our notion of the quality of life and so turn out to be, though incompatible, comparable after all.[16]

Are there, then, incommensurable values in the prudential sphere? Perhaps. As we saw, certain decisions (say, choices between saving life and relieving pain) are so opaque that it is not clear what goes on in them. But incommensurables are not pervasive in the prudential sphere. The better hunting ground, I think, is among moral values.

3. 'Values' (Moral)

Though I draw a line between 'prudential' and 'moral' values, the line is far from firm; the two sorts of values penetrate each other deeply. The prudential values that I have been speaking of so far, such as enjoyment or personal relations, do not direct action in any explicit way; they are things generally worth pursuing but leave open when, how, and to what extent we should pursue them. Certain norms, however, both prudential and moral, prohibit action.

As soon as action is at issue, the nature of agents is too. Prudential goods, to some degree, determine the content of moral norms, but the capacities of agents and facts about their social life begin to play a central role too. Now if moral norms are to be comparable across their range, we need an overarching framework, comparable to the notion of the 'quality of life' to which the various prudential values could all be seen as contributing—perhaps the notion of 'morality' itself, which might allow all norms to be ranked as to their moral 'weight' or 'importance' or 'stringency'. But do the determinants of moral norms provide a homogeneous or systematic enough background for that to be possible?

To answer that question, we have to open the large question of how moral norms get their shape.[17] One determinant is prudential goods. We have the moral norm, Do not deliberately kill the innocent, because we value life highly.

But appeal to the value of life explains only so much. It would give us the norm, Do not kill, which is too broad and indiscriminate. Even the norm, Do not deliberately kill the innocent, is too indeterminate; it should not be interpreted as applying to many particular cases: for instance, to directing the crippled airplane away from the center of town where it would kill many to the outskirts where it would kill only a few; to smothering the baby whose cries would give away the hiding place to the Gestapo; and perhaps even to eating the cabin boy to keep at least some of the survivors of the shipwreck alive. The value of life gives us a quite different norm for those cases: Limit the damage.

But then, as the notorious (and notoriously difficult) problem goes, should surgeons limit the damage by killing one person on the sly—a recluse, say, who will not be missed—to use the organs to save five? No, most of us would say; the norm, Do not deliberately kill the innocent, does apply here. But what is the difference? The answer to that question, I think, rests largely on certain facts about agents.

One fact is what human well-being is like. Prudential deliberation ends up with a list of values, such as enjoyment, understanding, accomplishment, deep personal relations, autonomy, and liberty. A striking feature of many items on the list is their long-term, life-structuring character. In that respect, they are quite unlike the one value in classical utilitarianism, which on the dominant interpretation is a mental state, an experience, and so is short term. To have deep attachments to particular persons is to acquire motives that shape much of one's life and carry on through most of it. To accomplish something with one's life requires dedication to particular activities that typically narrow and absorb one's attention. Many prudential values involve deep commitments—to particular persons, institutions, causes, and careers. One cannot live a prudentially good life, one cannot fully flourish, without becoming in large measure partial. That partiality then becomes part of one; it is not something that one can psychologically enter into and exit from at will.

A second fact is the limits of the human will. Evolution has planted in us both strong self-interest and limited altruism. How impartial can beings like us be? Some people say that we can overcome these limits by making our knowledge fuller or more vivid.[18] We can learn more about the plight of strangers, and our understanding will then prompt appropriate feeling and action. To some extent it will, of course; but seeing the problem as simply one about knowledge does not take the full measure of its difficulty. Famine-relief workers, who are not short of knowledge, seldom become impartial maximizers of the good. If humans do not become impartial just with the addition of knowledge, perhaps they can instead with rigorous training. We can train perfectly ordinary people to be soldiers prepared to risk their lives for their country. Why could not some well-conceived moral training make us fully impartial? Still, we bring soldiers to accept great potential danger by having a psychological apparatus of fear of the court-martial, shame before one's mates, and so on. We could, similarly, institute a kind of moral Red Guard to train us as children and keep us up to the mark thereafter. But there are two different sorts of doubts about that whole enterprise. First, to produce moral action by fear denies an agent autonomy, and loss of autonomy is the loss of an essential component of morality, as most of us now conceive of morality. Then, second, think what psychological forces are stacked on the other side. We naturally form relations of love and affection; we are committed to some causes and not to others. We think that these personal relations and these commitments are central to a good life. And these are attachments that cannot be entered into and exited from at will; they require a way of life in which partiality is entrenched. It is not easy to suppress these commitments or alter these beliefs about the good life, at least for long. The Red Guard enterprise aims at an unsustainable state. Many Chinese children who were model products of the Cultural Revolution turned up in the tents in Tiananmen Square.

These are enormously complicated empirical matters, and much more needs to be said than I can say here.[19] Most of us accept that 'ought' implies 'can'. What we disagree about is exactly what sort of 'can't' it must be to defeat 'ought'. How unconditional does the 'can't' have to be? It is an undeniable fact that some rare human beings sacrifice themselves for others. So they can. So humans can. So we can. And so the question, Ought we?, comes back to challenge us. In Auschwitz Father Maximilian Kolbe volunteered to take the place of another prisoner in a punishment detail and went to his death. But that Father Kolbe, with his religious beliefs, can sacrifice himself does not show that we, with very different metaphysical beliefs, can too. In any case, we do not need to look at religious believers for cases of self-sacrifice. Hundreds of students in Tiananmen Square autonomously went on hunger strike and were prepared to die 'to fight for the life that's worth living'.[20] But they were in special circumstances. They saw their lives as blighted, as not worth living. They saw an opportunity to change things, even if at a great cost to themselves, and when they gave up hope of change, they gave up the hunger strike too. Certainly people in exceptional circumstances can do exceptional things. Some mothers, when their children are threatened, can raise themselves to such emotional intensity that they acquire powers that they do not normally have. The hunger strikers had despair at their lives, hope that they could make a breakthrough, and the electric atmosphere of Tiananmen Square. But I doubt that we can use what people are capable of at the pitch of excitement as evidence of what they are capable of day in and day out, which is what a moral life needs. One special circumstance would be impending disaster; we expect great sacrifices if the alternative is dire enough: I ought, I think, to accept my own death to stop the lunatic from getting to the nuclear button. That the threat is so appalling should make the motivation follow more naturally.

What kind of 'can't', then, defeats 'ought'? There is 'can't absolutely': the human frame simply cannot deliver something that is asked of it. But one certainly cannot maintain that complete impartiality is impossible in this absolute sense; there are two many counter-examples. Then there is 'can't if one is living a prudentially good life in a nonoppressive society'. But this then would be a claim about the limits of the human will given some fairly hefty ethical assumptions. There is a lot of ground between these two senses of 'can't', and the relevant sense, it seems to me, lies somewhere there. Ethics must call on fairly settled dispositions. The dispositions must suit one for the variety of demands that life—in the particular society that one is in, in the most important roles that one is likely to play there—will make on one. Ethics must presuppose a sustainable social order—sustainable given the material circumstances of our life and, especially, given what is most enduring in human nature. The most relevant sense of 'can't' seems to me to be this: can't by someone in ordinary circumstances with suitable and settled dispositions in a sustainable social order. Most of us have to be prepared to raise children, or at least to have successful relations with other people, and more generally to be loyal and cooperative members of a community, and to care enough about our work to be productive. In short, we must live ordinary human lives; we must largely live as anyway we were going to live. A few people may turn out quite different from this; a very few of them, the ones who salvage some sort of sanity, might even be capable of effective impartial concern for all. But what is in the accessible psychological repertoire of the minute exception may well not be in the repertoire of the vast majority of humanity.[21]

Another determinant of the content of norms is the limits of knowledge. It would be helpful if we could tell how beneficial alternative forms of important social institutions, such as property, are, but their enormous complexity will eventually defeat us. It is not that we can never manage such calculations. We can certainly manage to assess the costs and benefits of smallish parts of large social institutions. And we can fairly reliably, if not very precisely, assess the costs and benefits of a whole complex social institution if its successes and failures are fairly plain. We can also advance our knowledge by trial and error. We can try, say, a centrally planned economy, and we might in time discover that it is inferior to a market economy in the efficient transmission of information. But that would leave us with very different forms of market economy still to be ranked, differing in their effects on the quality of life. The effects of an economic structure are pervasive and subtle; they shape, in ways that are beyond our grasp, not only economic performance but also political structures and personal relations—for instance, our sense of community, the extent of our altruism, and the forms of our competition. Many of the kinds of market economy will come into a band in which, though they differ in their costs and benefits, we shall not be able to rank them. We shall be unable to rank them not just for the present but probably in the future as well; we should need advances not just in economics, which may be forthcoming, but also in our understanding of how whole societies work, how individual psyches work, and how the one affects the other. There are, it is true, degrees of ignorance. We do not need certainty in order to act; reliable degrees of probability are enough. But at times we shall not have even that. There will still be a wide band in which our ignorance defeats even such judgments of probability. If we are wise, we shall then recognize our limits and live within, while also reforming, the society that seems generally satisfactory that we have inherited. What will then be behind the claim that we ought to do this or that will not (that is, not entirely) be the general good but that this is the way our society happens to work. Some moral norms are shaped by our own social tradition; we certainly do not create all our norms from scratch, but neither can we pass them all in review to sanction them as 'probable bests'. We work with the moral materials we have, changing what we can see needs changing.

These three facts about agents—the nature of their well-being, their limited wills, and their limited knowledge—go some way toward explaining the difference between the transplant case and the crippled airplane case.

If you are the pilot of the crippled plane, your moral situation is very simple: is the damage to be small (say, one dead) or large (say, five dead)? The salient policy in the situation, the only rational policy, is, Limit the damage. And the policy, Limit the damage, is modest, in two ways. It makes no great demands on knowledge (the policy is obvious), and it involves no ambitious program of action (we passively respond whenever, in exceptional circumstances, our hand is forced).

There is nothing like that modesty in the transplant case. Instead of passively reacting, the surgeons' policy is to go out into the world to find opportunities to limit the damage—that is, to promote preservation of life generally. And a policy like that makes enormous demands on knowledge. If the surgeons do it today, why not tomorrow? If this group of surgeons does it, why not others? If surgeons do it, why not, say, politicians when their moral sums come out the same? And, typically, we cannot know in the transplant case, even to a reliable degree of probability, what will most promote values. The transplant case is far from simple. The surgeons cannot know the consequences of killing the recluse. They cannot know whether, or how widely, people will learn what they have done. They cannot know how much fear and mistrust that knowledge will produce. They cannot do the calculation of total benefits against total costs. In any case, we are concerned now not with a particular case but with a policy. To do the calculations of costs and benefits if everyone—other groups of surgeons, politicians, and the rest of us—became entrepreneurs in life promotion is far beyond us. Anyone who aspires to a moral life based on such calculations aspires to Godlike knowledge. 'Ought' implies 'can'. Moral norms are shaped for agents with our limitations. So it is not surprising that we should use the norm, Limit the damage, in the crippled airplane case and the norm, Do not deliberately kill the innocent, in the transplant case. Those are the appropriate norms for the likes of us.

One thing that alarms us about the transplant case, I say, is that the surgeons would be 'playing God'. Why would you not also be 'playing God' if you directed your airplane to the suburbs? Your role in the airplane case would be, I say, a relatively modest, un-Godlike one. You are choosing, it is true, who will die, and that seems a pretty Godlike thing to do, but you are not arrogating to yourself anything approaching omniscience. The transplant case is different, I think, not just because the surgeons are deciding who is to die (that happens in the airplane case too) but because, in doing so, the surgeons are pretending to know that this is the best policy. They set themselves up as omniscient dispensers of justice in a situation in which there is no salient, obviously reasonable policy. So my suggestion is this: One thing that is objectionable about the surgeons' behavior is not intervention in the naturally unfolding course of events but pretension to be dispensing justice in doing so. Ethics, particularly ethics as conceived in modern universities, strikes me as often too ambitious. It usually fails to operate with a realistic conception of human agency. Ethics cannot do better for us in the transplant case than come up with norms for agents like us in the world so far as we are able to know it. One such norm is, Do not deliberately kill the innocent. And it takes some extreme case—some case, for instance, that is simple enough for another moral policy to be salient (though not error-proof)—for us to be justified in setting that norm aside. It would take, say, a plane headed for a crash.[22]

These thoughts move us in the direction of commonsense morality. Commonsense morality permits partiality to particular persons, groups, and causes; it tailors moral duties to our capacities. And, importantly, it provides no all-embracing system for our various norms; they seem to emerge from quite separate considerations, without any obvious single background consideration unifying them all.

System, however, is what philosophy, it might be hoped, will usher onto the scene. But the same facts about agents, I think, undermine certain important ethical systems. I want very quickly to look at one such system: utilitarianism. I shall be far too quick to say anything conclusive about it, but I want to give some idea as to why I have my doubts about a utilitarian system. (I also have my doubts about the more systematic forms of deontology and virtue ethics too, but I do not have time to go into them.)

 Consider utilitarianism as an illustration of how philosophy tries to introduce system. An obvious doubt about a direct form of utilitarianism is whether persons can have the commitment to their family, pursuits, and community that they must have for their lives to go well and yet be able to drop these commitments whenever utility calculation beckons. The central commitments of our personal and social life do not seem to leave us such freedom. Some commitments do not leave us the time even to notice chances for doing more good; others will not leave us able to take them up even if we saw them. Direct utilitarians can respond to these facts of life by including among their options becoming a person of commitments. But that would be a deeply subversive move; it would undercut, over a large swathe of the moral domain, their distinctive form of deliberation.

In contrast, an indirect form of utilitarianism can concede that the moral norms and relations that for the most part govern our lives are much like the ones that we find in an improved commonsense morality; all that it must stand out for is that they be sanctioned by the highest-level moral consideration, namely, the impartial promotion of interests. It proposes that we should act in accord with the norms, or from the feelings, that would promote interests in the whole society in the long run. But a doubt about indirect utilitarianism is whether we could ever perform the tremendously large-scale cost-benefit calculations that it requires or even arrive at probabilities reliable enough for action. We can do these calculations in fairly extreme or fairly small-scale cases, but often not otherwise.

Something else will then have to be at work producing determinate moral norms and relations. There are no moral norms outside the boundary set by our capacities. A moral standard that ignores human capacities is not an 'ideal' standard; it is no standard at all.

At this point, utilitarians might object that impartially promoting interests is not, in any case, meant as an action-guiding principle. There is an important distinction between a decision procedure (how we should go about deciding how to act) and a criterion (what makes an act right or wrong). Doctors, for instance, have protocols—procedures for diagnosis and treatment—which are different from their criterion of successful treatment, namely, health. Perhaps, similarly, the impartial promotion of the good is properly seen not as the consideration that we use to decide what to do, but as the criterion of our moral practice.

But I doubt that this reply helps utilitarianism. Although criterion and decision procedure can diverge, they are kept in the same general neighborhood by our capacities. Our decision procedures will, of course, be restricted by our capacities. But if a criterion becomes too remote from our capacities, it will cease serving as a criterion. Health can be a criterion for medical practice because doctors can often both act to bring it about and eventually find out whether they have. In parts of moral life, we can also eventually find out the important consequences of our acts, but in many other parts we never do. What most promotes interests cannot even serve then in a background position as a criterion. Our moral life cannot start from such an all-sanctioning background principle. We have to conduct it with what is within our reach.[23]

This is why one obvious utilitarian rejoinder to my line of thought is not, I suspect, strong enough. The rejoinder goes like this: We utilitarians are perfectly able to accept any facts about human nature or the workings of society, including (if they turn out to be true) your claims. We can, for instance, accept that moral life has to be conducted by appeal to fairly specific standards, in just the ways you say and for just the reasons you give. We shall simply incorporate all of this in the utilitarian calculation. Our question will become: What set of rules and dispositions will most promote interests, given agents of such-and-such a nature and a society that works thus and so?

But this rejoinder does not meet the strength of the claim that I have made. My suspicion is that *this* calculation is beyond us and that our moral life cannot therefore rest on it. Utilitarians cannot admit that our ignorance justifies the sort of reliance on tradition that I have defended. That concedes too much; it concedes that even indirect utilitarian thought is out of place in much of the center of moral life. If utilitarian thought is squeezed out of a quite large part of moral life, if there prove to be many situations in which the calculation of utilities cannot be done to a sufficient degree of reliability, then does enough remain to be called 'utilitarianism'?[24]

That is not a rhetorical question. It seems to be clear that *sometimes* utility calculation, even to a reliable degree of probability, is beyond us. And in moral life it may not be of much use that we can in the future extend our knowledge, say, by trial and error. If it takes virtually one's whole life to establish that one has tried the wrong policy, one cannot live one's life again. And if one's error has damaged the fate of others, they cannot live their lives again either. What we have to decide is just how often tolerably reliable utility calculations are beyond us and how central those failures are in moral life. What one finds will, to some extent, depend on the kind of utilitarian one is. If one thinks (as I do) that the most plausible form of utilitarianism is a highly indirect one, then at the center of one's moral thought will be some such question as, What set of rules and what set of dispositions would, if they were the prevailing ones in one's society, produce most utility over society at large and in the long run? But that is just the sort of question likely to defeat answer. We may know enough to identify fairly obviously inadequate rules and dispositions, but there will be many left that we cannot rank. And it is in the wide band that they would constitute that many of the hard choices in morality—choices, say, about the particular form that respect for life should take—would have to be made.

Utilitarianism seems to turn ethics into a project that fits badly the agents who are meant to carry it out.[25] The ambitions of utilitarian rationality, and thus one hope for the comparability of moral norms, seems too great.

4. The Source of Incommensurable Values

My doubts about utilitarianism, I admit, do not build up to a conclusive case against it. And I have not talked about other forms of consequentialism, or about deontology and virtue ethics. But my doubts about each of them point us more or less in the same direction.

My own view is that philosophers have not yet paid nearly enough attention to the nature of human agents. When we do, we find, I think, an explanation of the moral standards we have been talking about that gives them a standing that consequentialism does not, but without resorting to the further moral values that deontology posits but has trouble finding or to the primacy of moral dispositions that virtue ethics claims but has trouble justifying.

I have said that the norm, Do not deliberately kill the innocent, holds sway in all but extreme cases, because it is the only norm that agents like us can live by in those cases. My guess is that what stops us from accepting that conclusion is the myth of the morally right answer. We do not expect positive law always to have an answer; a situation may be so unusual that no law fits it, that even no legislator's intention fits it. We are prepared to accept the positive law as a fallible human creation, not always up to coping with the complexities of life. But behind positive law, we think, there is an ideal form of law, moral law, endlessly refinable, universally applicable, and never at a loss for an answer (though we may be at a loss to make it out). But moral law is limited in much the same way, and for many of the same reasons, as positive law. The myth is that there is always the morally right answer. Sometimes moral norms conflict, and there is no moral basis for a resolution. Sometimes we just have to stick to a moral norm, such as, Do not deliberately kill the innocent, despite all the nagging and, in a sense, rational worries weighing in on the other side—as in the transplant case—because, given our capacities, that is the only kind of moral life open to us.

There is another way, I think, in which morality is like the law. Purely moral considerations often leave us well short of determinate standards for action, and social agreement or convergence can enter to fill the gap. For instance, human rights have their moral grounding, I should say, in the great value that we attach to our status as persons, as agents. As persons, we deliberate about and choose our ends and then act to realize them. Human rights are best seen, on this Enlightenment conception of them, as protections of the values associated with personhood: our autonomously choosing a course through life, our having the basic wherewithal to achieve it, and others not blocking us. So one human right is a right to bodily integrity, because unless we have some security in our own bodies, we can have no security of action. But where is the line defining that right to be drawn? Does that right bar the state from forcibly taking one of my kidneys for transplant? Does it also bar a particularly accommodating state from demanding a pint of my blood, which, it says, it will take in my own house while I sleep and leave me to wake the next morning none the worse for it? What is clear is that, on its own, the relevant moral consideration—the value of personhood—is not up to fixing a determinate line. The personhood consideration would not protect me against the accommodating state after my blood. It is not clear that it would protect me even against the state that is after my kidney; after all, what I should lose from a kidney extraction is only a few weeks for convalescence (if my remaining kidney packs it in, there is a bank of them for me to have a transplant), and a few weeks of convalescence would hardly destroy my personhood. But the trouble is that the personhood consideration, unsupplemented, draws nothing even approaching a determinate line. And if the line is very indeterminate, we may be reluctant to say that a right yet exists. Its existence must, to some extent, depend on our being able to see it as a manageable, socially effective claim on others. So what sort of thing must we add to make it more determinate? A lot of practical considerations must go into fixing the line, such as how threateningly interventionist the political tradition of our particular society is, whether human nature is such that we should be well advised to leave a large safety margin, how simple and obvious the line has to be, and so on.

So we should not think that there always are fully defined moral norms standing behind laws or other social standards, which provide us with the ideal to which laws or social standards must measure up. It is not that there will be no rational grounds for assessing laws and social standards, but that they will not be entirely moral in content. They might, instead, be in terms of social or psychological probabilities. I am tempted to say that it is often the other way around: moral norms—that is, norms as far as purely moral considerations take them—are often highly indeterminate and need social agreement behind them to give them shape. Sometimes it is the law itself that will give them shape. More often, though, it is some nonlegal moral consensus. In this further way, moral norms are like laws. It is often society, through its conventions and decisions, that defines them and so gives them existence.

We follow the norm, Do not deliberately kill the innocent, unless we find a tolerably clear area of exception—as there is with cases covered by the norm, Limit the damage. And there is another area of exception, though its boundaries are hard to draw, for euthanasia. Legislators defining a policy on euthanasia have to face up to the fact that it will be applied by limited, fallible, temptable humans. Any legislation is bound to be a messy compromise with human nature and social needs. But it is not that behind the legislator's messy deliberation there is the moralist's purer thought. The two deliberations will be virtually identical: the same problems, the same compromises, the same vagueness and incompleteness.

I am not saying that moral norms are like positive laws in their content, but rather in the modes of deliberation used to arrive at them and in the considerations central to that deliberation, especially the limitations of agents and the solutions to actual social problems. On the contrary, one would hope that the content of moral norms would often not be identical to that of positive laws. One wants moral norms to provide ground for criticizing laws, and so they can if those who think about ethics keep a step or two ahead of legislators. It is just that when those interested in ethics think about human rights or euthanasia, they shall have to think about the same sort of messy considerations that a legislator does. Our job in ethics is not to have thoughts radically different from theirs, but to have them considerably earlier, or carried much further, than theirs. For instance, there is nothing stopping us from getting to a feasible norm about euthanasia before legislators do, and we can carry our deliberation to the highly specific or particular (say, in the cabin boy case) when legislators cannot. Nor is what I am saying especially conservative. It is certainly not a defense of commonsense ethics, which has always been inadequate in the past and must be still. We have powerful forms of criticism available to us: appeals to utilities, to rights, to the nature of agents. That there is no supreme background principle capable of bringing system to ethics does not mean that there are no modest background principles capable of sustaining criticism in ethics.

With moral norms' being grounded in such various considerations, with their answering such different needs, there can be no guarantee of comparability between them. When we wonder whether we have an exception to the norm, Do not deliberately kill the innocent, we have to decide whether there is a clear enough case for isolating another area of exception (as there may be for euthanasia) or not (as there is not for the surgeons' policy of life promotion). If we can reach either result, we have a solution. Still, the second sort of decision—the decision to stick to the norm—is not backed by a calculation of what most promotes interests. We do not know. Instead, the decision represents our acceptance that, by and large, our role is to respect life, not to promote it. We have the norm in the first place, it is true, only because of the value we attach to life. But that we are appealing, in this limited way, to prudential values is not the same as our appealing to some probabilistic calculation of overall promotion of those values. There are other cases, though, that are harder to resolve—cases in which we find ourselves more painfully suspended somewhere in the middle between two norms, with neither dominating. In the course of war we might wonder whether to retaliate against the civilian population of an enemy attacking our own; we might hope to limit the damage, without knowing at the time of decision or, given the complexity of the forces at work, perhaps even later, what the consequences of the action would be. Nor, I think, can we even say, as we could in the prudential domain with conflicting ends of life when precise calculation became difficult, that our options are roughly equal. What in the moral domain would be the unifying conceptual basis for such a judgment? It is likely that from time to time one will encounter incomparable moral norms and there will be no resources in any human repertoire to resolve the conflict.

❧3❧

Incommensurability:
Four Proposals

DAVID WIGGINS

1. Technical and recondite though they are—indeed in the continuing absence of explicit stipulation obscure—the ideas of commensurability and incommensurability have long since had a life of their own in moral philosophy. Their presence there reflects fears or expectations that are very familiar.[1] But it is doubtful even now whether the language of philosophy can simply carry them along and sustain an agreed signification for them. Explicit definition would be the best. On the other hand, so much has now been argued under their mysterious auspices and believed in their name that not just any definition will suffice.

In what follows I try to identify and to criticize a few salient ideas that have had some currency among adherents of claims of incommensurability. Then I redeploy them in an effort to pin down a little better what we ought to mean by "incommensurable". I hope that whatever survives this process will show the way to simpler, more refined proposals, as yet unformulated, that will carry with them the possibility of more widespread substantial agreement about what incommensurability is. Writing as an incommensurabilist, I have the further aim of persuading the reader that there are moral incommensurables. But this aim is subsidiary.

2. A familiar first proposal (not yet a definition, but rather, one might hope, the consequence of one) is this. We are frequently faced with situations where not every claim upon us can be satisfied. If the options *A* and *B* make incommensurable claims, then, whether you choose *A* over *B* or *B* over *A*, something will be lost. It is not sensible to expect that everything that matters about *A* and matters about *B* will always survive in the outcome of the wise exercise of practical choice between them.

So this is the first suggestion, preserving an echo of the discovery of irrationals—itself anonymous but following on from the theorem Pythagoras is said to have celebrated by the sacrifice of an ox—that moralists have long wanted to press into service in their account of our confrontation with the objects of appetition and conation: Option *A* is commensurable with option B if and only if there is a valuational measure of more and less, and some however complex property ɸ that is correlative with choice and rationally antecedent to choice and rationally determinant of choice, such that *A* and *B* can be exhaustively compared by the said measure in respect of being more ɸ and less ɸ;[2] where an exhaustive comparison in respect of ɸ-ness is a comparison in respect of everything that matters about either *A* or *B. A* is incommensurable with *B* just if *A* is not commensurable with *B.*

Where *A* and *B* made incommensurable claims in this sense—that is, where no measure and property simultaneously meeting these exigent conditions was available—it would be reasonable to expect that a choice between them would leave what Bernard Williams calls a residue. Even where you make the (in-context) right choice, something important may be left over for which the winning option can afford no compensation in kind.[3] For even by the uncontroversially right choice, some legitimate claim may go completely unsatisfied. The winning choice may not reflect all the claims—the valid claims—of the losing choice.

3. It is important not to let the claim that there are incommensurables in this sense lead one into the denial that a practical verdict arrived at by some means or other—the overall best one for the circumstances *C,* suppose—will effect *some ranking* between *A* and *B.*[4] That is not the right denial. The point the incommensurabilist should rather insist upon is this: The ranking read off a practical verdict will be a ranking in respect of overall choice worthiness under the circumstances *C, and only that.* An overall ranking of this kind need not represent a complete or exhaustive valuation of the alternatives *A* and *B,* or a valuation of everything that really matters about each of them.

At this point, I think the incommensurabilist may want to register a further point: that in real life, *A* may be more choice worthy overall than *B*—and may be seen as such—*otherwise* than on the basis of *A*'s representing more of something that *B* represents less of. For a comparison in respect of more and less "overall choice worthiness" may issue simply and directly from the scrutiny of *A* and the scrutiny of *B,* or from thoughts other than comparative or valuational ones. As a result of an agent's scrutiny of each of *A* and *B, A* may commend itself as required, for instance, and/or option *B* may seem to be out of the question. That is a special case. The general point is that the judgment "*A* is more choice worthy than *B* overall," coming after the decision, may well be the *only* comparison in respect of more and less that is to be discerned there. In such a case, it is the choice of *A* (or the considerations that ground the choice of *A*) that gives the ranking, not the ranking that gives the choice. The two-place predicate '*X* is more choice worthy than *Y*' plays no deliberatively useful role. It sums up a deliberation effected by other means. The predicate is certainly well defined, but that is guaranteed only because we can make practical choices in ways not allowed for by the ranking conception, and the extension of the said predicate can be determined wherever necessary by reference to the final choice that it recapitulates. *A fortiori,* the availability of such a universal predicate in this reacapitulatory role does nothing to suggest that there is just one overarching *deliberatively substantial* property: a single property that *grounds practical choice* and underlies all practical choices.

So, for the would-be incommensurabilist, this seems to be the state of play. Even if every practical choice *did* presuppose a comparison of options in respect of some antecedent deliberatively substantial property that subsumed all the relevant properties of the alternatives, *indefinitely many* such properties might (for all that anyone has yet shown) need to be invoked, depending upon the nature of the alternatives, the context, and so forth. Indeed, pending some argument to the opposite effect, the presumption has to be against there being only one deliberatively substantial property of choice worthiness. What is more, once the idea arises that there may be a plurality of such properties in play, the thing we shall immediately expect is that it will become *essentially contestable* which property should prevail in a given case or will trump all the others there.

4. These reflections put us into a position to formulate a second, and in some ways more satisfactory, definition of incommensurability, one which will mend a certain defect in the first proposal. For one might reasonably find fault with what that proposal stipulated about the comparing of A with B "in respect of everything that matters about either A or B". The defect is that if this means only that an exhaustive comparison between A and B *has regard* for everything that matters, then the denial that A and B were commensurable in the sense defined would be perilously close to the denial that one could choose sensibly between A and B at all. (Do we really want to confine our whole use of the notion of incommensurability to cases like that?) The claim of commensurability would then amount to rather little. It would simply remind us that a good choice must have regard for anything and everything that matters. On the other hand, if comparison "in respect of everything that mattered" about A or B meant that one could *recover* from the verdict "A is more ϕ than B" some condensation of all the information about everything that there was in favor of either A or B—if it meant that none of that information would be lost in the passage to a verdict in favor of one or the other—then the claim of commensurability would be improbably strong and the denial of A and B's commensurability would amount to little or nothing. For it would be absurd to expect such a mass of evaluative information about A and B to be recoverable from the overall verdict in favor of one or other of them.

The second proposal to which one is led by all these considerations runs as follows:

The set *(A, B, C, D, . . .)* constitutes an incommensurable set of options if and only if it is *not* the case that there is one property φ and one measure *M* of φ-ness such that φ and M satisfy all the following conditions:

(a) it is determined by *M* which is the more φ member of any pair *(X, Y)* consisting of options drawn from the set *(A, B, C, D, . . .)*,

(b) comparisons in respect of φ-ness ground correct deliberative choice between the members of each and every pair drawn from the set *(A, B, C, D, . . .)* and are antecedent in reason to choice between them,

(c) comparisons in respect of φ-ness reflect a proper regard for *every* choice-relevant feature of any member of the set *(A, B, C, D, . . .)*.

5. Does this definition of incommensurability inherit any title to minister to the thought that, where you rightly choose *A* over *B,* something important may nevertheless be lost by the choice of *B?*

Just to this extent. The relevant deliberative property φ' for the choice between *A* and *B* may have had relatively little regard for certain among the properties of *B,* and these less-valued properties might well have counted for much more in connection with a comparison in respect of another property φ", where φ" would not have been the right respect of comparison for the choice here between *A* and *B,* but might have been the right respect of comparison for the choice between *A* and (say) *C.*

This second conception of incommensurability can, to this extent at least, cast light on the classic or hackneyed examples, such as the choice here now between pursuing justice and pursuing commercial efficiency, or the choice between the lives of contemplation, of statesmanship and public endeavor, and of relaxation, privacy, and pleasure. Perhaps the most important thing about such examples is that there is no uncontentious choice of standard of comparison. Whatever standard you choose, someone else may, and in good faith, press for another. The second conception of incommensurability illustrates this vividly enough, just as it illustrates the fact that it may be sensible to refuse to see the different lives that different people choose as competing answers to some stable, unitary, and general question, with a stable and unproblematic sense, reference, and intended elucidation, "which of these lives is *the best overall?*" Even if we decide not to quarrel (here or now) with the myth that there is something general called value and comparison in respect of it fixes choice, we see that there is a further element of mythmaking in the idea that, in respect of sensible choice, there *ought* to be some not essentially contestable notion of "overall best" (or "overall best here now") that will serve to gloss the question that is at issue in the choice.

So the second proposal has some of the virtues that the first proposal was aiming at. It predicts that, for purposes of practical choice and the selection of the right dimension of comparison, it will in certain cases be agonizingly difficult to decide how to hold the right balance between the values that are preserved or promoted by one option and those that are preserved or promoted by the other option. It predicts this on the basis of the plurality of putative dimensions of comparison. Like the first proposal, it leads us to expect that the choice may represent a terrible challenge to the chooser. Bernard Williams, Peter Winch, and writers in other traditions, such as J-P. Sartre, have illustrated in convincing detail the nature and quality of challenges of this kind. There is much more to be said about them in the framework that is to be proposed later in this paper. (See below sections 13–14.)

One more advantage. Like the first proposal, the second has the effect of drawing attention to an important contrast between ordinary evaluations and practical verdicts. Whereas the verdicts of practical choice must often sacrifice something, pure evaluation, provided it makes a full use of all the resources of valuational thinking, need not lose or obliterate anything. Everything can register. We can say, "It would have been kind and it would have been benevolent to do act *A*, but unjust". Or we can say, "This work practice is time-consuming and costly, but it also achieves something distinctive, and it gives more people the experience and insight into reality that come from work. The point of persisting with it would not be that it was commercially efficient, though it does achieve something distinctive, but that it was just".

One last preliminary. The second proposal does not predict that every choice from a set of incommensurables represents a real dilemma or a case where the idea of the right practical choice is problematic. (Real or tragic dilemmas will be touched on in sections 13 and 14 below.) This nonprediction counts positively in its favor because, in given particular contexts, with varying senses of loss, we can and regularly do make such choices. (This is not to say that we always can.) In looking for the right dimension of comparison, we arrive, little by little, at rather specific reasons for our choices. How we do this and arrive at certain distinctive moral emphases in our practical and moral outlooks is an important part of the story of how we become what we become and make for ourselves the various different characters that we come to exemplify. The thesis of incommensurability is not a substitute for philosophy's effort to come to terms with all this, but it may usefully complement that effort.

6. How does the second of these two proposals relate to the fears and expectations that attach to the philosophical thesis of moral consequentialism? I ask because there are numerous writers who expect the existence of incommensurabilities, if there are any, to represent the chief escape route, if there is one, from the morally repugnant conclusions that flow from the consequentialist idea that practical decisions are to be arrived at by assessing states of affairs in respect of their total net desirability. Incommensurabilists expect such an escape route, and commensurabilists have come perhaps to expect that incommensurabilists will expect this.

Nevertheless, it is hard to believe that there is any notion of incommensurability that can provide this escape route. I say this because often, in cases where consequentialism outrages conviction, the considerations that stand behind the competing practical options seem all too easily comparable. There may be various numbers of deaths, lives, broken promises, and so forth on each side of the dilemma. We do not need to force these things or the options that comprise them into a common currency in order to compare and measure what lies within rival options. They may be in a common enough currency already. Comparison may be easy and may all too easily issue in morally repulsive directives.

According to Scheffler, moral consequentialism comes in two parts:

> First, it gives some principle for ranking overall states of affairs from best to worst from an impersonal standpoint, and then it says that the right act in any given situation is the one that will produce the highest-ranked state of affairs that the agent is in a position to produce. . . . Anyone who resists consequentialism seems committed to the claim that morality tells us to do less good than we are in a position to do and to prevent less evil than we are in a position to prevent.[5]

Insofar as our second conception of incommensurability sheds any light at all here, it does indeed cast doubt on whether there is just one deliberatively foundational principle of the sort Scheffler describes for ranking overall states of affairs from better to worse. That should never be taken for granted. (See section 3 above.) But how fatal that is to consequentialism would need to be argued. And in any case, the first question about consequentialism is not so much whether a single overall principle exists for ranking states of affairs as whether there is any positive and nonquestion-begging reason to espouse consequentialism in the first place.[6] What positive argument can the consequentialist offer for submerging the complex and distinctive deliberative procedures of an agent into "the impersonal standpoint"? To develop a good notion of incommensurability is a worthwhile aim, but it is no substitute for gaining an understanding of the distinction between questions of overall goodness or badness of states of affairs impersonally considered and questions that engage the agency of a person (questions of what it would be right or wrong, callous or kind, just or unjust, honorable or dishonorable, *for him or her* to do now here).

7. If the defects of the second proposal do not relate to its contributing so little to the examination of consequentialism, then they lie chiefly elsewhere.

First, the proposal perpetuates any unclarity there was about what kinds of thing they are that belong to sets of options that are counted as incommensurable.

Secondly, the proposal leaves us without any direct way of saying what we seem to want to say (however obscurely) when we claim that *A* and *B* themselves are mutually incommensurable.

Thirdly, the bare claim that there are incommensurable option sets *(A, B, C, ...)* is signally unsuggestive about what it is that a reasonable person will collate with what in arriving, by whatever contextually appropriate route, at defensible practical choices. It would be good if we could find an account of incommensurability that more explicitly related the incommensurability of incommensurables *A, B, C, ...* both to the standing concerns or commitments that sustain a reasonable person's interest in *A, B, C, ...* and to the contexts that activate these concerns. We need a proposal that is more deliberate and more explicit in its treatment of the *objects* and of the *occasions* of regret or anguish, for instance. (I mean the regret or anguish that ensues upon the 'payment' of what some like to call 'moral costs'.)

8. To this end, let us revert now to the thought that mutual incommensurables are things themselves, *A, B, C,* and not the sets that contain them. Let us try to preserve something from certain ideas that we began with: namely, (1) that incommensurability results from the way in which complete assessments of option *A* and option *B* may seem to underdetermine the decision between *A* and *B,* (2) that incommensurability should reflect the way in which a practical choice between the options *A* and *B* will often be either appreciably less or appreciably more than an all-inclusive valuational comparison between them. In order to achieve this end, let us be ready to supersede the thought that things that are incommensurable should be particularized historically determinate rival options. Abandoning these, let us rule instead that incommensurables are the relatively unspecific, rather general, potentially conflicting or rival objects of concern that historically determinate options import into the consideration of a given situation. Understood as things that can matter in some situation that makes claims upon us, incommensurables will be things that can be compared in a particular context, under the constraint of that context and for a particular purpose that obtains there. This is to say that often, in a given case, we *can* find a way to collate and arbitrate between the demands that impinge there of impartiality, benevolence, mercy, due process, and so on. There may, however, be no general method for doing this. And let us say that *A* is incommensurable with *B* in the new sense of "incommensurable"—and under the new understanding of what sorts of things *A* and *B* are—if there is no *general* way in which *A* and *B* trade off in the whole range of situations of choice and comparison in which they figure.

One clarification may be needed here. People of different characters will bring to bear certain distinctive moral emphases and seek to promote certain distinctive concerns. But according to the incommensurabilist, this is not to say that, even for one agent, any exceptionless (or helpful) statement applicable over a full range of situations can be made of his or her ranking of these concerns, or of his or her relative ranking of various combinations of these concerns. If it could, then very likely that would be a symptom not of the firmness or distinctiveness of an agent's character, but of his or her obstinacy or fanaticism.

9. Incommensurability in the sense we are now trying to pin down reflects the separateness and mutual irreducibility of the standing concerns that make up our orientation toward the distinct values and commitments (and whatever else) that impinge upon us in different sorts of situations. It reflects the fact that these concerns are not all variations on a common theme. According to our new account, incommensurability can indeed (as the first proposal insisted) have *application* to specific historically determined choices or options, or to sets of them (as the second insisted). But it does so only derivatively from the incommensurability (in the new sense) of the more general or persisting concerns to which we have standing, generally unranked attachments.[7]

How then, confronting these general concerns as they impinge upon particular historic contexts and situations, *do* we make our choices? The answer is that we have to make our choice in the light of our overall practical conception of how to be or how to live a life (both here and in general). We deploy these conceptions even as the variety of the contingencies that we actually confront constantly shapes or reshapes the conceptions themselves (a two-way flow). It will be no wonder if choice (as now described) is the exercise of an irreducibly practical knowledge, a knowledge that can never be exhaustively transposed into any finite set of objectives that admit of finite expression.

How, then, can the incommensurabilist who stresses the practical aspect of choice, and insists on the unlimitedness, distinctness, and separateness of the various values, concerns, and commitments that we care about, best mark or signal all these things and relate them to questions about the springs of action? Well, the claim is that one way for him to do this will be for him to say that, where *A* and *B* are incommensurable in our new and third sense, there is no correct (however complicated or conditionalized), unitary, projectible,[8] explanatory, and/or potentially predictive account to be had of how *A* and *B* trade off against one another in a reasonable agent's choices or actions, or within the formation of his springs of action. Where *A* and *B* are mutually incommensurable, the attempt to extrapolate from the actual choices that he makes between them under such and such circumstances (and under this or that constraint) and the effort this entails on the theorist's part to surmount the relativity of these choices to those circumstances (and constraints) will not succeed in establishing any determinate and projectible ratio of substitution between them.

10. Now that incommensurability is restored as something that concerns have to one another, let us be as explicit as possible. By the usage proposed, an incommensurabilist will not merely disbelieve that there is for each rational agent some in principle predeterminable and constant "ratio of substitution" that his valuational, ethical, normative outlook fixes in a projectible and counterfactual-sustaining fashion between all standing values or objects of concern that mean anything to him. To disbelieve that is to disbelieve a relatively simple and believable form of commensurabilism. The incommensurabilist will also reject a weaker, potentially more plausible conjunctive claim, namely this: that, given some rational agent possessed of a valuational, ethical, normative (etc.) outlook, there always exists, in principle, some account of how different sorts of objects of concern trade off for him, either at a constant ratio or at a systematically varying ratio of substitution, and this account is *explanatory, projectible,* and *counterfactual-sustaining.* The incommensurabilist will not, of course, deny that after the event, some such ratio might be hit upon. That claim is nearly vacuous, and the incommensurabilist will be foolish to deny the nearly vacuous.[9] The claim does not give any empirical content to the idea of maximizing anything. It does not represent a falsifiable claim about the agent's springs of action.

Maybe nobody will see any reason to assert what the incommensurabilist denies here. (If so, then see below section 11.) Maybe nobody at all will own up to believing the things the incommensurabilist disbelieves. However that may be, what the incommensurabilist holds (in defiance of any lazy scientism to which his adversaries cling in the privacy of the closet) is that for an ordinary agent to have a sane, reasonable outlook is not (in real life, in the real world) the same thing at all as it is for his outlook to amount to a preference ordering by reference to which the agent's well-considered actions may be seen as maximizing anything.[10]

11. Such then is the idea for the third proposal. The proposal under review could issue in definitions of incommensurability for a given agent and of incom-

mensurability for the rational agent. I postpone such refinements, however. It is more urgent to fill out the philosophical background for the denials that the incommensurabilist is issuing. Let us inquire also how reasonable beings do identify what is at issue when they decide in hard cases and arbitrate between the strident, mutually inimical rival claims of their various commitments, arriving thus at their choices—choices that may or may not command the acquiescence of other reasonable beings. What is it for them to do this better or worse?

Suppose—with Aristotle and common sense—that the subject matter of the practical is by its nature both indefinite and unforeseeable. Then there does not exist the option, which one might otherwise have supposed there would be, for an agent to measure in advance what exactly any kind of commitment lets him in for, either in and of itself or in relation to all his distinct commitments (whatever *they* may prove to amount to). It cannot be predicted in the real world how much scope one positive commitment will allow to others. (Contrast the acceptance of certain prohibitions, on which compare, e.g., Aristotle N.E.1110a29.) Nor can it be predicted what it will take to persist in a given commitment. If such is the condition of human agents, however, then theorists of practical reason ought to leave room for practical reason to propose to agents something other than that they should make as if to consult their preference function. The preferred picture must be that agents learn to decide about practical things by learning what it is they are to look to and learning how to interpret and reinterpret their given conceptions of the thing they are to look to. What we have to make speculative sense of is agents' making the best sense they can of their own positive concerns and commitments in the space not excluded by accepted prohibitions and of their striving to do this even in a world for whose countless and not exhaustively classifiable contingencies no decalogue or code of practice or statement of objectives could ever prepare them.

It will be useful to transcribe here, for the incommensurabilist's use, Aristotle's conception of the practical as it subsists in the real world. Aristotle describes this conception in Book Five of the *Nicomachean Ethics,* at chapter ten, which is on the subject of *epieikeia,* or equity:

> About some things it is not possible to make a general statement which shall be correct. In those cases then in which it is necessary to speak generally but not possible to do so correctly, the law takes the usual case, though it is not ignorant of the possibility of error. And it is not wrong to do so: for the shortcoming is not in the law nor in the lawgiver but in the nature of the thing, since the subject matter of the practical is like this from the outset. About some things it is impossible to lay down a law, so

that a particular decree is needed. For when the thing is indefinite, the rule also is indefinite, like the leaden rule used in making the Lesbian mould-ing: the rule adapts itself to the shape of the stone and is not rigid. So too a decree adapts itself to the particular facts.

Somehow, on the shifting ground that Aristotle describes here—his contention in this passage relates to problems of public legislation and adjudication,[11] but his perception of the nature of the practical is an entirely general one—individual agents do find a way to make real their conceptions of living and being. For they do deliberate, in the light of the good and the possible, about ends, about the constituents of ends, and about the means to ends. Somehow, despite the intractability and uncertainty of the subject matter of choice, agents do arrive at judgments about what is worthwhile or what can or cannot be done in pursuit of what. And somehow, from out of all this, they arrive at shared, partly inexplicit norms of reasonableness—and they set standards, not fully verbalized, by which people of good sense and good character can live. If these norms are only misdescribed when they are seen as norms of maximization, then the thing philosophy had best do is to desist altogether from the attempt to identify that which is to be maximized. It must attend instead to the various ideas that give the however essentially contestable content of reasonable agents' conceptions of the good. *Pace* the received misinterpretations of Aristotle, the main business of practical reason is ends and their constituents, not instrumental means. For an Aristotelian, the idea that a self-contained part of the concept of rationality can be bitten off and studied in value-free fashion as the rationality of means, leaving the rest, that is ends, to the taste or formation of individual agents, is a delusion, and a gratuitous delusion at that.[12]

12. I expect that a skeptic about everything that passes under the name of incommensurability or about our freedom to make and constantly remake our conception of the good may now join forces with the skeptic who doubts all the other things to which the new conception of incommensurability is intended to lend succor. The following declaration may be expected:

> Given any two options or packages and given a rational agent with desires and concerns of his own, either the agent will *qua* rational ascribe to the items equal overall utility or he will ascribe higher overall utility to one of them—where overall utility is the satisfaction of *all* the agent's diverse concerns, commitments (etc.) and relates in the obvious way to all the agent's various reasons to pursue this or that line of conduct. Surely the rational agent is one who unremittingly and consistently pursues this utility.

So far as I can see, this statement treats it as simply obvious that, for every rational chooser, there is something he or she is constantly seeking to maximize, namely the thing the objector calls "the chooser's utility". That is to say that the statement ignores almost everything I have said already. Despite that, I shall persevere with the objector, and shall even do the best I can not to repeat myself too much.

One difficulty for the utility thesis as it appears here I shall mention but then discount. This is the existence of weakness of will.[13] The objection, which I do want to insist upon, goes as follows: that insofar as the commensurabilist cum maximizing account of individual choice is not deprived of all empirical content and all explanatory or predictive interest (a privation that can easily escape notice in the postpositivist or postlogical empiricist phase of social theorizing), no reason whatever has ever been given to believe it—neither in the shape of telling conceptual considerations (for these would depend on the demonstration, still lacking, that the maximizing model furnishes the best way of characterizing a person's practical outlook or his springs of action) nor yet in the shape of empirical evidence. Indeed, in actual cases where a predictive or empirical theory is really needed and entrepreneurs also have something to lose by getting things wrong (e.g., in connection with the concern to make money by selling things that might be retailed at a profit), what we observe in the real world (or so I have been told by those who inhabit that part of it) is that nobody seriously proposes to make any distinctive use at all of rational choice theory or its modes of characterization of the springs of action.[14] In practice, the thing that is always deployed in the world of commerce is empirical phenomenology—or market research, to give it a more familiar name. This last is a modest, useful business, but it stands in no more need of the supposition that individual choices and the constraints on choices derive from the chooser's striving after a maximum than does advertising or any other method of persuasion on whose behalf market research can spy out the ground.[15]

13. Having come so far, let me recapitulate the third proposal and then paint in one further detail.

Suppose then that (as already claimed) our different valuations and pursuits are grounded in a multiplicity of distinct concerns, which are rooted in a multiplicity of different psychic structures, which make distinct and mutually irreducible claims upon us; suppose that a particular practical cum ethical outlook is something an agent works out in confrontation with the indefinitely varied contingencies (in the forms of opportunity and constraint) with which the world confronts him as he lives, as he acts, and as he responds to each new contingency in the light of past responses to past contingencies; suppose that there is not for each rational agent some general, predeterminable, and/or at least projectible rate (or yet some projectible systematically variable rate) at which different values such as honor, altruism, pleasure, safety, comfort, morality . . . will trade off for him against one another in the manner that is visually represented, for a given case involving *n* things, in given circumstances, under given constraints (budget, etc.), by an indifference map in *n* dimensions. We are to suppose, then, that there is no *general* (i.e., all context negotiating) way of arranging different quantities of honor, pleasure, safety, comfort, benevolence, justice, . . . into bundles that are valued equally by the agent. (As always, the denial depends upon taking projectibility seriously. Note also that the dots . . . are not the dots of laziness. We do not know how to complete this enumeration.) Suppose finally that we do arbitrate between such concerns constantly in our confrontation with whatever it is to which the world forces us to find our response, but that we do this not in the light of a postfactum construct called our utility but in the light of our ideas, our ideals, and our developing and essentially time-bound conception of that life (among the lives that we think it may be a realizable possibility for us to try to lead) in which we can best find meaning.

14. If we suppose all of this, then it provides precisely that which was (or could have been) presupposed by writers who have wanted to dwell upon tragic and/or morally impossible choices. Real dilemmas depend on various values' making autonomous, mutually irreducible demands upon us. The picture offered here suggests how over and over again, in normal life, we may reach accommodations between these demands and live with conviction the accommodations that we find. The picture makes room for the thought that this is a part of the process by which we acquire characters as we age, and so on. The extra thing that needs at this point to be added is this: that there *cannot be any guarantee* that, no matter what the circumstances may be, we shall always be able to find this accommodation. What is more, the picture that was offered earlier left room for that possibility. Where our concerns for *A, B* (which are incommensurable simply in the third sense) *cannot* in a given circumstance *X* be accommodated at all to our sense of how one should live and what one should do, where *nothing* seems to us, even for the context, bearable or livable, there *A* and *B* are also in a fourth and "tragic" sense incommensurable in *X*—or incommensurable for us in *X*.

We need both of these ideas of incommensurability—the third, which was introduced at section, 8 and our new sense. Let us distinguish them as the (common or garden) *incommensurable* and the *circumstantially cum tragically incommensurable*. (So for Sartre's young man, in the circumstances of World War II in occupied France, patriotism and filial duty were circumstantially cum tragically incommensurable.)

15. What, then, is rationality according to this conception, if there is nothing that rational agents need, simply qua rational, to maximize? The answer is that rationality in an agent is the disposition, episodically exercised (and occasionally no doubt not exercised), to prefer (and to persist in the preference for) an act or a belief or an attitude in the light of the standards of evaluation and normative ends and ideals that it is the substantive work of evidential, axiological, moral, and whatever other reflection to determine. The rich fabric of reason and reasonableness is not to be confected from the thin threads of plain consistency, or from any elaboration of such materials. (Indeed consistency only makes practical unreasonableness worse.) It follows that the standard of reasonable conduct that the philosophy of the practical derives from lived experience must attend to each value in its separateness and irreducibility to others. It must specify more and more closely what claims (including moral claims) each value makes on thought, feeling, and appetition. The philosopher of practice must render it as unmysterious as he can how the knowledge of such a standard is not exhausted by the verbalized generalizations or precepts of either agent or theorist. It is the existence of such knowledge that makes it possible, as Aristotle puts it, for the decision to lie in perception, that is, for the decision to depend on the exercise of judgment in confrontation with some actually given particular situation, even as the situation itself (with its larger context) is as specifically conceived by the agent as it is necessary for him to conceive it in order for him to realize or instantiate there his evolving conception of the life that it is for him to lead in the there and then.

What then, with regard to reason and rationality and reasonableness, is the business of philosophy? Surely, to participate in the critique of *reasons,* and to do so in a manner at once participatively engaged yet alert to the need to step off the treadmill, to stand back or to lower the level of optical resolution and look harder in search of scale, shape, and outline. The standards of reasonableness that philosophy can articulate from the critique of lived experience, or by reflection upon the claims that each value makes upon thought, feeling and appetition, will be a distillation from practical knowledge, knowledge not exhausted by the verbalized generalizations or precepts of either agent or theorist (cp. Aristotle, *Nicomachean Ethics* 1143^b, 1126^{b4}, 1109^{b23}).

16. The case for adopting the third and fourth accounts of incommensurability, like the evidence for the general picture presented here of action and choice, rests mostly on the evidence of phenomenology and phenomenological reflection, the last being undertaken in parallel with philosophical analysis of the language we already employ in the daily business of practical appreciation and decision. That language embodies the human account of what moves us. It helps us to make sense in our own way of what we all think and do. Of course, this is weak evidence. Rival accounts come in a far more impressive scientific cum mathematical livery, with countless fair promises of prediction and under-standing. Nevertheless, insofar as they make substantial empirical claims (and this is not a thing to be taken for granted) and insofar as these claims both relate to individual choice and go beyond the ordinary historical and philosophical platitudes concerning actions, beliefs, and desires, or insofar as these accounts enter normative claims about what it is reasonable for reasonable beings to aim for—well, here let us ask ourselves whether those rival accounts come with a shred of evidence, either empirical or conceptual, that is better evidence for them than it is for the working, untheoretical, open-endedly phenomenological account.

❦4❦

Is Incommensurability Vagueness?

JOHN BROOME

1. Indeterminate Comparatives

Which is more impressive: Salisbury Cathedral or Stonehenge? I think there is no determinate answer to this question. The dyadic predicate 'more impressive than'—the comparative of the monadic predicate 'impressive'—seems to allow indeterminate cases. Many comparatives are like that. Among them are many evaluative comparatives, such as 'lovelier than', 'cleverer than', and the generic 'better than'.

For many comparatives, the indeterminacy arises because the comparison involves several factors or dimensions, and it is indeterminate exactly how the factors weigh against each other. The impressiveness of a building depends on some combination of its size, its importance in the landscape, the technological achievement it represents, and more, and it is indeterminate how these factors weigh against each other. Many evaluative comparatives are indeterminate for this reason. They depend on a combination of values, and it is indeterminate how the values are to be weighed. The values are *incommensurable,* we say.

Not all indeterminate comparatives arise from incommensurable dimensions, however. 'Redder than' can also be indeterminate, even though it presumably does not involve several factors. Compare some reddish-purple patch of color with some reddish-orange patch, and ask which is redder. The answer may be indeterminate.

To make it clear, when I say a comparative '*F*er than' is indeterminate, I mean that for some pairs of things, of a sort to which the predicate '*F*er' can apply, there is no determinate answer to the question of which is *F*er than which. Neither is *F*er than the other, nor are the two equally *F.* This paper is about the logical structure of indeterminate comparatives and, in particular, whether they are vague. The analysis is intended to apply to all indeterminate comparatives, but my chief interest is in the structure of evaluative and moral comparatives. I am particularly interested in the structure of 'better than'. I shall argue that the indeterminacy of betterness is commonly misrepresented; it does not take the form that is most commonly assumed.

2. Standard Configurations

I am going to set up a standard framework to use in the investigation. Before doing so, I need to make a few preliminary points about the structure of comparatives. First, two formal features of the structure:

Asymmetry of 'Fer than'. For any x and y, if x is Fer than y, then y is not Fer than x.

Transitivity of 'Fer than'. For any x, y, and z, if x is Fer than y and y is Fer than z, then x is Fer than z.

I think these are principles of logic. If 'Fer than' is indeterminate, that is no reason to doubt them. They are only conditional statements. Asymmetry requires that *if* x is Fer than y, then y is not Fer than x. With an indeterminate comparative, it may turn out for some xs and ys that x is not Fer than y and nor is y Fer than x; this is consistent with asymmetry. Transitivity requires that *if* x is Fer than y and y is Fer than z, then x is Fer than z. If it turns out that neither x is Fer than y nor y Fer than x, than in this case transitivity is vacuously satisfied.

My next point is that no comparative I can think of is indeterminate between every pair of things. For some pairs of color patches, it is indeterminate which is redder than which, but for other pairs, one of the pair is determinately redder than the other. A red patch is determinately redder than an orange patch, for instance. Salisbury Cathedral is determinately more impressive than Bath Abbey. For most comparatives 'Fer than', we can form whole *chains* of things, each of which is Fer than the next in the chain. A well-chosen chain may run from things that are very F to things that are not at all F. For instance, we could form a chain of color patches, each redder than the next, starting from a pure red and running through orange, to a yellow with no red in it at all. Churches could be arranged in a chain, each more impressive than the next. The chain might start with St. Peter's and end with some unimpressive chapel. Stonehenge would not be included in this chain.

Take some chain ordered by 'Fer than'. Then take something that is not included in the chain, and compare it with each of the things that are in the chain, to see which is Fer. It may turn out that there is no determinate answer for any member of the chain. Compare Cantor's diagonal proof that the real numbers are uncountable with churches that make up a chain. Which is more impressive? You might conclude that proofs and churches in general are so different that they can never be determinately compared in terms of their impressiveness. Maybe so and maybe not. Things that are very different from the members of a chain are less likely to be comparable to these members than are similar things. But things that are not too different will normally be comparable to some extent. For instance, take a reddish-purple patch and compare it with the chain of patches I described that runs from red to yellow. The purple patch will be determinately comparable with some members of the chain. Patches at the top of the chain are redder than the purple patch, and the purple patch is redder than patches at the bottom of the chain. But somewhere in the middle there may well be patches where the comparison in indeterminate. To take another example, I think St. Peter's is more impressive than Stonehenge, and Stonehenge is more impressive than the gospel chapel in Stoke Pewsey, but for some churches in the chain, the comparison with Stonehenge will be indeterminate. So as we move down a chain from top to bottom, comparing its members in *F*ness with some object outside the chain, we may start in a zone where the members of the chain are *F*er, then move into a zone where the comparison is indeterminate, and finally come to a zone where the other object is *F*er.

The aim of this paper is to investigate what exactly goes on in the zone of indeterminacy. What is true of things in that zone, and what is not true? To focus the discussion, I shall concentrate on a particular type of example, which I shall call a 'standard configuration'. Here is one of the type. Take a chain of color patches ranging from red through orange to yellow, each patch redder than the next. In fact, let the patches form a continuum: a smooth band of color graded from red at the top to yellow at the bottom. Compare small patches or points of color from this band with a single reddish-purple patch, and consider which is redder. At the top are points redder than the single patch, and at the bottom points that the single patch is redder than.

A *standard configuration* for a comparative '*F*er than' consists of a chain of things, fully ordered by their *F*ness and forming a continuum, and a fixed thing called the *standard* that is not itself in the chain. At the top of the chain are things *F*er than the standard, and at the bottom things the standard is *F*er than. I shall refer to the things that make up the chain as 'points', whatever sort of thing they are.

Two matters of clarification. There may be a zone of indeterminacy between the members of the chain that are *F*er than the standard and those that the standard is *F*er than, and I am particularly interested in cases where there is, but the definition of a standard configuration does not require there to be one. The second point is that the continuum of points may not exist in fact; we may simply imagine it. For instance, actual churches do not form a continuum, but we can imagine a continuum of churches. Also, I have not defined what I mean by a 'continuum'; I hope I may leave that to intuition.

The color example is a standard configuration. Here is another. Suppose you have a choice between two careers, and you are wondering which is better. By this I mean: which would be the better one for you to take up. One offers travel and adventure, the other security and a regular income. Let us take the adventurous career as the standard and form a continuous chain out of the other by varying the amount of income it offers. At the top of the chain are secure jobs with a very high income, and let us suppose these are better than the adventurous career. At the bottom are secure careers offering poor incomes, and let us suppose the adventurous career is better than those. In the middle may be a zone of indeterminacy.

Here is a third example. A government is wondering whether to preserve a stretch of rain forest or open it up for commercial exploitation. Take as the standard the policy of preserving the forest. We can make a chain out of the exploitation option by imagining a range of economic benefits that might arise. Suppose that if the benefits are enormous, exploitation is better, and if the benefits are minute, preservation is better. Somewhere in between may be a zone of indeterminacy.

A standard configuration is illustrated in Figure 1. Graphed against points in the chain, the diagram shows truth values for the statements, 'This point is *F*er than the standard' and 'The standard is *F*er than this point'. At the top of the chain is a zone of points with the property that they are *F*er than the standard and the standard is not *F*er than them. At the bottom is a zone of points with the property that the standard is *F*er than them and they are not *F*er than the standard. That is a constant feature of any standard configuration. But what happens between the top and the bottom zones? There are a number of possibilities, which I shall describe in turn. In sections 9 and 10, I shall discuss which of the possibilities are realized in actual English comparatives.

3. No Indeterminacy

The first possibility is that there is no more than one point between the top zone and the bottom zone. It may be that, for every point in the chain, either it is *F*er than the standard or the standard is *F*er than it. Alternatively, there may be just one point for which this is not so. In both of these cases, there is no indeterminacy. Let us call these type (a) determinacy and type (b) determinacy, respectively. Figure 2 illustrates either.

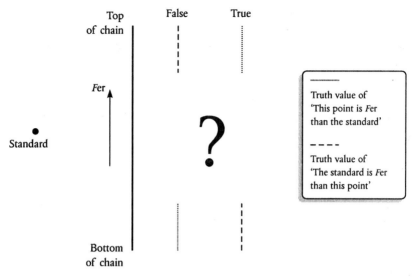

Figure 1   *A Standard Configuration*

In type (b) determinacy, I assume the unique point must be equally as *F* as the standard. That is why I say these cases have no indeterminacy: for every point, either it is *F*er than the standard, or the standard is *F*er than it, or it is equally as *F* as the standard. What justifies this assumption? Not much, I am sorry to say, but here is my reason for adopting it.

Take a standard configuration, and suppose one point in the chain is equally as *F* as the standard. Since higher points are *F*er than this point, and this point is equally as *F* as the standard, it follows that higher points are *F*er than the standard. This is an application of the principle:

> *Extended transitivity of* '*F*er than'. For any *x*, *y*, and *z*, if *x* is *F*er than *y* and *y* is equally as *F* as *z*, or if *x* is equally as *F* as *y* and *y* is *F*er than *z*, then *x* is *F*er than *z*.

This is a small extension of the transitivity principle, and I take it too to be a principle of logic. The same extended transitivity implies that if one point in a chain is equally as *F* as the standard, then the standard is *F*er than all lower points.

So if one point is equally as *F* as the standard, then for every other point in the chain, either it is *F*er than the standard or the standard is *F*er than it. I am inclined to believe the converse—that is, if for every point in a continuous chain bar one, either it is *F*er than the standard or the standard is *F*er than it, but for

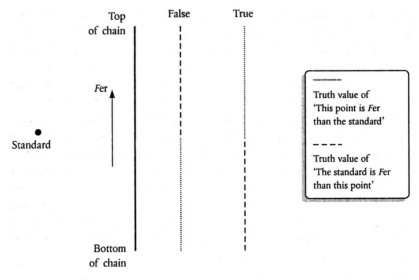

Figure 2   *No Indeterminacy*

one point this is not so, then I am inclined to believe this one point must be equally as *F* as the standard. In fact, I am inclined to believe that 'equally as *F* as' is not an independent notion at all but can be defined in terms of *Fer* than. I would say that '*x* is equally as *F* as *y*' means that *x* is not *Fer* than *y*, and *y* is not *Fer* than *x*, and anything that is *Fer* than *x* is also *Fer* than *y*, and *y* is *Fer* than anything *x* is *Fer* than. This is the basis of my assumption that in type (b) determinacy, the unique point is equally as good as the standard. I have no argument for it, but I can think of no counterexample.

Also, I can think of no examples of type (a) determinacy. I suspect it does not exist. This must depend on precisely what is meant by saying that the chain of points in a standard configuration is *continuous*. It has no gaps in it, but in what sense precisely? Since I have not given a precise definition, I cannot be sure whether type (a) determinacy exists. It does not matter in this paper.

4. Hard Indeterminacy

The next possibility is that there is more than one point in the chain such that it is not *Fer* than the standard and the standard is not *Fer* than it. All the points with this property form a central zone.

None of them can be equally as *F* as the standard. If one was, I showed in section 3 that all points above it would be *F*er than the standard and the standard would be *F*er than all points below it. Then only this one point would have the property that it is not *F*er than the standard and the standard is not *F*er than it. But our assumption is that there is more than one point with this property.

The whole central zone, then, constitutes a zone of indeterminacy. If there is more than one point in the chain such that it is not *F*er than the standard, and the standard is not *F*er than it, I shall say that '*F*er than' has *hard indeterminacy*.

Hard indeterminacy is not vagueness. It is definite that points within the zone of indeterminacy are not *F*er than the standard and the standard is not *F*er than them. However, it is natural to think there is often something vague about an indeterminate comparative. Take 'redder than', for instance. 'Redder than the standard' is a monadic predicate, and it is natural to think it may be vague, like the predicate 'red'. Start from the top of the chain in the standard configuration I described, which runs from red to yellow. Points at the top of the chain are red, and it seems implausible that as we move down the chain, we encounter a sharp boundary that divides these points that are red from those that are not red. Similarly, points at the top are redder than the standard (which is reddish-purple and not in the chain itself), and one might find it implausible that as we move down the chain, we encounter a sharp boundary that divides these points that are redder than this standard from points that are not redder than it. Instead, it seems there may be a zone of vagueness between the points that are redder than the standard and those that are not. For many comparatives '*F*er than', it seems plausible there is a zone of vagueness between points that are *F*er than the standard and points that are not. There seems also to be an area of vagueness at the bottom of the zone of indeterminacy, between points the standard is not *F*er than and those it is.

Is vagueness like this compatible with hard indeterminacy? At first it seems it should be. Hard indeterminacy simply says there is a zone where points are not *F*er than the standard and the standard is not *F*er than them. The vagueness I have just described is around the borders of this zone. The suggestion is that the borders are vague rather than sharp. The zone of indeterminacy is bordered by zones of vagueness. At first there seems nothing wrong with that. However, oddly enough, it turns out that this cannot be so. The boundaries of the zone of indeterminacy must be sharp rather than vague, for the following reason.

Take any point somewhere around the top boundary of the zone of indeterminacy. Clearly it is false that the standard is *F*er than this point, since this is false for all points in the zone of indeterminacy and above. If it is also false that this point is *F*er than the standard, then the point is squarely within the zone of indeterminacy. If, on the other hand, it is true that this point is *F*er than the standard, then it is squarely within the top zone. So if there is really a zone of vagueness, for points in this zone it must be neither true nor false that they are *F*er than the standard. But now we can apply something I call the *collapsing principle:*

> *The collapsing principle, special version.* For any *x* and *y*, if it is false that *y* is *F*er than *x* and not false that *x* is *F*er than *y*, then it is true that *x* is *F*er than *y*.

This principle is crucial to the argument of this paper. I shall defend it in the next section; here I shall simply apply it. I have just said that for a point in the zone of vagueness, if there is such a zone, it is false that the standard is *F*er than it, but not false that it is *F*er than the standard. Then according to the collapsing principle, it is true that it is *F*er than the standard. This implies it is not in a zone of vagueness after all. So there is no such zone.

Figure 3 shows hard indeterminacy. As we move down the chain from the top, starting with points that are *F*er than the standard, we suddenly come to ones that are not *F*er than the standard. Later, having found only points that the standard is not *F*er than, we suddenly encounter ones that the standard is *F*er than.

A comparative that has hard indeterminacy is a strict partial ordering without vagueness.

5. The Collapsing Principle

The proof in the previous section depended crucially on the collapsing principle. Now I need to justify it. My only real argument is this: If it is false that *y* is *F*er than *x*, and not false that *x* is *F*er than *y*, then *x* has a clear advantage over *y* in respect of its *F*ness. So it must be *F*er than *y*. It takes only the slightest asymmetry to make it the case that one thing is *F*er than another. One object is heavier than another if the scales tip ever so slightly toward it. Here there is a clear asymmetry between *x* and *y* in respect of their *F*ness. That is enough to determine that *x* is *F*er than *y*.

I find this obvious, and here is a thought experiment to reinforce its obviousness. Suppose you had to award a prize to either *x* or *y* for its *F*ness. Suburbs in Canberra are named after great Australians, and each new suburb has to go to the greatest Australian who does not yet have a suburb. Suppose there are two candidates for the next suburb, and you have to decide between them. Suppose that, on investigating their cases, you conclude it is false that Wye is a greater

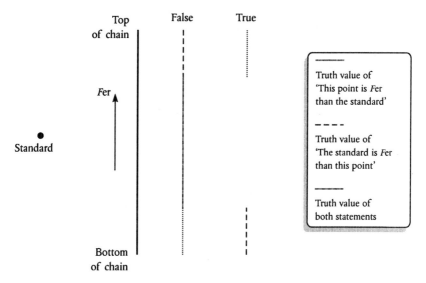

Figure 3   *Hard Indeterminacy*

Australian than Exe, but that it is not false that Exe is a greater Australian than Wye. This is not at all like the case where you conclude that Wye and Exe are equally great Australians, because then it is not clear who should get the suburb. You should probably toss a coin. Nor is it like the case where you conclude that neither Wye nor Exe is greater than the other and they are not equally great either. This is a case squarely in the zone of indeterminacy. In this case, it is once again not clear who should get the suburb, just because neither candidate is better than the other. Perhaps you should toss a coin in this case too, or perhaps some other procedure would be right. But when it is false that Wye is greater than Exe, but not false that Exe is greater than Wye, you need not hesitate. It would be quite wrong to give the suburb to Wye. Since the prize was for being the greater Australian, it could not be so obvious who should win unless that person was the greater Australian.

When it is false that *y* is *F*er than *x* but not false that *x* is *F*er than *y*, then if you had to award a prize for *F*ness, it is plain you should give the prize to *x*. But it would not be plain unless *x* was *F*er than *y*. Therefore, *x* is *F*er than *y*. This must be so whether you actually have to give a prize or not, since whether or not you have to give a prize cannot affect whether or not *x* is *F*er than *y*.

6. Soft Indeterminacy

What other options are there for the structure of a comparative 'Fer than'? No other option can allow the existence of points in the chain such that they are not Fer than the standard and the standard is not Fer than them (that is, such that it is false that they are Fer than the standard and false that the standard is Fer than them). That would be hard indeterminacy. But it might be possible for there to be points such that it is neither true nor false that they are Fer than the standard, and neither true nor false that the standard is Fer than them. There could be a zone of indeterminacy composed of points like this. I call this case *soft indeterminacy*.

None of the points in the zone of indeterminacy can be equally as *F* as the standard, since if a point was equally as *F* as the standard, it would be false that it was better than the standard, whereas it is not false. Therefore, the zone of indeterminacy must have more than one point in it. If there were only one point, I argued in section 3 that it would have to be equally as *F* as the standard. But I have just said this is impossible.

Unlike hard indeterminacy, which has no vagueness, soft indeterminacy is entirely vagueness. The zone of indeterminacy is also a zone of vagueness. For any point in the zone, it is vague whether or not it is Fer than the standard and vague whether or not the standard is Fer than it.

The possible structures of a softly indeterminate comparative are severely limited. Once again, it is chiefly the collapsing principle that limits them. One limit is that, for any point, it is neither true nor false that it is Fer than the standard if and only if it is neither true nor false that the standard is Fer than it. So the entire zone of indeterminacy necessarily has vagueness of both sorts; the comparison is vague taken either way. Here is the proof. First, suppose some point is Fer than the standard, and it is neither true nor false that the standard is Fer than it. Since this point is Fer than the standard, the asymmetry of 'Fer than' implies the standard is not Fer than it. This contradicts that it is neither true nor false that the standard is Fer than it. Second, suppose a point is not Fer than the standard, and it is neither true nor false that the standard is Fer than it. From this supposition, the special version of the collapsing principle, stated in section 4, implies that the standard is Fer than the point. That contradicts that it is neither true nor false that the standard is Fer than it. The rest of the proof is a matter of ringing the changes.

Another limit on the structure of softly indeterminate comparatives is imposed by a more general version of the collapsing principle. My statement of this version needs a preface. I intend it to be neutral between competing theories of vagueness. It uses the expression 'more true than', but this is not to be read as implying the existence of degrees of truth as they are usually understood. Its meaning is wider. For instance, if P is true and Q is false, then I would say P is more true than Q. If P is neither true nor false and Q is false, again I would say P is more true than Q. In this case, P is certainly less false than Q, and I intend 'more true' to include 'less false'. If P is definitely true and Q is not definitely true, I would again say that P is more true than Q. In general, I will say P is more true than Q whenever P in any way rates more highly than Q in respect of its truth. Now, the principle is:

> *The collapsing principle, general version.* For any x and y, if it is more true that x is *F*er than y than that y is *F*er than x, then x is *F*er than y.[1]

The argument for it is the same as the one I gave in section 5 for the special version. Remember that this principle is specifically about reciprocal comparative statements. I do not endorse the general claim that if any statement P is more true than another statement Q, then P is true, nor the different specific claim that if P is more true than its negation $\neg P$, then P is true. If someone is more dead than alive, I do not believe she is necessarily dead.

The general version of the collapsing principle implies that for no point in the zone of indeterminacy can it be more true that the point is *F*er than the standard than that the standard is *F*er than it. Nor can it be less true. This leaves open several possibilities, corresponding to different theories of vagueness. One theory is that when statements are vague, they have no truth value. Figure 4 illustrates how soft indeterminacy will appear from this point of view; I have called it type (a) soft indeterminacy. Evidently it is consistent with the collapsing principle. According to other theories, vague statements may have some other truth value besides true or false. It would be consistent with the collapsing principle for 'This point is *F*er than the standard' and 'The standard is *F*er than this point' to have the same truth value throughout the zone of indeterminacy. It might be 'indefinite', say, or some particular degree of truth. Figure 5 illustrates this possibility. I have called it type (b) soft indeterminacy.

7. Incomparable Truth Values

Both types (a) and (b) of soft indeterminacy fail to capture one natural intuition. For any point in the zone of indeterminacy, it is neither true nor false that it is *F*er than the standard. But intuition suggests that in some sense or other, the statement, 'This point is *F*er than the standard', is truer for points near the top of the zone than for points near the bottom. For points near the top, indeed, it

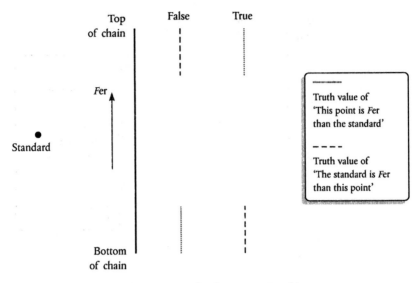

Figure 4 *Soft Indeterminacy Type (a)*

seems it must be almost true they are *Fer* than the standard, and for points near the bottom it seems this must be almost false.

This intuition clearly implies that statements can be true to a greater or lesser degree. So in order to discuss it, I shall have to give up my attempt to be neutral among competing theories of vagueness. For this discussion, I shall take it for granted that there are degrees of truth. Anyway, the study of comparatives suggests there are. Suppose x is redder than y. This implies that x has redness to a greater degree than y has it, so there are degrees of redness.[2] But it seems also to imply that x is red more than y is red, which in turn surely implies that 'x is red' is truer than 'y is red', so there are degrees of truth. I shall say more about this in section 8. Other sorts of comparisons perhaps point more clearly to degrees of truth, because they more clearly compare statements. 'It's raining more than it's snowing' seems clearly to imply that 'It's raining' is truer than 'It's snowing'.

One intuition, then, is that as we move from point to point up through the zone of indeterminacy, 'This point is *Fer* than the standard' becomes progressively more true and 'The standard is *Fer* than this point' progressively less true. At first, this intuition seems to be inconsistent with the collapsing principle. It seems to imply that as we move up through the zone, we must eventually encounter points for which 'This point is *Fer* than the standard' is more true than

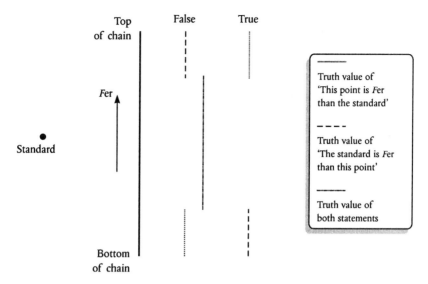

Figure 5   *Soft Indeterminacy Type (b)*

'The standard is *F*er than this point'. But then the collapsing principle will kick in and say these points must actually be determinately *F*er than the standard: they are not in the zone of indeterminacy after all.

However, a point made by Adam Morton can be used to show this need not happen.[3] It may be that the truth values of 'This point is *F*er than the standard' and 'The standard is *F*er than this point' are incomparable throughout the zone of indeterminacy, but nevertheless one of these statements may increase in truth value as we move up through the zone and the other may decrease. The reason this seems impossible at first is that we traditionally think of degrees of truth as numbers between zero and one. At least, we assume they are linearly ordered. If degrees are linearly ordered, every degree is comparable with every other. But degrees are not linearly ordered, and there really are incomparable degrees.

The evidence that there are incomparable degrees is this. I have already assumed that if x is redder than y, 'x is red' is truer than 'y is red'. We know already that in many cases it is indeterminate which of x and y is redder. In those cases it must be indeterminate which of 'x is red' and 'y is red' is truer. So because comparatives can be indeterminate, degrees of truth can be incomparable. Given that, there is no reason why it should not be indeterminate which of 'This point is *F*er than the standard' and 'The standard is *F*er than this point' is truer. This gives us a type (c) of soft indeterminacy. I have illustrated it as well as I can

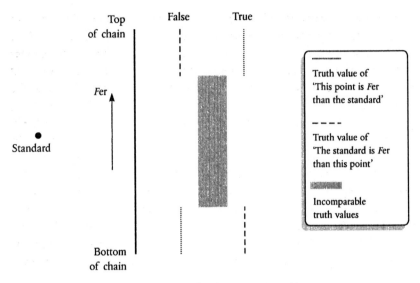

Figure 6   *Soft Indeterminacy Type (c)*

in Figure 6, but the illustration is inadequate because I can find no way of showing the truth values of the two statements varying through the zone of indeterminacy.

Type (c) indeterminacy raises a more complex question. If it is indeterminate which of two statements—specifically, 'This point is *F*er than the standard' and 'The standard is *F*er than this point'—is truer, just what sort of indeterminacy is this? This is a question about the structure of the comparative 'truer than': Does it have hard or soft indeterminacy in this application? I suggest it has soft indeterminacy, on grounds of uniformity. 'x is *F*er than y' implies 'x is *F*' is truer than 'y is *F*'. So if '*F*er than' is softly indeterminate, 'truer than' must be softly indeterminate between statements of the form 'x is *F*'. My suggestion is that it is also softly indeterminate between statements of the form 'x is *F*er than y' (such as, 'This point is *F*er than the standard') or equivalently between statements of the form "'x is *F*' is truer than 'y is *F*'". I also suggest it is softly indeterminate between statements at the next level of complexity: statements of the form "'x is *F*' is truer than 'y is *F*' is truer than 'y is *F*' is truer than 'x is *F*'". In fact, I suggest we find only soft indeterminacy as we iterate to infinity.[4] My reason is that I would expect 'truer than' to have a uniform structure wherever it is used.

Type (c) soft indeterminacy satisfies our intuitions to some extent, but not completely. One intuition is that as we move up through the zone of indeterminacy, it becomes progressively truer that the points we encounter are *F*er than the standard, and progressively less true that the standard is *F*er than them. Type (c) indeterminacy reconciles this idea with the collapsing principle. But another intuition is that as we get near the top of the zone, it becomes nearly true that the points we encounter are *F*er than the standard, and nearly false that the standard is *F*er than them. I think this really is inconsistent with the collapsing principle. If one statement is nearly true and another nearly false, it is surely undeniable that the first is truer than the second. Other degrees of truth might be incomparable, but the degrees 'nearly true' and 'nearly false' are plainly comparable. So the intuition suggests that, for points near the top of the zone, it is truer that they are *F*er than the standard than that the standard is *F*er than them. This drags in the collapsing principle in the usual way and leads to a contradiction. So even in type (c) indeterminacy, at the boundary of the zone of indeterminacy, 'This point is *F*er than the standard' changes its truth value sharply. At the top boundary, its value drops from true to some degree that is not nearly true.

8. Supervaluation

The most widely held theory of vagueness is supervaluation theory.[5] If we take this theory on board, what can we add to the analysis?

When a term is vague, there are various ways it could acceptably be made sharp. Suppose '*F*er than' is vague—softly indeterminate, that is—and in particular suppose it is vague whether x is *F*er than y. Then if '*F*er than' was sharpened in one direction, x would be *F*er than y, and if it was sharpened in another direction, y would be *F*er than x. I shall confine the word 'sharpening' to sharpenings that are *complete*: they are not themselves vague, that is. According to supervaluation theory:

> *Supervaluation.* A statement containing a vague term is true if and only if it is true under all acceptable sharpenings of the term.

The sharpenings of a vague comparative '*F*er than' will be comparatives. Since they are not themselves vague, they must either be fully determinate or have hard indeterminacy. Which will it be? I cannot rule out either possibility on logical grounds. A vague comparative may have as its sharpenings both determinate comparatives and comparatives with hard indeterminacy. Alternatively, a vague comparative may have only determinate comparatives as its sharpenings. However, I can show that no vague comparative can have only comparatives with hard indeterminacy as its sharpenings; at least some of its sharpenings must be determinate.

Here is the demonstration. Suppose every sharpening of *F*er has hard indeterminacy. Then each sharpening has two 'switch points', as I shall call them. The lower switch point is where 'The standard is *F*er than this point' switches from true to false as we move up the chain; the upper switch point is where 'This point is *F*er than the standard' switches from false to true. For every sharpening, there is a gap between these switch points. Now think about the top end of the zone of indeterminacy. Every sharpening must have its upper switch point within the zone, so every sharpening must have its lower switch point a definite distance below the top of the zone. Consequently, there will be some points within the zone that are above the lower switch point of every sharpening. (I shall ignore the mathematical possibility that there might be a sequence of sharpenings such that the distance between their switch points tends to zero; this is uninteresting.) For these points, every sharpening makes it false that the standard is *F*er than them. That is, every sharpening makes it true that the standard is not *F*er than them. Consequently, it is definitely true that the standard is *F*er than them. But in the zone of indeterminacy this is not so, so there is a contradiction.

Why does it matter what sort of indeterminacy the sharpenings have? If all the sharpenings of a softly indeterminate comparative were determinate, we could draw a striking conclusion. In every sharpening of '*F*er than', it would be true of every point that either it is *F*er than the standard, or the standard is *F*er than it, or that it and the standard are equally *F.* Since this would be true of every point in every sharpening, according to supervaluation theory it would simply be true of every point. Even when '*F*er than' is softly indeterminate, it would nevertheless be the case for every point that either it is *F*er than the standard, or the standard is *F*er than it, or it and the standard are equally *F.* This may seem puzzling, since for any point in the zone of indeterminacy, we know already it is not true that the point is *F*er than the standard, and it is not true that the standard is *F*er than the point, and it is not true that the point and the standard are equally *F.* Since none of these three things is true, how can their disjunction be true? The answer is, in the same way as the law of the excluded middle is true according to supervaluation theory. If *F* is vague, then for some *x* it may not be true that *x* is *F* nor true that *x* is not *F.* Nevertheless, according to supervaluation theory, the disjunction is true: *x* is either *F* or not *F,* since this disjunction is true in every sharpening.[6]

So, if every sharpening of a softly indeterminate comparative were determinate, the contrast between hard determinacy and soft determinacy would be particularly stark. In hard indeterminacy, no point in the zone of indeterminacy is *F*er than the standard, nor is the standard *F*er than it, nor are it and the standard equally *F.* In soft indeterminacy, for every point, either it is *F*er than the standard, or the standard is *F*er than it, or it and the standard are equally *F.*

Now, what version of soft indeterminacy does supervaluation theory support? Many supervaluationists refuse to recognize degrees of truth,[7] and that suggests they would adopt type (a) as their version. But I propose a small addition to the theory that I think should be readily accepted. I propose:

> *Greatervaluation.* One statement P, containing a vague term, is truer than another Q if P is true in every sharpening that makes Q true, and also true in some sharpening that does not make Q true.

When people dislike the idea of degrees of truth, I think that is generally because they assume degrees must be linearly ordered. Greatervaluation does not imply that.

I offer greatervaluation only as a sufficient condition for P to be truer than Q. It is not a necessary condition, as this example shows. Compare a reddish-orange patch with a pure orange patch. The former is redder than the latter. Consequently, it is more true that the former is red than that the latter is red. However, there is no sharpening of the language in which it is true that the former is red.

Now take a pair of points, one higher in the zone of indeterminacy than the other. Any sharpening that makes the lower point *F*er than the standard will also make the higher point *F*er than the standard, but there will be some sharpenings that make the higher point *F*er than the standard and the lower point not *F*er than the standard. So according to greatervaluation, it is more true that the higher point is *F*er than the standard than that the lower point is. Similarly, it is more true that the standard is *F*er than the lower point than that it is *F*er than the higher point. As we move up through the zone, then, it becomes progressively more true that the points we encounter are *F*er than the standard, and progressively less true that the standard is *F*er than them. This implies type (c) indeterminacy, so greatervaluation supports this type.

9. Ordinary Comparatives Are Softly Indeterminate

I have now laid out the possible structures a comparative might have. What structures do we find among our ordinary comparatives? I particularly want to ask what is the structure of 'better than'.

Without doubt, there are comparatives that have no indeterminacy. 'Heavier than' is one.

Are there comparatives with hard indeterminacy? A comparative with hard indeterminacy is a strict partial ordering without vagueness. There are plenty of such orderings around; the question is whether any of them are the comparatives of monadic predicates.

It may be possible to construe some of them artificially as comparatives, by deriving monadic predicates from them. For instance, let us say that one object is mucheavier than another if and only if it is more than one kilo heavier than the other. Then the relation 'mucheavier than' is a strict partial ordering without vagueness. Let us say it is the comparative of a monadic predicate 'mucheavy'. Then 'mucheavy' is a predicate whose comparative has hard indeterminacy. However, I am not convinced that the predicate 'mucheavy' really exists. The only property of objects that is involved in the relation 'mucheavier than' is their heaviness. The objects have no separate property that a predicate 'mucheavy' could refer to, and that suggests there is no such predicate. I do not think 'mucheavier than' is the comparative of any predicate; instead it is a fragment of the genuine comparative 'heavier than', the comparative of 'heavy'.

Or take another example of a strict partial ordering without vagueness. Let us say that one option is 'Pareto-better' than another if and only if it is better for someone and not worse for anyone. Pareto-betterness defined this way is a strict partial ordering, and for the sake of argument let us assume it is not vague. Could we define a monadic predicate 'Pareto-good' to have 'Pareto-better than' as its comparative? Once again I am doubtful. The only property of options that seems to be in play is their goodness. Pareto-betterness is best understood as a partial, sufficient criterion for 'better than', the comparative of goodness, rather than as itself the complete comparative of anything. There are people who think that Pareto-betterness is actually a *complete* criterion for betterness, so that one option is better than another if and only if it is better for someone and not worse for anyone. These people do not try to construct an artificial predicate out of the relation 'Pareto-better than'. Instead they think that 'better than', the comparative of the natural predicate 'good', happens to be extensionally equivalent to 'Pareto-better than'. If they were right, 'better than' would have hard indeterminacy, but I shall say in section 10 why I think they are wrong.

These examples suggest to me that constructing artificial comparatives with hard indeterminacy may not be as easy as it seems. But I do not insist they cannot be constructed. Perhaps they can. I am interested in our ordinary, natural comparatives. Do any of them have hard indeterminacy?

I find it implausible that any do. My reasons are these. First, the difficulty of finding artificial comparatives with hard indeterminacy suggests to me there is something fishy about hard indeterminacy in general. A comparative with hard indeterminacy is incomplete, and that suggests it may be a fragment of a complete comparative rather than a comparative in its own right. Second and more important, I showed in section 4 that if a comparative has hard indeterminacy, it cannot be vague. I find it implausible that indeterminate comparatives are not vague at all.

If a comparative has hard indeterminacy, then as we move down from the top of a chain in a standard configuration, there comes a point where 'This point is Fer than the standard' suddenly changes from true to false. So the monadic predicate 'Fer than the standard' is sharp and not vague. I find this implausible for indeterminate comparatives. Why? I do not think it is as obvious as the vagueness of many predicates. Take 'red', for instance. If we may move down a continuous chain of color patches from pure red to yellow, it seems obvious there is no point in the chain where the patches suddenly cease to be red. Therefore, 'red' is vague. But a predicate of the form 'Fer than the standard' cannot be quite so obviously vague, because it will not be vague everywhere. Take 'redder than the standard', for instance. Take the chain of colors from red to yellow, and for a moment let the standard be a patch that exactly matches some point in the chain. Then higher points are redder than the standard and lower points are not redder than the standard, and the transition is sharp. Since there is a sharp transition for certain standards, it is not perfectly obvious that there is no sharp transition for other standards.

Notice first about this example that it has no indeterminacy. The point in the chain that exactly matches the standard is equally as red as the standard. Higher points are redder than the standard, and the standard is redder than lower points, so this is not an example of hard indeterminacy. Moreover, I am sure there is no sharp transition when the standard is, say, reddish-purple and does not match a point in the chain. The reason is that if there is a sharp transition, I cannot tell where it is. I know no way of detecting where it is, and I know of no one who can detect where it is. If there is a point of transition, it is undetectable, and I do not believe redness can have an undetectable boundary of this sort. The same goes for every other natural indeterminate comparative I can think of, including evaluative ones.

I think ordinary indeterminate comparatives are softly indeterminate. Admittedly, even soft indeterminacy has a sharp boundary of a sort. There is a sharp boundary between points where 'This point is Fer than the standard' is true and points where it is not true. I find it hard to believe in a sharp transition of this sort. It is the collapsing principle that demands it, and this implication of the principle is paradoxical. The principle implies there are sharp boundaries where there seem to be none. I am recommending soft rather than hard indeterminacy as the lesser of two evils. It certainly is the lesser evil. In soft indeterminacy, the sharp transition is between points where 'This point is Fer than the standard' is true and points where it is not true. In hard indeterminacy it is between points where this statement is true and points where it is false. So the transition in soft indeterminacy is not so abrupt. Furthermore, in type (c) soft indeterminacy, 'This point is *F*er than the standard' becomes less and less true as we move down through the zone of indeterminacy. This makes the transition even softer. In this respect, type (c) is the least paradoxical type of soft indeterminacy.

10. Other Views

Many authors have described indeterminacy in a way that implies or suggests it is hard. Remember that in section 4 I defined a comparative '*F*er than' to have hard indeterminacy if and only if there is more than one point in a chain such that it is not *F*er than the standard and the standard is not *F*er than it. I explained in section 4 that none of these points can be equally as *F* as the standard, and I explained in section 3 that if there is only one point in a chain such that it is not *F*er than the standard and the standard is not *F*er than it, then it will be equally as *F* as the standard. So '*F*er than' has hard indeterminacy if and only if there is a point in the chain such that it is not *F*er than the standard, and the standard is not *F*er than it, and it is not equally as *F* as the standard. But most authors take it for granted that indeterminate comparatives will satisfy a condition like this. For instance, Christopher Peacocke argues that 'redder than' is indeterminate and says of two color patches that 'neither is red to a greater degree than the other, nor are they equally red'.[8] Joseph Raz says that when *A* and *B* are incommensurable, it is generally 'false that of *A* and *B* either one is better than the other or they are of equal value'.[9] When goods are incommensurable, I myself have said, 'Neither alternative will be better for the person and they will not be equally good for her either'.[10] I could find many more examples. All these authors seem to imply indeterminacy is hard.

But I doubt if many of them are seriously attached to this view. For one thing, there is a way of reading most of their statements that makes them consistent with soft indeterminacy. When Peacocke says that neither object is red to a greater degree than the other, and nor are they equally red, I read him as meaning it is false that either object is red to a greater degree than the other and false that they are equally red. But he could also be read as saying it is not true that either object is red to a greater degree than the other, and not true that they are equally red. This allows the possibility that these statements are neither true nor false, which is consistent with soft indeterminacy. (Raz, though, deliberately rules out this alternative reading.) More important, these authors have not realized that hard indeterminacy in a comparative is incompatible with vagueness. I am sure that once they realize it, they will have no inclination to believe in hard indeterminacy any more. I do not expect much controversy about my claim that indeterminacy is normally soft.

There is a tradition in economics, inspired by Amartya Sen, of representing certain comparatives by means of strict partial orderings without vagueness.[11] For instance, Sen himself uses a strict partial ordering to represent 'more unequal than' (applied to distributions of income),[12] and in another place to represent 'socially preferred to', which I take to mean simply 'better than'.[13] This seems to imply hard indeterminacy. But actually I do not think Sen necessarily has hard indeterminacy in mind. Let us look at one of his arguments.[14]

Suppose we have to compare various alternative arrangements for society, where some are better for some people and others better for others. To judge which are better than which, we have to weigh some people's good against others'. Suppose we cannot do this weighing precisely, but we can do it roughly. There is a range of weights we might give to each person; we should use weights from this range, but it is not precisely determined which. If, for each person, we picked one weight from her range, so we had a set of weights, one for each person, that set would determine a complete ordering of the options. If we picked a different set of weights, that would determine a different complete ordering. Suppose we go through all the combinations of possible weights; each will determine a complete ordering. Now let us say one option is 'clearly above' another if and only if it is above the other in all these orderings. 'Clearly above' is then a strict partial ordering without vagueness, and Sen takes it to represent betterness. Does this mean he thinks 'better than' is not vague?

I can see no evidence for that. Sen says one option is better than another if it is clearly above the other, but I doubt he would insist one option is not better than another if it is not clearly above the other. If neither of two options is clearly above the other, he does not tell us his views about their relative goodness.

If he had to tell us, it would be most natural for him to adopt soft indeterminacy. His explanation of how betterness comes to be a partial ordering is close to supervaluation theory. When applied to alternative arrangements for society, we can say that 'better than' is vague because it is indeterminate how we should weigh together the good of different people. Within the appropriate range, each set of weights constitutes a sharpening of 'better than'. Supervaluation says it is true that one option is better than another if and only if it is true in all sharpenings. Apparently Sen agrees. Supervaluation also says it is true that one option is *not* better than another if and only if *that* is true in all sharpenings. Sen does not state a necessary condition for one option not to be better than another, but it would be natural for him to agree to this too. If he did, he would have adopted soft indeterminacy. When Sen says betterness is a partial order, I do not think that is meant to be a complete account of betterness. If the account were consistently completed, it would amount to soft indeterminacy.

But what of the hard-liner who believes one person's good can never be weighed against another's to determine what is better overall? Suppose this person thinks one option is better than another if and only if it is better for someone and no worse for anyone. Between any pair of options that are not related in this way, suppose she thinks it false that either is better than the other or that they are equally good. She thinks the relation I called earlier 'Pareto-better than' is actually the whole of 'better than', the comparative of 'good'. It is a strict partial ordering, and let us suppose once again it is not vague. This person unequivocally thinks that 'better than' has hard indeterminacy.

My answer to this person is that her position is too implausible to be correct. I could understand someone who thinks there is no such thing as goodness, viewed from a neutral perspective, so that no option could ever be better than another—I mean plain better, rather than, say, better for a particular person. But our hard-liner recognizes the existence of goodness; she simply thinks it can never be determined by weighing one person's good against another's. Now imagine that some piece of good fortune could befall either of two people. Suppose neither of them has any particular entitlement to it. One would scarcely benefit from it at all because she has already received her fill of good fortune. The other would benefit tremendously; the good fortune would lift her from grinding poverty to a comfortable and enjoyable life. Would it be better for the first to receive the good fortune, or the second? If you do not believe in goodness, you will think this question meaningless. But if you recognize goodness, you cannot plausibly deny the question has an answer: the second person. So if goodness exists, then sometimes it can be determined by weighing together the good of different people. Once you acknowledge that, you will have to recognize borderline cases where it is indeterminate precisely how different people's good should be weighed. You will have to acknowledge vagueness in 'better than', and that makes it softly indeterminate.

11. Conclusion

So indeterminate comparatives are softly indeterminate, and that includes 'better than'. What conclusions can we draw? I shall talk about betterness only.

One conclusion is that the commonest formulations of indeterminateness are incorrect or at least misleading. When it is indeterminate which of two things is better, people commonly say that, of two options, neither is better than the other and they are not equally good either. This suggests it is false that either is better than the other, and false that they are equally good. But in a standard configuration, when a point in the zone of indeterminacy is compared with the standard, it is not false that it is better than the standard, and it is not false that the standard is better than it. Indeed, there are grounds for saying that either one is better than the other, or they are equally good. These grounds come from supervaluation theory.

In section 8, where I introduced supervaluation, I showed that some of the sharpenings of a particular comparative must be fully determinate. But I could not rule out on logical grounds the possibility that some of them might have hard indeterminacy. But by now I think I can plausibly rule it out on other grounds. I have not found any indubitable cases of hard indeterminacy even among artificial comparatives, and I very much doubt any exist among natural comparatives. So it seems reasonable to doubt they exist among the sharpenings of vague comparatives. If so, all sharpenings of 'better than' must be fully determinate. In that case, I explained in section 8 that for every point in a chain, either it is better than the standard, or the standard is better than it, or it is equally as good as the standard.

When it is indeterminate which of two things is better, their goodness is in a sense incomparable. But the conclusion I have just drawn makes it clear that in other senses it is not incomparable. Even if you reject this conclusion of supervaluation theory, just recognizing that soft indeterminacy is a sort of vagueness should make you recognize a sort of comparability. When it is indeterminate which of two things is better, it is not true that one is better than the other, but it is also not false. Furthermore, if the indeterminacy is type (c), then it is true to some degree that one is better than the other. And if one of the things improves a little, it will then be more true that it is better than the other. All these are facts about the things' comparative goodness.

❀5❀

Practical Reason and Incommensurable Goods

ELIZABETH ANDERSON

To develop a thought's meaning, we need only determine
what conduct it is fitted to produce.
—William James, *Pragmatism*

Call two goods incommensurable if neither one is better than or equal in
value to the other.[1] The possibility that some goods are incommensurable is
commonly held to pose serious problems for rational choice. This worry depends on two beliefs. One is that value judgments guide rational choice only
through the principle that one must choose a good better than or equal in value
to any alternative. This entails that there is no rational basis for choice between
incommensurable goods. But this would pose no problem if we could somehow
ensure that we could commensurate goods whenever we had to—that is, whenever we met them as *options*. Then the only incommensurable goods would be
such things as worlds governed by different physical laws, between which we
never have to choose. A second belief underlies worries about incommensurability: that the structure of values is independent of the requirements of practical
reason. Only then would the possibility that goods are incommensurable stand
to practical reason as the possibility that the external world is radically unknow-
able stands to theoretical reason: as a cause for alarm, confusion, and skepticism
about reason.

I shall argue that incommensurability poses no problems for rational choice
because both beliefs are false. Value judgments guide practical reason in many
ways besides the optimization principle. I call the theory that explains how this
can be so the *expressive theory of rational choice*. Moreover, the structure of values
cannot be intractable to practical reason because it is generated by practical
reason itself. I call the theory that explains how this can be so *pragmatism*. Pragmatism says that the meaning of a statement is exhausted by its practical implications. Whatever defects it may have as a general theory of meaning, it offers

an excellent account of value judgments. Pragmatism implies that goods are incommensurable whenever we have no reason to compare their values in practice. Sometimes it is boring or pointless to compare them, other times it makes sense to leave room for the free play of nonrational motivations like whims and moods, and sometimes goods play such different roles in deliberation that attempts to compare them head to head are incoherent. All of these cases generate incommensurabilities, but in ways that do not confuse practical reason, since they are its own conclusions.

Pragmatic theories of value are not widely understood. Debates about incommensurable goods have therefore focused on the optimization principle. But pragmatism offers the clearest way to ground alternatives to optimization. Kant constructed a pragmatic theory of value that proposed the same kind of Copernican revolution for practical reason that he attempted for theoretical reason: Instead of trying to establish that practical reason could handle an independent structure of values, he showed how the structure of values was a construction of practical reason. I devote the next section to outlining the general principles of pragmatism, Kant's version of it, and my own pragmatic theory of value, which responds to problems in Kant's theory.

Pragmatic Theories of Value

Practical reason is the power that agents have to adopt and revise their aims and attitudes in response to considerations they take to support or undermine them. Pragmatic theories of value claim that value judgments are constructions of practical reason that guide our reasoning about what to do and what to care about. This has two implications. First, value judgments have no proper application outside of practical reasoning, so it does not make sense to call things "good" that lack any relation to rational agents. To talk about what is good or to wonder how much value there is in the world outside of practical contexts is like talking about what is a point and wondering how many points there are in the world outside of sports and games. It does not make sense to affirm a value judgment that one thinks should never inform people's deliberations and attitudes. This is like supporting a rule that umpires should not count toward victory points fairly scored in an athletic contest. Just as there is nothing else for a point to be but something that counts toward victory in a contest, there is nothing else for a value to be but something that guides our deliberations and attitudes in practice.

Second, value judgments are justified by showing that they can perform their practical function well. This is done by showing that it is rational to use them to guide our deliberations and attitudes. So instead of saying that it is rational to value something because it is good, pragmatism says that it is good because it is rational for us to value it. Claims about what it is rational to value determine claims of value. Things are good in virtue of their bearing certain relations to principles of practical reason.

Kant invented the most important pragmatic theory of value. Begin with the thought that agents act for reasons. Reasons express the considerations that the agent takes to justify her end and the action taken toward it. They express the agent's understanding of what is valuable in her ends and actions. Kant called the agent's description of her intentions in and reasons for acting her maxim. A maxim has the form: "Perform act *a* in circumstances *C* because it will achieve end *e*, which I seek for reasons *r*." For an agent to judge something to be good is for her to incorporate it into her maxim as an end, means, or reason for adopting the end.[2] Her value judgment is correct if and only if her maxim is rationally justified. But what could rationally justify her maxim?

Most theories ground justification in the intrinsic value of the agent's ends. That her ends are good and her actions are effective means to those ends makes her actions good. That her actions are good makes her a good agent. To Kant, this account reverses the proper order of justification. What could make an agent's end, say, eating this apple, good? Some theorists would cite standards the end meets. The apple is good to eat because it is crisp, fresh, unblemished, and delicious. But what makes things meeting these standards good? It seems they are so because they appeal to our interests and desires. If we preferred to eat mushy old apples, the standards for being a good apple would reflect this. Some theorists, who identify the good with the satisfaction of desire, stop here. But we have many conflicting desires, some of which we find objectionable and refuse to incorporate into our ends. If we act rationally, we choose our ends for reasons we endorse. We do not just blindly go wherever our desires suggest. This is the autonomy of practical reason. So the satisfaction of a desire is good only if we autonomously adopt it as our end by incorporating it into our maxim.

We seem to be back where we started, except we now see that we cannot stop the quest for justification, for the condition that makes ends good, at a point external to practical reason. Practical reason is itself the condition that makes our actions and ends good. Kant took this conclusion to mean that practical reason (the goodwill, rational agency) is the only unconditional good.[3] Everything else is good only on condition that practical reason endorses it by its own principles. So an agent's maxim of acting is good in virtue of its conformity with these principles. Her act is good in virtue of its expressing a rationally justified maxim. And the end of her action is good in virtue of being the object of a rationally justified maxim. Things are good in virtue of their relation to practical reason, to rational principles of action.

But what are these principles of action? Reason seeks the conditions of anything being good until it finds the unconditioned. The above argument shows that reason discovers itself to be the only unconditional good.[4] Recall that to judge something good is to incorporate it into one's maxim as an end or reason for action. So to judge something unconditionally good would be to incorporate it into one's maxim as an unconditional end. In demanding that we regard practical reason as unconditionally good, practical reason thus requires us to incorporate a regard for rational agency as an end in itself, and never as a merely conditional end (a mere means), in all of our maxims. This is, of course, the Humanity as an End formula of the categorical imperative. Speaking intuitively, the categorical imperative commands us always to conform our maxims to practical principles that *express respect* for rational agency. This theory of value is pragmatic because it represents goodness as a feature that things have in virtue of their relation to practical reason. Values are nothing more than considerations that rationally figure in an agent's deliberations and maxims.

It might seem that this cannot be Kant's view. For Kant endorsed two kinds of value judgments that he thought could not or ought not to inform our deliberations. One is judgments about the supreme good, which is happiness in proportion to virtue. Since happiness is partly due to good fortune, over which we have no control, some judgments about the supreme good cannot figure in our deliberations. Another is judgments of natural beauty. Kant insisted that the judgments of beauty do not appeal to any interests or incentives, which means they do not motivate us, not even to preserve the existence of the beautiful object.[5] Judgments of the sublime in nature inspire awe; judgments of the beauties of nature inspire contemplative rapture. Neither state motivates us to do anything.

Kant's account of these judgments reveals how deeply pragmatic he is. He makes sense of them by situating them inside the imagined deliberations of a *postulated, nonhuman* agent. Pragmatism is the missing link in Kant's otherwise puzzling transcendental argument for the practical necessity of faith in God. To make sense of our judgments about the supreme good, we must postulate some agent for whom these judgments can count in deliberation, who can bring about the ends they prescribe. This can only be God.[6] Similarly, to make sense of judgments of natural beauty, we must postulate that *nature* acts according to a teleological principle. Our appreciation of natural beauties reflects our judgment that they embody imaginary ends of nature.[7]

Kant's attempts to explain these value judgments pragmatically are ingenious. I accept the pragmatic constraint, but think that less extravagant postulates can make more sense of the phenomena of valuation. The phenomena that challenge Kant's view are the value judgments that do not guide action, or that play rich roles in our lives apart from their action-guiding functions. Judgments of beauty and good fortune pose clear difficulties, as Kant recognized. We must also explain judgments of regretfulness. Most actions, even those we think are best, bring about some consequences we wish they had not. This is the ground of regret. Judgments of regretfulness are not action guiding. Even if we could go back and choose again, with these judgments in mind, we may still rationally choose the same way. Instead of postulating an agent for whom judgments of regret are action guiding, why not make sense of these judgments on their own terms? Judgments of regretfulness are, on their face, regret guiding. Many other types of value judgment tell us their pragmatic functions straightforwardly. When we evaluate things as wonderful, awesome, delightful, and charming, we are judging that it makes sense for us to be wondered, awed, delighted, and charmed by them. We can avoid the need to postulate fantastic forms of agency by assuming that value judgments guide our attitudes and emotions, not just our deliberations and actions.

I propose, then, that when we make value judgments, we are giving reasons for our attitudes, not just for our actions. We are applying standards for what merits our admiration, awe, pity, gratitude, delight, honor, shame, and other evaluative attitudes.[8] This activity remains within the domain of practical reason. Although we do not choose our attitudes, we do exercise the power to change our attitudes in response to reflections on the merits of having them. This is the power of practical reason. Call the attitudes susceptible to change upon such reflections the rational attitudes. Honor and contempt are attitudes responsive to reasons that can be offered for having them. One's attitude toward a Nobel prize winner may change from honor to contempt once one discovers that he plagiarized his research. Contrast these attitudes with nonrational attitudes such as appetites, mere tastes, impulses, and cravings, which do not respond to reasons. A smoker's craving for cigarettes does not diminish upon learning that smoking is bad for her health.

My theory of value, like Kant's, construes goodness as a function of an object's relation to rational principles. Begin with an agent's rational evaluative attitudes, such as respect, admiration, honor, affection, pride, and benevolence. A thing is valuable if it meets a standard we rationally endorse for guiding a favorable attitude toward that thing. Suppose we find ourselves admiring athletes for meeting high athletic standards. We judge that this attitude is rational if we reflectively endorse this attitude after examining it on all sides. Athletic standards get their status as norms for admiration and hence as standards of value from this reflective endorsement. The source of normativity is inside us, in the capacity for reflective criticism of our attitudes which is called practical reason.

Suppose an agent's attitudes toward what she values are rational. If it is rational to have an attitude, it is rational to express that attitude in appropriate circumstances. Most rational attitudes are nonpropositional; their direct objects are mainly people, and sometimes animals and things, rather than actions or states of affairs. People are, principally, what we care intrinsically about. The value of actions and states of affairs is derived from principles for *expressing* rational attitudes toward people. An action is good if it conforms to rational principles for expressing an agent's attitudes toward the people she cares about. A state of affairs is good if it is the aim of a rational action or the object of a favorable emotion that adequately expresses a person's rational attitudes toward someone. If James is fond of Sharon, it makes sense for him to anticipate eagerly her returning after a long absence and to drive to the airport to pick her up. His feeling joy in anticipation of seeing her again, and his aiming to pick her up, make sense because of the way he values Sharon. The state of affairs of seeing her soon and his action to bring it about are good in virtue of the relation they have to norms that rationally express his favorable attitude toward Sharon. I call this an *expressive theory of rational action,* because it identifies the rational act with the act that adequately expresses the agent's rational attitudes toward what she intrinsically values.

The proper scope of value judgments, then, is the whole domain of objects that can be taken up by rational attitudes. Kant failed to see this because he modeled rational attitudes after "pathological" motives, such as appetites, which are not responsive to practical reason. My analysis is pragmatic because it maintains an essential connection between value judgments and practical reason. In Kant's view, the practical function of value judgments is to guide deliberation according to our judgments of what it is rational to do. In my view, it is also to guide our attitudes according to our judgments of what it is rational to value. Both views explicate the justifiable content of value judgments in terms of judgments of practical reason. Kantians reduce "*x* is good" roughly to "*x* embodies or satisfies a principle of practical reason." I reduce "*x* is good" roughly to "it is rational to value *x,*" where to value something is to adopt toward it a favorable attitude susceptible to rational reflection.

Consequences of Pragmatism for the Structure of Values

Ethics raises many questions about the structure of values. Are there many kinds of value? What is the difference between intrinsic and extrinsic value? Does intrinsic value come in degrees? Can it be maximized? Are all goods commensurable? Pragmatism says that the structure of values is constituted by the structure of rational practices of valuation and justification. If our practices are rational, we can read the structure of values from the roles they play in them.

This does not make discerning the structure of values easy, for interpreting practices is a formidable task. But it does give us a general strategy for answering questions about the structure of values. Pragmatism implies that all authentic evaluative distinctions must play some practical role. So to evaluate a particular claim about the structure of values, we construct the kinds of attitude- or action-guiding principles that would enable it to serve a practical role. Then we ask whether it makes sense for us to guide our attitudes and deliberations by such principles. We construct the structure of values through the sorts of reason-giving principles that reflectively make sense.

Consider the distinction between intrinsic and extrinsic value. Intrinsic goods are said to have value in themselves, extrinsic goods to get their value from another source. This distinction marks the difference between considerations where justification comes to an end and considerations that call for further justification. If a consideration gets its reason-giving status from its relation to something else, it has extrinsic value. We saw this move in Kant's argument that practical reason is the only unconditional (intrinsic) good. My theory incorporates a different account of intrinsic value, tied to independence from particulars.[9] People have intrinsic value because it makes sense for us to care about them independent of our caring about any other particular thing. But states of affairs generally have only extrinsic value because our only reason for caring about them is that they concern the people we already care about. James has reason to care about seeing Sharon soon only because he is fond of Sharon. So the state of affairs in which James sees Sharon soon has extrinsic value. But James is fond of Sharon for herself, not because it makes sense for him to care about any other particular thing. So Sharon is intrinsically good. The order of justification determines the objects of intrinsic and extrinsic value.[10]

Consider next the structure of intrinsic value. We can ask whether intrinsic value is "scalar," that is, whether it is a magnitude, whether various mathematical relations and operations apply to it. For example, do objects have intrinsic value in different degrees? This idea could play a practical role only if it made sense to govern our attitudes by a principle that told us to adjust the intensity of our attitudes in response to the degree of intrinsic value in the object. In a Kantian scheme, such a principle makes no sense, because the attitude of *Kantian* respect cannot vary by degrees. There is only one way to express it: by obeying the categorical imperative. Because we cannot express a varied response to different degrees of intrinsic value, there is no practical role for a judgment that one intrinsic good is worth more or less than another. So, there are no differences in degrees of intrinsic value. This means that from the standpoint of moral respect, all persons are equals.

Now consider whether intrinsic value can be aggregated. Pragmatists interpret this as asking whether there is a justified principle that tells us to respond more favorably to more instances of intrinsic value. That is, does it make sense to adopt a principle to maximize instances of it? Kantians argue that there is no such principle. Respect for humanity as an end in itself does not demand that we bring more humans into existence or minimize their deaths. A public health official may not lie to the public about the dangers of fatty diets in order to save lives by getting people to eat differently. This is so even if reporting the true dangers would not scare people enough to change their habits. A maxim to minimize deaths in this way is wrong not because the lies have worse consequences than the deaths they avert (an implausible thought), but because the maxim expresses a paternalistic contempt for other rational agents, by substituting the official's judgments about their good for their own and by undermining the conditions for their own exercise of judgment.[11] Since there are no generally valid practical maximizing principles for intrinsic value, we say that intrinsic value cannot be increased by increasing the number of its bearers. So intrinsic value cannot be aggregated and does not vary by degrees. It is nonscalar.

My theory of value constructs the structure of intrinsic value differently from Kant's. In his scheme, there is only one kind of intrinsic value. My theory says that there are many kinds of intrinsic value, because it makes sense for us to value people intrinsically in many ways, such as by love, respect, honor, awe, and admiration. Some of these attitudes vary by degrees, so it makes sense to shade our expressions of these attitudes to the degree to which they are merited. If a critic judges one musician to be more admirable than another, it may make sense for her to praise the more admirable one more highly or more enthusiastically. So some kinds of intrinsic value do vary by degrees.

But little sense can be made of adding different instances of intrinsic value. How do you add the admirability of a musician to the adorability of a puppy? No rational attitude or action takes such a notional sum as its object. So no sense can be made of the claim that intrinsic values of different kinds can be aggregated. Nor does it generally make sense to speak of maximizing one kind of intrinsic value. For the practical role of intrinsic values is neither to prescribe an end to be maximized nor to prescribe an attitude toward an aggregate. It is to prescribe discrete evaluative attitudes that we should take up toward each of their bearers. For a value to be aggregative is for there to be a rational principle that tells us either to maximize it or to tie the degree of one's response to the total number of its bearers or to the total amount of value contained in all instances taken together. The mark of a maximizing principle is its support of trade-offs of one intrinsic good for another for the sake of increasing an aggregate. If the principle guides action, it tells people to sacrifice some instances of a value if this increases the total number of instances or the total value of all taken together. If the principle guides attitudes, it tells people to neglect some instances if this will optimize one's responses to all instances taken together.

The principles for expressing our evaluative attitudes toward most kinds of intrinsic goods are not maximizing and do not support these kinds of trade-offs. Instead, they typically have a *distributive* form. This is clearly true for respect, admiration, and love. For parents to express their love for their children adequately, they must show affection and concern to *each* of their children. Parental love is not truly expressed by parents' orienting themselves to some aggregate child collective. If it were, there would be principles that would tell parents to "maximize" the total "amount" of their love by trading off affection for one child for affection for another. To govern one's attitudes according to such a principle is to withhold love from one child, not to express it more adequately to all. It also represents a misunderstanding of parental love to treat it as a finite resource to be economized in a zero-sum game.[12] That principles for expressing favorable attitudes are typically distributive rather than maximizing explains why it generally does not make sense to say that intrinsic goods even of a single kind can be aggregated.

Incommensurable Goods: The No Good Reasons Principle

Now consider whether any goods are incommensurable. Two goods are incommensurable if neither one is better than or equal in value to the other. One can commensurate goods only in relation to some common valuable respect or "covering value."[13] So let us set aside nonsensical attempts to compare the intrinsic values of goods that are valuable in fundamentally different respects, such as the genius of a scientist with the honor of a gentleman.[14] To determine whether two goods are commensurable, pragmatists ask what practical attitude- or action-guiding function claims of commensurability can serve. There are two possibilities. Either it makes sense for us to take up a common attitude toward the objects being compared, and to adjust the relative intensity of the attitude to the relative values ascribed to the objects. Or it makes sense for us to justify a choice of one over the other in terms of these relative values.

This analysis implies a simple test for incommensurability. If there is no point to comparing the overall values of two goods, the comparative value judgment about them will serve no practical function. Pragmatism says that if a value judgment serves no practical function, then it has no truth value or warrant. And if a comparative value judgment has no truth value or warrant, then the goods it compares are incommensurable. Therefore, if there is no good reason to compare the overall values of two goods, the goods are incommensurable. Call this the "no good reasons principle" for incommensurability.

Our practices of making overall goodness-of-a-kind judgments reveal wide gaps that reflect the negligible interest we take in comparing the intrinsic worth of many goods of the same kind. If a kind of good is broad enough, there will be radically different ways of being a good of that kind. As the points in common among goods of a kind become fewer and more abstract, our interest in comparing their overall intrinsic values declines. Consider cross-modal aesthetic evaluations. Is Henry Moore's sculpture, *Recumbent Figure,* as intrinsically good a work of art as Chinua Achebe's novel, *Things Fall Apart?* What could be the point of answering such a question? It is doubtful that there are any illuminating *overall* comparisons of aesthetic worth here that help us refine our sensibilities or our understanding of art, or that reasonably guide any attitudes or actions. They are too different to support interesting comparative overall evaluations.[15]

Perhaps we could say that Moore's work is as good a sculpture as Achebe's is a good novel. Chang proposes that in such cases, we should say that the two goods are, if not equal, then "on a par," so still commensurable.[16] If the aesthetic values of all artworks were commensurable in this way, then something like a Michelin guide to *The Ten Billion Greatest Artworks of All Time,* ranking all works on a scale from one to ten, would have to be a sensible undertaking. But to what end? It would certainly be silly, boring, and arbitrary to draw a line between seventh- and eight-rate artworks. And is a first-rate limerick on a par with a first-rate concerto? With a fifth-rate concerto? No authentic aesthetic attitude would reasonably respond to such a unified ranking. Admiring contemplation is an aesthetic attitude that prevails in museums and classical concert halls. But aesthetic worth is not exhausted by the degree to which its bearers merit this attitude. Some music is aesthetically good because it makes you feel like dancing, limericks because they make you laugh. One could imagine various practical projects that could make use of such a guide. But these are the projects of philistines, snobs, and prigs, precisely those least open to a free exploration and development of their aesthetic sensibilities. If we have reason not to be such people, we have reason to repudiate the absurdly fastidious comparative value judgments they try to make. The project of comprehensively ranking all works of art in terms of their intrinsic aesthetic value is foolish, boring, and stultifying. Incommensurabilities are pervasive in the art world because we have no good reason to make many comparisons of aesthetic worth.[17]

The practical import of these incommensurabilities is, of course, negligible. We never confront a need to make a choice or adjust an attitude on the basis of such sweeping goodness-of-a-kind judgments. Even when on a leisurely Sunday I find myself with time either to read an Achebe novel or to see Moore's sculptures, I hardly make my choice on the basis of some crude commensuration of their overall aesthetic worth. Even when my interests are specifically aesthetic, and not just a matter, say, of seeing the sculptures to get out of the house, the relevant question for choice is not which option is aesthetically better but which option interests me more at the moment. Practical reason finds no difficulty confronted with choices among such incommensurable goods.[18] Neither choice is made on the ground that it is superior to the alternatives. Reason simply permits either choice to be made.[19]

Chang objects that if there is no rational basis for choice among incommensurables, then why not just flip a coin?[20] This may not be unreasonable for choices among Sunday enjoyments. Whether it is depends on whether such a procedure motivates. I may be afflicted with a groggy Sunday morning inertia, which the coin flip does nothing to solve. In that case reflection is still needed. But its point is not to reach a decision on the relative intrinsic merits of the alternatives. It is to imagine the respective incommensurable merits of each alternative vividly, so that one can engage my interest enough to get out of bed.[21] Incommensurabilities here signal an opening for the free play of moods, interests, whims, impulses, appetites, mere tastes, likings, and other nonrational motivations in my life. It is not irrational to follow the lead of these motivations wherever practical reason permits it. The claim of universal commensurability suggests, by contrast, that all of life's choices must be tied to the sober, rational demands of gradient climbing, leaving no room for the free play of these other motivations. This is a dull and rigid vision of human life.

Our need to make space for the free play of nonrational motivations could thus be seen as a rational ground for *not* seeking to make comparative value judgments at every turn. This is not an argument that it is rational to ignore some true comparative value judgments. If it does not make sense to guide our attitudes or actions regarding two goods on the basis of a commensurating judgment, no comparative value judgments hold in that case. Practical reason *makes* space available for other motivations by taking no interest in the construction of comparative value judgments. These incommensurabilities hardly pose difficulties for practical reason, since the nonrational motivations step in to help us decide what to do.

Rational Choice Among Incommensurable Goods: Beyond Optimization

The preceding discussion might suggest that the no good reasons principle makes incommensurable only those goods that may be chosen out of trivial or unserious motives. This is incorrect. Moods and interests may be important and serious. And even if one has no good reason to think that *A* is commensurable with *B*, one may have strong reasons to think that *A* is good and to choose *A* for those reasons. But there remain cases where we feel that the choice of *A* *over B* must be made on principled grounds, where reason does not permit either option to be chosen over the other from nonrational motives. Must we then choose on the basis of a commensuration of the values of the goods realized in choice? This thought reflects the first conviction behind worries about incommensurability that opened this chapter: that value judgments can guide rational choice only through the principle that one must choose a good better than or equal in value to every alternative. This conviction expresses an impoverished conception of the ways that value judgments guide choice. The expressive theory of rational choice provides alternative principles for choosing between options that do not require commensurating the goods contained in them. When this is the case, we still have no good reason to compare their overall values even when we need a principled basis for choosing between them.

Here is a typical case from Chang that is thought to require a principled resolution based on a commensuration of the goods contained in the options:

> Suppose the only way I can save my dying mother is by ending my friendship with Eve. It would be very odd to think, at least under normal circumstances, that it would be wrong for me to give up that friendship in order to save my mother. Clearly, I ought to trade the friendship for my mother's life. And it is just as clear that the reason I ought to trade the friendship is that my mother's life is more valuable. So my friendship with Eve *can* be compared with and properly traded off against the life of my mother.[22]

Certainly the choice at hand cannot be responsibly made on the basis of whims or tastes. But I find the thought astonishing that it must therefore be made on the basis of a comparison of the overall values of one's mother's life and one's friendship.

Ordinary moral thinking does not operate in this way. It finds Chang's predicament too radically underdescribed to offer any basis for rational choice. The right choice hangs crucially on what I intend in choosing to save my mother's life by means that end my friendship. Different means express different attitudes toward my mother and friend. Is it that I must spend so much time by my mother's side, far away from my friend, that our friendship will be attenuated from lack of contact? Or is my friend so neurotically possessive that he will interpret the energy I devote to my mother's care as a form of rejection and feel too wounded to permit reconciliation? Or is it that my friend's father, who disapproves of our relationship, will pay for my mother's lifesaving operation on condition that I never see my friend again? Or shall I get the money I need for the operation by betraying my friend, a celebrity, by revealing confidences to a scandal sheet? In the last two cases, I lose my friend through deliberate betrayal, in the first two, through regrettable circumstances or my friend's fault. These differences properly influence my choice.

My choice also depends on whether it would be a loving act to save my mother's life. Perhaps she is dying of a painful illness, and life-extending treatment would only continue her misery. Or suppose she has led a full life and is now elderly and prepared to face death. Ordinary morality counsels us to accept the limitations of human mortality. People need not destroy their special relationships to obtain or operate expensive life-extending technology for those who have already lived complete lives. If this is what my choice involves, my friend might not be neurotically possessive in reading my devotion to my mother's care as rejection. Perhaps it expresses an anxious dependency on her, with my life absorbed into hers in a way that undermines my ability to maintain independent relationships. Dropping my friendships to save my mother's life would thus express a failure to love my friends, not a failure to love my mother. Then none of the contemplated means to saving my mother's life would be justified.

Ordinary moral thought enables us to make choices in these cases without placing mother's life and friendship on a common scale and declaring one to be more valuable than the other. There is no common scale, no "covering value" here that justifies choice.[23] Instead, considerations of what we *owe* our mothers and our friends in different circumstances play a central role.[24] Sometimes we owe it to our friends not to do things that could save our mother's lives. Sometimes we owe it to our mothers to do things that will attenuate our friendships. The expressive theory of practical reason derives these principles of obligation from a nonscalar conception of intrinsic value. Suppose one recognizes both one's mother and one's friends as intrinsically valuable, as end points of justification. It is a short step from recognizing mother and friends as end points of justification to recognizing them as self-originating sources of claims on our attitudes and actions—that is, as sources of obligation.[25] The contours of these obligations are shaped by the respective expressive requirements of filial love and friendship. So to regard the values of mother and friends as expressed in principles of obligation is to regard them as original sources of value, as intrinsically valuable.

Contrast this with the way we would have to regard mother and friends if their values were scalar. Then they would figure in principles that tell us to maximize the number or endurance of their bearers. This is to regard mother and friends as valuable only for the ways their existence improves the state of the world. To regard one as more valuable than the other could be to accept a principle that one's continued existence is intrinsically more choiceworthy than the other's. So one can be sacrificed for the sake of the other, by *any* means that hold collateral consequences equal. This is to treat the sacrificed person as a mere means to getting desired consequences, not as intrinsically good.[26] Alternatively, to regard their values as scalar might be to accept a principle that tells one to adopt different degrees of the same attitude toward them. But mother is a proper object of filial love, one's friends of friendship. These forms of love differ in kind, not degree, and so mark their objects as intrinsically good in different ways, not just in different amounts.

Thus, there are no valid practical principles that express a regard for the values of mother and friends as scalar. So we have no good reason to try to compare the values of one's mother and one's friends, or of her life and one's friendships, in terms of some common value they possess to a greater or lesser degree. These goods are therefore not commensurable. Both are valuable—not more or less but in different *ways*. When we must choose between them, the basis of choice is not a judgment telling us which is more valuable but a judgment telling us how best to reconcile the expressive demands of the different kinds of concern we owe to and have for them. In the cases at hand, the bases of choice are principles of obligation, not a principle of optimization.

The belief that we cannot rationally choose between goods except by judging one to be better than the other thus rests on an impoverished theory of the way value judgments inform deliberation. On this theory, the sole practical role of the concept of value is to assign *weights* to goods, so that reason can choose what is weightiest or most valuable. It supposes that all values are scalar. The expressive theory represents intrinsic values as generally nonscalar. The practical role of concepts of intrinsic value is generally to assign a *status*, not a weight, to goods. Intrinsic value judgments tell us to treat goods according to the statuses assigned to them: to act with filial love toward family members, out of friendship for friends, with respect for human beings generally. The principles that express such attitudes generally take a distributive, not an aggregative or optimizing, form. They tell us to distribute our different kinds of concern to each of the intrinsic goods in our lives. Thus, choices concerning those goods or their continued existence do not generally require that we rank their values on a common scale and choose the more valuable good; they require that we give each good its due.

Hierarchical Incommensurabilities and Barriers to Trade

The preceding discussion may not satisfy those who feel that some comparative value judgment between one's mother and one's friends is still in order. After all, one's obligations to one's mother are usually deeper than one's obligations to friends. This intuition is right, but the vocabulary of commensurability, of more or less value, does not adequately express it. We speak instead of higher and lower values. Indeed, sometimes we deny that one good is more or less valuable than another precisely by insisting that it has an incomparably higher value altogether. One might say that loving relationships are of incomparably higher worth than anything money can buy. Some liberals say that human rights are of incomparably higher worth than money. Call such claims ones of *hierarchical incommensurability*.

Claims like these seem paradoxical: They seem to deny the possibility of comparison, yet then go on to make one. The paradox can be dispelled by identifying distinct practical functions for judgments of more and less value and judgments of higher and lower value. These two ways of speaking mesh with the metaphors of weight and status, respectively. Determinations of weight are continuous, require a common unit of measurement for the goods being compared, and place these goods on the same plane. This metaphor fits comparisons of goods of the same kind that have a common covering value. So in denying commensurability, claims of hierarchical incommensurability claim that the goods in question are of different kinds. They call for different attitudes, not different degrees of the same attitude. Weighting principles cannot capture the differences in how we should treat them. Determinations of status are discrete, require no common unit, and place goods being compared on different planes. This metaphor fits comparisons of goods that differ in kind, which may occupy one or more possibly cross-cutting status hierarchies. So in claiming that one good is of a higher kind than another, claims of hierarchical incommensurability compare goods in relative status, as meriting higher or lower kinds of attitudes.

Pragmatism says this hierarchical difference in attitudes must be captured by a difference in the practical principles that express them. Consider how Kant drew a hierarchical distinction between the values of persons and things in terms of a hierarchical distinction between the attitudes of respect and mere use. Respect counts as a higher attitude than use because it is expressed through principles that grant its objects a higher *status* in deliberation: Acceptable maxims must accord rational beings unconditional value, all other things having merely conditional value. That is, persons are treated as generators of principles of obligation, whereas the values of mere things generate principles whose reason-giving force depends on our desires for them. So it makes sense to deny that human beings are either more or less valuable than mere things; they have a higher value altogether. We refuse the language of "more" or "better"; we reject commensuration in favor of hierarchy, when the function of a comparative value judgment is to accord a higher *status* rather than a greater *weight* to a good in deliberation.

Endless confusion results from interpreting claims of status in terms of weight. Liberals often represent hierarchical incommensurability in terms of lexical orderings: We accord the value of humans an incomparably higher status than mere things by making human rights "trump" other goods such as economic growth or convenience.[27] Principles of right raise barriers to trade between higher and lower goods, thus repudiating maximizing logic. Consequentialists complain that it is either impossible or catastrophic to live up to these principles in practice. We cannot avoid trade-offs between the protection of human rights and other goods such as economic growth, for we cannot reasonably devote unlimited resources to human life and human rights by indefinitely expanding medical expenditures, police forces, and the like. Therefore, we cannot help placing a price on human life and human rights.[28] This objection interprets liberal principles of right as assigning infinite weight to certain consequences—states of affairs in which humans live or in which they effectively enjoy certain rights.

But liberal principles of right, properly interpreted, directly constrain the form of principles for justifying actions, not the consequences of those actions. They reject principles of justification that accord merely conditional value to human life and human rights by making respect for them contingent on others' desires, welfare, or convenience. We may not imprison people without trial just because an outraged crowd demands vengeance for alleged crimes. We may not deny disabled people access to city hall because it would be too expensive or inconvenient or discomforting to others to accommodate them. This is a difference in the reason-giving *status* accorded to rights claims in deliberation that cannot be translated into principles assigning weights to the consequences of actions justified by those rights. "Trade-offs" between money and human life, or money and the effective protection of human rights, may *happen* as a consequence of actions that respect human rights. They inevitably happen as a consequence of attempts by public bodies to reconcile competing obligations in the face of finite resources. But then what justifies the action that *results* in a trade-off of higher for lower goods is not a maximizing principle weighing the value of a human right against money but a distributive principle of obligation expressing what is due to others. This logic fits with the general form of expressive rationality: We justify actions not in terms of the value of the consequences, but in terms of the values of the people concerned with them, regard for which we express in principles that take a distributive rather than an optimizing form and that are often embodied in claims of right and obligation.

But then mustn't we adjudicate conflicting claims of obligation by assigning weights to them? This would reintroduce commensurability. Samuel Scheffler suggests that the higher values people place on loved ones over strangers can be captured by principles that permit people to weight intimates' interests by some constant multiple of the weight they accord to strangers' interests.[29] Such weighting principles do not come close to capturing the distinctive demands of friendship, filial love, parental love, and respect for strangers. They imply that we may properly take *any* interest of a stranger or friend as a reason for action. But some of those interests, for instance, personal health decisions or religious projects, may be none of our business, however important they may be to the person who has them. We are not entitled to participate in them even if we think we may help their projects go better. In contrast, some kin relations permit or oblige us to involve ourselves in such interests. Higher attitudes permit or oblige us to involve ourselves in interests of others that cut closer to the core of a person's identity or privacy. Which interests those are is determined not by a weighting principle but by the discrete social norms constitutive of different social relationships. Scheffler's weighting principle also implies that we must assign the same relative weights to people's interests in every social context. But people are not permitted to sacrifice their client's interests to their friends' in professional and business contexts, however much they may favor their friends' interests in personal contexts. A doctor may not refer a patient to a doctor friend she think is useless, just because the friend needs the business more than the patient needs treatment. Again, which trade-offs of strangers' for friends' interests are permitted and which prohibited are determined not by a weighting principle but by the discrete obligations and prerogatives constitutive of different (legitimate and adequately defined) social roles. The general rule is to prohibit only those trade-offs of higher for lower goods that express an inappropriate valuation of the people concerned in action.

This rule reflects the deliberative priority that expressive theories grant to the intentions or expressive meanings of action, embodied in the principles that agents use to justify them, over the consequences of action. Consequentialists and rational choice theorists interpret this to mean that such theories accord infinite weight to the "merely symbolic" meanings of actions, manifested in a supposed demand that we do our duty "regardless of the consequences." But to grant deliberative priority to the meanings over the consequences of action is neither to assign meanings a larger weight than the consequences nor to deny the consequences any weight at all. It is to assign them a different status in deliberation. It is to derive the role the consequences play in deliberation from the principles that express how we ought to value the people concerned with them. This means that the value of the consequences is extrinsic or derivative, not that their value is negligible or small. The value of promoting a given consequence, say, saving mother's life, depends on whether it would be a loving act to promote it, and on whether it would constitute a betrayal of a friend to promote it by the means at hand. Its value therefore varies with the intentions expressed in promoting it. But this does not preclude that its value is sometimes very large.

Since intentions and consequences play fundamentally different roles in deliberation, we never have reason to weigh the value of one against the value of the other. This is as incoherent as weighing the value of a recipe against the value of the ingredients. Recipes are neither more nor less valuable than ingredients; they tell us how to combine the ingredients to get the right results. Intentions or expressive meanings perform a similar organizing function: They tell us how to value the consequences so as to do right by the people we intrinsically value. They are therefore not commensurable with the consequences.

Conclusion

Failures of commensurability among goods are pervasive in our lives because we have no reason to weigh the values of many goods on the same scale. We may have no good reason to commensurate goods of the same kind because it would be boring or silly to do so, or because it makes sense to give free play to nonrational motivations in choices concerning them. It does not even make sense to commensurate goods of different kinds because value concepts here assign different statuses, not different weights, to them. Incommensurability may thus signal that the goods in question must play distinctive *roles* in deliberation that preclude setting them side by side for comparative evaluation. The need for commensuration where principled choices among goods are needed seems pressing only as long as we are bewitched by the idea that the sole principle of rational choice is to maximize value. Expressive theories of practical reason release us from this spell by showing us how concepts of intrinsic value directly generate principles of obligation and norms of conduct that have a distributive and intentional rather than an optimizing and consequentialist form.

One might object that in deflating the worry that incommensurability poses serious problems for rational choice, pragmatism denies only a particular *diagnosis* of these problems, which chalks them up to a kind of metaphysical mismatch between the demands of practical reason and the ontology of value—occasions where reason demands that we judge one good to be better than or equal in value to another, but where nothing in the world corresponds to these evaluative relations. Incommensurability cannot account for hard, tragic, or conflicted choices, since it appears in choices that are neither difficult, tragic, nor conflicted. Choices can be hard or tragic when the losses entailed by taking any option are calamitous, however commensurable the losses may be. And practical reason can be in conflict with itself when individuals are torn between the expressive demands of conflicting rational attitudes. To represent our conflict as a metaphysical absence of an evaluative relation does not illuminate our predicament. The source of conflict should be sought in irrationally constructed social roles, which give their occupants incompatible duties, or inside ourselves, in conflicts of attitudes that defy reflective equilibrium.

One may object that the structure of rational practices may not reflect the structure of values. Just because we find no good reason to compare the values of two goods, or good reason to refuse to do so, does not imply that the goods are really incommensurable.[30] Our reason-giving practices may mistake the true structure of values, or they may be justified as maximizing value indirectly. If bad consequences come from a practice that commensurates two goods, consequentialists tell us to refuse to commensurate them or even to believe falsely that they are incommensurable.[31] These objections reflect the thought that the structure of values must somehow exist externally to our reason-giving practices, so as to enable reflective criticism of or critical support for them.[32] Pragmatism offers a different route to reflective criticism and support of practices. It asserts the autonomy of practical reason, which takes no orders from a supposedly external structure of values. Practical reason has no need for such an external structure, for it is already self-critical.[33] We criticize practices not by consulting some metaphysical theory of value, but by seeing if we can reflectively endorse them. The sources and structures of value are to be found not in a mysterious external realm but inside ourselves, in our own self-understandings.

6

Incommensurability and Agency

JOSEPH RAZ

Incommensurability is the absence of a common measure. It has acquired currency as something of a philosophical term of art used in relation to a variety of topics and problems, depending on what is the measure whose alleged absence is of significance. The incommensurability that I will be concerned with is the incommensurability of value: the possibility that the value of two items, or that the goodness of two options, is incommensurate, in that neither of them is better than the other nor are they of equal value.[1]

When speaking of both items and options whose value is incommensurate, I will be referring to specific options or specific objects.[2] Occasionally I will refer to the value that possession of a certain property lends to an object or an option (e.g., that being sweet endows an apple with additional value). I will not be concerned, however, with the comparative goodness of abstract values, such as freedom, justice, beauty, fairness, and the like.

The essay will suggest that a proper understanding of human agency, and in particular of the relations between the role of cognition and volition in human agency, presupposes that there are widespread incommensurabilities of options.

1. Problems and Direction

An understanding of values is central to both our understanding of the world and our understanding of human action. This dual aspect of our interest in values and valuables is, of course, not accidental. Paradigmatically human actions aim at achieving some good or averting some bad. The capacity for human action is—I join many in believing—the capacity to act knowing what one is doing and doing so because something in one's situation makes this action a reasonable, or a good, or the right thing to do.[3] In other words, it is the capacity for intentional action, the capacity to act for reasons. Values "control" reasons in that one can have reasons for an action only if its performance is, or is likely to produce, or contribute to producing, good or if it is likely to contribute toward averting something bad.[4] Thus the concept of reason for action connects those of value and agency. I will approach the issue of the incommensurability of values from the perspective of the explanation of action. From this vantage point, the incommensurability of values is seen as leading to the incommensurability of reasons for action.[5]

I will contrast two conceptions of human agency, which I will call the *rationalist* and the *classical*. In broad outline, the rationalist holds that paradigmatic human action is action taken because of all the options open to the agent, it was, in the agent's view, supported by the strongest reason. The classical conception holds that the paradigmatic human action is one taken because of all the options the agent considers rationally eligible, he chooses to perform it. There are, I shall argue, three crucial differences between the two conceptions. First, the rationalist conception regards reasons as requiring action, whereas the classical conception regards reasons as rendering options eligible. Second, the rationalist conception regards the agent's own desire as a reason, whereas the classical conception regards the will as an independent factor. Third, the classical conception presupposes the existence of widespread incommensurabilities of reasons for action, whereas the rationalist conception, if not committed to complete commensurability, is committed to the view that incommensurabilities are relatively rare anomalies. The three differences come down to a contrast between the rationalist view that generally rational choices and rational actions are determined by one's reasons or one's belief in reasons and are explained by them, as against the classical conception that regards typical choices and actions as determined by a will that is informed and constrained by reason but plays an autonomous role in action.

The will is the ability to choose and perform intentional actions. We exercise our will when we endorse the verdict or reason that we must perform an action, and we do so, whether willingly, reluctantly, or regretting the need, etc. According to the classical conception, however, the most typical exercise or manifestation of the will is in choosing among options that reason merely renders eligible. Commonly when we so choose, we do what we want, and we choose what we want, from among the eligible options. Sometimes speaking of wanting one option (or its consequences) in preference to the other eligible ones is out of place. When I choose one tin of soup from a row of identical tins in the shop, it would be wrong and misleading to say that I wanted that tin rather than, or in preference to, the others. Similarly, when faced with unpalatable but unavoidable and incommensurate options (as when financial need forces me to give up one or another of incommensurate goods), it would be incorrect to say that I want to give up the one I choose to give up. I do not want to do so. I have to, and I would have equally regretted the loss of either good. I simply choose to give up one of them.[6] In the sequel I may on occasion refer to people deciding to do what they want from among eligible options. Such references should be qualified as meaning "what they want or what they choose without wanting".

My case for the existence of widespread, significant value incommensurabilities is connected to a way of understanding the role of the will in intentional action. This should not be surprising. If of the options available to agents in typical situations of choice and decision, several are incommensurate, then reason can neither determine nor completely explain their choices or actions. Nor can the action be predicted on the assumption that since the agents are well informed and rational, they would do what they have most reason to do. The bar to such predictions is not that people are not rational or well informed. Even if they are, this method of explaining and predicting action, which underlies so much work in the development and application of decision theory, is unavailable when the options that agents face, or some of them, are incommensurate. The will comes into play at this stage (though, as has already been noted, that is not the only role it can play in action), and typically agents choose from incommensurate options one that they want to perform. In any case, whatever they do, they do because they choose to, not because they ought to perform that action on the balance of reasons.

Rationalists would find this understanding of the relations between reason and the will distorted. They would gladly agree that the reasons for or against various options, the agents' own desires excluded, will often be incommensurate. But the agents' own desires are among their reasons for action. Some people think that ultimately the agents' desires are the only reasons there can be. Others may not go so far but will insist that the agents' desires are among the reasons that should and do guide their actions. Once we see that, we readily see that there is no room for incommensurabilities among the options open to agents, for when push comes to shove, the need to choose will concentrate the minds of the choosers, who will realize (or will think that they do) that they want one of the options more than the others.

Rationalists have powerful arguments to support that view of desires. The most compelling is that if they are not reasons, then the classical conception of action is right and there are widespread incommensurabilities. It is their abhorrence of incommensurabilities that makes rationalists what they are. They do not suffer this vacuum in the space of reason, and they have powerful arguments to deny its possibility. To rationalists, the fact that intentional action is undertaken in the light of the agent's understanding of his situation suggests that the agent must always be capable of finding an answer to the question, "What am I to do?"

There are always factors—we call them reasons—that guide the agent's choices and decisions. If there were incommensurabilities, then actions would be unintelligible to the agents who perform them. They would not be able to explain why they performed the action they did rather than one of the other options open to them. All they would be able to say is: "We saw that there is no reason to prefer *A* to *B,* or the other way around, and we did *A.*" The obvious gap in this explanation will baffle not only the observer who is trying to explain or predict people's behavior. It will defeat the agents themselves, who would regard their choices as a mystery, as something that happens to them rather than something they do. According to the rationalist, incommensurability is inconsistent with the fact that intentional actions are under the control of the agents, that they are determined by their choices.

2. Brute Wants

Practical reasoning, reasoning about what is to be done, has two aspects.[7] It is concerned to establish how things are and how—given that that is how they are—one is to act. I will be concerned with its second aspect only.[8] According to the belief/desire account of reasons for action, that aspect of practical reasoning has to do with determining what, in the instant situation, one desires most, or what is, or is to be, one's all-things-considered desire, given all one's desires and beliefs about how things are. As this account gives desires the most extensive role in practical reasoning, I will take a simple version of it as the target for my argument.[9] The simple version regards brute desires—desires that we have not because we see reason to have them—as the only kind of reason to perform an action, other than for instrumental reasons. In other words, according to the simple version of the belief/desire account, the only reason an agent has is to do what will satisfy his brute desires. I will rely on two arguments against it.[10]

The first argument concludes that the simple version assumes that people reason about what they should do, given that they have conflicting desires—desires that, the world being as it is, cannot all be completely satisfied—but that it is incapable of making sense of such reasoning. The simple version has to maintain that when facing conflicting desires, people should do what they most want to do. There is, according to that account, nothing other than desires that can be a reason for action, let alone a reason capable of adjudicating between conflicting desires. So the question of what to do in the face of conflicting desires must be settled by reference to those desires themselves, and as there is nothing in their content that could be a reason to prefer one of them to the others, it must be their strength to which agents must appeal when reasoning about what to do in the face of their conflicting desires. Their reasoning is, in effect, an attempt to establish what they want most.

The very thought of people deliberating about what they want most (unless it means—as I will later claim that it does—deliberating about what they should want most) is peculiar. It suggests a picture of people's wants being out of their control. They are givens that people are landed with, as they might be with tiredness or a passing depression. Given that people have the desires they have, the simple version assumes, they are concerned to satisfy them, and if it is impossible to satisfy them all, at least let the most powerful desires be satisfied. Were this a sensible view of people's wants, there would be no room for reasoning about what one should most want to do. Whatever one ends by doing, one wants most to do. In this picture of wants as powers somehow implanted in us, the winner is the want with the greatest motivational power. What else can "wanting most"—meaning the want with the greatest motivational power— mean other than the want that we end up acting on, at least if the action is not a mishap, not an accidental slip, but the action we intended to take? Admittedly there can be a question as to whether the action one took is the one conducive to achieving what one wants most to have or to be, but that is because of the possibility of cognitive failure in identifying the action most conducive to those further goals. When we ask what of the different things we want to have we want most to have then, barring cognitive failure, bad luck, or misfired action, it is just what we would have if the action we take bears its hoped-for fruit. Therefore, we can conclude that if the purpose of the part of practical reasoning we are discussing is to establish what we want most, the simple version of the belief/desire account would lead to the conclusion that we should not reason but act. In our actions, our strongest motivating desires reveal themselves.

This is, of course, no more than a caricature of the belief/desire account of practical reason. Its proponents do not think that the aspect of practical reasoning concerned with deciding what is to be done given that the agent has conflicting desires is an attempt to establish which desire is motivationally strongest. What we want most means to them something like: the satisfaction of which desire will give most pleasure, or avoid more frustration, or maximize our happiness, or contentment; or satisfaction of which of our desires will lead to those of our desires that cohere best being satisfied; or they may have a different interpretation of what the phrase "what we want most" means, and they may not even use this phrase but some other to hold this pivotal position in their account of practical reasoning. All these suggestions, I readily admit, are much superior to the caricature I criticized above. The point is that all of them suggest reasons for satisfying desires. None of them takes desires as inherently worthy of satisfaction. They are worthy of satisfaction to the extent that their satisfaction gives pleasure, or prevents frustration, or to the extent that it contributes to happiness, or to making a coherent whole of one's life. I do not wish to endorse the soundness of all these reasons, or of the others relied on in various versions of belief/desire accounts. (Why should people have a coherent life? In order to be all good, decent, middle-class folk?) Their soundness does not matter for the purpose of the argument at hand. What matters is that all of them transcend the self-imposed boundaries of the approach. All of them presuppose values whose normative force does not derive from the fact that people desire to pursue them. Were it to amount to no more than that, we would be back at the strength-of-motivation style of reasoning at one remove, with the added disadvantage that we will have acquired an additional false premise: that in the relevant sense, people desire pleasure, or the avoidance of frustration, or the coherence of their lives, or whatnot, more than they desire anything else. But if these values do not rest on desire alone, then there are values whose normative force is independent of being desired, and without them the belief/desire approach does not make sense, whereas with them it is no longer the belief/desire approach.

Notice that one cannot object that since such values are implicitly relied on in some belief/desire accounts, then their invocation must be understood as compatible with the approach once it is purged of incautious descriptions of its nature. For the moment we admit some desire-independent values, we open the floodgates to others. Why should practical reasoning give the sole role to the values of pleasure, avoidance of frustration, or the maximization of coherence in one's life? Why should it not give equal weight to friendship, loyalty, magnanimity, justice, and so on? And above all, why should it be dominated by one value, and deny the independent force of all others?

So much for the first argument. The second argument helps explain why the simple version of the belief/desire approach fails to account for deliberation in the face of conflicting wants. It does so because it mistakes the nature of the will.[11] What we want to do, be, or have, we want for reasons. The questions "What should we want most?" and "What do we want most?" are normally one and the same question. When we reason about what we want most, we reason about what we have most reason to want. Since the value or the goodness of things and options constitutes the reason for having them or for doing them, their value or goodness is also the reason for wanting to have them or to do them. Normally when we deliberate about what we want most, we deliberate about what it would be best for us to want because it would be best for us to have or to do.[12]

I will return to the qualification "normally" in the next paragraph but one. First, let it be noted that these remarks become compelling once we see that our wants are ours not merely because they are inflicted on us but because we conceived them and, as it were, endorsed them. For the most part, they are under our control, and that means that we have them only if we hold their objects to be worthwhile and that the wants disappear once that belief disappears. This feature of wants is central to them. It explains the sense in which they are under our control, rather than being states of mind visited upon us, like being overwhelmed by a sense of loss when hearing of the death of a friend. It also explains the sense in which we endorse or fail to endorse our wants. A want is ours so long as we have it because of a belief in the value of its object, and it would disappear were we to abandon that belief. Wants are not "ours"; they are compulsions, or addictions we suffer from, when we have them, even though we do not believe in the value of their objects or the desirability of satisfying them.[13]

Our wants are, in this regard, like beliefs. Beliefs too are under our control in this way; that is, we have them when we feel justified in holding them, and once that conviction evaporates (e.g., in the face of contrary evidence), we lose the belief. We cannot want what we see no reason to want any more than we can believe what we think is untrue or contrary to the evidence. Moreover, beliefs like wants can become irrational obsessions—thoughts that inflict themselves on us in spite of ourselves when they persist independent of the evidence.

Those remarks bring out the difference between belief and desire, as well as their similarities. We want to do or to have something only if we believe that it has some aspect that makes it worthwhile, makes it good or valuable. We want what we want inasmuch as it has that good aspect. We may at the same time want not to do the action or not to have the object inasmuch as they have other properties that make them worthless, or bad. In this respect, beliefs differ from wants. We cannot literally believe that *p* and that not *p*. But there is no contradiction in both wanting to perform an action or to have an object, and wanting not to do the action or not to have the object. This asymmetry, resulting from the aspect-dependent character of wants, should not blind us to the basic similarity between beliefs and wants, which results from the way both depend on judgment—about justification of the belief and about the worthwhile character of the object of the want. As was noted, in both cases we are familiar with pathological abnormalities. Sometimes people cannot help believing what they know to be false. Sometimes people cannot help wanting what they know to be worthless and entirely without merit. In those cases, deliberation about what we want most diverges from deliberation about what we have most reason to want.

But while the pathology of the will, like the pathology of belief, is important and revealing, the first and most important fact about it is that it involves pathological cases, whose understanding depends on understanding the factors that caused the deviation from normality. The pathological character of these cases accounts for the fact—to be commented on below—that in such cases, the agent concerned may well deny that he wants to perform the worthless or pointless action. Rather, he will say, he is driven toward it by a force that grips him and that he cannot control. And this too has its parallel in the cognitive case.

Some people reject the whole line of reasoning I have been pursuing. They believe that one can want anything, and not only what appears to one to be good or of value. This equates wanting something with an urge for it that attacks one. Urges, impulses, cravings, and their like are real enough, but it is wrong to take them as the basis for an analysis of wants and desires. (I am using "desires" in the way customary in philosophical writings. Its common use makes it far closer to urges and passions. But when so understood, its proper use is far too restricted for it to do its philosophical duty; that is, in its common use, it is false that whenever one acts intentionally, one acts because of a desire to do what one does.) Unlike urges, most ("philosophical") desires do not have a felt quality. My desire to get in time to a meeting on European democracy starting in an hour's time is typical of instrumental desires, and my desire to read Ivan Klima's new novel is typical of noninstrumental ones. Neither is a felt desire; they arose because of my belief that I have good reasons for both actions, and because something in me responded to these reasons and made me want to act on them.[14] If I do not get to act on them, that is most likely to be either because the opportunity did not arise or because when it arose I preferred to act for another reason. Either way, I am unlikely to feel frustration or any sense of loss. Naturally if I tried to satisfy my desires and failed, I may well feel frustrated. But that feeling of frustration is not a result of an unfulfilled desire but of a failed action, and is likely to be acute only if it is due to my clumsiness, thoughtlessness, incompetence, or the like.

Not all urges are pathological. Many of our desires are, if you like, endorsed urges. But normally we do not endorse them; they do not become our desires, unless we find them (and it may be no more than a rationalization) to be backed by reasons. If a force beyond my control propels me to take an action that I see no reason to take then, regardless of whether I actually take the action or not, it would be misleading to say that I want to take that action. Not infrequently we prefer to satisfy an urge or a craving as a way of ridding ourselves of it. In those cases, our reason is that the craving is troublesome and the action that satisfies it will rid us of it. Acting for such reasons is sometimes akratic, but it need not be. Either way it is action for a (good, albeit not necessarily sufficient) reason.[15]

So if I want to count the blades of grass in my garden, I do so because I think that this will take my mind off some upsetting event, or because the action has some other good-making property. If I find myself drawn to count blades of grass but cannot think of any reason for doing so, I would certainly deny that this is a desire of mine. It is a force that seizes me in spite of myself. If I am overcome by it and perform the action, I would be right to say that I could not help it, though in a way it would be an intentional action. All I say, to repeat the point made above, is that anyone will recognize this as a pathological case.[16] In the normal case, if I want to have a drink because I think that it tastes good, and am then convinced that it does not, then I no longer want to have the drink. No loss or regret is involved. The desire disappears with the loss of belief in the reason.

There is always a reason for any desire. The statement that one wants to paint potatoes green is incomprehensible, not least to the agent himself, unless there is something in the way he sees the action—in his beliefs about it, its circumstances and consequences—that makes it appear a sensible action to him. Not everything can be desired. Only what is seen under some aspect of the good can be.

3. Wants and Reasons

Still, the question remains: Given that there are things one has reason to do and does not particularly want to do, or feel like doing, is it not the case that if there are other things that one has reason to do and wants to do, one has greater reason to do them, other things being equal? If so, would it not show that wanting to do something is in and of itself a reason to do it, additional to the reason for doing it, which is one's reason for wanting to do it?

When put in this way, the answer seems to be yes both times, and yet the case is not so clear. First let us note that only desires that they currently have can be thought of as reasons for the people who have them. Consider the following case: I want to take up playing the piano after I retire. I want to do that because it would help pass the time in an enjoyable and rewarding way. I will enjoy facing new challenges, encountering music not merely as a listener, and so forth. All these are reasons for taking up the piano, and they are also reasons for wanting to do so. I am aware of them, and they are my reasons for wanting to do so after I retire. (I wish I could do so right away. It would be good to do it right away, but I cannot afford the time, and therefore do not want to do it now.)

Is the fact that I now want to take up the piano in thirteen years time an additional reason for doing so? Suppose that in the intervening years, I lose that desire and forget about it. At the time of my retirement, a friend advises me to take up the piano. Would he be missing one reason for doing so if he does not mention among others the fact that thirteen years earlier I wanted to do so? This example tilts the other way. My friend might mention my long-forgotten desire—not as a reason for taking up the piano or as a consideration that shows the good in doing so but as proof that once upon a time I agreed with him that there are good reasons for doing so, and also to show that the thought is not alien to me, that I can—or could—see myself doing it.

To suggest that an abandoned want is a reason is to put irrational obstacles to agents' changing their minds. As we know, our past conduct may bind us in the future. We may have entered into commitments from which we cannot now escape, except, perhaps, for good reasons. Or we may have built our life around certain goals and ambitions that it is silly to abandon, or worse, it may be a betrayal of all we ever cared about, of what our life was about. But these are special cases. They are not mere desires that we conceived for a while and then abandoned. If a desire is abandoned because we no longer believe that the reasons we saw for having it are good ones, it would be irrational to hold that even though we are right to abandon it, we cannot do so altogether, that it leaves a shadow, in the form of a reason to perform any action that will fulfill any of our now-defunct desires. But even if we did not change our mind about the reasons for the action, and even if the reasons themselves did not change, even if all that happens is that we no longer want to do what we felt like doing before, we are—as it were—within our rights to change our mind or our will like that. There can be no rationale for holding us bound to pursue dead desires, not even when this is subject to the "other things being equal" proviso.

But if dead desires are not reasons, nor are future desires. That is, the fact that I now want to take up the piano when I retire is no reason for me to take up the piano when I retire, or to prepare for taking it up at that time. As we saw, if when I retire I no longer desire to take up the piano, the fact that once I had such a desire will be no reason to do so. Therefore the belief that the fact that I now have the desire to take up the piano in the future is a reason for doing so (in the future) and therefore for preparing for doing so (now) can be sustained only if we have reason against changing our desires. To hold that there is such a reason is to put arbitrary obstacles to possible changes of mind. Why should my current desire commit me to its perpetuation unless I have a good reason for a change of mind? What is wrong with losing a desire to do something just because one no longer feels like doing it, even though one's judgment of the merit of the action has not changed? Of course, if my desire results from a belief that it is supported by reasons that defeat any alternative, I should not abandon the desire unless I come to believe that it is no longer supported by such reasons or that it never was so supported. But when it is merely a desire to do one of many things one could rationally do, there is no reason why I should not change my mind or inclination. The presumption in favor of continuing with one's existing desire cannot be more plausible than its opposite: the presumption in favor of periodically changing all one's (nonrationally compelled) desires. Each of these presumptions will appeal to people of a certain temperament, but neither of them is sanctioned by general principles of rationality.

It is still possible that while I have a desire, it is a reason for the action that will satisfy it.[17] One way in which this, if true, may be thought to be significant is in clarifying the way we think of resolving conflicts between our various desires. Wants and desires are to be distinguished from wishes. They indicate a disposition to perform the action, given appropriate circumstances. At the same time, one may have conflicting desires. If desires are reasons, a rational agent should, other things being equal, follow the desire (or combination of desires) that is the most stringent reason. But in what sense can one desire be more stringent than another? Presumably the desire that is backed by the weightier reasons (those whose satisfaction would be best), or whose satisfaction will give most pleasure, or whose nonsatisfaction would be felt most acutely, or the desire supported by some combination of these factors, is the most stringent one. But if that is the measure of the stringency of a desire, then its stringency is determined by reasons other than itself. This is obvious in the case of the reasons that back it and the same is true for securing pleasure and avoiding frustration. Pleasure is not a general concomitant of satisfaction nor is frustration a general concomitant of nonsatisfaction of desires. We may be unaware that something we strove to achieve was realized. But that does not mean that our desire was not satisfied, nor does it generally diminish the good done by its satisfaction. We campaigned for a cause and—unbeknown to us—as a direct result of our campaign, our cause has won. The good thus done is unaffected by our ignorance of it.[18]

The case of frustration is even clearer. For the most part, frustration is the result of failure in an attempt to satisfy the desire, but many desires remain unsatisfied because the opportunity for their satisfaction does not arise, or because when it does, one has better reasons, or one just chooses to do something else instead. One can feel frustrated in such circumstances, but this is not an inevitable concomitant of the desire, and I believe that it is in fact not at all common. For example, I want to spend a summer in Chamonix. This may be quite a strong desire if by that one means a desire I would not let pass unsatisfied given a decent opportunity to satisfy it. But if I never have the opportunity, I will not feel frustrated. I am aware that I have many desires of this kind; there are many things I want to do or to experience and I am aware that many, indeed most of them, will remain unfulfilled (even too many places where I want to spend a summer). It would be silly of me to feel frustrated every time I realize that all hope of satisfying one of them has passed forever.

If the stringency of the reasons that desires (allegedly) constitute is determined by other considerations that are reasons in their own right, and would count anyway—that is, would count even if we deny that the desire itself is a reason—what sorts of reasons are desires? Perhaps the answer is that prima facie desires are not reasons, but that one's all-out desire is a reason. That would seem to fit with the only reason we have seen so far to think that desires are reasons: that if of a range of acceptable options one wants—and this must refer to one's overall want—to pursue one, it would be irrational to choose one of the others. But the thought that while prima facie desires are not reasons for action overall desires are is riddled with difficulties. First, an overall desire is just a prima facie desire that encounters no opposition from conflicting desires or that defeats the opposition. How can its being a reason depend on whether it is opposed by other desires? I am offered a pear and a banana. I want to eat, but I cannot have both. I want to eat a pear. That fact is a reason for eating a pear if I do not want to eat a banana more than a pear. But if while wanting a pear I want a banana more, then wanting the pear is not a reason. Not merely is it a weaker reason than my desire for the banana. It is no reason at all.

Second, what I want most to do may conflict with what I know that, but for the fact that I have a conflicting desire, I ought to do. The situation of a person who wants to do something that he ought not to do, all things considered, is familiar and unproblematic. In that case one will, on pain of irrationality, do what one has a conclusive reason to do, perhaps reluctantly or with regret that one's want remains unfulfilled. The question is: Is it possible that an action that, barring one's desire to perform it, one ought not to perform (one has a conclusive reason to avoid) is a permissible action just because one wants to perform it? Can one's desire for an action, or for the consequences of an action, change the balance of reasons from conclusively against to that action being as well supported by reason as any alternative?

A variety of will-related factors may indeed have that effect. That one does not want to do what one otherwise has to do may mean that one will not do it well, and therefore it may be better not to do it at all. One's disappointment and frustration at having one's desire remain unsatisfied may tip the balance the other way.[19] Naturally, the fact that doing what one wants to do will be enjoyable or pleasurable is a reason for doing it, which may tip the balance. We are familiar with these and with other ways in which factors sometimes connected with the agent's desire may affect the balance of reasons. But none of them can be equated with the fact of his having a certain desire, nor is any of them a necessary concomitant of having an overall desire.

I suspect that desire in itself cannot tip the balance of reasons and that to the extent that we are inclined to think otherwise, this is because we think of other factors that are (contingently) related to desires. "Proving" this point is, however, difficult. All one can do is analyze examples and rely on a shared understanding. Consider the following case. I want to do something. I know that unless my desire tips the balance, I should not engage in the action, for it will hurt the feelings of someone, call him George, whose feelings I should not hurt. That factor is no more than a prima facie consideration against the action. It can be overridden or defeated by other considerations. The action may be necessary for my health, or for my prospects of promotion, or something else. In all such cases I am called on to compare the stringency of the reason I have not to hurt George's feelings (how much he will be hurt, the nature of my relations with him, etc.) as against the stringency of the conflicting reason (what damage to my health will ensue, how certain it is, etc.). We often call such comparisons "weighing the reasons against each other". But if the only "reason" I have for doing the hurtful act is that I want to do it, is such "weighing" appropriate, or even possible? It is not just that wanting it seems an inappropriate consideration even to mention as weighing against the hurt it will cause George.[20] The problem is that it is not clear what, in the circumstances, could count as weighing my desire against the reason I have not to hurt him. I can, of course, take account of the strength of my desire. But that merely sends me back to how much frustration or inner disruption its nonsatisfaction will cause, how much effort (and what will be the costs of the effort) overcoming the desire will require, and so forth. These—I have allowed earlier—are reasons for action, but they are not to be identified with the desire itself, and they do not accompany all desires.

I have argued above that in the normal case, a desire disappears[21] when the reason for it seems insufficient. Formally I cannot rely on that conclusion at the present juncture. It begs the question we are considering: whether the desire can tip the balance and thus not be insufficiently supported by reason. But the point is nevertheless relevant. The thought that my overall want can both be a reason in its own right as well as dependent for its continued existence on the balance of reasons is paradoxical. It requires too much by way of mental gymnastics.

The following objection may be raised: The way to assess the weight that having a certain desire has is simple. As I rightly argued earlier—the objector would say—it is determined neither by the strength of the felt force propelling one to satisfy the desire, nor by the frustration caused by its nonsatisfaction, nor by the pleasure its satisfaction gives. It is determined by how much one is willing to forgo in order to have it satisfied. A desire one would give up one's career for is greater than a desire one would only give up a week's holiday for, and so on.

This objection may have occurred to the reader in connection with my dismissal of the simple version of the belief/desire account. There I took motivational strength to be the only meaning a supporter of that account can assign to the notion of a strong desire. The reason that was so, the reason that the simple version cannot avail itself of the "option value" of a desire as a measure of its strength (as I will call the objector's suggestion that the strength is determined by how much the agent is willing to forgo for the satisfaction of the desire), was that according to the simple version, options have no value except inasmuch as being desired endows them with value. The person who would not sacrifice a chance for promotion at work to save the life of his child is simply a person for whom the value of his child is less than the value of his career. It does not show that he is giving up more when he sacrifices his child, for his child has little value for him. Therefore, that he sacrifices his child to earn an extra $1,000 a year does not show that he wants money very much, for he is giving up something very valuable to get it. So long as we regard wants as the only determinant of value, we cannot resort to some independent source of value by which to measure how much one wants one thing or another.

At the present stage of the argument, however, we have left the simple version behind. We allow that value and reasons do not derive entirely from desires. Does not the objection succeed at this stage in the argument? One's first response is that the same problem is still with us. In the preceding paragraph, I assumed that if desires determine the value of options, they determine not their value *tout court,* but their value to those who have the desires. This assumption is necessary to avoid contradiction, since the same option can be open to various agents, of whom some want it and some want to avoid it. Some may say that even though we are admitting that value is not determined by desires, value for an agent is. That is, if a person would rather give up his child than forgo an extra $1,000 a year earnings, then the child has less value for his life than the money. If this is so, it is still impossible to use value to determine strength of desire. But if this is so, nor is it ever possible to criticize a person for wanting something that is bad for him. In the next section I will suggest that what is good for someone is not determined by that person's desires. This allows for the objection to stand. It allows for a desire-independent value of what is good for an agent, which enables us to measure the strength of the agent's desire by its option value to him.

So far we can go along with the objection. We can agree that the strength of a desire can be measured in this way. This is not to accept this as the sole measure of its strength. We do assess the strength of desires in a variety of ways, and we have already encountered several of them. Their motivational force and the frustration that their nonsatisfaction will cause are both among the determinants of the strength of desires. The problem we encounter in taking desires as reasons is not that we cannot make sense of the notion that desires have strength but that we have no reason to take their strength as desires as indicating their weight as reasons. This remains the case with the "option value" measure of desires. It leaves untouched the basic point that since desires are reason dependent, their persistence depends on persistence of belief in the reason and that necessarily those who have them want the strength of their desires to reflect the weight of the reasons for them, and accept criticism if it does not. This implies that they do not want desires to be counted independent of the reasons that they see as backing them, and they do not want them to count at all if those reasons do not exist. You may question why I suddenly attribute importance to what people want, when my aim is to discount the importance of wants. I rely not on what people contingently want, but on what is necessarily implied by whatever they want since it is an implication of the very notion of a desire, an implication of the way it is based on belief in reasons. There is, therefore, nothing to the objection.

All the considerations canvassed over the last few pages suggest that a bare desire is not a reason for the action that will satisfy it. But they do not altogether dispose of the argument. There remains the simple point that if of two acceptable options one wants one thing and does the other, one is acting irrationally. If when offered a pear or a banana, I have reason to take one and it does not matter which one, then if I want the banana but take the pear, I have acted irrationally. Moreover, in situations of the kind just described, one can explain and justify taking the banana by pointing out that one wanted the banana, and not the pear. In such contexts we refer to what we want as we do to reasons. Here they function as reasons. In these circumstances, wants are reasons, though in being limited to this case they are very peculiar reasons.

4. Values and Reasons

Wants, I have argued, are not reasons for action—not in the normal sense of the word. They are neither independent reasons in the sense of being by themselves a consideration in favor of the action that satisfies them, for we cannot have wants except where we believe there is a reason for it, nor do they carry any weight in themselves, independent of the reasons that support them. A want can never tip the balance of reasons in and of itself. Rather, our wants become relevant when reasons have run their course. Once the verdict of reason is that one option should be pursued, we can do so willingly or unwillingly, and of course we can defy reason and follow a different option through either the impetuosity or the weakness of our will. Likewise, once reason has failed to adjudicate between a range of options, we normally choose one for no further reason, simply because we want to. Sometimes, however, we choose what we do not want. This usually manifests an unconscious desire for punishment, self-hate, self-contempt, pathological self-doubt, or something else. And such manifestations are irrational. In that sense, and in those circumstances, doing what one wants is the rational thing to do. Of course, in such cases the question, "What should I do?" does not normally arise for an agent aware of the nature of his situation. Yet it makes sense for an agent in that situation to ask: Given that that is how things are, would it be all right for me to do what I want? And the affirmative answer suggests that wants are here reasons. But given the concerns of this essay we can put such cases aside and accept the conclusion that wanting something is no reason for the action that satisfies it.

The fact that options have a certain value—that performing them is a good thing to do because of the intrinsic merit of the action or of its consequences—is the paradigmatic reason for actions. My wanting something does not make it good or valuable and is therefore not a reason for action. But does not the fact that I want something make it good for me?

As before, we have to avoid confusing wanting something with other features, sometimes associated with some desires. We have to distinguish what I will call "goals" from desires. Typical examples of goals are success in one's career, success in one's relationships, possessing the entire set of nineteenth-century French stamps, or qualifying as an International Master in chess. For those who have these goals, they are, of course, things they want to do or to accomplish. But they are not mere desires. Goals are our goals because in our actions we have set on pursuing them, because they play an important role in our emotional and imaginative life, because our success or failure in pursuing them is going to affect the quality of our life.[22] The fact that goals are integrated with central aspects of our lives, that they represent what matters to us in life, makes them constitutive of our well-being. We have reason to do whatever will facilitate the pursuit of our worthwhile goals, and often we would also want to perform actions that we believe facilitate pursuit of our goals. But not everything we want does contribute to the pursuit of our goals; sometimes what we want will retard and hinder their pursuit, and not always do we want to do what would in fact facilitate pursuit of our goals, even when we know that it would. While we adopt goals through our actions, and mostly through our willing actions, we do not always feel like doing what would serve our goals any more than we always feel like doing our duty, even when we know that it is our duty.

Some goals are reasons, but the fact that achieving a high level of competence on the piano is John's goal does not make it a more valuable achievement or accomplishment than it would have been had it not been John's goal. Does not that show that the value or goodness of options is not the only fact that can be a reason for action, that goals—some goals—are reasons as well? While the fact that competence on the piano is John's goal does not affect the value of such competence, it does affect its value to John. It makes that competence something the achievement of which is good for him. In general the achievement of a goal is good for the person whose goal it is only if the goal is worthwhile.[23] In this respect, goals are like desires; having them implies belief that there is value in them, that there is a reason to pursue them independent of the fact that one does or wants to pursue them. To take up stamp collecting, or playing the piano, or being a lawyer implies believing that these are worthwhile activities or pursuits. Yet once a person has made something his goal, it acquires special importance for him. He has a reason to pursue it that he did not have before. I believe that writing poetry and teaching are both valuable activities. But as a teacher who has never taken up poetry, I have reasons for teaching that arise out of my commitment to teaching, and I do not have similar reasons for writing poetry.

This suggests a certain complexity in the relations between value and reason that cannot be explored here. For present purposes, I have to confine myself to the suggestion that the difference between the value of an option and its value to the agent covers the point we are concerned with, and lends further support to the supposition that the value of options (in general or to the agent) is a reason for performing them, whereas desires are not reasons for the actions that satisfy them.

5. Reason and the Will

Most of the argument of this essay was designed to show that the fact that a person wants something is no reason for that person to perform the action that is most likely to facilitate the satisfaction of the want. My suggestion was that the fact that wants are not reasons for action makes it most plausible that typical reasons are facts about the value or good of options.

Given that the fact that an action satisfies the agent's desires does not endow it with value, it seems inevitable that in typical situations in which an agent faces various options, the value of some of them will be incommensurable. This is certainly not always the case. Even in typical cases, there will be options that are inferior to others. But typically once they are eliminated, agents are still left with a number of options that are incommensurate in value. If this is so, then reasons for actions are better characterized as making actions eligible rather than requiring their performance on pain of irrationality. In typical situations, reason does not determine what is to be done. Rather it sets a range of eligible options before agents, who choose among them as they feel inclined, who do what they want to do or what they feel like doing. Much work needs to be done to analyze the different ways in which our will leads us to do one thing rather than another. My only concern was to suggest that in all of them, the will plays a role in human agency separate from that of reason, a role that neither kowtows to reason by endorsing its conclusions nor irrationally rebels against it by refusing to endorse them.

This leads to a vindication of the classical conception of human action. If reason leaves room for an independent role of the will, this is because reasons merely render actions intelligible. And that is so only if normally choice situations include a number of undefeated incommensurate options. If desires are not reasons, it is much more likely that that is indeed so. There are few credible sources of commensurating value left.[24] To be sure, much further argument is needed to make this conclusion secure. But we should by now be immune to the fear of vacuum in the space of reason that, I have suggested at the outset, is the strongest argument for rejecting the possibility of widespread incommensurabilities of options, and the classical conception of reason of which it is a part. That phobia was fueled by the thought that wants are intelligible to those who have them. The argument of the essay embraced this point and showed that the intelligibility of our wants is secured by the fact that they are based on reasons. That does not fully explain why we want one thing rather than another. Explanations by reference to reasons do not explain everything. Our chemistry rather than our rationality explains why some like it hot. That variability between people, like variations between what people want at different times, is not fully accounted for by reason. The intelligibility of our desires does not require that. It does, however, require that we have reasons for our desires and that is inconsistent with the rationalist account of the will, which is itself prey to the objection it raised against the classical conception.

The argument of this essay for the classical conception of human agency with its reliance on widespread incommensurabilities gains support from ordinary human experience, which teaches us that quite commonly people do not survey all the options open to them before choosing what to do. Rather, they find an option that they believe not to be excluded by reason and that appeals to them and pursue it. At the very least, the case for this conception of practical rationality is to be taken seriously. That suggests that incommensurability of the value of options is a pervasive feature with far-reaching theoretical consequences.

❧7❧

Value, Comparability, and Choice

DONALD REGAN

In this volume I am the "designated eccentric", appointed to take a position no one else would touch with a barge pole. I believe in what I shall term "the complete comparability of value" (or "complete comparability" or even just "comparability" for short). Specifically, I believe the following two propositions.

1. There is one and only one sort of value that matters to practical reason in the final analysis. This unique final value is G. E. Moore's "good".
2. Given any two items (objects, experiences, states of affairs, whatever) sufficiently well specified so that it is apposite to inquire into their (intrinsic) value in the Moorean sense, then either one is better than the other, or the two are precisely equal in value.

The thesis of "complete comparability" is both stronger and weaker than its name might suggest. The thesis is very strong in that it posits a complete weak ordering. There is no appeal to any sort of intransitive relation such as "rough equality", which some have recently suggested is an important mode of comparison. On the other hand, the thesis says nothing at all about how far comparability obtains with respect to any value predicate other than Moorean "good". In that way, the thesis is, if not weak, then at least drastically limited.

It is clear that my claim about the existence and centrality of Moorean good is far more significant and problematic than any specific claim about comparability. For myself, the only issue of comparability that I have more than a puzzle fancier's interest in is the issue of comparability in terms of Moorean good, which most philosophers claim to find unintelligible. In the end, the crucial issue is not comparability but the nature of value, and how judgments of value figure in practical reasoning. Other chapters in this book, notably Elizabeth Anderson's, also make it clear that to deal properly with the matter of comparability, we need a full-fledged theory of practical reason.

Unfortunately, I cannot simply produce at this point a complete theory of practical reason. Instead, I shall proceed as follows. In section 1, I shall offer some very sketchy remarks designed to clarify to some degree what I mean by Moorean good and why I believe in it. Then, in succeeding sections, I shall discuss three arguments for comparability. Very briefly, the first argument (section 2) is that a belief in (complete) comparability fits better with other things we believe about the possibilities for comparison than does a belief in incomparability. The second argument (section 3) begins by defending a picture of ideal agency as responsiveness to reasons, and then points out that this picture supports the thesis of comparability. The third argument (section 4) is that choice between incomparable goods is not intelligible to the agent; I shall confront directly the contrary claim of Joseph Raz in this volume.

In arguing for complete comparability, I actually have two sorts of opponent (at least): on the one hand, "hard-line" incomparabilists or incommensurabilists like Joseph Raz,[1] and on the other, believers in "rough equality" like James Griffin and Thomas Hurka.[2] The first of my three arguments below tells about equally against both sorts of opponent. The second and third arguments are directed much more against the hard-liner than against the rough egalitarian.

If more of my arguments are directed at the hard-liner, one reason is that I disagree with more aspects of this position. I disagree with both the hard-line incomparabilist and the rough egalitarian on the basic structure of value. In addition, I disagree with the hard-liner about the possibility of genuine deliberation over a choice between incomparable goods. But on this point, the rough egalitarian, who says the choice between roughly equal goods is a matter of indifference,[3] seems closer to my position than to the hard-liner's. I can imagine that the rough egalitarian might endorse completely my argument against the hard-liner in section 4 about the unintelligibility of choice between incomparables.

In fact, I suspect the rough egalitarian needs something like my argument in section 4 if he is to establish his claim that the choice between roughly equal goods is a matter of indifference. To my mind, one of the most interesting aspects of this whole debate is the question of what we mean by the claim that some choice is a matter of indifference. In the end, I think this claim is often best interpreted as asserting the unintelligibility of deliberation over the choice in question, and I do not think equality of value, rough or otherwise, settles the issue.[4]

Raz says that even though two goods are incomparable (or, in his terms, incommensurable), it may make sense to ponder at length the choice between them.[5] A moderately successful life as a clarinetist is neither better nor worse, Raz suggests, than a moderately successful life as a lawyer. (Nor are they equal in value.) Still, Raz says, if I am trying to decide whether to be a clarinetist or a lawyer, expecting moderate success in either pursuit, then because the lives are so different, it matters greatly which I choose, and it makes sense to deliberate about which to choose. The central point seems to be just the great qualitative difference between the two options. How could a choice that makes so much qualitative difference to the way my life unfolds, to what I am, *not* be a choice to spend hard thought on?

If this is indeed Raz's point, then claims about equality, rough or precise, are beside that point. Even supposing that my anticipated life as a clarinetist and my anticipated life as a lawyer are roughly equal in value, they are still so different that I cannot be indifferent between them. I must take the choice seriously, and I must be doing something intelligible when I ponder it. For that matter, even if the two lives are *precisely* equal in value (as I think they could be, however great the qualitative difference), Raz could still deny on the same ground that the choice is a matter of indifference.[6] What we need to answer Raz is the sort of argument I give in section 4, about whether the undeniable qualitative differences suffice to provide a content for genuine deliberation.

So much for explaining my differing stances vis-à-vis the hard-line incomparabilist and the rough egalitarian. I cannot say that I regard the arguments I shall offer for comparability as overwhelmingly persuasive. But then, I find the arguments for incomparability less persuasive still. (Incidentally, although I begin with remarks on Moorean good, I think my arguments on comparability should have some interest even for readers with no patience for Moore.)

1

Moore suggests, correctly in my view, that the fundamental concept for practical reasoning is an unanalyzable, nonnatural "good". This is a predicative "good". It is not "good of a kind", or "good in a way", or "good from a point of view", or "good for someone". (Nor, of course, is it "instrumentally good". Nor is it in any way compounded out of "goods for" different individuals. "Good", not "good for", is the basic concept for practical reason.) To say of something that it is good (*simpliciter*, in Moore's sense) is to say of that thing that, considered by itself, independent of its causes or consequences or external relations, it ought to exist.[7] (Which is perfectly consistent with the thought that if its existence would have sufficiently bad costs or consequences, we ought not to promote its existence.)

The proper ultimate aim of practical reason is to produce the best state of affairs possible (which depends on our feelings as well as our acts) given the circumstances in which our choices occur. This is what I mean by saying Moorean good is the only sort of value that matters to practical reason in the final analysis. Of course, all the other notions of good I have mentioned—good of a kind, good in a way, good from a point of view, good for, instrumental good—may be useful tools for reasoning with. Any sane consequentialist (*pace* readers who will regard that as an oxymoron) must believe in a "two-level" theory in some fashion and must admit that deliberation does not proceed always and only in terms of what is *ultimately* valuable. Many decisions may quite properly be made without any conscious attention to the ultimate good at all. But when it comes to justifying habits of mind, or modes of deliberating, that do not attend consciously to the ultimate good, it is to the ultimate good that any justification must finally appeal.

To most philosophers nowadays, this whole approach seems quite dotty. Consequentialism—by which I mean simply the claim that the ultimate aim of practical reason is to produce the best state of affairs possible—is bad enough, and consequentialism with Moorean good as its goal is worse still. I can neither defend the view nor even expound it adequately here. But I want to say just a word about the *nature* of the argument for the existence of Moorean good that I find persuasive.

Briefly, I think a belief in Moorean good is the only view that really allows us to make sense of deliberation and choice. One of the things we deliberate and make choices about is what projects to make central to our lives. We all engage in activities like studying philosophy, singing in choruses, playing amateur hockey, collecting coins, working for the preservation of wetlands or of the art treasures of Venice, and so on. What are our grounds for developing and maintaining the commitments we have to projects of this sort? It would be foolish to suggest that at any point in our lives we survey the entire menu of possible, or plausibly available, projects and decide which is best. We drift into things; we are led and pushed in various directions by all sorts of chance circumstances; some projects that we might pursue with great pleasure and success we are turned aside from by an initial bad experience; and so on. Still, if we are reflective, we ask ourselves from time to time whether we are spending our time in worthwhile ways. If we are unable to believe that we are, we feel some compunction. We feel some pressure to reform our habits or redirect our energies.

What does it mean, this question whether we are spending our time in worthwhile ways or, more briefly, whether our projects are worthwhile? In the end, I think there is nothing this question can plausibly mean except, "Are my activities in pursuit of these projects good in Moore's sense? Ought they, *ceteris paribus,* to exist?" (I am assuming that what we are concerned with for the moment is projects that are justified, if at all, not by their consequences but by what they are in themselves.)

To sustain the claim that a belief in Moorean good is necessary to make sense of deliberation and choice, I would have to explain, among other things, why I reject the accounts of the good given by neonaturalists, neo-Kantians, neo-Aristotelians, and neoexpressivists. That is a project for a book, not for this essay. But I do think all those accounts are seriously inadequate. I make this observation, not to engage in gratuitous sniping at admirable work, but to emphasize that one can follow Moore because doing so seems to allow the least unsatisfactory account of reflective choice. One need not claim to have met the Good face to face.

The standard objection to Moorean good is that its metaphysical status and the nature of our epistemological access to it are completely mysterious. This is true, and I regret it. Much of recent moral philosophy has consisted of attempts to make moral concepts metaphysically and epistemologically respectable. But the attempts seem to me to have failed. Where respectability has been achieved, it has been purchased at the price of misrepresenting or ignoring what it is like to deliberate. For the present, it seems to me better to have virtually nothing to say about the metaphysical and epistemological questions than to adopt any of the proposed answers I am aware of.

So, if we need Moorean good to make sense of deliberation, what does deliberation in terms of Moorean good look like? As Moore pointed out, we must distinguish between the questions, "What does 'good' mean?" and "What sorts of thing are good?" The central activity of practical reasoning is the attempt to answer the second question, to figure out what sorts of thing are good. (As Kolnai tells us, "Deliberation is of ends.")[8] The basic truths we are trying to discover, about what sorts of thing are good, must be regarded as synthetic *a priori* truths, available to a faculty of perception or intuition. This faculty, though potentially veridical, is neither limited to immediate judgment of particulars (we may adjust our judgments by comparing various objects of judgment in our imagination in a reflective equilibrium process) nor infallible (however careful we are, we may sometimes get it wrong).

Well, what sorts of thing *are* good? Speaking generally, the sorts of thing that are good are pleasurable experiences of appreciation of appropriate objects. Examples would be the contemplation of a beautiful painting, a beautiful landscape, or the beauties of physics or mathematics; or equally, spending time in conversation with a friend. By far the most important point for present purposes is that there is no natural property that is the sole measure of the goodness of various good states of affairs. (In particular, neither pleasure nor anything like intensity-of-desiredness is such a measure.)

It is worth emphasizing that on my view, just as there is no natural property whose occurrence we are trying to maximize, so also the point of promoting the best possible state of affairs is not to maximize the occurrence of the *non*natural property "good". The point is not to maximize the occurrence of any property at all. *The point is simply to produce the best state of affairs we can.* To put it another way, we do not promote certain states of affairs because they are somehow carriers of something else (good, or value) that we *really* care about. Rather, we care about promoting these states of affairs because, in view of what they are, they are good. They are to be promoted. It is probably a mistake even to think of good as a property in a metaphysical sense, however convenient it is to treat it as a property grammatically. If "good" is the name of anything, it would seem nearer the truth to think of it as naming a ranking of possible objects or states of affairs in terms of to-be-promotedness. In his repeated references to good as a property, I suspect Moore was making his own view harder to grasp.

The idea of a nonnatural "ranking of states of affairs in terms of to-be-promotedness", however mysterious, does not seem *more* mysterious than a nonnatural property "good". And this much mysteriousness I have suggested is unavoidable if reflective deliberation and choice are to make sense. But the question remains just what the nature of this ranking is and how complete it is. That is the question of comparability.

2

Comparisons between goods of the same kind are relatively unproblematic. Nobody, I think, would balk at the idea that an extensive knowledge of Hittite archaeology is more valuable than a paltry knowledge of the same topic, even if the person with only a smattering knows a few isolated facts that have escaped the expert (so that there is no relationship of strict inclusion between the goods being compared). But how can we compare a knowledge of the Hittites and a knowledge of the halides? Or harder still, how can we compare, say, a friendship and research on beetles? Such different things may both be valuable, but how can we possibly say one is more valuable than the other?

The first thing to notice is that we often are willing to say things of just this sort. Imagine that what we are comparing is a deep and passionately committed knowledge of beetles, such as might result from a life's study, and a modestly rewarding but not especially intimate friendship, such as any fortunate person can expect to have a goodly number of. Whatever our worries about how comparisons of value are possible between such different things, do we really doubt that the knowledge of beetles is more valuable? (The reader who hesitates may just think knowledge is not all it is cracked up to be, and human relations are the very stuff of life. This reader should compare a richly developed friendship with a modest familiarity with, say, scarabaeids. If the reader says the friendship is more valuable, while conceding the knowledge some value, my basic point is made.) James Griffin has given us some other examples. As he points out, we sometimes judge without hesitation that some accomplishment is worth the pain it required.[9] Or we may give up some amount of political freedom to live in the country of someone we love.[10]

Michael Stocker, an eloquent proponent of value pluralism, is nonetheless quite explicit that plural values may be comparable.[11] In a specific example, he suggests that a particular increase in wisdom may more than compensate in value for the suffering by which one acquires it (even though he does not accept the maximizer's inference that if that is true, one ought to seek the wisdom at the price of the suffering).[12] Joseph Raz, who believes in the incomparability of some goods, nonetheless says that "more of one thing may be better than a certain amount of another, even if less of the first is incommensurate with that amount of the other."[13] In context, the point is that a highly successful life of one kind may be more valuable than a modestly successful life of another kind, even though modestly successful lives of the two kinds might be incommensurable. So far as I am aware, no one in this volume claims that plural values are always incomparable. Such a claim would fly in the face of very common ways of thinking and talking.

It seems to be widely acknowledged, then, that we can often compare great values of one type against relatively slight values of another type. It could still be true, of course, that *most* intertype comparisons, between values from the middle of the scale in both types, should be impossible. (More precisely, it could still be true of most pairs of goods, where the members of the pair represent different types of value, that neither is better than the other, nor are they precisely equal in value.)

But the concession that intertype comparisons are sometimes possible seems to me to give away a great deal, and indeed to make it unclear why they should ever *not* be possible. Why should it not be so, that a particular middling-successful life as a clarinetist must be either better than, equal in value to, or worse than a particular middling-successful life as a corporate lawyer? The failure of comparison cannot be attributed to the *general* impossibility of intertype comparisons; that has already been abandoned. Nor does it seem that the failure of comparison can result from an insufficient fine-grainedness in the value scales. If we are comparing various lives-as-a-clarinetist with each other, it seems we can imagine gradations in value as small as we like (including gradations much smaller than it would normally be worth worrying about in practice, but that is a quite different point). The same is true of lives-as-a-corporate-lawyer. So if *some* comparisons are possible between particular lives-as-a-clarinetist and particular lives-as-a-corporate-lawyer, and if the scales of value within each type of value are indefinitely fine-grained, why should it not be possible in principle, however difficult in practice, to make indefinitely fine-grained comparisons between the two types of lives, so that any life-as-a-clarinetist and any life-as-a-corporate-lawyer are comparable?

These remarks are my first argument for comparability. I do not imagine that they constitute any sort of proof. What I am suggesting is that a belief in comparability seems to fit better with other things we believe—the possibility of some intertype comparisons and the fine-grainedness of intratype comparisons—than does a belief in incomparability. So why not believe in comparability?

It may seem that I am ignoring the precise point of John Broome's very interesting central example, where we have fine-grained comparisons of redness on the red-orange spectrum and fine-grained comparisons of redness on the red-purple spectrum, and comparability in respect of redness between color patches from opposite ends of the two spectra, but no comparability in some cases where we try to compare a patch from the red-purple spectrum with a patch from roughly the same location on the red-orange spectrum.[14]

There are two reasons why I am not persuaded of value incomparability by Broome's example. First, unlike red, good is objective. Actually, it is unclear whether we should regard red as an objective property defined by complex facts about the reflectivity of surfaces (in standard cases) or as a subjective property defined by human perception. But whatever tendency we have to believe in incomparability with regard to red seems largely attributable to viewing red as a subjective property. It seems much less likely that a plausible objective definition of red would give rise to incomparability. Since I regard good as objective, not subjective, the example of red suggests no reason, to my mind, for believing in incomparability with regard to good.

The second reason I am unmoved by Broome's example is less fundamental but may be more interesting. When I first encountered the example, it did not occur to me to question the claim that, given a red-purple patch from somewhere in the middle of the spectrum, I would be unable to identify a point on the red-orange spectrum that was exactly equally red. This seemed very plausible. Then as I thought about it, I became less certain. It might not be immediately obvious where the "equally red" point was on the red-orange spectrum; I might have to puzzle a bit; I might never be absolutely confident of my judgment; and yet it seemed that I might after all be able to identify such a point.

I do not have an expert's eye for color. Some readers may think that only someone unusually obtuse about color could even imagine finding a red-orange patch exactly as red as the red-purple patch. So I asked a painter friend if she thought she would be able to identify a point on the red-orange spectrum that was exactly as red as a given red-purple patch. Her answer was yes. She pointed out that painters who are critiquing each other's work discuss this sort of question all the time. (Her first example was the question of the relative redness of a particular patch of green and a particular patch of blue.) She said that of course another painter, given the same red-purple patch, might initially pick out a different point on the red-orange spectrum as the "equally red" point. But she suggested that further discussion between them (about such matters as how to allow for the fact that the red-purple patch would almost certainly have a lower value, in the painter's sense, than the disputed red-orange points) could be expected to bring them closer together, and perhaps to agreement. Finally, she said that even some residual disagreement would not convince her that there was no right answer to the question which was the equally red point on the red-orange spectrum.

What all of this suggests is that the more refined our perception, whether of color or, I would say, of goodness, the less often we are going to find ourselves unable to make comparisons. Indeed, stated in such general terms, this proposition seems utterly undeniable. The question, of course, is whether a perfectly refined perception will be able to make comparisons in every case. I have no way of demonstrating that it will. But remembering that perceptions in most areas are subject to a great deal of education and refinement may make us slower to jump to the conclusion, when we do not see how to make some comparison, that it cannot be made.

Despite what I have just said, the incomparabilist's strongest argument is still the exhibition of examples where making a comparison seems virtually impossible. Some of the examples that are regularly used to establish incomparability have quite specific features, such as the variants on the problem of deciding how much money a friendship is worth, or whether it could be appropriate to avoid one's friend for a period of time in return for a sum of money. I have discussed these particular cases elsewhere, so I shall say no more now.[15] But beyond these specialized cases, we can imagine innumerable hard choices. Can we really determine (we may ask ourselves) whether a moderately successful life as a clarinetist is more or less valuable than a moderately successful life as a lawyer? Whether the intimacy with friends forgone to pursue my amateur study of beetles would or would not have been more worthwhile? Whether an evening with *Waverley* would be better or worse, in a Moorean sense, than an evening of bridge? I can only repeat, we should not conclude because making some comparison is difficult (or even because we can hardly see how to start) that no comparison can be made. Making value comparisons requires refined perceptions. It takes practice. A lifetime may not be long enough for us to arrive at really confident judgments on all the value questions that confront us.

The incomparabilist may not content himself with pointing out that comparisons such as these are extremely difficult. He may go on to say that if we consider how deliberation actually proceeds in cases like these, we can observe that we do sometimes treat the competing options as incomparable. In the incomparabilist's picture, if I understand it, deliberation often proceeds in two stages. First, we find we can decide quite quickly that the options we are choosing between are incomparable. Then, if we continue to deliberate, as we often do, when we are trying to do is merely to decide which option we want, or which we feel like. These two claims are thought to support one another. If we have once decided the options are incomparable, there is nothing left to do but try to decide which we want. Similarly, if at some point we realize we are doing nothing more than trying to figure out what we want, then we have passed beyond concern with *reasons* for one choice or the other, so we have implicitly decided that reason will not determine a choice (because of incomparability).

This picture seems to me wrong on both counts. Let us start with the second stage. I agree that in deliberating about whether to choose a life as a clarinetist or as a lawyer, the agent might after some point spend almost all of her time trying to figure out what she "wants" to do, in some sense. But, as I shall have numerous occasions to remind us, "want" is a chameleon among concepts. To inquire into what we want may not be to leave questions of value behind at all. In asking what she "wants" to do, the agent may be asking what she will enjoy most, which is highly relevant to the question of comparative value, or she may be asking which pursuit she will find it easier to devote her energies to, which is similarly relevant to the anticipated value of her achievements. Even if the agent decides fairly early on that what she "wants", in one or both of these senses, is likely to be the crucial determinant of which life will be more valuable, and even if she never explicitly returns to the question of comparative value, the question about comparative value continues to be the organizing principle of her deliberation. So, thinking about what one "wants" need not be abandoning the attempt at comparison.

This suggests that the incomparabilist is also wrong in supposing that incomparabilities are ordinarily easy to identify. (If incomparability followed simply from plurality of value, then of course it would be easy to identify, but we are still assuming, with many or all incomparabilists, that plural values are sometimes comparable.) Even if we assume there are some cases of genuine incomparability, it seems very likely that an agent might work long and hard at trying to figure out what her life as a clarinetist and her life as a lawyer would be like, and how the values would compare; and she might still find, after she had spent as much time and effort as seemed reasonable even for such an important choice, that she could not be entirely confident *either* that one life was the more valuable, *or* that the lives were equally valuable, *or that the lives were incomparable.* She might be leaning toward one of these conclusions but still not be certain. And, of course, her not being certain that one life was better or that they were equally valuable would not mean she was certain that neither of those possibilities was true; so it would not mean she was certain of or even leaning toward belief in incomparability. If the agent concludes her deliberation without final certainty on these questions, it will have been her working hypothesis all along that the lives might be comparable, and her object will have been to figure out how they compare. And this may be true, we have seen, even if much of her explicit attention has been to questions about what she "wants". Viewed from within, her deliberation will offer no evidence for the incomparabilist.

3

I turn now to another argument for comparability. The crucial premise from which the new argument begins is that the perception of a reason motivates an ideal agent (and therefore *ought* to motivate an actual agent). I would not have expected this premise to be controversial, but Raz and (less clearly) Stocker seem to reject it, so a brief argument seems appropriate.[16] (To forestall a possible misunderstanding, let me emphasize that even though I am asserting a connection between reasons and motivation, I am not defending any sort of Humean internalism. To put the point crudely, it is not a defining feature of reasons that they must motivate some agent; rather, it is a defining feature of ideal agency that the agent must be motivated by whatever reasons there are.)

Let us consider a standard philosopher's example. Jones sees an unattended baby about to drown in a wading pool. Jones can save the baby with no significant inconvenience to himself. There is a reason for Jones to pull the baby out of the pool. Indeed, we may plausibly assume there is conclusive reason for him to do so. That means that if Jones is to behave as reason requires in this case, he must pull the baby out. Furthermore, if his pulling the baby out is to be the action of a rational agent and not to be a manifestation of automatism or delusion, he must be *motivated* to pull the baby out. In some sense, rational agents must want to do what they intentionally do, and in that sense Jones must *want* to save the baby. This is yet another sense of "want", different from those discussed in section 2. Of course, I am not saying Jones must expect to get pleasure from saving or having saved the baby, nor that he must have any sort of warm, fuzzy feelings surrounding the thought of his saving the baby. He need not "feel like" saving the baby in any ordinary sense. All I am saying is that if Jones is to act rationally and as reason requires, he must be moved to save the baby by the perception that there is conclusive reason to save it.

But if we should be motivated by reasons when they are conclusive, should we not be motivated by the same reasons when they are not conclusive but merely present? Any reason, however strong, can be overborne in some circumstances, and any reason, however weak, can be conclusive in others. Our motivational response to one reason should not depend on the accident of what other reasons are present. Of course, whether we should do the action the particular reason supports does depend on what other reasons are present. But our action will be the result of motivations that may conflict, and the fact that the weaker ones generate no overt behavior is no ground for doubting that they are present, or that they should be.[17]

I can imagine only one possible reason for denying that nonconclusive reasons should be motivating. Someone might suggest that what we really ought to be motivated by is not the first-order reasons themselves (conclusive or not) but rather a second-order reason to do whatever there is conclusive first-order reason to do, if there is such a thing. This suggestion would indeed get rid of motivation by nonconclusive reasons, but it seems wrong-headed. To be motivated only by the second-order reason to do whatever there is conclusive first-order reason to do is to focus excessively on one's own "getting it right". Of course, one wants to do the right thing, and if one is appropriately responsive to the first-order reasons, one will do the right thing. (Acting on the first-order reasons, one will be led to do what the second-order reason requires.) But one's primary concern should be with whatever features of one's choice situation *make* one choice or other the right thing, that is to say, with the first-order reasons. One's primary concern should not be just a solipsistic concern for one's own moral rectitude. So the first-order reasons ought to motivate us, and in that case, they ought to motivate us whether they are conclusive or not.[18]

It may trouble some readers that I began with Jones and the drowning baby. It is such an extreme case. The controlling reason is so strong, and it is other-regarding to boot. Does an argument that begins from this case really have any application to the choice between being a clarinetist or a lawyer, or to the other choices mentioned above? I think it does. It is irrelevant that in Jones's case the reason he ought to be motivated by is other-regarding, unless other-regarding reasons differ from self-regarding reasons in the nature of their claim on rational agents' motivation. But why should there be such a difference? If self-regarding reasons really are *reasons* that make *claims* on us (as I think they are), and if they ever properly compete with other-regarding reasons (as I think they do), then I cannot see any ground for doubting that self-regarding reasons make the same sort of demands on our motivation as other-regarding reasons.

So far I have argued that an ideal agent is motivated (and an actual agent should be motivated) by the perception of a reason, conclusive or not. We can now add that the ideal agent will be motivated (and an actual agent should be motivated) *to the appropriate degree*. There is a right strength for the motivation, which is what the ideal agent will feel. Only if the ideal agent is motivated to the right degree by the various reasons she perceives will she be certain to be motivated on balance to do the action there is strongest reason for. Jones must not only be motivated to save the baby; he must be more strongly motivated to save the baby than to wander off in search of an ice cream cone while the baby drowns.

Now consider again Smith, deciding whether to be a clarinetist or a lawyer. Smith sees the value in her imagined life as a clarinetist, which is a reason (or a bundle of reasons) for choosing that path. If she is an ideal agent, she will be motivated to choose that path, and motivated to the appropriate degree given the strength of the reasons. On the other hand, she also sees the value in her imagined life as a lawyer, and she is motivated, to the appropriate degree, by that perception to choose that path. If she now chooses in accord with the stronger motivation, is not the relative magnitude of the values revealed? The point, of course, is that even though the values considered separately may appear to lie along different dimensions, still, in a particular context each represents an incentive to a particular resolution of a binary choice problem. The choice must go one way or the other, and the result, whatever it is, answers the question of how the values compare.

Notice that I am not making the argument that every actual choice by an actual agent suffices to "compare" the values involved for that agent.[19] In my picture, how the values compare is revealed by the choice of an *ideal* agent (or an actual agent imagined to be acting as the ideal agent would). The ideal agent's choice reveals a non-agent-specific comparison of non-agent-relative values precisely because the ideal agent recognizes and is motivated appropriately by whatever real values really are relevant.

The crucial point is just this: *Values, properly apprehended, motivate.* (I have argued that reasons, properly apprehended, motivate, and I assume that values constitute reasons.) When motives conflict, one or the other prevails (except in the rare case where they are of exactly equal strength). It is the connection between value and (ideal) motivation that shows that values must be comparable.

The rough egalitarian might object that if values are fuzzy or indeterminate, then the "appropriate degree of motivation" for the ideal agent will be fuzzy or indeterminate also, in which case there may be no definite fact of the matter about how the ideal agent would choose.[20] That seems right (*if* values are fuzzy or indeterminate), and that is why I said in my introduction that the present argument tells less strongly against the rough egalitarian, who relies on fuzziness, than against the hard-line incomparabilist, who relies on something like multidimensionality to generate indeterminacy, not of values, but only of intertype comparisons.

Even as directed against the hard-line incomparabilist, there is an uncomfortable air of sleight of hand about my argument. What precisely is the role in the argument of the ideal agent? I have spoken of her choice as revealing the correct comparison of the conflicting values. Does her choice really *reveal* the comparison, or does it *constitute* it? If her choice constitutes the correct comparison, then the ideal agent is playing a role so important that I ought to have more to say about what she is like and what her motives are. On the other hand, if the ideal agent's choice merely reveals the correct comparison, then it ought to be possible to state the argument without bringing in the ideal agent at all, so why don't I?

I do mean to claim that the ideal agent's choice reveals the correct comparison. As I noted earlier, in my view reasons are not constituted by their ability to move agents, but, rather, the ideal agent is one who responds accurately to whatever reasons there are. So the real problem is whether I can restate the argument without reference to the ideal agent. The answer is yes, although perhaps not so persuasively. Bringing in the ideal agent and focusing on a particular choice highlights the significance of the fact that value is "to-be-promotedness". This is what guarantees that values bear on, and in most cases determine, how choices ought to be made. "To-be-promotedness" comes in degrees, but it is unidimensional, as it were. The role of the ideal agent in the argument is to help us see this. Of course, this means that the present argument for comparability depends on a highly controversial claim about the nature of value. True enough. As I have said, we will not get to the bottom of the issue of comparability without dealing with much larger questions.

A more specific objection to my argument here is that even if the ideal agent is motivated, and motivated to a particular degree, by the values in conflict, she may *also* be motivated by such considerations as her wants. As a result, different ideal agents with different wants may choose differently, and we cannot look to choice by an ideal agent to determine comparative value. The response to this objection is complicated by the multiple meanings of "want" and must to some extent anticipate the argument of the next section, but the basic point is this: If the "wants" in question are reason-generating (like the dispositions to enjoy or to be energetically committed discussed in section 2) or reason-generated (like Jones's required motivation to save the baby discussed already in this section), they will mirror the values involved, and they will have no distinct effect on the outcome. (Different morally ideal agents may indeed have different talents and inclinations, which can properly lead them to choose different lives. But that is because different possible lives are available and are being compared.) If the "wants" in question are not reason-generating or reason-generated, then although they might derail the choice of a nonideal agent (who may, for example, be weak of will), they will have no influence on the choice of an ideal agent. The first responsibility of the ideal agent is to reasons. Even if we concede for purposes of argument that an ideal agent might be guided by reason-independent wants when reasons have run their course, what I have been arguing is that reasons rarely run their course without determining an action. The reasons' proper "course" includes motivating the agent, and except in the rare case of a tie, some choice will be determined by the competition of the motives so produced.

The picture of agency as responsiveness to reasons that I have appealed to in this section is repugnant to some incomparabilists, who complain that it leaves no room for exercise of the will. The objection seems to be that if reason, responding to considerations of value, dictates a unique right act in every choice situation in which I find myself, then I am demeaned by having no room for originality or self-creation. This is an argument that has never had any force for me at all. It is no easy matter to discover the Good and guide one's feelings and conduct by it. It seems to me the attempt to do so is a quite sufficiently ennobling pursuit for a human being (and quite sufficiently involves self-creation, in forming for oneself a reliably reason-guided character), even if there is a best choice, given one's talents, inclinations, and opportunities, in every situation.

As the preceding sentence suggests, the idea that agency is responsiveness to reasons not only supports an argument that values, if determinate, must be comparable; it also entails that insofar as values are comparable, our goal should be to choose the best that is available to us. How does this follow? Ideally, we will be aware of all the reasons relevant to any choice we make, and ideally, we will be motivated to the appropriate degree by all those reasons. The upshot is that (ideally) we will do not just something that is good enough, but what is best, what there is most reason for. So that is what, as actual agents, we should aim at.

In practice, of course, we can never be perfectly informed, and we must adopt various strategies to deal with the unavailability or the cost of information, strategies that may include terminating certain deliberations when we have come up with a choice that is good enough, or even not deliberating at all in some cases. Nor is this caveat about imperfect information the only one that is necessary. We are also imperfect in our motivational capacities. Without caving in, we must learn partly to work around and partly to accept our limitations, moral or temperamental as well as physical and intellectual. Still, our goal in principle remains doing the best that is practically possible.

This is not the place to canvass the objections that have been raised against the idea that we should do the best we can (against "maximizing", if you will). But I do want to insist that the right argument *in favor of* doing the best we can is the argument I have sketched in this section. The argument depends on the idea that we should be responsive to reasons. It does not depend on any claim about the "rationality" of maximization in the abstract.

4

My third argument for comparability is just that choice between incomparables is unintelligible. Faced with a choice between two incomparable goods, the agent will see that there is reason to choose the first and also reason to choose the second, but there is no adequate reason to choose the first over the second, or vice versa. This does not necessarily mean the agent will be paralyzed, like Buridan's ass. But it does mean, I think, that if the agent finds herself pursuing one of the goods, she will have no way of making what happened fully intelligible to herself as her choice. Choice is based on reasons. Choice between two specific goods must be based on reason to prefer one of the goods to the other. Where there is no adequate reason for preference, there can be no real choice. A decision to go one way rather than the other will be something that happened to the agent rather than something she did.[21]

Even if what I say is true (more on that presently), what sort of an argument is this for comparability? Either values are always comparable, or they are not (someone might say); if there are incomparabilities, and if that renders some "choices" unintelligible to the agents who make them, that's tough. That's just the way it is. From one perspective, this seems right; the unintelligibility of choice between incomparables is no argument against incomparability at all. On the other hand, it is not at all clear whether values are always comparable or not; and so long as it is unclear, the costs of incomparability (and surely the unintelligibility of choices to the agents who make them is a cost) do incline us toward belief in comparability. In any event, the question of the intelligibility of choice between incomparables is interesting in itself. So I shall proceed.

Consider an example from Raz.[22] I am offered a pear or a banana. I can have either but not both. I am hungry for fruit, so I have reason to take the pear, and also reason to take the banana. On the other hand, the experiences of eating the pear and eating the banana would not be the same, and the values of each are incomparable. As it happens, I want the banana, and I do not want the pear. So I take the banana. As Raz says a bit further on, "our wants become relevant when reasons have run their course."[23] (I hope it will not seem that the pear-banana example is too trivial to discuss, or that it is an example of my want determining a choice that is *de minimis* rather than a genuine choice between incomparables. The attraction of this example is simplicity and ease of discussion. Even so, I would not use it if it did not seem reasonable to read Raz as suggesting that the values are genuinely incomparable, however small the stakes. I would make exactly the same arguments I make here about choices like that between being a clarinetist and being a lawyer.)

The notion that I choose the banana because I want it may seem straightforward enough, but in fact I think it does not suffice to make the choice intelligible, even to me as chooser. "Want" is an extremely slippery term, a fertile source of confusion. If we try to be clear about just what we mean by "want", I think we will discover that there is no sense of "want" that actually makes choice between incomparables intelligible.

There is one crashingly obvious sense of "I want the banana", which may seem to be just what we need. Perhaps I expect to enjoy the banana (and I do not expect to enjoy the pear). The trouble with this suggestion is that if I would enjoy the banana but not the pear, my experience of eating the banana would be more valuable. There would therefore be a reason, in the fullest sense, for choosing the banana but not the pear. This would not be a case where "reasons had run their course" without dictating a choice; it would be a case where reason clearly dictated the choice of the banana. If our goal is to find a way in which I can choose intelligibly on the basis of what I want after reasons have run their course, we must not interpret "want" in such a way that we introduce into the case previously unconsidered reasons. (Raz's point cannot be just that enjoyment-based reasons become relevant when other reasons have run their course. That claim would be trivial and uninteresting insofar as it was true, and also seriously misleading, since enjoyment-based reasons do not have to wait for other reasons to vacate the field before they matter.)

This is the point to recall another sort of "want" that came up along with the expectation of enjoyment in the discussion in section 2 of the choice between being a clarinetist or a lawyer. I refer to a "want" that is a disposition to pursue energetically one project or another. This sort of want is not likely to matter in the choice between the pear and the banana, but it is highly significant when we are choosing long-term goals. As we saw before, this sort of want, like the expectation of enjoyment, affects the value of what we will achieve by our choices, and therefore it affects what we have reason, in the fullest sense, to choose. So this sort of want also cannot help us after reasons have run their course.

A quite different sense of "I want the banana" involves what I shall call a "reason-tracking". We assume there is reason to want the banana. We saw in section 3 that if I perceive this reason, and if I respond as I should, I will be motivated to choose the banana. *In just that sense,* I "want" to choose the banana: I am moved to choose it by the perception that there is reason to do so. This reason-induced motivation is what I mean by a "reason-tracking" want. (Notice that the reason that induces the motivation *could* even be the fact that I will enjoy eating the banana, though of course it need not be. Being aware that I will enjoy eating the banana, if that is indeed the case, and being moved on that ground to eat the banana, are not the same thing. We often slide from positing an expectation of enjoyment to positing a motivation to seek that enjoyment, and this may be good general psychology; but the fully reflective agent will realize that it is appropriate to be moved by the prospect of enjoyment only when that prospect really is a reason, and not, say, when it is a counterreason, as it would be if we are talking about the prospect of enjoyment from a sadistic revenge.)

Reason-tracking wants are not enough to make it intelligible why I choose the banana instead of the pear in the sort of case we are interested in. There is a reason to choose the banana, so I will have a reason-tracking want for the banana. But by hypothesis, there is also a reason, and a reason no less weighty, to choose the pear. So I should have a reason-tracking want for the pear as well. If I do not have a reason-tracking want for the pear, my failure to have such a want is essentially unintelligible to me. After all, I see that there is reason to choose the pear, and indeed that there is no less reason to choose the pear than to choose the banana. (A case of simple mistake on my part about what reasons there are is obviously beside the point.) If I see that there is no less reason to choose the pear than the banana, I know I should want (in the reason-tracking sense) to choose the pear no less than the banana. If I do not, I will be unable to understand myself as a properly deliberating agent.

It is worth comparing what appears to be Raz's central notion of "want" or "desire" with reason-tracking wants as I have described them. Raz raises the question how our desires can be intelligible to us (or, in formulations he treats as effectively equivalent to this, how they can be "under our control", how they can be truly "ours" as opposed to being mere compulsions). Raz's answer is that our desires are intelligible if they persist only so long as we believe we have reason for them.[24] The theme here seems to be that wants are intelligible when they are appropriately responsive to reasons. The analogy to reason-tracking wants is clear.

But there is a striking asymmetry in Raz's discussion. Raz tells us what makes it the case that a desire I *have* (like my desire for the banana) is intelligible (is under my control, and so on), but he never considers the intelligibility of a *failure* to have a particular desire (like my failure to desire the pear). What Raz seems to have in mind, then, is something which is like a reason-tracking want in being dependent on the perception of a reason, but which is optional, so that the failure to have a want based on some perceived reason simply raises no issue. Given this conception of wants, I might see a reason to choose the banana, and see a reason no less weighty to choose the pear, but I might simply be moved by the former and not by the latter. So I would want the banana and not the pear. And because wanting the pear was optional, even in the presence of a reason to want it, my responses would be unexceptionable.

The trouble with this is that wants that are to be rendered intelligible by their dependence on reasons are not optional. An agent ought to be moved by the perception of a reason. (Perhaps it is worth noting explicitly that this is true even when the reason is the expectation of an appropriate pleasure. If I correctly expect that I would enjoy both the banana and the pear, it is not acceptable, or intelligible, for me to be moved by the former expectation but not the latter, and to choose the banana on that ground. Of course, if I would enjoy only the banana, then the choice of the banana is intelligible. But as I pointed out earlier, this is a case of reason dictating a specific choice.) Raz is right to ground the intelligibility of desires in dependence on reasons. But having done this, we must regard as unintelligible the failure to have a desire that there is reason for. My desire for the banana cannot be made truly intelligible by my perceiving a reason to eat the banana, if at the very same time I perceive a no-less-weighty reason to eat the pear but have no desire for it. (In choosing the banana, if there really is incomparability, I may not go against reason. But that is not the present issue. The issue is whether my choice of the banana instead of the pear is intelligible to me. It is not.)

There are a few other possible senses of "want". One possibility is that "I want the banana" means "I contemplate with pleasure the idea of eating the banana". Notice that "contemplating with pleasure the idea of eating the banana" is different from "expecting pleasure from eating the banana". (If it were not, then what we have already said about the expectation of pleasure would apply here.) Precisely because "contemplating with pleasure" is different, it invites the question how my wanting the banana, if that consists just in contemplating with pleasure the idea of eating the banana, is supposed to be a reason for actually eating it. It seems to be a reason for continued contemplation but not for anything else.

Another possibility is that my wanting the banana is a pure dispositional fact about my tendencies to choose. My wanting the banana just consists in the fact that, offered a banana, I tend to choose it. (To be of interest, the tendency we are now talking about must be independent of, though it may be cumulative with, any reason-tracking want I have for the banana. The reason-tracking want also involves a disposition to choose, but a disposition with a specific origin in the perception of a reason. Reason-tracking wants we have already discussed. It is other dispositions, with no such grounding, that I am concerned with now.) The trouble with this suggestion is that it is hard to see how such purely dispositional wants can figure in my deliberation, or why they should. That I have such a dispositional want may not even be known to me before I act. And if the disposition is known to me, why should I regard it as something to be guided by in my deliberation, as opposed to something that I just happen to know is going to push me around willy-nilly, perhaps even something to struggle against? I do not see how I could be said to reasonably choose something on the ground that I know I have a disposition to choose it (barring indirect explanations such as that resisting this disposition will cost me too much effort or will cause neurotic anxiety in the future).

What we are finally left with is a possibility so evanescent I can hardly describe it, although it seems to be what philosophers who are not pure functionalists often have in mind when they talk about desires. The idea is that wanting the banana is just "feeling like" choosing or eating the banana. If this is to be a significant new possibility, it must be clearly distinguished from the earlier notions of want involving either expectation of pleasure or pleasure in contemplation, although I think many philosophers are careless about these distinctions and are thus prey to confusion about how desires figure in deliberation. I cannot emphasize too strongly that what we are now left with is what is *left*, if anything, after the other possibilities we have discussed are set aside for the reasons already canvassed.

Paradoxical as it sounds, I have no idea what these pure "feeling like" desires are supposed to *feel like*. (It is interesting that Raz says that most desires of the sort he is centrally concerned with have no felt quality.)[25] Like everybody else, I have occasionally caught myself wondering whether I "feel like" orange marmalade or blackberry jam on my morning toast. But if I try to see what really goes on during my fleeting, semiconscious "deliberation" on this question, it seems that what I am doing is trying to imagine how each conserve would strike me in the eating that morning and, specifically, how fully I would appreciate and enjoy its particular qualities. This brings us back to (what I have loosely referred to as) the expectation of pleasure and to full-fledged reasons for one choice or the other. The more self-conscious my decision process becomes, the clearer it is that I am inquiring into something besides the pure momentary state of my "feelings". (If it is suggested that this sort of self-conscious attention to what is going on *changes* what is going on, my response is that probably it often does. But surely if our concern is with the intelligibility of choice, we are interested in decision processes that could operate in the light of self-consciousness.)

It may illuminate the unintelligibility of "feeling like" desires if we look briefly at a phenomenon in which they might be supposed to be operative. Raz insists that any account of deliberation must leave room for my changing my mind in regard to choices between incomparables.[26] But what exactly happens when I change my mind about whether to have a pear or a banana? At all times, I see the reason for having a pear and the reason for having a banana, and I believe that neither reason is conclusive. Up to the point where I change my mind, I feel like the banana. And then, suddenly (or gradually) I no longer feel like the banana. Instead, I feel like the pear. Assuming incomparability, none of this violates the requirements of reason. In that sense, there is nothing wrong with what has happened. But this account hardly makes changing my mind intelligible as something I do. I hardly seem to be in control.

I am not saying that changing my mind is never something I do. Quite the contrary. In what seems to me the standard case, I change my mind about some choice because I discover new reasons, or I improve my appreciation of reasons I already knew about, with the consequence that I change my belief about what reason requires. Here my changing my mind about what to choose is completely intelligible and fully under my control in the relevant sense. But this is completely different from the case where my inclination changes without any change in my underlying beliefs about the reasons. In such a case, if I am asked why I took the pear after previously saying I was going to have the banana, I might respond, "I don't know. I just changed my mind." But this would be an admission of defeat. It would concede that my volte-face was no more intelligible to me than to my interlocutor. (Alternatively, and perhaps more likely in practice, "I just changed my mind" might mean, "From causes unknown to me, my expectation of what I would enjoy most changed." But that, of course, points to an [unexplained] change in what I thought reason required.)

In sum, I see no way to make choice between incomparables intelligible by elaborating the suggestion that when reasons have run their course, I choose what I want or what I feel like. What is needed, if such a suggestion is to work, is a kind of "want" that is both reason-grounded (since reason-groundedness is the source of intelligibility) and available to step in after the deciding force of all relevant reasons has been exhausted. The very specification of the need virtually compels the conclusion I have been arguing for: that there is no sort of want that can do the trick.

Before leaving this topic, let me emphasize that I am not denying the relevance of wants (in appropriate senses) to deliberation. I am not even denying the relevance of unreasoned wants. It may just be a brute fact about me (though there will presumably be some deep explanation) that I can enjoy some activities and not others, or that I can bring myself to pursue with energy and commitment some projects and not others. These facts about my wants are highly relevant to what to choose. But they are relevant because they affect the value achievable by various choices; they affect what reason directs me to do. Raz, if I understand him, would give wants some further role in deliberation. So far as I can see, the further role is neither necessary to account for the importance of wants nor intelligible.

5

Nothing I have said will change the mind of someone who just finds it obvious that goods are often incomparable. I cannot even retort that *I* find it obvious they are always comparable. To me, nothing is obvious in this area. Still, for reasons I have tried to suggest, I am inclined to take comparability as my working hypothesis.

8

Incommensurability and Practical Reasoning

ELIJAH MILLGRAM

Worries about the incommensurability of ends or of values arise when practical reasoning—that is, reasoning directed towards decision or action, contrasted with reasoning that aims only at arriving at belief—seems to run out; the thought that ends or values are incommensurable is prompted by facing a decision in which they must be jointly brought to bear, and it is not clear how this is to be done. If the difficulty persists, frustration may give rise to the thought that there *is* no way to do this, that one *cannot*, here, reason one's way to a practical conclusion, and that this is because the relevant considerations cannot be measured or weighed against each other. So far, so familiar.

I myself do not know what 'values' are; like William Bennett, when I hear the word 'values', I reach for my Sears catalog. So I am going to consider only the incommensurability of ends (or equivalently, as I will claim, the incommensurability of desires), on the supposition that the incommensurability of values is a closely related phenomenon, and that a treatment of the former could, if necessary, be adapted to the latter. "Incommensurability" is a word applied to a number of distinct, though related, phenomena. I will use it, provisionally, to say of pairs (or sets) of ends or desires that one is not more important than another (or the others) and that they are not equally important. And I will restrict myself to the case in which all ends or desires in question are those of a single human being.

I will first show how the worry that ends are incommensurable is framed by a widely shared model of practical reasoning. I will then suggest that the standard way of introducing incommensurability as a philosophical problem has things backwards: commensurability is the result, rather than the precondition, of practical deliberation. I will give two examples of ways in which desires or ends are commensurated, and show how they indicate imprecise, but rather near, boundaries to the effectiveness of practical reasoning. Then I will consider how, despite the nearness of these boundaries, it can be brought about that practical deliberation provides an agent resources sufficient to negotiate the decisions he faces. Along the way, I will try to indicate the role that the achievement of commensurability plays in the constitution of the practically unified agent; if I am right in thinking that commensurability is a product of practical deliberation, practical deliberation is important not only for successful action, but for the construction of an acting self.

1

Failure of deliberation is one thing, and incommensurability (on the etymology, failure of measurement) is another. We need an explanation for their being so often connected, evidently one identifying practical deliberation, or some central part of it, with measurement. I take the explanation to lie in the widespread, if often only implicit, acceptance of an instrumentalist model of practical reasoning, by which I mean the following.

In the formal mode, instrumentalism is the view that to justify an action or a plan or a goal, one must adduce a further goal, such that attaining the former goal (or performing the action, or executing the plan) would be a means (or a satisfactory means, or the best means) of attaining the latter. (I will from here on out mention only ends or goals and will omit such qualifications as 'satisfactory', 'the best', and so on.) In the psychological mode, it is the view that all practical reasoning consists in, or can be without loss reconstructed as, deriving a desire (or intention, or action; again, I will not continue to repeat this) from another desire via a bridging belief to the effect that attaining the object of the former desire would be a way of attaining the object of the latter desire. I desire to lower my cholesterol levels, and I believe that the best way of doing this is to cut back on eggs and butter and cheese. So I come to desire to cut back on eggs and butter and cheese. In the formal mode: the goal of lowering my cholesterol levels, together with the fact that cutting back on the butter and so on will lower them, justifies my goal of cutting back. On the instrumentalist model, all practical reasoning, and all practical justification, while perhaps more elaborate, comes to something very much like this; practical deliberation consists *only* in means-end reasoning. The point of practical reasoning, on this model, can only be to satisfy some already existing desire or attain some already adopted goal, and practical justification can do no more than exhibit the fact that some action or desire serves the satisfaction of some further desire.

That instrumentalism is more or less the received view, and that it is mistaken, are claims I will not argue for now.[1] Rather, I want to consider problems that arise within the instrumentalist model, and how addressing these problems leads to the idea that ends may be incommensurable.

We live in a world in which ends or goals or desires can conflict, that is, in which desires that one has cannot be jointly satisfied. Such conflicts are pervasive; it is *normally* true that, for any desire one has, one has a conflicting desire. A purchase requires money with which I could buy something else I want; activities compete for time with other activities. So a sane instrumentalism must supplement the raw claim that practical reasoning consists in finding ways to satisfy one's desires with an explanation of how conflicts between desires can be resolved.

Now instrumentalism is an exclusionist doctrine: it counts *only* deliberation directed toward the satisfaction of desires as practical reasoning. Since only desires give rise to practical reasons, conflicts between desires must be adjudicated by appeal to features of those desires whose satisfaction deliberation can address. At this point, the notion of the strength or weight of a desire enters the picture, as an intrinsic feature of the desire that can be used to resolve conflicts between desires. Some desires are intrinsically more demanding than others; conflict between desires is resolved by satisfying the stronger of the conflicting desires or, in more complicated conflicts, by satisfying the desires that have the greatest summed strength or weight.

This version of instrumentalism requires that we be able to determine the weights or strengths of desires or goals in a way that allows them to be compared, one to another and in larger groups: deliberation proceeds by measuring and comparing the respective weights or strengths of one's ends. It is in this context that failure of deliberation is construed—is bound to be construed—as failure of commensuration. If one is clear about what is a means to what—and attaining this kind of clarity is not, it has been pointed out, properly speaking practical deliberation at all[2]—then the remaining locus of difficulty is the task of comparing weights or strengths of ends or desires.

Naive instrumentalists—early utilitarians, perhaps—might have thought that desires resembled sensations and came with their strengths somehow inscribed on them; and if desires *did* come this way (and if the view of sensations that tends to be relied on in this context were satisfactory), then incommensurability would be quite unusual. But the sophisticated instrumentalist realizes that "desire", in his use of it, must be a term of art, the correlate in his moral psychology of a goal or end, and that there is no particular phenomenological aspect it must wear. A desire need not *feel* like anything at all, and so its strength need not feel like anything at all either. The strength of a desire, considered logically rather than phenomenologically, is simply a way of expressing or summarizing the relations of comparative importance in which the object of desire stands to other objects of (actual or possible) desire.

Expressions like "strength" or "weight" normally indicate a quantitative conception of the comparison-enabling intrinsic feature of desires. I will return to the link between the comparison of ends or desires and the measurement of quantities associated with them below. For now, note that a quantitative conception of the relations of importance among an agent's desires requires only that those relations satisfy a few familiar formal conditions.[3] But because the instrumentalist wishes to *explain* those relations in terms of features internal to the desire, when he believes those formal conditions are satisfied, he will be pressured to construe the comparison-enabling features as measurable quantities of something within the desires (their strengths or weights), and ascertaining the presence of the feature as measuring.

There is no reason to expect that when an agent conceives an interest in some object, he at the same time considers and settles the relations of comparative importance in which it stands to all other possible objects of desire. (When you decide you want a piece of apple pie, do you ask yourself whether you would prefer it to an order of vegetable samosas? If samosas are not on the menu, probably not; and even if for some reason you do consider the samosas, there are indefinitely many items that you do not consider, at least if you are ever to get around to ordering.) A desire is formed in a particular practical context, and we should not expect its content to address demands not made by that context. Of course, desires will quite often come with contents supplemented by habit, or by references to judgments of relative importance invoking previously formed desires, as when finishing the pie is unproblematically overridden by a babysitter emergency. But a newly formed desire will generally not contain within itself the resources needed to adjudicate conflicts between it and many other actual and possible desires. Desires have only the contents that are put into them, and since human beings are finite creatures, those contents will be quite limited.[4] So, because it is characteristic of human beings to find themselves in circumstances in which desires conflict in novel ways, we should expect desires to be frequently incommensurable.

This is not to say that one *could* not form only desires that contained the resources needed to adjudicate arbitrary conflicts—for example, by making a real number intended to be used for all such comparisons part of the content of each desire. But our desires are normally not like that, and there is a reason they are not. Someone who *did* form desires equipped with these resources—whether in the crude way just mentioned or in some more sophisticated fashion—would be foolishly committing himself to a position whose practical upshots he could not have seriously considered. Forming desires in this way would be imprudent, thoughtless, and rash.

The instrumentalist take on practical reasoning is an essential ingredient of the problem. If I have already formed a desire that allows me to choose between *A, B,* and *C,* and another desire that allows me to choose between *D, E,* and *F,* why can I not repeat the procedure when a situation arises that requires me to face the hitherto uncontemplated choice between *A, D,* and *G*? The difficulty is that instrumentalism insists that if the way in which the choice between *A, D,* and *G* is made is to count as practical *reasoning,* it must be justifiable entirely by reference to the already available desires; simply *coming to have* a further desire is not reasoning. If we accept the instrumentalist model of practical reasoning, the pervasiveness of conflicting desires and the inevitability of novel conflicts, the severe limitations on the deliberative resources we can suppose are located within reasonably adopted desires, and the consequent pervasiveness of incommensurable desires, we must conclude that practical reasoning should almost *never* work. If the optional member of this package is instrumentalism, then the price of instrumentalism is quite high.

That one cannot successfully navigate one's life by rational deliberation alone is a conclusion that might be accepted with composure. Faced with decisions between incommensurable options, it will be suggested, we have resources other than deliberation. For example, one can decide on impulse, and there are presumably more sophisticated methods of adjudication. If the considerations supporting the competing options are genuinely incommensurable, then one's choice will, at any rate, not have been *wrong.*

Against this counsel of complacency, let me briefly indicate the kind of trouble into which choice on the basis of incommensurable considerations is likely to get one. Selection techniques whose results are not entirely explicable in terms of their sensitivity to what is important in the choice situation will to that extent produce results that are arbitrary with respect to what is important in that choice situation; they will rehearse, piecemeal, the foolhardiness of forming desires whose demands significantly outrun the thought that one has put into them. And experiment with such techniques shows that there are further problems. Choice that does not reflect a resolution of the competing considerations should not be expected to be consistent across choice situations; for example, an agent acting on a systematic policy of impulsive choice—the most naive member of this family of techniques—would be almost bound to end up at cross-purposes with himself. Because the competing considerations are not decisively resolved, it is easy to find oneself reconsidering one's choice and discovering that the overridden consideration now seems more salient, more central, and simply more important. Such reconsideration is likely to give rise to a family of related and not always distinguishable forms of impaired agency: vacillation, akrasia,[5] an inability to free oneself of second thoughts and to commit oneself to a single course of action, and, last but not least, regret avoidable only by a cultivated blindness to the persisting merits of the discarded choice.[6] That is, choice on the basis of incommensurable desires undermines unified agency in one of several ways: by either successively propelling the agent in different directions, or encouraging indecisiveness, both of which prevent the adoption of coherent and effective approaches to practical problems; or where an agent is able to avoid indecisiveness and waffling by dint of the sheer determination not to change his mind once it is made up, by committing him to a dogged and unintelligent response to as-yet-unanticipated circumstances; or where the agent props up the arbitrary choice by adopting an equally arbitrary way of viewing the choice situation, by trading in akrasia for self-deception.[7]

Faced with this catalog of the risks taken in using alternatives to rational deliberation to bridge the gap between competing desires and choice, the instrumentalist might reply that not all candidate techniques have been considered. (These techniques might add new desires to one's stock or modify those already in it; or they might select an action while leaving one's desires and evaluative judgments unchanged. If one cannot settle which option is better, one can always flip a coin, or ask one's mother.) Perhaps a technique will be found that does not involve these risks—a method sufficiently intelligent, even when systematically applied, to support rather than weaken agency; sensitive enough to its surroundings to deflect charges that its use is ill considered; and so on. But when a technique that deserves these encomiums is found, the time will have come to ask whether the instrumentalist is not being dogmatic in refusing to call it a form of practical reasoning.

2

Within the instrumentalist model of practical reasoning, the bases for comparison of desires are their intrinsic features, and so one can determine whether given desires are commensurable simply by examining them. Ends or desires considered generally are either always (or almost always) commensurable—so that instrumental practical reasoning is in principle equipped to solve the problems it is given—or they are often incommensurable, so that practical reasoning must frequently be unsuccessful. An instrumentalist who has not realized how quickly the resources available in desires run out is bound to ask which option we are stuck with.

On the one hand, he may observe that many ends do not, when carefully and sensitively considered, seem to be commensurable. Should I become a lawyer or a clarinetist? Exactly how much money should Judy take her friendship with

John to be worth, anyway?[8] If a prospective graduate student attends institution A, she will live in Los Angeles, with its automobile-oriented lifestyle, study with the teachers at institution A, and become much closer with her LA-dwelling friends and acquaintances. But if she goes to institution B, she will live in the Bay Area, with its more bohemian lifestyle, receive a very differently flavored education, live in proximity to a number of relatives, and so on. Would it be better to study with the Wittgensteinian at A or the philosopher of physics at B? How much better? If one teacher is preferred to the other, how is the difference between them to be weighed against the availability of used books and an endless supply of perfectly prepared cappuccinos? The ends being compared seem resistant to measurement and even to ranking, both within and across categories of goods. From the observation that many ends are plausibly incommensurable, an instrumentalist is likely to draw the conclusion that there are many questions that practical reasoning cannot answer. Choices have to be made, and they will be made without sufficient reason.

On the other hand, an instrumentalist might observe that, even in circumstances of this kind, deliberation quite often terminates in reasoned choice. The considerations presented at the outset may seem incommensurable, but we deliberate and decide anyway. The prospective graduate student visits the respective institutions, talks to friends, advisers, and other students, searches her soul, decides—and is subsequently able to justify her decision. Since, on the instrumentalist's view, getting the answer right through rational deliberation requires commensurability, the apparently incommensurable considerations must have been commensurable after all. The problem is then to explain why the considerations had been mistakenly thought to be incommensurable and to reconstruct the underlying metric.[9]

On the one hand, we have convincing examples of agents faced with considerations that do not contain within them the means of commensuration; on the other, we have agents successfully completing deliberations in equally difficult circumstances, and who are subsequently prepared to pronounce on the relative importance of the considerations that entered into their decision. The competing arguments that proceed from these observations are mirror images of each other; each argument requires dismissing the opposing and recalcitrant observation. We should accommodate both observations if we can; they can be reconciled if we suppose that the considerations to which deliberation appeals *are* incommensurable at the outset of the deliberation, but that the process of deliberation *renders* them commensurable. The prospective graduate student begins deliberating unable to commensurate her desires to study under the guidance of the teachers at institution A with her desires to study under those at B, and these desires with other goals having to do with the way she wants the texture of her day-to-day life to feel. Eventually she decides to attend one of the two, having on the way seen how to commensurate the conflicting and initially incommensurable ends. Commensurability is not the precondition but the *product* of successful deliberation. At any rate, I propose to proceed on this hypothesis.

Some philosophers have come this far only to conclude that deliberation must be self-deceiving. In an influential but under-discussed paper, Aurel Kolnai writes:

> However enlightened by reason and based on or rather supported by reasons, choice is shot through with arbitrariness . . .
>
> Placed before significant choices, man cannot but deliberate, weighing ends as if they were means, comparing them as if they were fixed data accessive to theoretical measurement, whereas their weight depends on the seesaw of his own tentative willing and on his emergent *parti-pris* as well as the other way around. In some sense, it is an inherently deceptive, not to say deceitful operation, with loaded dice as it were; the agent cannot help weighting what he is weighing, though neither can he do the weighting without a vague but imperative reliance on the results of his weighing, some would say the illusion of his manipulating fixed weights.[10]

If competing ends do not have content sufficient to resolve conflict between them into a choice, choice proceeding from resolution rather than impulse, or something on a par with impulse, will involve *augmenting* the content of those ends, for example, by arriving at fixed weights for them. That is to say, choice in the face of incommensurability involves deliberation of ends. Kolnai's difficulty is that deliberation is, as he affirms, of ends, but he takes rationality to be of means: deliberation's "primary habitat and starting-point is indeed, so Aristotle's dictum remains valid, the consideration of means in view of ends."[11] Deliberation of ends was required because instrumental rationality did not have enough to go on; but deliberation of ends, on Kolnai's view, amounts to a form of instrumental rationality. So he concludes that obtaining results in the face of incommensurable considerations must involve some sleight of hand.

We saw earlier that, within the instrumentalist model, successful practical reasoning presupposes commensurability. So it is not surprising that accepting the suggestion that commensurability is the product of practical reasoning will force an instrumentalist to construe the practical reasoning that produces commensuration as dishonest. If we want to continue to explore the suggestion, we will have to leave instrumentalism behind.

Abandoning instrumentalism means revising our provisional notion of incommensurability. Instrumentalism entails that whenever we are able to render a judgment as to the relative importance of the objects of our desires, we can do so on the basis of the desires themselves; consequently, when we cannot render such a judgment, we can determine that we cannot simply by examining the competing desires. So an instrumentalist can use the notion of commensurability without distinguishing between ends or desires standing in relations of relative importance in whatever way, and their standing in relations of relative importance specified by the desires' contents. When we reject instrumentalism, we need to make the distinction and to decide what the term 'incommensurable' is going to label. Continuity suggests adhering to the following revised usage: Desires or ends are incommensurable when they do not contain within themselves the resources to resolve conflict between them into a judgment of relative importance or into choice.

3

The next item on the agenda is to lay out reasonably representative examples of practical deliberation that manages to commensurate initially incommensurable ends. Consider a standard case of conflicting desires. My roommate has announced that we are welcome to the raspberry chocolate cake in the refrigerator; it is from Rosie's, and is bound to be delicious. However, I am on a diet, and the cake is fattening. It may help to think of the two considerations as the major premises of competing practical syllogisms ('Eat delicious things' and 'Do not eat fattening things'). A practical syllogism proceeding from one major premise might well be defeasible by the major premise of the other: if something is delicious *enough,* and the occasion special enough, making an exception to the diet is probably the right thing to do; conversely, if something is fattening enough, I should make an exception to my policy of eating delicious items. I know that both of these considerations are important to me, but the cake is both delicious and fattening, and faced with it, I realize that I do not know *how* important the two considerations are with respect to one another in this particular case. I want this, I want that, and I cannot tell which one I want more. How do I resolve this very practical problem?

There are many ways one might address a question like this; let me run through one. Desires, as Anscombe pointed out, come with desirability characterizations; or, equivalently, major premises of practical syllogisms have *points.* What are the points of my competing major premises? The point of eating delicious things will be the sensual pleasure involved; that seems clear enough.[12]

And while there are, of course, many kinds of diets, mine is a response to my body image. I am fat, and ashamed of how I seem to others, especially when I dwell on my thighs, of which I am particularly conscious. Because I do not believe that anyone could find me attractive, I don't date. I feel guilt for my body and contempt and hatred for myself. A successful diet would change my body (and, I perhaps naively think, my body image) for the better.

How can I bring these two desirability characterizations to bear on each other? One thought that might occur to me is that my body makes me so unhappy that I should not deny myself this bit of pleasure. But this thought is self-pitying, and realizing this may lead me to examine more closely the pleasure that I will experience when eating the cake. It might occur to me that there are, after all, different kinds of pleasure: on the one hand, the expansive, joyous pleasure that I might have sharing dessert with old friends, and, on the other, the pleasure of escape: alone in my kitchen at night, the only light that from the open door of the refrigerator, hunched over and completely absorbed in the cake I am greedily devouring, I can forget, for as long as I am eating, that I am ashamed of my body and unhappy with myself. Now I realize that as long as I see myself the way I do, it is the latter pleasure, rather than the former, that I would experience on eating the cake. And once I realize this, my mind is made up. The pleasure of escaping from my body into food is a pleasure I do not want; it is part of the life of self-hatred I am striving to be rid of. It is not that this pleasure has undesirable side effects (though I imagine it does); not all pleasures are intrinsically good, and this, I firmly believe, is one that is not. I will forgo the cake.[13]

In this example, deliberation has rendered initially incommensurable ends commensurable, and done so by enriching their contents. I can now say that my diet has turned out to matter more than the pleasure of eating the cake, and I can say this because I have developed a more articulated picture of the objects of my desires. My indiscriminate desire for sensual pleasure has become a more nuanced family of attitudes toward different varieties of sensual pleasure.[14]

Here is a second example. I am trying to choose between two potential roommates. One of them, I can see, will be clean to a fault, but her conversation loud and uninteresting. The other is quite personable, well read, and clearly will be fun to talk to, but admits to leaving half-full cups of coffee on the floor, dishes in the sink, and laundry on the furniture, often for weeks on end. I know that I care about both aspects of a roommate's behavior, but find myself unable to say which is more important. The competing considerations are incommensurable.

When the summer is over, I *know* which is more important. I shudder when I think about the kitchen sink. My roommate and I have settled into a kind of trench warfare over taking out the garbage. And I find myself saying things like, "I had no idea that cleanliness mattered so much." It is clear to me that a dull conversationalist who has learned to pick up after herself is much to be preferred to a witty slob.

Here it looks like I have *discovered* how much cleanliness matters. I could not have simply made up my mind, enriching my desire by conceiving a further interest, as it were, in one quality or the other. And the problem is not, or not obviously, something I could, at the outset, have reasoned or imagined my way through. (The story could just as easily have been told the other way; I might have found slovenliness tolerable, but dull and whiny conversation obnoxious and infuriating. Ahead of time, there is no way to tell which of these imaginable outcomes I will be brought up against by events.) Rather, I learn what is important (and *how* it is important) in the way I learn many other things: from experience.[15]

If so, then one form that practical deliberation can take is something analogous to inductive or experimental reasoning. In cases like these, we are unable rationally to decide—and the competing considerations are incommensurable—because we simply do not yet know enough about how they matter. Experience and inductive deliberation may supply the information that content-poor desires could not.

Aristotle holds that *phronesis,* or practical intelligence, comes only with experience. We can now give reasons for thinking him correct on this point. Practical intelligence is in large part a matter of being able to choose correctly in the face of competing considerations; on Aristotle's view, intelligent choice appeals to a conception of what matters (which he calls *eudaemonia*).[16] By determining how the different ways in which our ends are important fit together, this conception commensurates the major premises of one's practical syllogisms. But the agent's conception of *eudaemonia* is an achievement. It is acquired piecemeal, beginning with parental instruction, and is supplemented by experience when disappointment and pleasant surprises supply one with new premises for one's practical syllogisms, or correct and augment premises already accepted. When circumstances press one to resolve conflicts between one's ends into a locally coherent understanding of what, in the case at hand, matters more, one articulates, bit by bit, the gradually more global, coherent, and systematic conception of what matters that serves as a guide to subsequent choice. That is, the process of rendering ends commensurable is the process of acquiring one's conception of what matters.

4

I have suggested that incommensurability works to undermine agency. I now wish to claim that rendering competing considerations commensurable is a central part of the process through which unified agency, or the practical unity of the self, is achieved.

Consider the would-be agent whose would-be practical syllogisms are not at all defeasible by competing considerations—that is, a creature equipped with reflexes rather than the logical apparatus of the practical syllogism. In such a creature, the joint acknowledgment of the major and minor premises of a practical syllogism suffices for forming the intention or executing the action that is its conclusion. The major premise functions as an exceptionless rule, and where rules conflict, conflicts must be resolved in an arbitrary manner—perhaps simply on the basis of which rule happens to be triggered first. Decision making of this kind is familiar enough: Skinner's pigeons, unwieldy bureaucracies, and rule-based expert systems are examples. We think of the behaviorist's conditioned pigeons and rule-bound bureaucracies as mindless, and it is instructive that expert systems, although now a commercial technology, are considered one of the dead ends of the field of artificial intelligence, precisely because intelligence was what they could not be made to exhibit.

Now a rough-and-ready rule of thumb for use in discussions of unity of the self at a time (or synchronic as opposed to diachronic personal identity) might be this: if two thoughts belong to the same mind, then there are trains of thought they could both figure in. And since unity of the self is a matter of degree, we can add that the mind's unity is in part a matter of how *likely* it is that, when thinking that deploys one thought makes it appropriate to invoke the other, the other will in fact be invoked. If this is right, then unity of agency— the practical dimension of personal identity at a time—will be exhibited in the agent's ability to bring to bear in a train of thought leading to a practical conclusion his various desires, concerns, and so on, as they become relevant. But this ability is just what makes the difference between reflex and that essentially defeasible inference pattern, the practical syllogism: so achieving unity of agency is a matter of transmuting one's reflexes into practical syllogisms. However, bringing competing considerations to bear in the course of deploying a practical syllogism—contrasted now with the mere juxtaposition of impulses—requires commensurating its major premise with the various considerations that are its potential defeaters. Consequently, a central part of the enterprise of attaining unified agency is commensurating one's ends or desires.

Like our conception of *eudaemonia,* unified agency is an achievement—in fact, the same achievement, seen from a different point of view. The process resembles the day-to-day activities of a sculptor I know. He begins work with a pile of found metal objects—rebar, cotter pins, washers, steel plate, and so on—which he pieces together to form larger units: the head of a hoe is joined to a length of bent reinforcement rod, and is now a hand. Similarly, we start our practical lives with haphazard collections of desires so poor in content as to amount to no more than reflexes—some innate, some conditioned, and some supplied by adults around us. Pressured by experience to resolve practical conflicts, we weld disparate desires into larger and more structured practical judgments. When we do, they are transformed in two not entirely distinguishable ways. First, the desires may be reshaped, just as the sculptor might cut or bend the hoe to make it fit its role as a hand. Second, the desire acquires a role or location in a larger whole, in roughly the way the hoe has; this location is displayed in the defeasibility of the practical syllogisms in which the desire figures.

We are now in a position to reconnect measurement and commensurability. My deliberations regarding the relative merits of diets and cakes, or different kinds of roommates, allowed me to say, retroactively, that my diet and a roommate's cleanliness mattered more than their competitors. But these conclusions did not involve a judgment, or at any rate a very precise judgment, as to *how much* more they mattered. A quantitative conception of the competing merits does not seem to have figured large in my deliberations.

That is in part because of the locality and small number of comparisons. As more of the judgments of relative importance that make up one's picture of what matters are put in place, it will often happen that more patterns of comparability will seem to be expressible using notions of measurement.[17] Recall the sculptor: as parts of the sculpture are assembled, a scale is gradually brought into play with respect to which parts of the sculpture can be too big, or too small, or against which one can be bigger than another, and bigger by such and such an amount. (The respective *physical* sizes of the pieces do not themselves determine their respective sculptural sizes. Painting two physically identical pieces of metal red and blue, respectively, will typically have the effect of making one larger with respect to the other. For comparison, think of the way adding painted items to an initially blank canvas creates the perspectival space in which the items have their relative pictorial sizes.) Similarly, the development of an overall and coherent conception of what matters gradually puts in place a background against which one can judge not only that one consideration is more important than another, but *how much* more important.

Now if, as the instrumentalist has it, the direction of explanation proceeds from what is already there (that is, from the contents of one's desires) to comparisons, then the ability to perform the full range of comparisons presupposes that this background is fully in place, and a background with enough structure to guarantee the feasibility of the full range of possible comparisons is normally one that supports measurability. This is why the strengths or weights of desires are thought of as *quantities,* and it explains why commensurability has so often been thought of as a question of what quantities are measurable against what other quantities. But if the instrumentalist has the direction of explanation back to front, and the contents of one's desires are constructed, piece by piece, through the deliberation of ends, then quantitative measurability will be a cumulative by-product of successive commensurations. Over the course of one's deliberations, one constructs a conception of what matters, and in doing so, one may come to an understanding of some things mattering measurably more or less than others.

Measurability of this kind will appear only when the successive commensurations produce results that satisfy the formal conditions required for a quantitative construal. We should not expect that this will always occur—just as we should not expect every sculpture or painting to put in place enough perspective and scale to determine fully the absolute and relative pictorial and sculptural sizes of all their elements.[18] A satisfactory conception of *eudaemonia* is more likely to look like Matisse's *Red Room* than Raphael's *School of Athens*.

5

We began with the worry that incommensurability threatens the effectiveness of practical reasoning. Now we can see that we have better things to worry about: that the ineffectiveness of practical deliberation might threaten the commensurability of ends and thus the practical unity of the self. And, it seems, there is reason to worry. I am not going to claim that all commensurating practical deliberation looks like one or the other of the two examples of section 3. After all, we do not have the theory of practical reasoning it would take to underwrite such a claim. But I do think that instances of deliberation that resemble them are not unusual, and if they are not, then practical reasoning is likely to run out precisely when we need it most.

First, experience has a way of coming along too late to be of use. I discover that cleanliness in a roommate is more important than wit only after I have made my choice of whom to live with. To be sure, the lesson I have learned here may stand me in good stead in similar future choices, and if so the experience will not have been wasted. But if it is the case that the larger the decision to be made, the less likely it is to be repeated, then the larger the decision to be made, the less likely one is to come to it prepared by experience. And, of course, the larger the decision, the more important the ability of practical reasoning to resolve it will be.

Second, recall the way in which the competing considerations relevant to eating the chocolate cake were brought to bear on each other. The approach to the problem was opportunistic and *ad hoc*. It seems to follow that my arriving at a solution was a matter of pure luck. It was fortuitous that I noticed that there were relevantly different kinds of pleasures at stake in the problem, fortuitous that one of these was disqualified as an end, and fortuitous that this disqualification solved the practical problem. While it is possible that surveying more examples and developing a theory to account for them would bring to light a general technique guaranteeing solution, I see no reason to expect such a guarantee, and I am going to push forward on the assumption that there is not going to be one. Although we may on occasion be lucky enough to find a way to square one end with another, it looks like we should count on being left high and dry most of the time.

Third, notice that in this example the number of relevant considerations was quite small. To arrive at a practical conclusion, I had only to make clear the relation between my interest in my diet and the kind of pleasure that wolfing down the cake would entrain. The more complex the situation, the harder it will be successfully to bring the respective considerations to bear on each other in this kind of way—and not only because we can only keep seven or so items in mind at once.[19] It will simply be less likely that there *is* a story that does the job of showing how, here, this decision would be the right one. If this is right, then in order to be successful practical deliberators, the number of considerations facing us in each of our choices must usually be few. But the situations in which we need practical guidance most are bound to be the ones in which the considerations are multifarious.

It appears that we are back very near where we started. Incommensurability looks to be the rule rather than the exception, and successful practical deliberation the odd lucky hit. All we have succeeded in doing, it might be thought, is reversing the direction of explanation: instead of explaining the failures of practical reasoning by appealing to the prevalence of incommensurability, we are now explaining the prevalence of incommensurability by adducing the failures of practical reasoning. And if this is the position we are in, then there is something we are not seeing. The reason is that if we are to take it for granted that we *are* more or less unified agents, our successes in commensurating competing considerations must be much more frequent than the argument so far has led us to suppose.

Our stake in our own agency should lead us to treat this as a *practical* problem: how can sufficient commensurability be brought about to make integrated persons the rule and fragmented would-be agents the exception? If the problem is that arbitrary desires and goals will be too infrequently amenable to deliberative commensuration, then evidently the solution is to ensure that the competing considerations that we face are not simply drawn at random from the space of possible desires and goals. If the machinery of practical reasoning is effective only for a relatively narrow range of inputs, we can safeguard the unity of agency that depends on successful practical reasoning by making it likely that practical reasoning by and large receives inputs on which it is likely to be effective.

While there are steps the individual can take toward this end, I want now to consider social dimensions of the solution to this problem. Christine Korsgaard has pointed out that one of the more important functions of social organization is to remove occasions for means-end reasoning: when I want to fly to Prague, instead of spending time and effort considering how this is to be done, I call my travel agent. There is a parallel point to be made about the role of social organization in making possible deliberation of ends. We ought to judge social arrangements in part by the degree to which they provide the missing guarantee that the premises of competing practical syllogisms can be (often enough) commensurated.

Many of the major premises of our practical syllogisms are *bequeathed* to us by our social surroundings. (Parents and friends play a particularly important role in this regard.) By contriving to equip our children with aims, maxims, and evaluative judgments that we know to be amenable to joint commensuration, we will have stacked the deck in favor of successful practical deliberation. Now we know that ends, evaluative judgments, and so on are amenable to joint commensuration if we have derived them from a unified and systematic conception of what matters that captures a way in which they can be commensurated. This suggests telling our children to do and value those things that belong to our own picture of the well-lived life—remembering, of course, that we should not expect them simply to reconstruct, in the course of growing up and deliberating, precisely the conception of *eudaemonia* from which these dicta were derived.

If we need experience in order to discover what matters and why, then proper upbringing will involve not just the right parental injunctions, but arrangements that ensure the range of experience that an agent needs to develop his practical intelligence. Saying what the appropriate range of experience would be is not a task I want to take up now; in any case, it will vary with the deliberative demands the agent is likely to face later on in life. But there may well be an argument in the vicinity of this point against our current practices of committing childhood and youth almost entirely to formal schooling.

Lastly for now, a social organization must arrange matters for those who live in it so that they are presented with manageable choices, both with regard to the number of considerations involved in any particular choice and to the ability of the agent to square considerations of particular kinds with one another. Policies to the end of presenting agents with manageable choices do not need to be carried to extremes: our choices need not be quite as predigested as those we are given on commercial airlines. ("Sir? Would you like the chicken or the beef?") Choices can be prestructured and remain genuine choices. Such policies may smack of paternalism, but there is a Kantian argument for paternalism of this kind. If autonomy consists in resolving or, at any rate, a willingness to attempt to resolve, practical problems by bringing to bear the resources of practical rationality, respect for autonomy demands doing what one can to make sure the resources of practical deliberation are not too often swamped. For when they are, failure to deliberate successfully will normally result in heteronomous choice, and consistent failure will lead the agent to abandon deliberation as quixotic and simply surrender himself to heteronomy.

If we are adequately unified agents, we may conclude that we have been given starting points that are good enough and choices that are manageable enough. That is no surety for the future. Unified agency is fragile: technological and social change may force us into choices that we are unequipped to make; a personality that counts as a unified and practically intelligent deliberator when faced with one menu of options may be irrational, habit bound, and impulse driven when faced with a different menu. It is up to us to do our best to make sure that the menus we face are the right ones and that we come equipped to meet them as rational deliberators.

6

Experience shows that the account I have been sketching is likely to prompt a number of related objections; I will conclude by briefly addressing these. Taken jointly, they amount to a dilemma.

On the one hand, I have claimed that incommensurability can often be resolved by appealing to experience. This suggests that what I have been describing as a problem arising from incommensurable desires is actually a problem of incomplete information about something like values, where these are thought of as mind-independent objects of perception and theorizing. But if this is the right way to think about the problem, experience will be able to help square incommensurable desires only if the values they reflect or express are themselves commensurable; and if so, the commensurability of values will be the prior, and deeper, philosophical problem. Moreover, if this *is* the right picture of the problem, my suggestion that we can adequately respond to the threat posed by incommensurability to unified agency by supplying agents with ends made to be commensurated should seem beside the point. If what matters is the responsiveness of our practical judgments to an already-existing Good, it is not merely unhelpful but positively pernicious to supply agents with motivational materials that they will fit into patterns that do not correspond to that Good. (The point of moral education, on such a view, must be the transmission of a discovered truth.) Finally, if one can simply *observe* what matters more than what, one would expect a good deal of agreement about what matters. But different people can have different—even conflicting—yet nonetheless adequate understandings of what matters, and these differences are often to be accounted for in terms of the agents' differing deliberative histories.

On the other hand, I have been suggesting that deliberation that commensurates ends is something like the construction by the agent of a conception of what matters—and, implicitly, a scale against which relative importance can be, sometimes, measured—out of raw materials such as desires, ends, preferences, and reflexes. But if *this* is the right picture of the problem, why isn't the process of commensurating competing desires or ends after all only a sophisticated member of that camp of strategies, represented by choice on impulse, to which it was supposed to be an alternative? How can it differ from the self-deceiving deliberation of ends characterized by Kolnai? And, last, if an agent's conception of what matters is his own construction, how can it be experience- and observation-driven as well?

As I remarked at the outset, I do not understand what 'values' are. But I suspect that if there *are* items to which the much-abused term can be applied, they arise out of and in the course of the kind of experience-driven deliberation at which I have been gesturing. So the question is whether there are processes of noninstrumental deliberation that sidestep the dilemma; since an answer will have to wait on a far more definite characterization of the usable deliberative techniques than I can give here, I will just say what I think. It is a mistake to imagine that experience can play a role in the construction of a picture of what matters only if that picture is taken to be a *copy* of something else. (Think of the role of experience in painting, when painting is not merely a mimetic exercise.) It is also a mistake—the same mistake—to suppose that if something is not meant as a copy of something else, then there is no possible source of correction to and constraint on it. (Think again of painting or, for that matter, of mathematics.) Whether the impression of constraint is genuine rather than self-deceiving, and what forms the evaluative by-products of choice that commensurates incommensurables are likely to take, depend on whether there are in fact patterns of noninstrumental practical reasoning, and what they look like. If this is right, the next step in understanding the achievement of commensurability, of conceptions of *eudaemonia,* and of unity of agency is to advance an account of the forms that noninstrumental practical reason can take.

9

Leading a Life

CHARLES TAYLOR

I

The word 'incommensurability' tends to crop up in the discussion of two different kinds of predicament in ethical life. The first is where we have to make a choice with two different goods at stake—goods that are different enough that we have difficulty knowing how to weigh them together in the same deliberation. For instance, in an example designed by Bernard Williams, the act with the best consequences may conflict in some situation with the demands of my integrity.[1] Or the demands of benevolence to others may conflict with those of my own fulfillment. Or the demands of justice may conflict with those of mercy and compassion.

The second kind of context is increasingly common in our world. It is where we somehow have to weigh together, perhaps even adjudicate between, demands emanating from the ethical outlooks of very different cultures and civilizations. Here we tend to struggle without being able to find any common ground from which to reason in a way that people from both cultures could be induced to accept.

As Ruth Chang has incisively shown in her introduction to this volume, to speak of 'incommensurability' here is often sloppy and overly simple. We need to make a number of important distinctions in this domain. I am taking her argument as granted, and I want to explore the first of these contexts. I want to try to say something about what it is to reason when very different goods are at stake. I shall not go into the second context, though some of the things I say about decision between goods may cast light on the problem of reasoning across the boundaries of cultures.

II

A basic idea with which I start the discussion of the first context is that any adequate account has to do justice to both difference and unity. We are brought up short in these contexts and forced to recognize the diversity of goods. But at the same time, we seem to be able at least to struggle toward making nonarbitrary choices in these predicaments, and that indicates that in some way unity is something that we can strive for in ethical life.

Of course, this starting point is far from uncontested. In the philosophical world, big battalions follow views that rather deny the diversity of goods and make unity unproblematic. I am thinking of the various forms of utilitarianism, on one hand, and the theories inspired by Kant, on the other. In reaction, critics arise who declare values to be unarbitrably diverse. The most popular views of this kind today are the various flavors of "postmodernism".

I think both of these extreme positions ignore crucial and undeniable features of our ethical life. These have often been pointed out, and I will be doing some more of this in the following pages, but my main aim goes beyond the negative one of refuting these one-sided positions. I would like to help us move toward a plausible view of moral reasoning that reflects both its inescapable diversity and its continuing struggle for unity.

The polarized philosophical scene reflects in the first place the powerful impact of the theories of unity on post-Enlightenment thought. The theories of diversity arise in reaction to this near hegemony. The appeal of the former is readily understandable. The theories seem to introduce both clarity and decidability into ethical life.

They bring clarity in somewhat the way that scientific theories do. They show a diverse array of moral intuitions and felt obligations to be the realizations of a single purpose, like the greatest happiness of the greatest number, or the deliverances of a single criterial test, like the attempted universalization of the maxim of one's action. This unity brings with it decidability. Either we weigh different actions in the light of the single overall purpose, or we simply see which actions are permissible by the criterion. If more than one is, then by definition we are faced with a nonmoral choice between them.

The clarity was won not just by uniting the diverse demands but also by excluding some, or at least relegating them to a position of lower priority. Utilitarianism articulates our sense of the importance of what I will call "benevolence", using the eighteenth-century term—the call we feel to help our fellow creatures live and flourish, to prolong life and reduce suffering. But it does not seem to have place for the goals of personal fulfillment or for our aspirations to realize in our lives other goods than benevolence: to be people of integrity, sensitivity, feeling, and love (except insofar as this instrumentally serves benevolence). This is why the demands of, say, integrity can be taken as a challenge for utilitarianism.

The various theories inspired by Kant certainly give articulation to our sense of justice. But they too demote personal fulfillment to a lower rank among our objectives. First, the demands of justice must be served; then the pursuit of the "good life" will be in order.[2] We get a tight circumscription of the domain of morality, with a very clear criterion for right and wrong, but that is partly because we expel from the precincts of morality a number of aspirations that are now classed as merely personal, and hence not obligatory in the same sense.

This move is in an important way overdetermined. It is motivated by both epistemological and moral reasons. I have already mentioned the epistemological attractions: the clarity, the sense of decidability, the insight seemingly conferred into the bases of morality by relating all obligations to a single principle. But the moral grounds are equally, if not more, important. Modern liberal, post-Enlightenment culture has given justice and benevolence a centrality and importance in ethical life that seems unprecedented in human history. The issues that are of supreme importance turn around these. The transgressions that seem the most grave and shocking, which earlier ages might have identified as blasphemy, or treason to one's tribe, or infractions of the family sexual code, now are identified as violations of human rights. In the post-Enlightenment stream of thought, even sexual morality undergoes a displacement of its center of gravity. Wrong now is not defined in terms of personal impurity but as infringement of another's rights, as in issues of sexual harassment, or in the new radical feminist condemnation of pornography as a mode of violence against women.

So a number of things come together: first, a moral temper that exalts issues of benevolence and justice over all others, even to the point of making them the whole of what is properly called "morality"; then a corresponding focus on our obligations toward others: morality is concerned with "ought". And along with this is an unprecedented clarity in moral affairs—a clarity in that the boundary of the moral is so sharply marked, and also in that the issues within it can be decided by a definite procedure.

This clarity is won by relegating outside of moral deliberation certain historically important domains of ethical thinking. Two closely connected domains are relevant to this discussion. When we start reflecting on the ethical life, and perhaps questioning the injunctions handed down to us, we can start by trying to define what is really important.[3] This reflection can actually be more radical than I have just made it sound, because it is not assured at the outset that one has an already clear and defined notion of importance and that one just needs to discover what things have this property. On the contrary, as one looks at different ethical theories, one is struck with how differently they understand what I am rather vaguely calling here 'importance', and in particular with the very different kinds of boundaries they draw between what is important and what is not. In some cases, the frontier is very sharp, like a cliff, separating high-altitude matters of real moral moment from a low-lying plain of ordinary desires. In other cases, we have something more like a gentle slope interrupted by many plateaux, representing a finely graded hierarchy of goals, none of which stands out starkly from all the rest. Kant's theory seems to fit more the first model, Aristotle's the second.

This level of reflection is concerned with defining what I have called "life goods", that is, what actions, modes of being, virtues really define a good life for us.[4] Is it devotion to God, or steadfast courage in the face of adversity, or heart-felt concern and benevolence for our fellow human beings, or some combination of these and still other qualities? This level connects to a second where we try to clarify what it is about human beings, or their place in the universe, or our relation to God, or whatever else, that makes it the case that such and such are the highest life goods. Thus, devotion to God makes sense in the context of seeing ourselves as creatures of a loving God. Austere courage makes sense within a vision of a universe that is hostile or indifferent, and of a human being defined by the capacity to maintain the dignity of remaining uncowed by this hostility. It requires a certain kind of picture of the universe, our capacities, and the possible stances toward this universe they make possible for us. The focus on benevolence can have a number of backgrounds—some theistic, some atheist, some not classifiable in terms of this contrast—yet they have in common that they see love, or something like it, as our highest capacity, and they see human beings as worthy objects of this love, whether as children of God, or beings with inherent dignity, or whatever else.

This further definition of our nature, or position, or relation to some higher power, articulates what I want to call "constitutive goods". I call them so because whatever is defined at this level is what constitutes our life goods as such. Reflection at either of these levels is hard to carry on without touching on the other. This is patent in the case of a theistic ethic: How can I see my life goal as devotion to God without some sense of being his creature? But it is just as much the case in connection with "disenchanted" ethics of austere courage. Part of the background that makes sense of this is the view that we live in a disenchanted universe, as well as being creatures with certain capacities. I distinguish the levels because it is possible to describe the articulations separately—for instance, to lay out what you think the good life consists in. But to make full sense of this good life, and hence to win through to the insight in the first place that this is the good life, you need to be operating on both levels.

It is characteristic of a great deal of moral philosophy today that it stays clear of these linked domains. It simply starts with our intuitions and then finds a formula that can claim to generate them, perhaps refining them in the process, until we reach reflective equilibrium. Such was the procedure of an important contemporary Kant-inspired theorist, John Rawls. Kant himself did not similarly restrict the scope of his theorizing. He is clear about the status of human beings as the only rational agents in the universe, and hence as (1) bound to live up to the demands of rationality in the realm of practical reason and (2) commanding a kind of respect as bearers of dignity that nothing else in the world does.[5] But Rawls's aim was to re-edit something of the Kantian theory, without the "metaphysics".[6] And it is this move that effectively relegates the reflection on life and constitutive goods to extra-philosophical darkness.

Similarly, Habermas claims to be able to show that the standard of a discourse ethic is binding on us by showing how we are already committed to it in virtue of talking with each other the way we do. We can bypass altogether reflection on the good.

In the case of utilitarianism, the refusal takes a rather different form—that of claiming that it is obvious that only one thing is important: human happiness, or pleasure and the avoidance of pain, or actual human preferences, depending on the formulation. In a sense, there is something less puzzling about this than the Kant-derived theories, because plainly all of them are making an assertion about importance. Those flowing from Kant are giving justice, or respect for my fellow human beings, a paramount position and relegating everything else to a lower priority. It seems odd that they think that they can just establish this priority in the very structure of their theory, without even formulating it as a proposition about importance, let alone arguing for it. At least utilitarians have an official position on this, and even something like an argumentative strategy. This consists of taking advantage of the temper of unbelief and suspicion that surrounds not just faith in God or nirvana but all the various aspirations to self-transcendence, at least within the post-Enlightenment culture, to defy their opponents to name anything else than just plain human happiness and suffering, to which comparable importance can be attached. And then they wait for their interlocutors to condemn themselves as fusty, woolly minded, and perhaps even misanthropic reactionaries.

And so we have an influential style of thinking in modern moral philosophy that gives vent to the widespread sense that justice and benevolence are of supreme importance, thus also reaping the rewards of clarity and decidability that flow from this restrictive move, while at the same time closing off the entire area—which in a post-Enlightenment culture must appear epistemically "soft"—within which such definitions of importance can be made and argued. Moral philosophy can now deal with such "hard" and decidable issues as the calculation of benefits, or the theorems of rational choice theory, or the derivability of certain intuitively binding injunctions from some procedure, and can stay altogether out of the murky domain within which these intuitions can be articulated, refined, or overturned. This style of thinking covers wide differences of opinion. Most notably, there is a long-running dispute between utilitarians and Kantians. But the very fact that each of these identifies the other as its main opponent says a great deal about what binds them together and removes them as a group from moral philosophers who want to open the closed areas.

Of these, there are also two main families in today's philosophical world: those, often inspired by Aristotle, who want to redefine an ethic of the good and of virtues, and those who, following Nietzsche, want to challenge the hegemony of benevolence altogether, some even going as far as the master in rejecting the whole post-Enlightenment emphasis on reducing suffering and cruelty as an attempt to imprison and control the Dionysian play of our being.

Many neo-Nietzscheans are as shy about owning their antihumanist stance as a frank judgment of importance as the post-Enlightenment theorists are in their humanism. They develop complex quasi-epistemological reasons out of Nietzschean perspectivism as to why judgments about the good have no alethic value, are merely reflections of stances of power, and the antihumanism is made to emerge out of the supposedly universal fact that all intellectual orders are imposed on chaos, and hence the struggle between them is one in the end of power. In this (like their neo-Kantian opponents), they are less forthright than their master (although possibly more consistent).

All this explains why rational and responsible attempts to articulate goods, both life and constitutive, are not in very good repute in contemporary philosophy. But it is exactly in this domain that we could hope to come clearer about how we recognize a diversity of goods and how we try to make a unity of our lives in the face of them. It is not surprising that we are unclear about this. Between those who have dictated without discussion a premature unity, and those who see all unity as arbitrarily imposed, there remains only a relatively narrow band of thinkers who are even able to discuss the issue.

III

It seems to me that the issue cannot be avoided. We do face a diversity of goods and often have to make all-in judgments of how to act where more than one of them is at stake. Of course, we have the move, originating with Kant, of declaring that all other goods except the favored ones have a systematically lower priority, are not part of morality, and are to be considered only when the demands of morality are met. But this will not do.

In saying this, I am not taking a stand on the substantive issue. I am not saying, for instance, that justice is unimportant, or less important than Kantians think—much less am I embracing the antihumanism of neo-Nietzscheans. One can have the strongest views about the paramountcy of justice, but still a systematic priority will be difficult to justify. By systematic priority, I mean one that says, Answer all the demands that belong to domain *A* (say justice, or benevolence) before you move to satisfy any demand of domain *B* (say, personal fulfillment). What makes this kind of rule unlivable in practice is what I want to call differences of weight. Within any domain, there will be issues of vastly different importance. The domain as a whole may be of great importance, in the sense that you may judge that it is here that the value of your life is really decided. But within that domain, there will be matters that are central, and others that are more peripheral, questions where what makes this domain important are centrally at stake and others where something relatively minor is in play. Under the rubric of justice fall such weighty issues as the preservation of basic human rights, or the avoidance of brutal exploitation, on one extreme, and on the other, whether you took your fair share of the housework last week.

Of course, we frequently see, among those who want to make a certain good preeminent, the attempt to level out all issues connected with it, and to give them identical weight. When it comes to sacrificing to the gods, we might say, the neglect of even a trivial detail is as grave as the refusal to honor them altogether. This kind of homogenizing of a whole issue area by promoting the trivial to the rank of the vital can work up to a point for a while, but sooner or later life reasserts itself, and people begin to make distinctions. That is because the sense that there is an obligation or call on us comes from our sense that something important here is at stake and in the end has to be sensitive to this perception of importance. Now there are differences of importance not only between goods, but also between occasions when what we are calling the same good is invoked.

That is why systematic priority leads to pragmatic absurdity. Perhaps justice, or benevolence, is in general more vital than personal fulfillment; perhaps there are lots of cases where I ought to sacrifice my fulfillment for the sake of justice or to save another. But this does not mean that in any case in which an issue of justice, however trivial, occurs together with an issue of fulfillment, however weighty, I have to give priority to considerations of justice.

Imagine a tropical republic governed by a red-green coalition. The leader of the Green Party (call her Priscilla) is the minister of natural resources, vowed to protect Tropicana's rain forests from total destruction. But the relation of forces is such that it becomes clear that the only way to avoid much worse destruction is to give over x square miles of the forest to the chain saws of a large multinational corporation. Priscilla is intellectually convinced by this argument and realizes it would be irresponsible to sabotage the arrangement, but she asks to be relieved of her portfolio, so as not to be the person who actually introduces the necessary legislation and guides it through the chamber. What is at stake here is something like integrity; this act would go against the whole direction of her life and the causes it has been dedicated to.

The example is complex, of course, because integrity is also a political asset. Priscilla realizes that this will be bad for her profile before the public and will jeopardize her ability to communicate what she is about in politics. But integrity is a political asset only because it is also a personal good, and she also feels this deeply. She has her role to play in the scheme of things, but this cannot override a certain fidelity to a fundamental bent of her life, of her commitments; she would feel the overriding of this as a kind of violation.

Now some members of the coalition (utilitarian social democrats—there are, alas, lots of these) try to convince her to stay. They realize that there will be less trouble from the factious elements in the Green Party if their leader is actually taking responsibility for the scheme. But Priscilla resists and is given another portfolio.

Very different kinds of goods are in play here: on one hand, the results of consequentialist reasoning about the common good; on the other, the demands of personal fidelity. They are very hard to compare. Indeed, it would be hard to know what to say if they were to be ranked in abstracto. When E. M. Forster said (as has been alleged) that if he had to choose between betraying his country and betraying his friends, he hoped he would abandon his country, he was making the kind of rhetorical gesture that it would be absurd and disastrous to translate into a statement of systematic priority. Without knowing the nature of the treason, what rides on it, what this shows about one's friend, the nature of your relationship, how can one just state a blanket priority?

But in this case, Priscilla can decide, and feel she is right to decide. Of course, we can disagree. But it is also clear that the confidence she feels, and even that we may feel in disagreeing, is very much dependent on the particular weights of what is at stake in each domain. Perhaps if the whole scheme was sure to unravel without her taking charge of the bill, and if as a result the entire rain forests of Tropicana were sure to be razed, Priscilla would have stayed at her post. One might say that almost certainly she would. In fact, as it turns out, some support is required of her; she has to go on supporting the government, even perhaps serving it in another portfolio, but this she judges is not such a direct disavowal of her basic convictions, so she is willing to do it. Again, if what was at stake in refusing the deal were much less, she might not have gone along with it at all and taken her party into opposition. Everything here hangs on the details.

As another example, in John 12, it is related that while Jesus was at the house of Martha and Mary in Bethany, Mary took a pound of ointment and anointed his feet, wiping them with her hair. The then equivalent of the utilitarian social democrats grumbled and said: "Why was not this ointment sold for three hundred pence, and given to the poor?" (John 12:5; the speaker is identified as Judas Iscariot, not the highest recommendation for this stance). An act of devotion, meant to foreshadow the imminent death of Jesus ("let her alone: against the day of my burying hath she kept this," John 12:7); what price? In a sense, none. It is not in the same register as calculations about what can be given to the poor, but the rightness had something to do with weights here. The act of devotion here could find expression only through something of value. But something whose use would condemn to poverty masses of people would be obviously wrong to use here. The rightness of the action also has something to do with its one-off character ("For the poor always ye have with you; but me ye have not always"; John 12:8); as a steady, continuing priority, it would be a different matter.

IV

How can we reason between goods that are so different? How do we manage to reach nonarbitrary conclusions? If our model is the possession of some metric for actions, such as utilitarians claim to have, we will give up in despair. But if we turn to the way in which we articulate relative importance in our lives, we will see that we are not without resources.

It might sound as though our judgments of relative importance across different kinds of goods, in the absence of something like a metric, have to be quite inarticulate. But this is not so. Of course, they will not be fully *articulated,* but this is a different matter. The point is the one made famously by Aristotle in his discussion of *phronêsis,* or practical wisdom, in Book VI of the *Ethics.* We cannot lay out fully what it is that induces us to make this choice rather than that in contexts where deliberation requires practical wisdom. That is, we could not set out a sufficient condition for this being the right action in this case, which we would then have to apply mechanically, as it were, that is, without further deliberation or thought, to other cases where this description applies. Or put differently, any such sufficient condition would have to be on a level of generality where it was utterly unhelpful (e.g., that the action was "the right thing to do").

This is so because the contexts of action, the kinds of goods in play in a given case, and the particular weight of each kind in this precise case, are infinitely variable. Any general rule, derived from one set of cases, will have to be considered again and finely tuned in some other situations.

In this, Aristotle differs from the modern theories of obligatory action I have been discussing. Both utilitarianism and Kantianism can claim to have defined an informative sufficient condition for rightness, for example, being the action producing the greatest utility consequences, and proceeding from a universalizable maxim. Of course, critics have claimed that these are not unambiguously applicable in practice; notoriously, the universalizability criterion has been taxed with being empty. But these criteria are meant to pick out the right action in each case, without requiring modification or riders.

The fact that the rightness of an action can never be fully articulated in this sense does not mean that we do not make use of articulation, even that our degree of practical insight may be partly a function of our articulations. That these never suffice of themselves to pick out a unique solution does not say that they may not be crucial in guiding us.

I have already talked about one kind of articulation: that in which we identify different life goods and judge them as more or less important. This articulation is given further depth and richness by our pictures of the constitutive goods that lie behind the life goods. Of course, when I speak of "articulation" here, I mean more than formulation in what might be recognized as theoretical terms, in some philosophical or theological doctrine. Our sense of both life and constitutive goods is fleshed out, and passed on, in a whole range of media: stories, legends, portraits of exemplary figures and their actions and passions, as well as in artistic works, music, dance, ritual, modes of worship, and so on. A Bach cantata articulates a certain mode of Christian piety, in a way that cannot be substituted for by treatises on theology, just as Camus' *La Peste* sets out what it is to practice a certain mode of austere integrity in a disenchanted world, more effectively than a lot of philosophical writing about the death of God.

But beyond this, I want to talk about another aspect of our sense of good and right, which we also manage to articulate. This is not so much a matter of the relative importance of goods, but of a sense of how they fit together in a whole life. In the end, what we are called on to do is not just carry out isolated acts, each one being right, but to live a life, and that means to be and become a certain kind of human being. An ethical outlook that might seem to deny this— might say, for instance, that precisely what we should aim at is just being able to do the right thing in each new situation, and nothing else—would simply confirm this point. It would be telling us to become the kind of person who *can* (which you and I manifestly are not now) dedicate ourselves thus totally to the rightness called for at this moment.

Your life is something you "lead", in the telling expression of ordinary speech, which Richard Wollheim explicates in his insightful book,[7] which involves both the sense that one's life is moving somewhere, perhaps in many directions at once, and that one is trying in some degree to guide this movement (or these movements). So an inescapable category—or perhaps one might say, register of our ethical thinking—is our life, as our moving, changing, becoming, with its own nonuniform temporality, embodying different rhythms: some phases are regular, involving repetition of a routine through slow, almost imperceptible change—change that we may wake up to only afterward and recognize in retrospect. Other phases seem critical; a lot is at stake in a fateful moment. In a trice, something irreversible has taken place. It is in the very nature of a life to contain such kairotic passages.

But insofar as we have some sense of our lives, of what we are trying to lead, we will be relating the different goods we seek not just in regard to their differential importance, but also in the way they fit, or fail to fit, together in the unfolding of our lives. These goods may play different roles and have different places (and this also may mean different times) in our lives. And grasping this may help us decide what we ought to do.

So to return to Priscilla, something like this may have been her reasoning: An important part of the point of my life is to act as effectively as possible for this endangered cause—the world environment as whole, of course, but in my case what I can do something about is Tropicana's threatened rain forests. This cause will take all our efforts and even more, outnumbered as we are and nearly overwhelmed in the world political balance of forces. In a sense, we ought to say that no personal sacrifice is too great in this cause. So perhaps then I shouldn't resign. After all, my colleagues have a case that this *might* endanger this deal, which we all see to be the best hope of avoiding disaster.

But on another level, why are we doing this? Why are we engaging in this fight? Yes, undoubtedly because the issue is important, because a lot is at stake here. But there is also something else: we know that we human beings are capable of responding to these issues, although we most often fail to respond adequately. We know that we are capable of feeling that the world, and the whole sphere of life, commands our admiration and even reverence, although we often block this out and pursue just our own projects and seek to maximize our instrumental efficacy. We want to become the kind of human who can fully feel and live this reverence, a goal that is not easy to reach.

We want to win our fight for the rain forests, but this is not all. We also want to cherish and develop a certain way of understanding and responding to the world—in short, a certain reverence. It is not so much a question of ranking these goods as of seeing the way they fit together, the way they are complementary. Just cherishing reverence without action would be unbearably precious. One would even wonder about the quality of the reverence if it could accommodate supine surrender to the lumber companies. On the other hand, single-minded pursuit of the results, without any concern whatever for what kind of people we are becoming, would be more than questionable.

It would be in effect to treat ourselves like gods, who could give their single-minded attention to the disposal of things in the world, because they did not need to concern themselves with what they are becoming—their nature being fixed, invulnerable, not for them the continuing need to cherish the good in order to avoid becoming monsters. To throw oneself into winning the result alone, as though it did not matter what kind of human one might become, is an act of hubris, a leap beyond the vulnerable human condition. I (this is Priscilla speaking still) can see how the philosophy of disengaged reason that develops with the modern world can encourage this stance of the morally invulnerable agent, concerned only to control the world. But this is the illusion that stands behind everything I am fighting. And the history of our century has shown how political revolutionaries, in the name of total efficacy, can throw the ordinary human restraints on action to the winds. This same history has shown what monsters they can become. The hubris brings its terrible nemesis.

But what has all this got to do with resigning or not resigning? asks Priscilla's impatient, down-to-earth, and unmetaphysical friend, who, we might imagine, is trying to help her make up her mind on this question. Well, answers Priscilla, someone else might be able to do it, but for me, taking such a direct part in an act of desecration of our rain forests (if you will allow me to be a little hyper-dramatic) goes so deeply against what I am becoming, and *what I am striving to become,* that it does a kind of violence to me. Perhaps if I were further advanced, perhaps if this reverence I seek were more deeply rooted in my being, perhaps then I could take the legislation through the chamber without a tremor. But granted where I am in my striving, this is impossible. To do this, I would have to take a step toward becoming one of those dissociated, hubristic, deracinated agents of pure instrumental reason, whose blindness has helped to put our civilization in this dire pass. I must resign.

Thus reasons Priscilla—or a possible Priscilla; there are other available reasonings. But I have developed this one because it shows a sense for how different goods relate. What is important here is a kind of complementarity between goods that nevertheless can be in conflict. The crucial reasoning that brings about the decision has to do not so much with weighting here, but with a sense of the complementarity and of how it may be threatened at some point by the overwhelming of one side in the name of the other. Where this point lies has a lot to do with the particular person and case. Priscilla even admits that it depends on her level of ethical or spiritual development. But at a certain point, she feels she has to act in order to safeguard one side of the complementarity, and that is what induces her to resign. There is a kairotic element here; at another period of her life she might be able to act differently, but she cannot now, given where she is.

When it comes to general ranking, Priscilla may agree that the cause in a sense comes first—that is, that one ought to be ready to sacrifice a great deal, including fighting down one's own squeamishness at various crucial moments. But the path of becoming a being capable of reverence is something one should never abandon. It is not an insight about ranking that yields this decision, but one about the complementary relations of goods in a life.

A similar point can be made about Mary's action. Pouring the ointment was an act of devotion, but so is giving to the poor if it is done out of agape. We have enough examples in our day of this help to those in need being torn not just from the context of agape but from any equivalent context. I mean by this one that would also, from whatever grounds, theist or atheist, nourish a sense of the dignity and human worth of the recipients. Modern history sometimes dramatically, and often in more humdrum ways in the life of the modern welfare state, has shown what destruction can be wrought in human lives when this kind of context is lost. Among modern writers, both Nietzsche and Dostoevsky have contributed immeasurably to our understanding here.[8]

But all this has no direct bearing on Mary's perhaps impulsive action. We can suppose that she had a powerful need to express her love and devotion, and knew that there are moments when this cannot be repressed. We might say there are moments where its repression helps rather to make us less capable of love. The kairotic context of this action is all too obvious. She senses that the rabbi will soon die.

V

I have been discussing a context of the ethical life where people have been tempted to talk of incommensurability, where people make decisions between rather different goods. The goods are different enough so that it seems difficult to find a common measure, not only in the clear and obvious sense of a metric but even some rough ordinal scale. And yet we seem to manage to make nonarbitrary (albeit contested) decisions in these cases.

The view that I have been advancing is that we have potentially rich resources at our disposal to help us in such decisions—ones that have tended to be ignored by modern moral philosophy. These include not only the articulation of goods and a sense of their relative importance, but also our sense of the shape of our lives, and how different goods fit together within it—their different places and times.

If we neglect this, then outside of the ordered and well-surveyed terrain of modern philosophies of moral obligation, which solve the problem of plurality by denying it; once, in other words, we recognize that these fortresses of top priority, all-trumping morality cannot be defended, what overwhelms us is the diversity of goods, seemingly unarbitrable.

I am not saying that all conflicts are arbitrable. Far from it. But our resources for arbitration are greater than they are normally supposed to be in moral philosophy, and they lie partly in our sense of our lives as a whole, the lives we are leading. I have touched only a small part of the picture here. There are a great number of different ways that goods relate to each other, beyond the particular complementarities of doing and being that I explored through the examples I introduced. In particular, there are a great many ways in which supposed "highest" or "supreme" goods relate to others in a life, beyond simply that of displacing them to a lesser rank and priority.[9] I have just opened one little segment of a vast terrain, but it is enough to show how the intuition of diversity of goods needs to be balanced with the unity of life, at least as an inescapable aspiration. We return, as so often, to an Aristotelian theme. Some people have objected that Aristotle seems to fall into a confusion—or perhaps pulls a fast one on us—in the discussion of the supreme good in *Ethics* I.vii. He talks first as though there might be one, but there might also be several such ends.[10] Later he seems to slip into assuming that there is just one final aim.

I am suggesting that some move of this kind has to be made. There are in fact two separable stages of reflection, which Aristotle perhaps does not separate here: We can determine what we think the goods are that we seek "for their own sakes" and also their relative ranking, if any. But even if we see a plurality of final ends of equal rank, we still have to *live* them; that is, we have to design a life in which they can be somehow integrated, in some proportions, since any life is finite and cannot admit of unlimited pursuit of any good. This sense of a life—or design or plan, if we want to emphasize our powers of leading here—is necessarily one. If this is our final end, there can only be one.

Real ethical life is inescapably led between the one and the many. We cannot do away either with the diversity of goods (or at least so I would argue against modern moral theory) or with the aspiration to oneness implicit in our leading our lives. I would argue that Aristotle knew this, and it is another one of those basic insights of his that we moderns have spent too much time forgetting.[11]

❧10❧

Comparing the Incomparable:
Trade-offs and Sacrifices

STEVEN LUKES

In this paper I ask a number of questions about the incommensurability of values in the hope that they may take us some way beyond the impasse that the discussion of this issue seems to have reached. That impasse, as I see it, consists in a confrontation between those who resolutely deny that values can be incommensurable, who hold that whenever we look for incommensurability we will find incommensurability, and who hold that to deny this is cant[1] and even morally dangerous[2] and those who believe that incommensurability between values and kinds of value is ever present in our lives, in both trivial and serious ways, and that failure to recognize this betrays an impoverished theory of the way in which value judgments inform deliberation. The former insist that we not only can but constantly do engage in a practice that the latter maintain is often meaningless, pointless, or inappropriate. In defense of their views, those on each side of this dispute say much that is plausible and appeal to intuitions that are compelling, which suggests, first, that what we have here is a live philosophical issue and, second, that there are still complexities to explore and further questions to be asked.

Following Griffin, I shall maintain that incommensurability is neither nonadditivity on some cardinal scale nor incompatibility, nonsubstitutability, irreplaceability, or uncompensatability[3]. Following Raz, I shall say that two alternatives are incommensurable if they are incomparable: that is, if neither is better than nor equal to the other[4] (I leave aside the issue of quantitative measurability and the question of whether there can be scales or metrics that can range across types of goods). Following Chang, I shall say that comparison is best thought of as holding between 'particular bearers of value' —'between *goods, acts, events, objects,* and *states of affairs* that instantiate or bear value (or disvalue), not between abstract values themselves. Thus we want to know whether, with respect to the goodness of places to live, an economically poor community with breathtaking landscapes is better than a moderately prosperous community blanketed with unsightly features and smokestacks—not whether, with respect to the value, goodness of places to live, the value of beauty is better than the value of prosperity'.[5] (We may want to know that too, but knowing the first does not amount to knowing the second. Too often in the discussion of these issues, it is taken for granted that to choose between valued alternatives is *eo ipso* to decide on the relative standing of the values they instantiate.) I also agree with Chang that any such evaluative comparison must always be in terms of some 'covering value': something can be better than, or equal to, another only in some respect, in virtue of some value, explicit or implicit.

The first question is: What does incommensurability, or incomparability, thus understood, amount to? When it is claimed that valued alternatives are incommensurable, *what* is being claimed? Three possibilities suggest themselves. One is that it is *meaningless* to assert that relations of betterness or equality hold between them. A second is that it is *pointless* to do so. A third is that it is *inappropriate* to do so.

The first possibility, that such relations are meaningless, need not detain us long. Incommensurabilists do not focus on unintelligible comparisons, but on what they claim to be mistaken ones. Moreover, incommensurabilists typically deny (and therefore understand) the comparisons that commensurabilists endorse. Nor, second, does the apparent pointlessness of a comparison (such as cross-modal aesthetic evaluations, comparing, say, an Achebe novel with a Henry Moore sculpture) seem to be the crucial issue. The fact that such comparisons may be philistine, snobbish, priggish, and even 'foolish, boring and stultifying'[6] does not show that what they compare is incomparable, or even that they have negligible practical import:[7] They may be important to practices that are, in turn, pointless. Such comparisons may, however, be inappropriate, revealing those who make them to have a poor, distorted, or corrupted understanding of the value of what it is they are seeking to compare.

This is how I shall understand the claim of incommensurability: It is the claim that someone who makes certain comparisons with respect to the worth of valued alternatives thereby exhibits, at the very least, misunderstanding—misunderstanding that may in turn merit condemnation, as we shall see. The fact is that we do sometimes refuse to commensurate or compare alternatives, both of which we value, and I believe Raz is right to say that such a refusal can display our understanding of what is involved in certain relationships and commitments.[8]

Why do we so refuse? What is wrong with comparing the value of a friendship with the offer of a sum of money, or with the pleasures of new acquaintances, or with asking how much trouble or discomfort a loving relationship is worth maintaining for? Why is it shocking if a person facing the death of a close relative determines how much to spend on medical resources to keep that relative alive? Or if a fishing community should deliberate how much time and resources to devote to fishermen lost at sea?[9] Why was there such outrage when the Ford Motor Company failed to withdraw the Pinto car after discovering a design fault that caused deaths and injuries on the basis that the estimated costs of the latter were less than those of modifying the car?[10] Why would we be appalled at sending convicts to work in extremely hazardous industries or denying the aged hemodialysis?

In all of these cases, what shocks us is the overt and evident failure to respect valued relationships and ways of behaving that have, or are supposed to have, a special place in our lives. Such failure is expressed by the very willingness to make honoring them a matter of comparative evaluation—by the disposition to treat them in the same way as other valued practices to which such comparison is appropriate. We rightly think that friendship, love, maintaining safety, protecting the vulnerable, and treating people as equals are valuable in special ways—that they have a special status, not just greater weight.[11] We mark that special status by holding them apart from more mundane goods. Incommensurabilists are inclined, therefore, to say that they are 'incommensurably higher' and speak of 'hierarchical incommensurability'. Commensurabilists, by contrast, insist that such locutions are just ways of lending emphasis to comparative judgments in which certain valued alternatives are accorded infinite or very great weight. Such cases, they may say, are cases of lexical superiority between values or types of values, or, more subtly, they may say that they exemplify emphatic comparisons that obtain between specific bearers of value that form a network of judgments (relating, say, different friendships to different sums of money).[12] They reject the idea that some commitments and relationships may have the kind of value for us that typically requires us to shun the making of certain comparative evaluative judgments.

There are three common grounds for resisting that idea (there are doubtless others). One is the pervasiveness of choice. We do, after all, have to face the choices indicated: of saving the friendship or accepting the offer, of paying the increasing medical costs or not, of sending search boats out for the lost fishermen day after day. Ford had to decide whether the design fault justified withdrawing the car. Choices must be made that assign risks and allocate medical resources. Doing nothing is, of course, always just one such choice. But choosing between alternatives is not the same as a judgment about their comparative worth. The mere fact of taking, or having to take, a decision between options does not show that that decision is based on a judgment as to the relative worth of the options, even if the decision is part of a systematic pattern of such decisions and is not arbitrary.

The second ground is the theory that value just is wholly constituted by revealed preferences and that therefore choosing between alternatives is all there is to affirming the superior value of one. Despite the centrality of this theory to social decision theory, it is a poor theory, of which several effective critiques exist, and I shall not discuss it further here.

The third ground is a view of reasons and reasoning, according to which if a choice between alternatives has been made rationally, it must involve a comparative evaluative judgment of the kind that incommensurabilists resist. Such a view has been called 'scalar'.[13] On that view, values are magnitudes and are subject to various mathematical operations, notably addition and subtraction: Objects have value to different degrees, and disvalue can be minimized and value maximized.

I shall not discuss this theory directly here but will, rather, comment on the pervasive metaphors that derive from it, by means of which evaluative choice between alternatives is typically described, in both academic and colloquial parlance. We speak of *weighing* goods, of *balancing* considerations, and, very often, of *trade-offs* that must be made when values clash: that is, when a choice must be made between valued alternatives that instantiate different and incompatible values. Indeed all thought about these questions that is based on or influenced by economic thinking typically takes the (never analyzed) idea of a trade-off for granted as an adequate characterization of what such evaluative choice between valued alternatives consists in.

Yet these metaphors are neither straightforward nor innocent. Consider, by contrast, the metaphor of *sacrifice*. We often speak of 'sacrificing' one good for another and normally see no difference in meaning or connotation between this and the aforementioned metaphors. Yet, as I shall argue, it not only has a different provenance; it suggests, or can suggest, an alternative way of thinking about the phenomenology of choice.

Compare, in particular, the notions of 'trade-off' and 'sacrifice'. The one is an economic, more specifically a commercial, metaphor; the other is a religious metaphor. Trade-off suggests *exchange* of valued objects at an equivalent price (either in terms of money or of one another): The last gun is worth (equivalent to) the last pound of butter forgone to obtain it. Sacrifice, by contrast, suggests the *forsaking* of a valued object because this is required by a sacred source of authority. Jehovah commands the sacrifice of Isaac; the monastic life demands celibacy. Trade-off suggests comparison, calculation, and estimation, bringing points of view together. How much do I value guns (or the last gun)? How much do I value butter (or the last pound of butter)? Sacrifice suggests total and one-sided commitment to one point of view, with its associated background of belief and faith. What painful loss does my God or my vocation require of me? Trade-off suggests that we compute the value of the alternative goods on whatever scale is at hand, whether cardinal or ordinal, precise or rough and ready.[14] Sacrifice suggests precisely that we abstain from doing so: Devotion to the one exacts an uncalculated loss of the other.

All of this suggests that the values that the attitude of incommensurability protects are sacred values. 'Sacred things,' wrote Durkheim, 'are those which . . . interdictions protect and isolate; profane things those to which these interdictions are applied and which must remain at a distance from the first.[15] To be sacred is to be valued incommensurably. This is not, however, to suggest that such evaluation must be an unconditional, unquestioning, unreasoning commitment, though of course it may be. As Kierkegaard observed, Abraham's attitude to the authority of Jehovah was religious in this sense. But goods can also be valued as sacred in a fully reflective and self-reflective manner. In short, though religious in origin, sacredness can take a religious or a secular form.[16] It may apply to interpersonal or public and civic commitments, and it spans the spectrum of worldviews and ideologies. It is not only believers, particularists, conservatives, romantics, and traditionalists who treat their favored values as sacred; liberals do so too. Thus Kant's notion of respect and his distinction between dignity and price are meant to protect the sacredness of persons conceived of as ends in themselves from a variety of mere uses. Emile Durkheim applied this notion during the Dreyfus Affair in a striking polemic against the anti-Dreyfusards, in which he argued that Dreyfus's right to a fair trial was simply not to be considered in relation to or weighed in the balance against what they took to be the demands of social peace and the maintenance of the established order, since Dreyfus's rights were sacred and central to the 'religion of individualism'—which was the only basis for social cohesion in a modern industrial society.[17] John Stuart Mill's 'higher pleasures' were not merely more valuable, even lexically prior; they were constitutive of the very individuality that a progressive liberal order was to protect and encourage and that a culture that favored 'lower' pleasures would threaten. Contemporary liberals are also, I suggest, using the notion of sacredness when they seek ways of characterizing how rights and the inviolability of persons are to be seen as typically set apart from all-things-considered judgments, as constraining or 'trumping' consequentialist, and in particular utilitarian, considerations.

We treat values as sacred when we devote ourselves to maintaining or furthering the goods that instantiate them without calculating the loss involved, by omitting or refusing to commensurate the benefits against the costs. We also do so through the attitudes of discomfort, embarrassment, shock, outrage, or horror that we display when such calculation or commensuration is engaged in by others. Yet it would be quite mistaken to suppose that such behavior and attitudes must be irrational and unreflective. On the contrary, careful, discriminating thought is needed to determine what values are at stake in any given situation of choice, especially if one or more of the values is sacred. Both Chang and Anderson demonstrate this in their discussions of the exemplary case of ending a friendship for money. In the case introduced by Chang, in which I can save my dying mother only by ending a friendship with Eve, two sacred values are in conflict, and I fully agree with Anderson that the issue cannot properly be understood in terms of a comparison between them in order to determine which is more valuable. What is needed, rather, is closely discriminating attention to what filial attention and friendship demand in *this* situation.[18] (My only quarrel with Anderson is her apparent assumption that there must, more often than not, be an obligation that delivers a nontragic solution in such a case.)

Sacred values must have a limited scope; indeed sacred values make sense only against a background that is nonsacred or mundane. In a secular world, sacredness can play only a relatively minor part in most people's lives. Moreover, in a secular world in which values are both plural and conflicting, we cannot devote ourselves without limit to the values we deem central or preeminent and must indeed calculate, or rely on others to calculate, where those limits lie.

The demands of friendship are not limitless. Indeed, we might say, only those able to realize this are capable of being friends. At a certain point, set by cultural norms, uncalculated devotion to a friend becomes pathological or unjust, a case of servile dependence or exploitation. At a certain point, those looking after a sick relative may have to consider the consequences of their declining resources on, say, the education or health of their children. After several days (how many?) of fruitless search, the fishing community will have to decide whether it can afford the cost of bringing in helicopters, as the chances of survival of those lost lessen. We assume and expect car companies to make cars as safe as possible within limits that are both legally permitted and financially costed. What was shocking about the Pinto case was in part that the price put on human lives and injuries seemed so low and in part that that price was made public. We will spend vast sums of public money to save particular victims of a single mining disaster or on a well-publicized case of a child needing heart surgery, but expend only limited sums on risk control and the allocation of medical resources, which we expect to be carefully calculated and costed.

In short, our commitment to sacred values is norm governed. Cultural norms (which may indeed be legally codified) provide answers to a series of highly interesting questions—answers that are by no means always uncontested. *Which* values are held as sacred, and *by whom,* and against comparison with *which others* are they protected? *When* and *where* do people omit or refuse to make such comparisons? *Whom* do we expect *not* to refuse to do so and *in what circumstances?* *How* are such comparisons of the otherwise incomparable to be made?

Values that we treat incommensurably as sacred may be *partial* or *impartial.* Values are partial when the goods that instantiate them are exclusive to particular relationships, practices, or ways of life. What makes them valuable is their contribution to the survival or flourishing of these. In treating a partial value as sacred, we are giving incommensurable value to *this* vocation or friendship or marriage or family or community, whether local, regional, or national. We may, moreover, treat partial values as sacred *concretely* or *abstractly.* We do so concretely when what we value are the actual memories, experiences, and aspirations inherent in a given relationship, practice, or way of life. We do so abstractly when what we value is the *idea* of such goods.

Our devotion to sacred partial values is normally contained within strict limits. Those who do not respect such limits we tend to see as fanatics or extremists. But contrary to the prophecies of some, the role of such values in social and political life does not seem to be on the decline. In particular, the contemporary politics of identity, focusing on 'authenticity' and 'recognition', seeks to give them renewed and added emphasis, whether this be in terms of religion, gender, ethnicity, or nationality. Such politics may treat such values more concretely or more abstractly, or ideologically. One way of drawing the distinction between patriotism and nationalism, for instance, is to view the former as valuing concretely what the latter values abstractly.

Partial values may be limited in two ways. On the one hand, they may be subjected to commensuration and in this way desacralized: put in the balance, weighed, traded off against other valued goods, as when immigrants assimilate, valuing (and thereby transforming) the loyalties they bring with them in comparison with the requirements of success and acceptance in the host society. Alternatively, partial values may be limited by impartial values, commitment to which requires the acceptance of principles that favor no particular relationship, practice, or way of life but are rather meant to apply to persons whatever their partial or particular loyalties or commitments. With respect to impartial values, the distinction between concrete and abstract does not make sense—or perhaps we should say that such values are by their very nature abstract, since to be committed to them is to be committed to a set of abstract principles, though these are embodied in concrete, living institutions.

Some have argued that there can be no impartial values—that the very idea of such values is a myth.[19] Thus it has become fashionable to criticize liberalism, or particular defenses of it, as promising an unachievable (and perhaps in any case undesirable) universality, objectivity, or neutrality. Liberalism, it is said, is just another partial tradition with its own history, and its claims to *adjudicate* between, or offer principles that do justice to, alternative and rival forms of life and conceptions of the good are and must be spurious.[20]

The truth in this criticism is, I believe, that impartial values must always take on culturally distinctive forms and that, when treated as sacred—when the goods that instantiate them are valued incommensurably—this is always within variable but well-defined limits that indicate when, by whom, and how they may be overridden. In the remainder of this paper, I shall seek to show (with particular reference to the works of Calabresi and Bobbitt) that impartial values, culturally defined, are treated as sacred in contemporary societies but that norm-governed limits are placed on the pursuit of these sacred values. I shall show this in respect of two impartial values taken to be incommensurable with others in modern liberal societies: the value of human life and the value of equality.

Human life is often said to be priceless, but only in certain contexts. Treating it as sacred—proclaiming the ideal of saving life at any cost—is appropriate in certain situations but denied in others. Symbolically asserted or implicit in official documents, such as charters of human rights and civil constitutions, and in speeches by statesmen and clergymen, this ideal is also suggested by the manner in which certain public policies are presented. Thus, in situations in which choices must be made that involve the saving of some lives and not others (for example, deciding how many iron lungs are to be built) these may be presented, or framed, as 'life validating': that is, as only *saving* lives, since the lives of all those in a certain defined category will be seen as being saved. This mode of framing decisions gives the impression of 'sufficiency'—that enough is available for all, that everyone in a definable category is being saved, thereby suggesting that the choice of *whom* to save has been avoided, and deflecting attention from the fact that other opportunities of saving lives (of those in other categories) have been forgone. As Calabresi and Bobbitt have observed, such a way of framing choice reaffirms the pricelessness of human life: 'Since many other values depend on valuing life as an incommensurable and since these values are constantly being eroded by decisions which, in fact, place a low value on human life, substantial benefits accrue from any demonstration by society of its devotion to life's pricelessness'.[21] In fact, as this quotation suggests, in many contexts the value of life is 'constantly' being compared or traded off against others—often, as by the Occupational Safety and Health Administration in the United

States, explicitly and officially, albeit not openly. It is done, as Griffin graphically puts it, by the French government when it maintains tree-lined boulevards at the cost of a determinable number of road accidents[22] and when governments in general decide when 'to stop putting resources into lifesaving medical procedures in order to support education or the arts' and when 'to divert funds from saving lives into relieving pain'.[23] It is done on a regular, routine basis by policymakers and administrators in the fields of health, industrial safety, transport, and urban planning, by private companies in the costing of safety features and by insurance companies.

Human lives are, as commensurabilists insist, constantly costed, albeit in ways about which most of us prefer to know little. This is most rationally done when based on extrapolations from the risks we actually take and the judgments we actually make.[24] We rely on others to take on the burden of assessing how many lives the various goals we value are worth, even though that burden is normally lessened by treating such lives as statistical rather than actual.[25] We elect politicians and pay administrators to do the dirty work of trading off our health, our safety, and sometimes our lives for economic growth, profitability, administrative efficiency, and tree-lined boulevards.

Equality is also treated as a sacred value in contemporary societies, which, however, give it differing political and cultural interpretations. To treat people equally is not to discriminate between them, but what counts as discrimination is open to different understandings. Egalitarianism can, for instance, focus on merit, need, or the provision of a basic minimum, prohibiting discrimination that violates the associated rights: the right to fair and equal opportunity, the rights to health, education, and welfare benefits, the right to a minimum income or standard or quality of living. Market liberals treat as sacred the equal right of individuals to reap whatever rewards accrue from whatever they own: their property, including whatever skills or talents they have acquired or may be lucky enough to possess. The politics of identity treats as sacred the equal right of individuals qua members of particular groups or categories to special treatment that expresses recognition of what is claimed to be distinctive of these.

In their book, *Tragic Choices,* Calabresi and Bobbitt suggest that, as well as these political differences of interpretation of equality, there are also significant cultural differences that mark how different societies interpret the value of equality and different ways of making choices that nevertheless violate it. Italy, they suggest, inherits from the French Revolution, which totally reshaped its legal structures, an 'absolute or simple' egalitarianism, expressed in the Constitution and in legal rules, proclaiming 'equality of status and treatment' for all citizens. Hence, for example, universal military training is the rule, and there is a universal right to public education. But such rules are 'viewed as expressing ideal goals and not programmatic guidelines. Italians commonly joke that many laws, at least those that are *regolamenti* (administrative regulations) are meant to be broken'[26], since, given their general nonobservance, it would be absurd to follow them. Yet this 'allegiance to a sentimental egalitarianism' leads to a 'substantial distrust of money markets' and also of discretion on the part of judges and independent decision-making bodies that are seen as 'unprincipled' and 'obviously corruptible'[27]. The result is a 'complex system of subterfuges by which the results of simple egalitarianism are avoided'.[28]

By contrast, the authors characterize the United States as subscribing to what they call 'qualified egalitarianism which strives for efficiency but corrects the efficient result to mitigate socioeconomic disadvantages'.[29] More specifically, in respect of the allocation of scarce medical resources, they argue, the United States 'generally permitted allocations based on therapeutic and other efficiency considerations so long as the results did not coincide with well-recognised patterns of race or class discrimination.'[30] The principle, in short, seems to be that 'persons ought to be treated as equals if they are similar according to generalised efficiency criteria, but also if not treating them as equals displays a disfavoured group in some prominent way'.[31]

England, the authors argue, seems to represent a 'third alternative': 'formal egalitarianism designed to achieve a result which can be termed efficient'.[32] In England, they suggest, poor risks are excluded on the basis of exterior, observable therapy-related criteria. The criteria are applied unswervingly, and damn the implications for general equality. Thus hemodialysis is allocated so as to achieve the highest rate of success, given a limited number of kidneys available.[33] What is operative is a kind of 'mechanistic efficiency', which 'reduces itself to getting the most life-years out of the limited number of machines. Everyone's desire to survive and live in treatment is assumed to be equal. So is society's desire to have each one live'.[34]

Calabresi and Bobbitt suggest that 'each of the societies has a peculiar affinity' for the conceptions indicated.[35] Moreover, each society exhibits a distinctive way of making decisions that compromises its sacred principle in making the tragic choices of allocating kidney machines (or did until their cost fell sufficiently to make their scarcity less significant). In Italy, in typical Italian fashion, the actual allocation was produced by a 'complex system of modifications of . . . guidelines' favoring status and money, administered by bureaucrats and officials. Italy thus 'sought to avoid a tragic conflict by simply not applying, without ceasing to proclaim, principles of absolute equality'.[36] In the United States, the authors trace a sequential development over time. First, kidney machines were allocated by doctors and hospitals to those in whom the kidneys were most likely to work or in whom there was a substantial experiment interest. As the circle of availability widened, it started to seem that 'some medical bets were surer than others because of previous or present wealth advantages'.[37] A first-come, first-served system was set up, but this in turn came to seem arbitrary and open to corruption. Then the so-called 'Seattle God Committee'—an independent body of 'selected representatives of various groups' assisted by medical experts—was set up to choose 'those who, considering the relative chance of success, were most deserving to live', but without applying explicit rules or giving public justification for their decisions. This mode of allocation was subject to 'an avalanche of criticisms', chief among them that the sanctity of life was being explicitly denied. Other approaches were discussed and tried, but, in the meantime, the price of kidneys declined significantly, so as to enable provision of 'hemodialysis for all who might benefit'—a formula that the authors describe as 'another subterfuge', since it distinguishes those dying from renal failure from 'those dying from other diseases, who for similar expenditures could also have been saved'.[38]

As for the English pattern, this was to assign to doctors and hospitals decisions that were supposedly purely clinical, based on 'a sort of mechanistic, Newtonian efficiency-determined egalitarianism'.[39] Insofar as this system was what was really operative, it could perhaps be seen as exhibiting a merely 'formal' or 'utilitarian' egalitarianism and a way of compromising either of two sacred conceptions of equality: that which regards each human life as equally priceless and that which, as in the United States, focuses on the rights of disfavored groups.

In a world in which plural values conflict, we attach a special importance to sacred values in both private and public life. We mark that importance by holding them apart from commensuration with others, both in what we privately and publicly say about them (and proclaim in official documents) and in how we behave in certain contexts and within certain limits. In a secular world, our commitment to sacred values is conditional. Sacred, or incommensurable, values thus play a central, if limited, role in our interpersonal and public lives. Would it not, after all, be better if they did not? Would we not be better advised to carry further what Max Weber called the disenchantment of the world and to follow Thomas Schelling's advice, coolly subjecting all our choices, including those involving such emotional matters as friendship, the saving of lives, and nondiscrimination, to cost-benefit analysis, as we do when we make decisions about insurance?[40] Would it not be altogether better if we reduced the temperature and realized that all of life, including its hard and tragic choices, consists in trade-offs rather than in sacrifices?

The truth in the incommensurabilist position is that such a proposal expresses a misunderstanding of the partial and impartial values we treat as sacred and of how we relate to the persons and the goods that embody them. We do not treat them as strategic ends for which we select the most efficient means and which we seek to secure at the lowest cost. If we were to do so, we would express a debased, impoverished, or corrupted understanding of what makes them valuable. Yet the commensurabilist is also right. Friendship makes its demands within calculable limits, and as Schelling rightly insists, public policy requires ever more complex cost-benefit calculation, without which resources, such as medical resources, will be maldistributed and policy choices will be made irrationally.

The incommensurabilist's position, taken to the limit, as by so-called fundamentalists, proposes the sacralization or resacralization of interpersonal and public life.[41] The commensurabilist's position, taken to the limit, proposes its technicization, the colonization of the life world, and the public sphere by instrumental reason. The point, perhaps, is not to ask which side has the better of the argument that continues to divide them, but rather to fear and resist the advent of a world in which either has won it.

❧11❧

Abstract and Concrete Value: Plurality, Conflict, and Maximization

MICHAEL STOCKER

In this paper, I discuss incommensurability, conflict, and maximization by examining their entanglements with a currently popular view of ethics: the *abstract action-guiding view of ethics.* I will show how this view conspires with and also against these issues to generate a misunderstanding of ethics in general and of these three issues in particular.

1. Abstract, Action-Guiding Ethics

In section 2 of *Principia Ethica,* G. E. Moore writes that "conduct is undoubtedly by far the commonest and most generally interesting object of ethical judgments." In section 89 he writes that "the assertion 'I am morally bound to perform this action' is identical with the assertion that 'This action will produce the greatest possible amount of good in the Universe'."[1] Many contemporary philosophers agree with his first claim, holding that ethics, or at least its most interesting part, is concerned near enough only with conduct: that ethics, or at least its most interesting part, is action guiding. Many also agree with Moore's second and maximizing claim, even if they do not put it in terms of meaning.

Some also see maximization as required by rationality. Donald Davidson and many others characterize the irrationality of weakness of will in terms of knowingly doing a lesser act.[2] They claim that such action is surd: It defies reason, precludes interpretation, and can only be explained. And many others think it near enough impossible to understand, even in this way, how one might fail to do what one thinks best. Further, as noted by R. Jay Wallace, many contemporary philosophers see maximization as one of the unproblematic forms of modern-day, non-Kantian, and broadly Humean practical reasoning.[3]

I call these maximizing claims *abstract* because they are made without any attention to the concrete nature of The Good, or the various goods. We are told that whatever goodness is like, (what has) more of it is more obligatory than (what has) less of it. All we need to know about an act to know that it should not be done—for either moral or rational reasons—is that doing it would prevent us from doing a better act. For example, to know whether it is right or wrong to do a given act, we do not need to know—nor will it really help us to know—which of such contrary values as pleasure or pain, life or death, caresses or torture, trust or betrayal, wisdom or ignorance it involves. All we need know—because it is all that is relevant—is whether there is a better incompossible act. We are thus told to be concerned with value, not values. And value is—or might as well be—treated monistically; the only relevant differences among values or instances of value are differences of amount, not kind.

I think this is mistaken and that concrete values—plural values in their concreteness—play a substantial role in ethics. But if the important question about conduct is whether an act is best, these values, considered as plural—their specific and peculiar qualities as values—are not important. What is important is simply whether an act is best in an indifferent and general way. For we are not concerned with concrete values, but with the amount of some indifferent and general value.

2. Conflicts

Let us now turn to conflicts, starting with conflicts of duties. (For simplicity, I write as if the conflict is between only two, rather than more, incompossible duties, acts, or whatever else.) For example, in E. M. Forster's case, one has to betray a friend, thus violating a duty of friendship, or alternatively betray one's country, thus violating a duty of citizenship.

How will an abstract, maximizing account of ethics allow for such conflicts? On that view, ethics is concerned with conduct and is concerned with what act is best to do. If there is a third act better than each of the conflicting acts, neither should be done, and thus there is no conflict. And if one of the two acts is better than the other, how can the other be one's duty and be part of a conflict?

Some suggest that there are conflicts where the incompossible acts are equal best—that is, where no other act is better than either of the incompossible acts and each of them is as good as the other—for example, swerve one's car and run over one infant, or not swerve it, thereby running over another. I think conflicts involving top-ranked acts are rare. But no matter. For the abstract maximizing view to show how such cases involve a conflict, it must show why it is not completely all right to do just any top-ranked incompossible act. After all, in some cases this is perfectly all right. Suppose that the two top-ranked acts are taking this portion of vanilla ice cream or alternatively taking that equal portion of the very same vanilla ice cream.

The abstract maximizing view must show how the two pairs of top-ranked incompossible acts—swerving or not, taking this or that portion of ice cream—differ so that only the former presents a moral conflict. I think its explanation would be similar to mine: The swerving case is a conflict because of the horror, albeit equal horror, of each of the acts. But to speak of the horror of each act is to speak of each act, on its own. And this goes beyond a comparison of how each act stands to incompossible acts.

I think conflicts between equal top-ranked incompossible acts are rare, and I want now to turn to what I think is a far more common and important sort of conflict. This is a conflict where it is clear which incompossible act to do, but not doing the other incompossible act is nonetheless somehow wrong—where it is clear that a given act should be done but, nonetheless, because of what it precludes, it is therefore somehow wrong.

This formulation answers to many clear cases of dirty hands and other conflicts—for example, betraying a friend for overriding political reasons, or one's country for overriding personal reasons; during World War II, bombing German cities, and thus killing innocent German civilians; leaving a marriage that has gone dead for you but not for your spouse; and Aristotle's case in the *Nicomachean Ethics* III.1 of someone's having to do something base to save his family from a tyrant.

In such cases, I suggest, it can be clear what one should do. I do not mean that it is clear just from these descriptions. The clarity comes from the particularities and details of the cases. Despite the clarity, however, doing the act that should be done can be conflicting. It can be clear in those circumstances that Aristotle's man should do that base act and save his family. But even having seen, after careful reflection and so on, that this is clearly what he must do, he can be terribly torn and conflicted. Even though he does what is and what he thinks right, he can see and feel that he also does something base and thus wrong.

As Bernard Williams recently put it, there is a remainder of wrongness, within and despite the rightness of the right act.[4] And some forty years earlier, this is what Ross suggested in *The Right and the Good* when he said that sometimes even where the stronger prima facie duty clearly overrides the weaker, forgoing the weaker should involve compunction.[5] Here, the weaker and overridden prima facie duty remains as a consideration—not for guiding action but for grounding the moral emotion of compunction.

How will abstract action-guiding ethics make sense of this? And given their understanding of ethics as action guiding, why should they? What action-guiding purpose can be served by being told that the right act has a part, a remainder, that is wrong—for example, that a justified act is also base or involves a betrayal? What point is there in being told this if to avoid doing that wrong part, one would have to avoid doing what is overall right? These theories' exclusive concern with guiding action is thus one important reason they have trouble with conflicts.

A second reason, already given, is that they are concerned with abstract and general value—with what is simply and generally better. To this extent, they can be seen as at least quasi-monistic theories of value. (And, of course, some of them are straightforwardly monistic.) They thus cannot even allow for, much less give an account of, conflicts that involve remainders and compunction. Plural values are needed for this.

To be sure, there are certain sorts of conflicts that do not require plural values. Monisms can allow for conflicts between top-ranked incompossible acts. Monisms can also allow for a sort of conflict even between acts that are ranked differently. Even on the assumption of a monistic hedonism, I can be conflicted over having to choose between two dishes of ice cream, even if they are equally attractive. After all, I might want the pleasure of both portions. Whether I dither, am paralyzed, or simply choose, I can clearly be conflicted by having to choose.

Other forms of irrational conflict, such as akrasia, also seem possible on the assumption of evaluative monism. This is a controversial point, disputed in important work by David Wiggins, Martha Nussbaum, and others. Since my general case against abstract maximizing theories would be even stronger if akrasia did require plural values, let me simply note that we all agree that akrasia requires plural objects of attraction. They think that these must involve plural values. But I think that plural objects of desire, which need not involve plural values, are sufficient.[6]

So far I have suggested that monism can allow for at least certain forms of nonrational conflict. I now want to suggest that the sorts of conflict we are concerned with—those involving remainders and compunction—require plural values.

The reason these conflicts involve plural values has to do with their internal structure. In such cases, whichever act we do, we forgo something of value, which would have been achieved had the other act been done. This forgone value helps to constitute the conflict and ground the regret peculiar to conflict. The absence of the forgone value is the remainder and the ground of compunction. In Aristotle's case, if the man rescues his family, he gives up his honor, and if he saves his honor, he gives up his family. And even if he clearly sees that he must save his family, and thus that he must give up his honor, he can regret the loss of his honor. The loss of honor is regrettable even if losing it is entirely justified, perhaps obligatory. So too, of course, losing one's family would be regrettable, even if justified or obligatory.

In these conflicts, there is a strong, evaluative reason to do each conflicting act rather than the other. This goes beyond saying that each incompossible act has value. After all, choosing each dish of ice cream has value. But this does not give one any reason to choose a lesser or an equal dish rather than the other. The point here is one about monism, not simply about trivial choices. If the very same value will be achieved by doing each of the incompossible acts, there seems no evaluative reason to do one act rather than the other, unless it is better than the other. This, it should be clear, allows both that there can be a reason to do either, rather than neither, and also that there can be a reason to do both, rather than either.

In our cases of conflict, there is a reason to choose and do each conflicting act rather than the other. Even if one of the acts clearly should be done, doing the other act would achieve something of value not achieved by the act that should be done.

This last is not what makes a conflict a conflict. For in many cases, perhaps most cases, where we have to choose between plural values—for example, finish dinner or go to a lecture on Aristotle—there is a reason to do each incompossible act rather than the other. But not all such choices involve conflict.

Thus we see that we cannot accept the popular account of conflicts given in terms of the mere incompossibility of values or valuable acts. Mere incompossibility does not guarantee what is needed: that the forgone value ground compunction or other form of serious regret. But we need not go into what distinguishes those choices among plural goods that involve conflicts from those that do not. For what we were concerned to see is that conflicts of a certain sort involve plural values.

To make it clearer what is in question here, I want to pursue these issues. Even if it is agreed that many conflicts involve plural values, it might be thought that there can be conflicts without them. So we might be asked to consider a case where the agent has to choose between helping one person or another, or keeping one promise or another. Certainly, doing one of the acts rather than the other may be a source of compunction and conflict. But the worry is, why should we think that helping one person rather than another, or keeping one promise rather than the other, must involve plural values? Couldn't it, for example, involve exactly the same sort of benefit?

One way to put this is to hold that instead of there being plural values here, there are only plural modes or sorts of one value, benefit to a person.[7] This claim might be making either an ontological point relying on claims about values and their modes, or it might be making a somewhat related evaluative point. I will deal with these in turn.

I do not think our ontological theories give us *one* answer to, "What is it to be *one* value, and what is it to be a *mode* of a value?" Some theories will answer one way, others another, and others will find the questions too confused. This is so about these cases of promise keeping and benefiting different people, and about other cases too. To turn to another case, consider the pleasure of discussing philosophy and the pleasure of a good meal. Ontologically speaking, how many values and how many modes of values are there here? Some ontological theories will see them as different sorts or modes of one value: pleasure. Others will see them as different values. Still others will see each of them as incorporating plural evaluative considerations, where, say, the "one" pleasure of a good meal really contains evaluatively plural pleasures of anticipation, of satiety, of different parts of the meal, of different cuisines and dishes, and so on. (This last is to see them as *spurious monisms,* discussed in *Plural and Conflicting Values.*)[8] And still others—perhaps after cautioning us against the fallacy of "one name, one thing"—will tell us that, on their view, there is no fact of the matter here and perhaps that the questions are irremediably confused.

We must also recognize the fallacy of "different name, different thing" and the correlative possibility of spurious pluralisms. Not everything that is ontologically plural is also evaluatively plural. The pleasure of a good meal could be evaluatively the same as that of philosophy, even though one involves food, the other, inquiry.[9]

This lack of ontological fixity does not tell against my pluralism. Even if what is plural is only a mode or sort of "one" thing, that plurality remains. As such, it can pose all the problems of plurality that have worried philosophers— preeminently, worries about having to weigh and combine different evaluative considerations. For what philosophers find troublesome about pluralism is not the ontological nature of what is plural—whether they are values, or modes of values, or something else, such as the ways they must be taken into account—but the plurality of what must be taken into account. And this plurality is precisely what my pluralism is about. It is about the evaluative fact and problems of plurality, not the ontological nature of what is plural. My pluralism is just as much a pluralism if there are only plural evaluative modes as it is if there are plural values.

Let us now turn to claims of evaluative sameness. In the case of benefiting different people, we can see that qua benefit, there need be no difference between these acts. But as I see matters, for there to be a conflict here, it must make a moral difference whether this person rather than that one receives the benefit, and as I further see things, this moral difference cannot be accommodated by monism.[10]

We can see this, I think, by contrasting sketches of two theories. The first is clearly a monism. It holds that there is only one good—benefit, say. It also holds that in choices of distributing benefit in different ways, all that is evaluatively relevant for evaluating what the agent should do and should feel is the total amount of benefit. It denies any (other) relevance to who is benefited and what amount or proportion of the benefit each beneficiary receives. The second theory also holds that there is only one good—again, benefit. But it holds that even where the amount of benefit is the same, who receives the benefit can make an evaluative difference. Even where there is the same total benefit, there can be action-guiding considerations, perhaps of justice, in favor of making one distribution rather than another. For example, a fair distribution might be favored over other equally large total distributions. Or nonaction-guiding considerations might ground different feelings about different distributions, depending on the nature of the distributions or who the recipients are. For example, I might hold that I should make the greatest total distribution but nonetheless regret that it is not a fair one; or I might hold that I must make a fair distribution between a stranger and my child but nonetheless regret being unable to give all the available benefit to the child without regretting being unable to give all to the stranger.

As it seems to me, we can make sense of this latter theory only if we see it as pluralistic. This holds especially for making sense of the ways it differs from the first. (And we can readily imagine a "charge" of pluralism, leveled by adherents of the first.) To be sure, its pluralism is not found on its "value" side. It recognizes only one good: benefit. Its pluralism is found in the *function* it uses to move between value and how we should act or feel. This function is pluralistic in that it tells us to treat the same value in different, plural ways, depending on who the beneficiary is. (On my view, the distinction between value and function may be more notional or notational than real, as is the similar distinction between axioms and leading principles in systems of logic.)

It might still be claimed that this theory deserves the name 'monistic', because it involves only one good: benefit to someone or other. The proper response to this, I think, would not be just that this is simply a claim about technical terminology, about how to use 'monism'. For it also shows that theories can be monistic or pluralistic in different ways and at different locations within the theory: in regard to value, in regard to act evaluations (whether action guiding or not), and in regard to the function between the two. It also shows that the significant dispute over monism and pluralism cannot be limited to just the value or values of a theory. It must also include the monism or pluralism of and in its act evaluations and function. Thus, I would say that the second theory either takes each person's benefit to be a distinct good, or it counts benefit pluralistically, in terms of both quantity and whose it is. Either alternative is enough to make the theory pluralistic.

I want now to make several additional points about how plural values allow for conflicts. Some hold that plural values, or at least those grounding conflicts, are incomparable—indeed, that plural values allow for conflicts because of incomparability. Some think incomparability is a simple consequence of plurality, holding that if values are plural, they must be incommensurable; and if incommensurable, incomparable. I agree that if values are plural, they must be incommensurable, since I understand 'plural values' to mean pretty much the same as 'incommensurable values'. But incommensurables can be comparable. The side and diagonal of a square are incommensurable but comparable. Indeed, the diagonal is provably longer than the side.

Even if plurality does not entail incomparability, the plural, incommensurable values involved in conflict might still be thought incomparable. If so, this could be taken as suggesting that maximization does not preclude conflicts. The thought here would be that where there is incomparability, conflicts would not violate the strictures of maximization. For somewhat similar reasons, Joseph Raz holds that only on the assumption of incomparable values can there be conflicts with their attendant losses and choices.[11] I think we must reject that suggestion, for I think we must reject the claim that if the values are incomparable, there is no rational way to choose which to pursue, and thus that in pursuing one, another will be forgone—and this forgoing constitutes the conflict.

First, as already noted, the fact that one will forgo a given value that one could have achieved by doing an incompossible act is not peculiar to conflict. It is common to near enough all choice involving plural values. Such choices are, at least generally, choices of which value to pursue and which to forgo. So, I may have to choose between the gustatory pleasure of finishing dinner and the increased understanding gained by attending a lecture on Aristotle.

Second, some conflicts do not involve incomparable values but are conflicts between equal and top-ranked incompossible acts. However, if the values of the conflict are incomparable, what is to be made of the claim that they are of equal value?

Third, and more important, if the values involved in conflict are incomparable, it seems impossible to make sense of those conflicts I think are both common and important: cases where it is clear what to do but where, nonetheless, because of what that act involves, it is somehow wrong—for example, Ross's cases of compunction. In such cases, we can make comparisons strong enough to see that a given one of the acts is to be done and the other is not to be done. The agent may see that there is no moral choice but to do the base act, but may nonetheless find doing that act conflicting.

Fourth, trying to understand conflicts in terms of incomparability makes it difficult to understand conflicts of weakness of will. In these cases, agents are tempted by, and indeed do, what they see as the lesser rather than the better act. But if the values are incomparable, how are we to understand talk of the lesser and better?

Recourse to incomparable plural values thus seems not to help us understand conflicts. But recourse to plural values that are comparable does help us. If the values are comparable, then we may well be able to judge and, thus, choose sensibly which value to achieve—which act to do. And if the values are plural, that makes this possible in a way that also allows for remainders: by allowing for goods that at once are forgone in doing what one should do and also which, because *they* are forgone, ground compunction. Insofar as maximizing, abstract, action-guiding theories do not allow for plural values and remainders, they cannot allow for, much less explain, conflicts, nor therefore can they tell us everything of importance about ethics or even about conduct.

At this point, supporters of these theories might make a concession, two objections, and then a backhanded compliment. The concession is that I have shown that those theories have not told us everything of importance about what we ought to do—for example, about remainders and moral emotions. The first objection is that I have not shown that the theories are at all mistaken about which acts we ought to do. The second is that we could simply add what I have shown those theories do not tell us about what we ought to do to what they already do tell us about conduct. These objections lead naturally to the backhanded compliment: that my account of conflicts, unlike many other accounts, does not argue that if—or since—there are conflicts, ethics must be inconsistent or incomplete: inconsistent if, when there are conflicts, it tells us both to do and not do the same act, and incomplete if, when there are conflicts, it does not tell us what to do.

Putting the point in terms of remainders, our ethical theories have not talked about remainders, but remainders do not determine what we ought to do. They ground moral emotions, especially about what we forgo in doing what we ought to do. And our ethical theories could simply be enlarged to take note of this.

Put somewhat concessively, it could be said that enlarging our ethical theories this way would help repair the unfortunate recent division of ethics into one part that deals with conduct and another that deals with agents, including moral emotions and moral psychology; and it might even help restore the second part to the importance it was accorded in pre-twentieth-century ethics. This needs to be done, in any case, not just to accommodate conflicts, for we need to allow, *inter alia,* that motives, not just outcomes, of acts are evaluatively important— that, for example, an act's being done out of malice is itself morally important, independent of how that bears on the act's outcome.

Now I do think both that our ethical theories must be enlarged and that this restoration must take place. Otherwise the notion of conduct figuring in ethical theories is, instead of being "the commonest and most generally interesting object of ethical judgments," rather, a barren notion of action and conduct— barren precisely because it is devoid of moral-psychological elements. Put another way, one reason we need that enlargement and restoration is that agents, moral emotions, and moral psychology are among the most interesting objects of ethical judgments.

Although I do look forward to an enlarged ethics, giving importance to moral emotions and moral psychology, I do not look forward to such a theory made by the simple addition of those missing elements to our abstract, maximizing, action-guiding theories. I think that those theories are wrong even about conduct—and conduct understood in their own terms.

The best way to show this is by a frontal attack on their claim that they correctly tell us what we ought to do. So, let us now turn to maximization.

3. Maximization

I will here argue against maximization in ways that help show the plurality of values. A popular mode of criticizing maximization—or consequentialism, now its most prominent version—starts with a maximizing theory and then argues for various limitations and qualifications.[12] Some see this way of proceeding as killing by a thousand cuts, especially since there are many such limitations and qualifications. But contrary to what was intended, this criticism can also suggest that maximization holds except when those conditions hold. And this can suggest that maximization is right in general form, needing only the sorts of qualifications almost any theory needs to apply to all cases. It may also suggest that we need to apologize for or justify what is nonmaximizing. It thus can give life to the hope that there will be a new and improved maximizing theory allowing for those qualifications, but now on maximizing terms. Much the same holds for arguments that we should be *satisficers* rather than maximizers.

Antimaximizers need to present alternative ways of thinking about value and of engaging in practical reasoning. From the outset, these ways must be through and through different from maximization, not just qualifications or modifications to maximization. In what follows, I can indicate only some of these alternatives, restricting attention to those depending on the plurality of values. Many of my points are thus intended to show both how we can and should describe justifiable courses of action that are not maximizing in terms that do not invoke maximization—whether or not limited and qualified, whether or not satisficing—and also that these courses of action are justifiable and nonmaximizing.

To bring out the first sort of nonmaximizing evaluation, let us use the grammatical distinction between absolute and relative superlatives. 'The best' as understood by maximization is a *relative* superlative: To be best in this sense, there can be no better in the relevant comparison class. To be best *absolutely*, the item must be, of its kind, excellent—satisfying, or coming close to, ideals and standards. For examples of absolute superlatives, we can look to the notions of a most excellent person, the best of friends, the best work in philosophy, the best of times, or the best of lives. Someone can be a most excellent person even if there are better people; friends can be the best of friends even if they could be, or we could have, better friends; we could be having the best of philosophical discussions, even if this or other discussions could be better; I could be having the best of times, or even the best of lives, even if I could have a better one.

One way to put the contrast is that a given item can be best absolutely even if there are better instances. And even if a given item is best relatively, it need not be best absolutely; none of the available members of the comparison class may be good enough.

A second and related nonmaximizing form of evaluation appeals to, for example, a good life, or a good part of a good life, or a good project. As I will suggest, we can justify an act, both morally and rationally, by showing that it helps bring about or constitute a good life, or good part of a good life, or a good project. I will further suggest that such justification does not require that the life, part, or project be the best available to the agent. Nor does the justification require that the act in question be the best one for that life, part, or project. The act need only be good enough, and the life, part, or project need only be good enough.

These two nonmaximizing forms of evaluation can support each other. For one of the important ways to show that the project or life is good enough is by showing it is absolutely, even if not relatively, best. And one of the ways to show that something is absolutely best, especially in ways that do important work in evaluative and rational justifications, is by showing that it is a significant feature of a good life.

I will start my criticism of maximization by using these two sorts of non-maximizing considerations to show that maximization is not morally or rationally required and also to show the need for plural values. Toward the end of the discussion, I will mention two other, related nonmaximizing forms of evaluation that also show the need for plural values: narrative justification and justification by exemplars.

Let us start with several cases. In the first, I am content because I have achieved a good life. I am offered an opportunity to make my life even better by changing jobs. I think that it need not indicate any moral or rational failing to decline the offer. I can hold that although the change would make my life better, the improvement will not be worth the effort.[13] Second, I have gained considerable wisdom by reflecting on the painful ending of a love relation. Although I am certain that the value of the wisdom outweighs the disvalue of the pain, nonetheless, I would rather not have suffered that way, even though I am also certain that I would then not have acquired the wisdom.

It might be thought that these cases are just about amounts of value: The benefit to myself is not worth the cost, even though the value of the benefit more than outweighs the disvalue of the cost. I think this account is inadequate, even though it tells against maximization. What also seems important, in the first case, is that I have achieved a certain sort of life—a good life—and that having achieved such a life, it is now "up to me" whether I try to make my life even better. What justifies my doing what is nonmaximizing is how doing that fits into my life—a life that is good enough, and that is good enough because of what it is like, not because it is better than other lives open to me. Similarly for the second case—with focus on the nature and extent of the suffering.

Let us now turn to a case highlighting plurality: Suppose that my university career is one of the central large-scale goods and projects of my life. Suppose further that I have worked hard on this project, for both myself and my university department, and now that I have some free time, I see that learning classical Greek would be very good for me, but learning logic would be even better. My present suggestion is that if I am more interested in learning Greek, and if learning Greek would be good enough, then for these reasons, I can be justified in studying it rather than logic. Again, even to describe this case requires plural values.

Maximizers typically are unconvinced by these examples and reply in one or more of the three following ways. The first claims a moral defect in me, holding that if I choose one option because it is easier or interests me more, I thus show that I am weak willed, lazy, weak, or the like. The second and third claim that I am really maximizing. The second holds that I give enough value to the ease or interest to make the complex that includes it better than the other, or alternatively that what I want to maximize is the value of some desired activity or state, for example, doing what interests me. The third, making a point not about the act but a policy or rule, holds that it is maximizing to allow for nonmaximization in certain areas, and this is one of those areas.

I find these replies objectionable or unhelpful. It is clear why the charge of such defects as weakness of will, laziness, and the like is objectionable. But the claim that I give such a high value to my ease or interest is also objectionable—if it imputes to me the evaluative arrogance or stupidity of claiming that I think my ease or interest more valuable than alternatives I choose not to pursue. I can see that my ease or interest is less valuable than some alternative option, while also thinking that I am justified in pursuing it.

I find the second reply objectionable—if it holds that the precept "From among those lives (projects, acts, . . .) that interest you, choose the best one" is a maximizing precept. This is not a maximizing precept. Its very point is to allow us not to do what is best, unless it so happens that that is what interests us. At the extreme where one wants to do a particular project, act, and so forth, it tells us just what "do what you want" tells us to do. We might also note that it is a precept that strongly suggests plural values: the values one is interested in and the others.

As to the third reply, I grant the possibility. But I think it mere hopefulness— one might say, mere liberal hopefulness—to think that it holds for these cases. To modify a point just made, it may well be that we would prefer a policy allowing us to exercise our nonmaximizing preferences, but I see no reason to think that in general or here such a policy is itself maximizing.

Let us now turn to some issues about rationality. When reasoning or giving advice, maximizers seem to have a principled answer to the question of what is to be done, "Do the best." The best, they say, is a natural and final stopping point. In contrast, they claim, nonmaximizers are on a slippery slope or in yet other ways caught up in arbitrariness. They advise doing something with less than a maximal amount of goodness. But they can have no reason that that particular less-than-maximal amount is fixed on rather than a larger or smaller amount. Do nonmaximizers perhaps expect us to pursue only a certain proportion of the available good—two-thirds, say? And if so, why that particular proportion? It might thus seem that nonmaximizing acts cannot be interpreted as intentional, much less rational, for there is no reason for choosing the nonmaximizing over the maximizing act. This, of course, is to say that a nonmaximizing act cannot be the conclusion of practical reason.

Maximizers see the choice in question in terms of quantity of value, where the only relevant difference between acts is whether one is better than the other.[14] The assessments for such ranking, they remind us, have already given full weight to the difficulties, hardships, opportunity costs, discovery costs, and so forth of the acts—and thus these cannot be counted again.

To make sure that we are considering a choice just in terms of ordinal ranking, we might consider a philosopher's case: Simply by giving the nod to one act or a different one, we can have something that is good (perhaps in a certain way) or something else that is better (in that very same way). Maximizers expect us to agree that where the only difference between options is amount of value, one would have to be silly and perhaps irrational to forgo the better and choose the lesser. They also expect us to agree that since reasons for acting are given just by considerations of ordinal ranking—whether this act is better than that one— this argument can properly be generalized to show that it is always silly and perhaps irrational to choose the lesser over the better.

Another way to put the argument is that practical reason is concerned just with value. More specifically, the only difference between acts relevant to choice is which is better. All other differences between them are irrelevant. Further, it is a requirement of rationality that one choose the better rather than the lesser.

Indeed, many think that we can reject this claim about rational relevance only by severing the connection between reason and value in a way that would endorse arbitrariness or irrationalism. Although I disagree with them, I do think that the argument is persuasive. But I now want to suggest that this persuasiveness has to do with a specific and nongeneral feature of the argument: the elimination of all but quantitative evaluative differences. Remember that we were asked to consider two cases that differed only in that one is better than the other. This feature was required to ensure that the options differed only in regard to value and thus to ensure that the argument could be generalized to value and reason taken generally. But what it rather does is have us focus only on abstract value, not on value and reason, that is, not on values and reasons.

This abstractness is found in the fact that the argument looks only at value taken generally and indifferently, and not at the particular value or values concerned. It asks simply which option is better, and not what is good about the options and why one is better than the other. Similarly, it talks about reason and what reason singles out, and not about the content of the reasons. Quite naturally, then, the argument sees nonmaximizers as advocating—almost in so many words—doing what is less than the best or what is good enough, perhaps even what is second best, if not second rate.

But nonmaximizers can instead be understood as advocating concrete sorts of lives, projects, courses of action, friendships, and so on. These are advocated because of what they concretely are—that is, the sorts of lives, projects, and so on they are. For example, I do not choose to study Greek because of its abstract value. My reason is neither that it is less than maximally good nor that it achieves some proportion of available value. Rather, I choose it because of the concrete ways it is good: how it will fit into my life, what I will then be able to do, and so on.

To explain what I mean by this—and to help clarify what I mean by forms of evaluation that are through and through nonmaximizing—I want to show that it is a serious mistake to think that what is less than the best is, at best, second rate. Rather, what is second best may well be first rate. This, of course, is to say that reason is not, nor does it require, maximizing. I will take philosophy as an example, since it is an important example, at least for philosophers, and one that can easily be generalized.

Let me start by seeming to accept maximization. We quite naturally write, 'It could have been better,' on a student's paper to criticize it. Anything less than the best may seem second rate, a failure. I do not want to reject those claims. Rather, I want to show that maximization seriously misunderstands 'the best' as used here, as it similarly misunderstands the justification of philosophy.

To show that philosophy is worth doing—for example, by a particular person, discipline, or profession—do we need to show that doing it is, in a comparative and maximizing way, best? I hardly think so—not least because I have no idea of how anyone would go about even trying to show that. Will it be held that only a world that includes the doing of philosophy can be the very best world? This seems, at best, anthropocentric and philosophico-centric puffery.

Here we would do well to reflect on Aristotle's claim about our wish for the good or the best for ourselves: "For existence is good to the good man, and each man wishes himself what is good, while no one chooses to possess the whole world if he first has to become someone else (for that matter, even now God possesses the good); he wishes for this only on condition of being whatever he is" [*NE* IX.4, 1166a19–22].[15] This is to say that I want to live *my* life, and I want *that* life to be good or best. I do not want to live another life—become someone else or even God—whether or not that life would be better for the world. Similarly, I wish what is good or best for my friends. But even if it would be best for the world, I do not want my friends to become other people or Gods. Were that to happen, they would not be my friends, but would be other people or other beings.

Our desire for a good or best life for ourselves or our friends is thus nonmaximizing: It is not concerned with what is good or best for the world. Indeed, such a desire would be subject to a *reductio ad absurdum:* On a maximizing understanding of value, a commitment to the best will almost certainly not involve a commitment to be "whatever he is." This, of course, depends on the reasonable assumption that what is best for any given person is almost certainly not best for the world.

To be sure, not all maximizing theories are concerned with what is best for the world. Some are concerned with what is best for some lesser "group," such as the agent alone or the agent and those close to the agent. They are, in short, concerned with what is best from among a restricted range of options. Restricting concern that way is, almost certainly, not maximizing. It allows and may require choosing what is best from among what is not best. Put more emphatically, it allows and may require choosing what is *not* best. But it might well allow one to be "whatever one is."

Nonetheless, Aristotle's claim can be made to apply to many of these and other (somewhat) maximizing theories. For, insofar as 'good life' and 'best life' figure in this desire, they are not to be understood comparatively, as required by maximization. They are to be understood absolutely.

To see this, let us continue with how we evaluate philosophy. We justify the doing of philosophy by arguments that it is a fine and truly human activity. We justify it by describing good lives, good polities even, that make room for philosophy, where, further, these lives and polities owe some of their goodness to making room for philosophy. And we show a life to be a fine and truly human activity by detailing what it involves, what it is like, what activities and relations make it up, what interests the person has and develops, and so on. There is little, if any, appeal to what is relatively, abstractly, and maximizingly best and many appeals to what is absolutely and concretely best or concretely good.

To justify particular people's lives of doing philosophy—for example, to show that they are thus living a good life—we do not appeal to maximizing considerations. It is not required that they do the best philosophy possible—for example, the equal of Kant or Aristotle. Nor is it required that these people do the best philosophy they could. Indeed, that might well require a monastic dedication to philosophy, precluding a life that also makes room for family, political, artistic, athletic, and other interests. Nor, for their life of philosophy to be justified, is it required that their whole complex life of philosophy and other interests be the best one they could live. Nor, for that matter, would that be sufficient. Because of their particular limitations or circumstances, their best may not be good enough to do good philosophy.

Rather, what comes at least close to being sufficient is that they meet proper and reasonable standards of philosophy—for example, those we are pleased if our advanced students are beginning to meet, and those we expect ourselves and our colleagues to meet. Correlatively, for one's philosophical works to be justified—for one to be justified in producing them, as, for example, part of one's life work or as a more occasional activity—the work need not be the best the person could do.

After all, Aristotle surely could have made the *Nicomachean Ethics* better by precluding the worries about seeming to move from "every activity has a goal" to "all activities have a goal." On a maximizing understanding of 'it could have been better,' we see that the *Nicomachean Ethics* could have been better. But we also see something of greater importance, at least for our present concerns: that 'it could have been better' is not to be understood in terms of maximization, as indicating that what was done was not maximizingly best. Were 'it could have been better' understood that way, it would apply to every work, no matter how magnificent, by Aristotle, Kant, Bach—and indeed, by any person. Nonetheless, to state the obvious, not all human works are failures or defective, nor are their agents unjustified in doing them rather than something better.

Some may object that we have no reason to believe that, say, Aristotle could have avoided that worry and made the *Nicomachean Ethics* better, except at too great an expense, by turning away from other work that would benefit far more from his attention. And thus we have no reason to believe that he could have done better. This seems like mere hopefulness in support of a theory, maximization. But in any case, it can be used to show, yet again, that 'it could have been better' is not to be understood in terms of maximization. For we still criticize work by our students, colleagues, and ourselves, saying of it, "it could have been better," even where we know that the authors had more rewarding uses of their time than redoing the work to avoid problems.

My rejection of maximization thus does not involve accepting, much less hallowing, the second rate. Rather, it shows that maximization does not give a correct understanding of evaluative standards—for example, a concern for good or even the best philosophy. Making use of Aristotle's claim, it shows that many, if not most, maximizing theories are forced to give an account of best philosophy such that those who claim commitment to that are, of all things, really committed to giving up philosophy and doing something better.

Meeting standards of excellence is, of course, only one nonmaximizing way of justifying an activity, life, or whatever else. Narratives are another, even if related, way. Here justification involves making sense of an activity, a life, or something else, seeing and creating significance: for example, being able to comprehend and accept one's life with equanimity and perhaps pride.

Much work must be done to show how such narratives proceed and how they establish that one's activity, life, or something else is good. But from the outset, I think it clear that much of what is involved here has little, if anything, to do with comparative, abstract value, and much less maximization. A narrative is constructed out of plural values and their interrelations (which constitute still other values), and it can show one's life to be good, even absolutely best, without showing it to be comparatively best.

The last form of nonmaximizing justification I want to mention is justification by exemplar. I think it is clear beyond doubt that we do justify or criticize lives and courses of action, as well as emotions, forms of attachment, and so on by appeals to exemplars. To mention a few, we speak and evaluate in terms of the wisdom of Solomon, the loving concern of Saint Francis, the charitableness of Mother Teresa, the intellectual dedication of Kant or Wittgenstein, the depravity of de Sade, and so on. We also recur to ideal types, such as moral saints and heroes.

Lacking time to argue for two further points, I will simply assert them. First, these examples involve plural and concrete values. Second, the role and power of these exemplars is not to be understood in terms of maximization. This latter is relevant for the controversy between Susan Wolf and Robert Adams over moral saints.[16] Adams may well show Wolf mistaken in charging that moral saints cannot lead attractive and exemplary lives. However, his arguments tell not against her antimaximizing arguments, but only against understanding moral saints in maximizing terms—even if negatively, as 'nonmaximizing.'

I will conclude by examining an important objection.[17] It might be thought that in urging an appeal to standards or exemplars—for example, those set by and in the *Nicomachean Ethics*—I run the risk of urging something akin to economic protectionism or an antiquarian concern. The objection can be put in terms of several, related questions: What if there is an improvement in philosophy and if what becomes recognized as good philosophy is better than the *Nicomachean Ethics*? In general, shouldn't we be alive to every possibility to make what we do better, rather than remain fixed—stuck or mired—in the past? What would have happened, if we had remained entranced with Aristotelian science, and continued to judge science by those antique standards?

These are serious and difficult questions. But as I see matters, it is a mistake to think that standards do or should change to accommodate every chance for betterment. We already know how to get, and how Aristotle could have given us, a better *Nicomachean Ethics:* Eliminate the concern over the move from 'each activity' to 'every activity'. But that change is already countenanced by the standards we already use, which take the *Nicomachean Ethics* as a paradigm of good philosophy.

Further, there is a large distance between a concern to improve standards, paradigms, exemplars, and so forth and a concern with what maximizers understand as the best. And there remains the serious danger that a commitment to maximization will involve a commitment to stop doing those activities, which are, nonetheless, absolutely good or even excellent.

It might be thought that this danger can be averted by maximizing theories explicitly including those absolute goods. This moves relative bestness toward absolute bestness. I do not have time to argue that this would not be just something of a concession for maximizers, but—by including absolute goods—an abandonment of maximization.[18] I will simply note that it clearly involves plural, incommensurable values.

Further, I do not think that incorporating absolute goods will give an adequate theory. The new theory cannot tell us to pursue the best philosophy. For as seen, when understood maximizingly, this gives implausible directives and evaluations. The theory, in its determination of the best, might instead allow trade-offs among these different goods, telling us to pursue the best mix of these goods. But a commitment to this best can, and often will, involve a commitment to stop doing a particular good or even excellent activity. Modifying Aristotle's words, this commitment will often not allow us to pursue philosophy whatever it might be. And it may often require us to pursue an entirely different activity.

This, of course, requires that, even at their best, doing philosophy, lives of philosophy, and so forth are often not maximizingly best—not even in a new, extended sense. This may seem too pessimistic about the value of philosophy. If so, it should be noted that my antimaximizing argument is also sustained by a far more modest and unexceptionable claim: that doing philosophy, lives of philosophy, and so on are often justified, even though they are not maximizingly best.

If this claim does hold, then not even extended maximizations get things right. For that, we need plural, incommensurable values and absolute, nonmaximizing evaluations. Given my use of Aristotle, it is fitting to note that, as this also shows, we must understand *'eudaemonia'*, 'best life', and 'good life' in absolute, nonmaximizing ways—if they are to play the supreme justificatory roles he claims.

In conclusion, then, understanding value concretely shows how we can and why we should reject maximization. This complements and uses the earlier arguments that understanding value concretely helps us understand the nature and importance of moral and rational conflict, as well as the serious errors of abstract, action-guiding ethics.

❦12❦

Commensuration and Public Reason

JOHN FINNIS

A classic explanation of law calls it a measure: *quaedam regula et mensura actuum,* a kind of rule and measure of actions.[1] The law's own terms, like its makers and officers, hold out its principles and rules as a (nonoptional) standard for comparing options and ranking them as obligatory, permissible, or impermissible, or as legally valid and enforceable or unenforceable, voidable or void, and so forth. The law is indeed a set of publicly adopted reasons for adopting or rejecting proposals for action, public or private. In this essay I consider law as a paradigm of public reason and choice, and use this paradigm to illustrate the bearing of (in)commensurability on decision making in the public sphere.

Obviously, law does not deserve the place it claims in our deliberations unless it, too, meets some standards. Though we need law, and though anarchy as a form of life has little intelligible appeal, the Hobbesian redefinition of "justice" as conformity to the law strikes everyone as impoverishing our lexicon profitlessly. For what are requirements of justice if not the standards of reasonableness in dealing with others? And must not law measure up as reasonable, if it is to earn the respect of its subjects as providing standards for action which are rightly directive in their deliberations?

Before a law is taken up in its subjects' deliberations, it has itself been deliberated on by those who made it. (Among *lawmakers* are also those who can and do decide, with some authority, that the legal materials relevant to some issue shall be taken to mean this rather than that.) The lawmaker's deliberations ended in choice; alternative practical possibilities—including, perhaps, just leaving things be—will have had some attraction, been options. Those deliberations will have sought, at least purportedly, to *compare* and *rank* the options as better and worse, as involving respectively greater and lesser good (or perhaps lesser or greater evil). In turn, the lawmaker's assessments, comparisons, and rankings, whether adequate or not, can and will be tracked and reassessed by critics, reformers, supporters, and everyone wondering whether the law is justified and, more radically, whether it is reasonable to take the law, and/or this particular rule of law, as the normal measure, the standard for evaluating in conscience one's own day-to-day options.

I

It was law reformers—notably, Beccaria and Bentham—who proposed that the legislator's assessing of options as better and worse can and should be by commensuration in a stricter sense. As one might put the principle they offered: Aggregate the pluses, subtract the minuses, and pursue the option with the highest balance. For the founders of the aggregative tradition in individual and political ethics, the unit was pleasures (pains being presumed, too casually, to be a negative quantity on the single scale supposed to run from exquisite pleasures down to atrocious pains).[2] And desire for pleasure, as Bentham learned from Hume, is not a *reason*. Still, the principle that good (pleasure) is to be maximized and bad (pains) minimized was conceived and offered as a principle of reason.

Utilitarianism was addressed not to those whose only concern is to get what they happen to want, here and now or in any other horizon they fancy, but to those interested in being guided by reason, that is, by reasons.[3] So too is utilitarianism's self-appointed successor in legal theory, the normative Economic Analysis of Law. In its uncompromised forms,[4] this takes as the supreme, and indeed exclusive, measure of law's rationality the goal of "efficiency", that is, of efficiency in maximizing social wealth or value, as measured by what those concerned would be willing and able to pay for in money.

Like other theories of justice, all such notions of guiding social choice by measuring and comparing the expected net value of alternative foreseeable outcomes are the target of a popular objection. Options (and their outcomes), it is said, are incommensurable because evaluative perspectives are irreducibly plural. The ideals, ideologies, and interpretations and forms of life to be found in a modern society are radically and insurmountably diverse. The "interpretive incommensurability of values",[5] in excluding any significant collective ranking of options, precludes also the utilitarian or economistic proposals for ranking.

But this denial of commensurability fails. It fallaciously deduces a conclusion about what are or are not good reasons for action from premises which refer only to facts—facts about public opinion, the sheer plurality of views, and the like. Or else it simply misses the question of good reasons for action, as that question is raised in or with a view to deliberation and choice, and instead discourses about another matter (the existing and foreseeable diversity of opinion about them). Or, if it does attend to reasons for action "from the internal point of view" (practically) and commends a political option (say, neutrality among the "incommensurable" conceptions of the good life), it fails to show that (say) utilitarianism errs in envisaging a social conversion, critical education, and reform by which the truth about individual and social good could overcome the supposedly "ineradicable" pluralism of uncritically accepted worldviews.

The assertion that worldviews are incommensurably plural because opinions seem ineradicably diverse overlooks the commensurability of truth with untruth, of attention to evidence with inattention, of insight with stupidity and oversight, of sound with unsound reasoning—in short, the commensurability of reasonable with more or less unreasonable grounds for making the judgments involved in a worldview or a conception of human goods and human fulfill-ment. And the implications of asserting this sort of incommensurability of opinions are typically glossed over. Where there are no reasonable grounds for disagreeing, agreeing, and resolving disagreement, the only bases for social co-operation are subrational motivations such as lust or terror, self-preference or inertia. If worldviews are incommensurable, we have no *reason* to accept a scheme of social decision making, a constitution, a Rule of Law. For each person, then, the challenge is simply to become and remain one of those who are in charge. Domination will be bereft of justification, for no combination of wants and preferences, even when considered from the internal point of view ("I want . . .", "I prefer . . ."), can constitute or entail an *ought*, a *reason* justifying or *demanding* a course of conduct.

In a Kantian critique, on the other hand, the utilitarian aspiration to guide individual and social choices by commensurating the goods and bads in alternative options is censured precisely for conceding too much to the noncognitivists and relativists. Morality and right are matters of practical reason. But what the utilitarian proposes to maximize is not any sort of reason, but rather something subrational—desire, sensible impulse, "sensuous motives",[6] "happiness",[7] in short merely "empirical grounds" from which one can derive no "ought".[8] So utilitarian conclusions offer deliberating subjects no rational norms by which to measure as right or wrong their acts of free choice (the supreme concept of the metaphysics of morals),[9] or by which their wills could be given any sort of direction capable of being called "categorical", that is, unconditional, "binding", or "obligatory".[10]

So far, so good. But the criteria proposed by Kant to replace utilitarian maximization of satisfaction fail to supply the rational measure of right and wrong in choosing. Most well known is the criterion of universalizability of the maxim of one's chosen action (that is, the universalizability of the intelligible content of the proposal which one adopts by choice). But what does it mean to say that a maxim *cannot* be universalized? What sort of modal is this? Kant's way of dealing with ethical issues makes it clear that the (im)possibility he has in mind is essentially logical: A choice is wrong if its universalized maxim contains a *contradiction*. This attempt to explain immorality as a form of illogicality yields no fruit. Whether in the *Grundlegung*'s well-known examples[11]—suicide, borrowing on false promises, neglect of talents, and indifference to others' interests—or in the *Rechtslehre*'s—courts of equity, the deduction of rightful possession, swearing to beliefs, subjection of rulers to coercion, punitive war, and prescriptive acquisition on the basis of abandonment or long use[12]—no contradiction is found without premising principles of the very kind the arguments were meant to validate.

Its official master principles being empty of rational guidance, Kantian ethics and theory of justice measures deliberation only with makeshift "principles" such as that "nature's end" should be respected.[13] (Here Kant, foiled in his attempt to find principles for the moral order in the logical order, illogically uses as premise for a moral conclusion a proposition pertaining to another nonmoral order, the natural in the sense of "natural" that we use in speaking of the natural sciences.) Moreover, in the "casuistical questions" which he quietly puts to himself at the end of his famously rigorous reaffirmations of the Western moral tradition on killing the innocent, sex, lying, intoxication, and so forth, Kant employs a mix of intuitionistic and consequentialist considerations[14] like nothing so much as late twentieth-century academic ethics.

For intuitionism, though officially dead and buried with Prichard, Ross, and their generation of philosophers, is in fact very much alive. The ethical ("metaethical") skepticism of the 1950s having officially perished (in the Vietnam War?), the staple of academic discussion of individual and political morality is now the appeal to "my" or "our" *intuitions* about specific types of conduct. The term "intuition" claims respectability for positions which are defended not by *reasons* but by the more or less tacit appeal to consensus. But as a response to questions and objections, appeal to consensus is fallacious and rationally futile. Against objectors it merely insinuates that *we*, not they, are in charge around here.

Setting relativist, Kantian, and intuitionist objections aside, therefore, there remains a sound response to notions that social choice can and should be guided by measuring the expected value of alternative foreseeable outcomes. The response has several elements.

II

The first element is this. Commensuration of the goods and bads in alternative available courses of action is possible insofar as the deliberation about alternatives remains in the technical domain. This is the domain proper to cost-benefit analysis. Here, (1) goals are well defined, (2) costs can be compared by references to some definite unit of value (for example, money), (3) benefits too can be quantified in a way that renders them commensurable with one another, and (4) differences among the means, other than their measurable costs, measurable benefits, and other aspects of their respective efficiency as means, are not counted as significant.

The response's second element is this. Because none of those four features obtains in the case of morally significant choice as such, it is not possible to commensurate—though it is possible to compare in some other important ways—the goods and bads in alternative available courses of action considered as options between which an individual or group has occasion to make a morally significant choice. In particular, it is not possible to make the type of commensuration required by utilitarianism in any of its forms, or by its consequentialist or proportionalist or economistic successors. (When I refer hereafter to commensuration and incommensurability, it is this type I have in mind, unless the context shows otherwise.) So since the making of a law is always a morally significant social act, engaging the moral responsibility both of the individuals who participate in it and of the group for whom they act, and self-determining both for these individuals and for the group, the incommensurability of the goodness of alternative options is of great importance for legal thought and practice. Indeed, as we shall see, it is an essential element in the grounding of the inviolable human rights which are properly the law's backbone.

The response has two elements because the technical and the moral are irreducibly distinct domains. That distinction is not grounded on some moral principle or norm. (If it were, the defense of that principle or norm against objections and "exceptions" by utilitarian, consequentialist, proportionalist, or other commensuration-presupposing moral theories would be question begging, as would appeal to the principle or norm in critiques of such theories.) Rather, it is grounded in the realities involved in freely chosen human action. Any philosophical reflection on morality and law must give careful attention to those realities. Still more so must a reflection on incommensurability in morality, public reason, and law. No one should assume that there is a general theory of incommensurability, or indeed of incomparability, such that what is true of commensuration or comparison in the domains of nature, logic, or technique is also true in the domain of deliberation about *options*. The question whether or in what ways X and Y are (in)commensurable and/or (in)comparable must always turn on *what X and Y are*.

In morality and law, X and Y are, generically, options: proposals for action which could be adopted by choice. Throughout this essay I mean by "option" just such a proposal: one that comes up for deliberation and adoption or nonadoption, not *as* a possible move within the confines of a game or other technique as such, but as an apparently eligible answer to the unspoken question, What shall I, or we, *do* with this part of our one and only life? That being so, and the making and following of law being always a matter of such real-life options, the question of incommensurability in law turns on the prior question: What are the realities involved in any and every choice—in any and every adopting of one proposal (option) for action in preference to another or others?

Whether it be large scale (such as the choice to marry, or to become a lawyer rather than a philosopher) or small scale (such as the choice to write a friendly letter to an opponent, or to spend a week of one's life reflecting and communicating one's reflections on commensurability), every human choice is a step into a new world. To be sure, the proposal adopted by one's choosing will involve more or less definite goals. But the content and the significance of the choice are not exhausted by these goals. For the choice anticipates benefits (the very reasons for the choice and action) that are open-ended—capable of being instantiated not only in the envisaged and intended goals but also in further developments, opportunities, payoffs, many of them as yet envisaged only dimly, if at all. And the choosing itself has a further significance.

Determinisms hard and soft to the contrary notwithstanding, choices can be free.[15] In free choice, one has reasons for each of the alternative options, but these reasons are not causally determinative. One's having these reasons is a necessary but (even when morally sound and obligatory) not a sufficient condition for making one or the other choice. No factor but the choosing itself *settles* which alternative is chosen. So there is real creativity in free choice.

And this creativity is also self-creative, self-determining, more or less self-constitutive. One more or less transforms oneself by making the choice, and by carrying it out, and by following it up with other free choices in line with it. One's choice in fact *lasts* in, and as part of, one's character. In this respect, it is analogous to the insights which last as one's habitual knowledge (for example, of arithmetic, logic, or history) and are parts of that knowledge (and effective in guiding one's further inquiries) even when rarely or perhaps never consciously recalled and put to use. But choices differ from habitual knowledge in that they can be reversed by subsequent, inconsistent choices, especially choices to repudiate or repent of the former choice. Still, until such reversal, they last. That lasting of choices, which shapes character (and further choices) around those persisting adoptions of proposals, is a real effect of the choice—classically called an "intransitive" effect, to mark its radical difference from every effect which transits beyond the chooser's will. To choose is not only to set out into a new world; it is already to become a person (or society) more or less different from the person (or society) that deliberated about the goods and bads in the alternative available options.

Such, in bare outline, are the realities which Aristotle, notwithstanding his obscurities about the freedom possible in choosing, discerned clearly enough (on the whole) for him to insist on the basic distinction between *praxis* and *poiêsis,* between doing and making, and correspondingly between the ethical and the technical as irreducibly[16] distinct domains.[17] Life—the life one lives through one's chosen activities and lives well by (in large measure) one's acting well— neither is nor has a goal that one might sometime *have accomplished* by one's acts as one can accomplish one's technical objectives through skilful and unimpeded deployment of one's art/technique.[18] If you are tempted here to reply (as Aristotle perhaps was) that the goal is "obtaining or realizing human goods or human fulfillment", think again about the aspects of human fulfillment that prevent obtaining it being the description of such a goal—the aspects sketched in this section.

And the same is true, even more evidently, of the life of groups such as politically and legally ordered societies. Every student and practitioner of law becomes aware of its open-endedness—of the ceaseless change in rules and institutions, changes which are guided by more or less stable principles and policies and in many cases have a specific goal, but which are not measured by their efficiency in moving society toward an overarching goal which might, even in principle, be attained by "one more change". The intransitive effect of choice on individual character has its clear analogue in the effect that every change in the rules on one subject matter is liable to have—by way of arguments about coherence and integrity—on the rules and argumentation on other subject matters.

In many respects the law (the legal ordering of a political society) is a technique, and many aspects of legal reasoning are, for good reason, technical—a manipulation of cultural artifacts for specific goals (such as effecting a transfer of property or change of status) which can be successfully accomplished and finished off. But as the debates around legal positivism and interpretation have made amply clear, the law is also a moral undertaking by society and by each of those individuals and groups whose acts go to constitute, maintain, put into effect, and develop the law, guided by many reasons of principle and/or policy but by no specifiable goal.

It is, above all, this open-endedness of individual and social life that makes impossible (not merely impracticable) the commensuration of the goods and bads in alternative available courses of action considered as options between which an individual or group must make a morally significant choice. When Socrates and four other Athenians were ordered by their government to help liquidate a political opponent, the four went off to do the job but Socrates simply "went home".[19] A game theorist, a utilitarian, or a proportionalist would try to commensurate the goods and bads in "states of affairs"—presumably the states of affairs most obviously likely to eventuate from the two most obvious alternative choices for Socrates: go on the liquidation mission *versus* go home and therefore quite probably be liquidated oneself (two lives lost instead of one).[20]

But either choice was a step into a new world: either the world in which Socrates was a participant in what he judged to be murder (choosing to help kill the innocent) or the world in which Socrates put into practice his own teaching[21] that it is better to suffer wrong than to do it. Our world today is (and tomorrow, though changed, will still be) a world which Socrates shaped by choosing to go home. The proposal to evaluate the alternative choices facing Socrates by commensurating the goods net of bads in *our* world with the goods net of bads in the hypothetical world(s) into which Socrates chose *not* to step would be senseless even if our world were not itself being changed by the choices we are making. Why pick our world as one term of the comparison, given that (1) our world has been shaped by many free choices and events besides Socrates' acts, (2) the state of affairs which we call our world has no special priority of rational significance over the various states of affairs which lie between Socrates and us and the indefinitely many states of affairs which lie in the future though still somehow affected for good and ill by Socrates' choice, and (3) there is no theory of probability, subjective or objective, which could even in principle have identified for Socrates the relevant consequences of his choice, let alone assigned to our world some priority in his assessment of risk, still less settled the comparative weight of probabilities and values or disvalues?[22] Nor would the proposal be saved by stipulating that a proportionalist Socrates himself need be concerned only with "foreseeable effects". For Socrates could foresee as well as anyone that choice will necessarily (and therefore, in principle, foreseeably) have self-constitutive intransitive effects on the chooser, and on all who condone or admire the choice and accordingly employ in their own deliberations what they take to be its rational principle(s). And he could equally well foresee that the irreducibly different kinds of effects of his choice would ripple out through history, in ways affected by many other free and self-constitutive choices, some affected and others unaffected by knowledge of his own choice. He had no reason whatever to think that the accounts, however rigged or simplified to produce a bottom line, should be drawn up in, or by reference particularly to, the state of affairs in 1997. And nor do we. None of this open-endedness of Socrates' choice, of course, prevented him from choosing, and choosing (as we shall see) quite rationally!

Why did no substantial philosopher before the Enlightenment entertain the notion that moral or legal reasoning can and should be guided by some principle of commensurating and maximizing the net overall goods promised by alternative options? The answer must, I think, have much to do with an insight more or less lost in the Enlightenment's adoption of more or less scientific models of human nature, individual and social action, and historical development—the insight that the subject matter of deliberation toward free choice (moral reasoning) differs from that of technical reasoning in the ways which I have summarized as "open-endedness".

Hume treated as an admirable novelty his insight that "ought" cannot be derived from "is". (He ignored or flouted it in his own affirmative work in ethics and metaethics.)[23] But there were earlier philosophers who had better understood that the moral *ought,* the directiveness of reason in deliberation toward choice and action, cannot be derived from (or reduced to) the *is* of nature, or the logic of noncontradiction, or the how-to (including the how-to-measure) of any technique. Aquinas thought this so important that he began his commentary on Aristotle's *Ethics* (and thus also his *Politics*) by pointing out the four irreducibly distinct types of order with which our reasoning is concerned: the "natural" (for example, natural scientific), the logical, the moral, and the technical.[24] Where Kant confused the moral with the logical (eked out with the natural), utilitarian and other aggregative theories for guiding morally significant choice confuse the moral with the technical. The confusion lends its spurious support to (and is supported by) the mistaken notion that, prior to moral judgment, the goodness in a morally significant option and the goodness in any alternative available option must be commensurable by reason as, all things considered, greater and lesser (or, perhaps, equal or approximately equal).

III

Of course, technical reasoning and technical commensurability are often of great importance to moral deliberation. Whenever technical reasoning can show that proposal X has all the beneficial features of proposal Y *and some more,* the latter proposal ceases to be a live *option.*

Technical commensurability of this kind is not restricted to the obvious instances of economics or engineering (where Y costs more, delivers less, and is less safe). It includes also legal considerations, as where argument *Y* relies on a statute that can be shown to have been repealed or a holding that has been overruled.

In all such cases, proposal *X* can be preferred, adopted, and carried out without the need for any *choice* (in the strong, morally relevant sense of "choice") between *X* and *Y*, and without the need to appeal to the sorts of *justifying reason* we call moral (including legal principles and rules insofar as they address the deliberations, the consciences, of judges, officials, and citizens).

IV

What, then, is the source and character of the justifying (and the critically demanding and excluding) reasons which do give us standards for comparing *options*, "weighing" those options (as the loose phrase goes), and finding reason to prefer one to another—reasons that direct but do not determine choice? If lawmakers, as I said at the outset, must evaluate and rank options as better and worse, how can they do so?

The reasonable standards for comparing and, so far as possible, ranking options are moral standards. Each of them is itself a specification, a making specific, of the following idea: everybody, all human persons and their communities, being fulfilled in all the basic human goods—integral human fulfillment. Integral human fulfillment is not some gigantic synthesis of all the instantiations of human goods in a vast state of affairs such as might be projected as the goal of a worldwide billion-year plan. Human goods and their instantiation through creative free choices are open-ended. Yet wishing for everybody, present and future, to flourish in all the goods intrinsic to human persons, while it does not amount to forming an intention, is not empty.

On the contrary, that wish is the only rational response to the directiveness of the reasons for action, the practical reasons, which each of the basic human goods provides. What gives reason for action is always some intelligible benefit which could be instantiated by successful action, benefits such as the basic forms of human opportunity and need. Each of these basic goods (basic reasons for action) is desirable for its own sake as a constitutive aspect of the well-being and flourishing of human persons in community (and none is unqualifiedly commensurable as more or less valuable than the others).[25] (Kant's ethics and doctrine of right remain empty precisely because, failing to break with empiricist assumptions, he did not differentiate the basic goods, the basic reasons for action and principles of practical reason, from the subrational inclinations and desires which are, in truth, the data for practical understanding's original, underived insights into these intelligible goods and reasons, insights articulated as principles of reason.)

The combined or integral directiveness of all these basic practical reasons, these first principles of reasonable deliberation and practical reasonableness in choice and action, is not another good or additional reason for action to add to the list. (In that sense of the elusive term, it is not a "covering value".) Rather, that integral directiveness of all these reasons for action is articulated in—their interplay, unfettered and undeflected by emotions is, so to speak, moderated by—the rational principle which is the conceptual content of a sufficiently reflective wish for integral human fulfillment. The principle can be formulated thus: In all one's deliberating and acting, one *ought* to choose and in other ways will—and other persons, so far as satisfying their needs is dependent on one's choosing and willing, have a *right* that one choose and will—those and only those possibilities the willing of which is compatible with integral human fulfillment.[26]

That principle is the first, master principle of morality, in its most abstract formulation. All other moral standards are specifications of it. The Kantian imperative that in every act one regard oneself as legislating for "a kingdom of ends" (a "whole of all ends in systematic conjunction")[27] is an intimation of that first principle; Christianity's love of neighbor as oneself for the sake of the Kingdom is another; the utilitarian injunction to seek "the greatest good/happiness of the greatest number" is another attempt, unhappy precisely because of its several confusions about commensurability.[28]

How, then, is the first principle and measure of morality specified into less abstract moral principles and norms? How is its rational prescription shaped into definite responsibilities? Well, what that master principle itself prescribes is that one not narrow voluntarily the range of people and goods one cares about, by following nonrational motives, that is, motives not grounded in intelligible requirements of the basic *reasons* for action, the basic human goods. Now, one type of nonrational motive is hostile feelings such as anger and hatred toward oneself or others. A person or group motivated by feelings of, for example, revenge does not have a will open to integral human fulfillment. So a first specification of the master principle is: Do not answer injury with injury. This principle is treated as foundational in all decent legal systems and is quite compatible with principles of just compensation (even by self-help) and of retributive punishment to restore the balance of fairness between wrongdoers and the law abiding.

Another specification of the master principle is the principle which every form of consequentialist, proportionalist, or other purportedly aggregative moral theory is tailor-made to reject: Do not do evil—choose to destroy, damage, or impede some instance of a basic good—that good may come. The previous principle excludes making harm to another one's end; the present principle excludes making it precisely one's means (as distinct from causing it as a side effect of what one intends and does). In such a case, one unreasonably treats a good end as justifying the bad means. For: the instantiation of good which one treats as end (call it *E*), and for the sake of which one acts *against* the reason constituted by that instantiation of a basic good which one is choosing to harm (call this reason *M*), could not constitute a *reason* thus to act against *M* unless *E* could be weighed and balanced against, commensurated with, *M* and—prior to moral judgment—*rationally* judged to be greater, more weighty, the greater good (or, where both reasons concern avoiding evil, the lesser evil). But by virtue of, inter alia, the considerations set out in section II, *that* sort of rationally commensurating *judgment* is not possible. So one's preference for *E* over *M* is motivated not by reason but by differential *feelings* as between *E* and *M* and violates the master principle of morality. The feelings which thus motivate the judgment that *E* is the greater good or lesser evil may well, of course, be veiled (more or less in good faith) by rationalizations or by conventional "wisdom," which prescribes or licenses some narrowing of horizons or ranking of persons or other way of making the incommensurable seem rationally commensurable.

The principle that evil may not be done for the sake of good, interpreted in this way, is the foundation of truly inviolable (absolute) human rights and is the backbone of decent legal systems. For a decent legal system excludes unconditionally the killing or harming of innocent[29] persons as a means to any end, whether public or private. On the basis of other specifications of morality's master principle, it also excludes the use of perjured testimony, the choice to render false judgment, judicial or other official support of fraud, resort to sexual seduction as an instrument of public policy, and chattel slavery. These unconditional norms, and the associated absolute or truly inviolable human rights not to be mistreated by the violation of any of those norms, give the legal system its shape, its boundaries, the indispensable humanistic basis (at least some necessary conditions) for its strong claim on our allegiance. Without these norms, and respect for the underlying principle, the legal system becomes an organization of powerful people willing to treat others as mere means.[30]

This principle excluding all *intentional* harm to persons (in any basic aspect of their wellbeing) also rules out the economistic ambition to explain and justify the main institutions of our law as devices for maximizing economically assessable (commensurable) value. For central to Economic Analysis of Law is the assumption, or thesis, that (though there might be a difference in the purchase price) there is no difference of principle between buying the right to inflict intentional personal injury even on nonconsenting persons and buying the right not to take precautions which would (supposedly) eliminate an equivalent number of injuries caused accidentally.[31] But in every decent legal system, the former right is not available, whether by purchase or otherwise. For a decent legal system is in the service of human persons, and its first and most fundamental service is in protecting and vindicating their right not to be made the object (end or means) of someone's will to harm them.

A third principle giving relative specificity to the master principle of openness to integral fulfillment is the Golden Rule, the core principle of fairness: "Do to others as you would have them do to you; do not impose on others what you would not want to be obliged by them to accept". For a will marked by egoism or partiality cannot be open to integral human fulfillment. This rational principle of impartiality by no means excludes all forms and corresponding feelings of preference for oneself and those who are near and dear (for example, parental responsibility for, and consequent prioritizing of, their own children). It excludes, rather, all those forms of preference which are motivated only by desires, aversions, or hostilities that do not correspond to intelligible aspects of the real *reasons* for action, the basic human goods instantiated in the lives of other human beings as in the lives of oneself or those close to one's heart.

Although fairness is thus a rational norm requiring one to transcend all rationally unintegrated feelings, its concrete application in personal life presupposes a kind of commensurating of benefits and burdens which reason is impotent to commensurate. For, to apply the Golden Rule, one must know what burdens one considers *too great* to accept. And this knowledge, constituting a premoral commensuration, cannot be a commensurating by reason (see part II). Therefore, it can only be by one's intuitive awareness, one's discernment, of one's own differentiated *feelings* toward various goods and bads as concretely remembered, experienced, or imagined. To repeat: This is not a rational and objective commensuration of goods and bads. But once established in one's feelings and identified in one's self-awareness, this commensuration by feelings enables one to measure one's options by a rational and objective standard of interpersonal impartiality.

Of course, it is implicit in what I have said that the feelings by which someone makes the commensuration identifying what it is fair for that person to choose or otherwise will (for example, to accept as a side effect) had better be the feelings of someone whose deliberation and action is open to and in line with integral human fulfillment and each of that master principle's specifications. That is what is sound in Aristotle's pervasive methodological principle of ethical and political theory: It is the mature person of fully reasonable character who is the standard and measure, *kânon kai metron,* of what is and is not truly worthy, worthwhile, and enjoyable.[32]

Analogously, in the life of a community, the preliminary commensuration of rationally incommensurable factors is accomplished not by rationally determined judgments but by *decisions* (themselves presumably based ultimately on commensuration of alternative options by feelings). And these too had better be made within the framework established by complete consistency with the other specifications of morality's master principle. Is it fair to impose on others the risks inherent in driving at more than 10 mph or in planting trees near the roadside? Yes, in our community, since our community has by custom and law *decided* to treat those risks and harms as *not too great.* Have we a rational critique of a community which decided to limit road traffic to 10 mph and to accept all the economic and other costs of that decision? Or to have no trees along the road? Or not to have the institution of trusts, or constructive trusts? No, we have no rational critique of such a community. In short, the decision to permit road traffic to proceed faster than 10 mph, or to plant trees along the verge, or to define trusts just as English law does was rationally underdetermined.[33]

But we do have a rational critique of someone who drives at 60 mph but who, when struck by someone driving at 45 mph complains that that speed is per se negligent. Or of someone willing to receive the benefits (for example, the tax breaks) of trusts but not willing to accept the law's distinction between trust and contract in bankruptcy. And, in general, we have a rational critique of those who accept the benefits of this and other communal decisions but reject the correlative burdens as they bear on them and those in whom they feel interested.

Fundamental to the working out of the Golden Rule across time are expectations such as that those who have received the benefit of a scheme of cooperation involving onerous burdens will shoulder the burdens when it is their turn to do so; or that we who have shouldered the burdens will in due course receive, and not be deprived of, the reasonably expected benefits. Claims based on appeals to fairness in view of such expectations vary in rational force, according as, for example, the collaborative enterprise is subject to risks of success or failure arising from factors external to it and independent of the intentions (that is, outside the control) of its participants. Where the nonaccrual, or the confiscation, of expected benefits arises because one of the parties to the collaboration intends to deny or confiscate the benefit, it cannot fairly be treated as merely the crystallizing of a risk which, just like risks of the kind referred to in the previous sentence, could (and should!) have been discounted by putative beneficiaries when considering their "investment in" (assumption of the burdens of) the collaborative enterprise. Economic Analysis of Law errs again here in equating confiscation with other forms of loss of expected benefit, commensurating all these forms of loss by reference to one factor assumed to be quantifiable: probability or degree of foreseeable risk of loss.[34]

In this part, I have identified three of the measures or standards of reasonableness that are intermediate between the supreme moral measure of choice and action and the specific moral norms which give more determinate guidance and which in some but not all cases, are taken over and applied more or less directly by the law of any decent community. There are other such intermediate, high-level principles, but they are not so directly constitutive of justice between persons and thus not so central to the understanding of legal systems, rules, institutions, and practices. What I have said is sufficient to establish that the failure of utilitarian and other consequentialist or proportionalist attempts to guide moral judgment by commensurating the goods and bads in options does not leave reason impotent to evaluate options and rank them as, if you will, better and worse, or as involving respectively greater or lesser evil. Because morality is nothing other than integral, unfettered reasonableness, an option which violates one or more of the principles I have mentioned and so is morally wrong can always be described as "worse" compared to options which are not morally wrong. Because even morally upright choice, fully in line with integral human fulfillment, can never definitively avoid side effects more or less harmful to the goods constitutive of human fulfillment, a morally upright action which involves no *choice* of evil (no intent to do harm as an end or a means) can be described (though not without risk of being misunderstood as supposing an impossible consequentialist commensuration) as choosing the lesser evil.

Indeed, since the consequentialist project of commensurating is impossible, but rational deliberation must go forward and be articulated, we often find such a nonconsequentialist usage on the lips of avowed consequentialists. Thus Justice Oliver Wendell Holmes in the Supreme Court of the United States:

> We must consider the two objects of desire, both of which we cannot have, and make up our minds which to choose. It is desirable that criminals should be detected, and to that end that all available evidence should be used. It is also desirable that the Government should not itself foster and pay for other crimes, when they are the means by which the evidence is to be obtained. . . . We have to choose, and for my part I think it *a lesser evil* that some criminals should escape than that the Government should play an *ignoble* part.[35]

"Lesser evil" here either (1) merely expresses an opinion *consequent* on choice, rather than a moral judgment antecedent to and suited to guide choice, or (2) implies an appeal to a prior, nonconsequentialist moral standard according to

which covert manipulation of legal rules by officers of the law violates the
Golden Rule and perhaps even the principle that evil may not be done for the
sake of good, and for either reason, or both, is something "ignoble", especially
for professional guardians of the law (whose appeal is to reason and whose
authority is thus from morality).

Law can effectively provide a community with a common "rule and measure"
for guiding and evaluating the actions of its members (including lower-level
communities within it)—and thus for attaining the benefits of cooperation—
only if it provides those members with a standard which each can adopt and use
just as if it were his or her own scheme of action autonomously excogitated and
adopted. It can provide this standard only by establishing more or less content-
independent criteria for assessing the validity of rules and thus the validity
and/or legality of the acts those rules regulate. These criteria refer us to past acts
and other facts (of types picked out in other rules), which often are exercises of
the *technê* of rule making (by any of the three constitutional branches) but need
not be (as in the case of the emergence of customary rules) and in any case
are evaluated by the *technê* (not exclusively a lawyers' craft) of rule finding. In
an important sense, a legal rule just *is* the relation between such a past act or
fact and my present deliberation, choice, and action as a member, official or
otherwise, of the community that measures its conduct by looking back to such
past acts and facts. But in another important sense, a legal rule just *is* the relation between the master principle of morality (and the ideal of integral human
fulfillment) and that same deliberation, choice, and action of mine, insofar as
that master principle has been given specificity not merely in the intermediate
principles and other norms of morality but in the particular choices of the rule
makers acting as rule makers, *including* the choices of those who settled the
constitutional criteria of validity of other legal rules.

Judges in superior courts in the common law world have (relatively determinate) authority not only to find, declare, and enforce the existing rules but also
(relatively indeterminate) authority to reshape them and/or make new rules.
Moreover, the complexity of the judicial system, and of the cultural materials
relevant to judicial rule finding, makes it necessary (and therefore morally and
institutionally possible) for rule finders to treat some of the relevant materials as
lacking the authority which would otherwise be attributed to the past acts (say,
of rule finding and declaring) of the author(s) of such material. So there emerge
the two dimensions on which to compare and evaluate the rival interpretations
of a particular part of the law in dispute between the parties before a court: the
dimension of fit with the legal materials and the dimension of moral soundness.

One could say that a *hard* case is one in which one interpretation of the law
is the best of all rival interpretations on the dimension of fit, while another is

best on the dimension of soundness. I have argued in the past that fit and soundness are incommensurable, so that there cannot be a *uniquely* right interpretation in a hard case so understood (though countless interpretations can be identified as wrong because inferior to the right, that is not-wrong, interpretations on both dimensions).[36] Insofar as fit is simply a matter of understanding and applying the technical criteria of validity of rule making or other ways of generating legal rules, it is indeed incommensurable with the moral considerations relevant to soundness. The cultural-technical order as such shares no common measure with the moral as such.

But fit, and indeed the whole technique of rule making and rule finding to which "fit" synoptically refers, is in the service of the community's common good. Indeed, the technique was instituted and is maintained for the sake of a morally required (and therefore sound) end, the common good attainable by a fair and peaceful cooperation which fully respects the rights of every member of the community (including the rights which properly must be respected and prevail whatever the circumstances). Ultimately, rule finding is no mere game or technique, but a morally significant act which, like all other choices to act, will be fully reasonable only if in line with integral human fulfillment. So there is a measure common to the two dimensions: moral soundness.

It was not a mere mistake to speak of two dimensions, the one being concerned with such morally significant considerations as the disappointing of expectations, the overriding of acquired legal rights, and the desirability of like cases getting like treatment by the various tribunals disposing of them; the other being concerned with the merits of the alternative ways of dealing with these parties (and future parties in like case) and of guiding the conduct of citizens and officials generally. These "substantive merits" can never reasonably be considered entirely in abstraction from the network of other substantive principles and rules legally adopted in that community.[37] But they can be considered in abstraction from the technical authoritativeness of the alternative solutions, respectively. The possibility of doing so is the possibility of there being two distinguishable dimensions or moments of the one, ultimately moral assessment.

Does it follow that, morality being a matter of unfettered reasonableness, there is in truth a uniquely right answer even in hard cases at law? No. Although I was mistaken, I now think, in contending that the two dimensions are simply incommensurable, it remains that assessing the moral significance of differing degrees of fit and soundness will usually be a matter of fairness. And fairness, though a rational requirement, is one whose content in any given circumstances is determined, as I have argued above, in part by *feelings* ("How would I like it if . . . ?" and so forth). The commensurating here must be done by discernment of one's feelings. It is not reason, whether moral or technical, that settles for each judge the stance he or she will adopt on the great strategic questions whose answers do dispose of hard cases—whether to uphold national/federal power or constitutionally legitimate state/provincial interests, whether to countenance judicial reform or defer to the legislature, whether and when to swim with and when to breast a tide of judicial opinion one thinks technically inferior or based partly on morally unsound arguments, and so forth. In such cases, reason does no more (and no less) than hold the ring, disqualifying countless "solutions" as contrary to reason and wrong, but identifying none as *uniquely* right.

   Many cases at law are not hard but are settled easily by reason. Of these, many are settled by technical considerations of validity and authoritativeness, and the rest by moral considerations, for example, of inviolable rights. Where a moral right is entailed by "Do not return harm for harm" or "Do not do evil (choose precisely to inflict harm) for the sake of good", it is truly inviolable and itself entails what some have called a "hierarchical incommensurability"[38] or "lexical priority" or genuinely[39] "trumping" status, in relation to all other technical and/or otherwise morally relevant considerations. Where a moral right results from the Golden Rule of fairness, it trumps all considerations of technique or interest except where those considerations themselves create, in the relevant circumstances, a moral responsibility and/or countervailing fairness-based right. This priority of moral considerations over all, but only, *nonmoral* considerations in deliberation is the source and content of the "constitutive incommensurabilities" which Joseph Raz's work has highlighted. One does not rightly exchange one's friend for cash, however much cash (where "cash" stands for interest and advantage); that moral truth is a constitutive element of the relationship of friendship. But there can be a moral responsibility to take and use cash for good purposes, even at the expense of friendship.[40] So that sort of "constitutive incommensurability" is bounded by the commensurability of each moral consideration with all others.

   The same boundedness obtains in somewhat analogous relationships such as patriotic allegiance. One does not rightly give up one's allegiance for cash. But the moral obligation to obey one's country's laws—an obligation derived from multiple considerations of fairness,[41] and constitutive of a decent relationship of allegiance and citizenship—is measured by moral principle, and so is defeasible by other serious moral responsibilities.

VI

In sum, talk of incommensurability takes its measure from a presupposed concept of *measure,* and talk of measure is not univocal but highly analogous. Law is a measured measure; its immediate rational measure is the common good of the community whose law it is. That common good is a kind of specification (relative to a particular group) of integral human fulfillment, the primary rational measure of all human action. The ideal of integral human fulfillment does not measure our deliberations in the way that goals enable us to measure the efficiency of means, nor does it provide a unit of aggregation. It measures rather by another kind of specification (relative to the ways in which emotion can subordinate rather than support reasons), a specification in and of the standards of fully reasonable conduct, including the conduct of lawmakers. Within the rational/moral limits fixed by those standards, much remains to be settled by individual and group commitment in accordance with discernment of feelings and fair procedures of collective or representative decision making. The essential role of feelings and emotions in individual life and action is closely paralleled by the essential role of procedures for decision making in the life and action of communities; in each case, that role is beneficial so long as subordinated to the fundamental reasons for action (basic human goods) and to the standards of unfettered practical reasoning (moral principles and norms). Feelings and commitments (including such collective or community commitments as constitutions) enable individuals and groups reasonably to compare and rank, and in that sense commensurate, many options which by reason's own standards are incommensurable. So the incommensurabilities with which deliberation must contend, and which necessitate morally significant *choice,* do not prevent our choices being in a genuine (though not game-theoretical) sense instances of *rational choice.*[42] Choice between options neither (or none) of which is required by reason's principles and norms should nonetheless respect all of those requirements and be made, so far as possible, for relevant reasons.

A sound understanding of practical reason, then, denies many of the types of incommensurability implicit in unsound conceptions. These include the incommensurabilities that result from a pure "will" theory of law which, as in Kelsen's final works, denies that legal directives need be coherent (noncontradictory); the incommensurabilities implicitly embraced by value-relativist and ethical-intuitionist rejections of the possibility of rational unity of principle; and the incommensurabilities implicit in every method of practical reasoning which proposes, with whatever subtlety, to guide deliberation by aggregating value, and so for want of a rationally defensible understanding of *value* remains at the mercy of its exponents' diverse and shifting preferences, conventional opinions, and nonrationally determined horizons of concern.

✻13✻

Incommensurability and Kinds of Valuation: Some Applications in Law

CASS R. SUNSTEIN

Many people claim that values are plural and diverse and that human goods are not commensurable. These claims raise many questions, but if they are right, they should have important consequences for law. Some of the most influential approaches to legal theory and practice have insisted that values are unitary and that goods are commensurable. A recognition of the plurality of kinds of valuation, and of problems of commensurability, helps cast light on disputes in a wide range of apparently unrelated areas in law.

For example, the traditional liberal effort to use law so as to create diverse social spheres—families, markets, politics, religious organizations—makes space for different kinds of valuation. Certain features of political liberalism are illuminated by attention to this issue. Consider the exclusion of religion from politics, the principle of civic equality, and the puzzling notion of rights as "trumps." An understanding of issues of commensurability helps explain why some exchanges are blocked. Some otherwise puzzling anomalies in the theory of environmental protection—and in the theory of rational choice, as shown by Kahneman, Tversky, and others—tend to dissolve if we attend to diverse kinds of valuation. An understanding of these issues will also help in understanding some features of practical reason in law, especially in the old area of analogical thinking, but also in new areas involving the theory and practice of the regulatory state. Most generally, an understanding of diverse kinds of valuation draws attention to the *expressive function of law,* a function that has frequently been overlooked by students of jurisprudence and legal theory.

By focusing on the plurality of values and the problem of incommensurability, I want to show some distinctive ways in which economic analysis of law, and some forms of utilitarianism as well, miss important commitments of a well-functioning legal system. I hope also to suggest that many legal disputes can be illuminated by an understanding of debates over appropriate kinds of valuation. To see goods as incommensurable, and to emphasize that people are really disagreeing about appropriate kinds (not levels) of valuation, is not by itself to resolve legal controversies. It is necessary to say something about the right kind of valuation and to investigate the particulars in great detail, in order to make progress in hard cases in law. But an understanding of these problems will make it easier to see what is at stake.

I. Kinds of Valuation[1]

Human beings value goods, things, relationships, and states of affairs in diverse ways.[2] Some things are for use; consider (most) hammers, or forks, or money. Other things have intrinsic value; consider knowledge or friendship. Intrinsically valued things produce a wide range of responses. Some bring about wonder and awe; consider a mountain or certain artistic works. Toward some people, we feel respect; toward others, affection; toward others, love. Some events produce gratitude; others produce joy; others are thrilling; others make us feel content; others bring about delight.

Negative valuations are similarly diverse. We might be horrified by an act of cruelty, disgusted by an ugly scene, shocked by a betrayal of friendship or love, made indignant by a failure of respect, frightened by the prospect of loss, angered by the infliction of a wound, saddened by undeserved hardship, or frustrated by the failure of our plans. These various terms themselves include a variety of experiences that embody diverse ideas.

We could categorize qualitatively different valuation in many different ways. For purposes of law, it might make sense to focus on such things as love, affection, respect, wonder, worship, and use; these notions come up in many legal disputes. But each of these terms captures a range of qualitatively distinct features of human experience. Love for a parent is different from love for a child, which in turn is different from love for a friend, a spouse, a pet, or a house. We might feel wonder toward an act of selfless courage, and also toward a musical performance or a beautiful beach. How, and how finely, we should categorize kinds of valuation depends on the uses to which the categories will be put. For law and politics, Henry James is not a good guide; for these purposes, the number of useful categories is undoubtedly smaller than it is for ethics, literature, or poetry, which may be especially concerned to offer finely grained accounts.

Distinctions among kinds of valuation are highly sensitive to the particular setting in which they operate. In one setting (say, the workplace), the prevailing kinds of valuation might be quite different from what they are elsewhere (say, the home or the ballot box). Moreover, particular goods do not admit of a single kind of valuation. The prevailing kind has everything to do with the relationship among the various actors. A cat might be valued in a certain way by its owner, but in a different way by a landlord, and in a still different way by a government agency. Much of social differentiation is connected with this point. So too, several kinds of valuation might be directed toward a single object. A person might, for example, both love and respect a friend.

Conflicts among diverse kinds of valuation permeate private and public choice. Suppose that Jones has arranged to have lunch with a friend today, but that he has become very busy and would like to cancel. Suppose Jones thinks in this way: If I cancel, my friend will be disappointed, because he would like my company, and also a bit insulted, because it is cavalier and disrespectful to cancel lunch at the last minute. Maybe I should make it up to him, or provide compensation, by offering a nontrivial cash payment. This would clearly be a hopelessly inadequate response, even if the payment is very high. A cash payment would be inconsistent with the way that someone values a friend. The point helps explain the social norm requiring that sometimes gifts should not take the form of cash, which is regarded as excessively impersonal.[3]

Or suppose that we feel awe toward something. If we do, we will not believe that it should be valued in the same way as its cash equivalent. The judgment that a mountain is "really worth" $10 million may well be right in an important sense, but it is inconsistent with the way that most people value the mountain. This is because the mountain is valued for different purposes from the $10 million. The former produces awe and wonder, whereas the latter is for human use—though admittedly $10 million may produce a (different) sort of awe and wonder as well. The point does not suggest that pristine areas cannot be degraded, nor does it suggest that $10 million is not the right amount to pay for preservation of the mountain, nor does it challenge decision theory in its modern form. But it does have consequences for how participants in the legal system might think about environmental protection.

An understanding of diverse kinds of valuation helps explain the anticommodification position for law or social norms—the view that some things ought not to be tradable on markets. The objection to commodification is simply a special case of the general problem of diverse kinds of valuation. The claim is that we ought not to trade (for example) sexuality or reproductive capacities on markets because economic valuation of these "things" is inconsistent with their appropriate kind (not level) of valuation. The claim is not that markets value sexuality too much or too little; it is that markets value these activities in the wrong way. People who support legal barriers to exchange may well be concerned that exchanges will affect social norms in a pernicious way. These points do not mean that the law should forbid prostitution and surrogacy; questions of this sort cannot be assessed in the abstract. But controversy over appropriate kinds of valuation, and over the effects of law on existing norms, plays an important role in the debate.

Thus far I have dealt with cases in which the kind of valuation expressed through cash payments is believed to be wrong. But we can think of many examples not involving the issue of monetary equivalence. Imagine, for example, that John treats a beautiful natural object in the same way that most people treat friends, or that Sandy values her car like most people value art or literature. All of us know people with occasional tendencies of this kind. Indeed, all of us *are* people with occasional tendencies of this kind. But sometimes an improper kind of valuation seems odd, or disrespectful, or even pathological. Sometimes law is concerned to ensure against improper kinds of valuation and the social norms that valuations, proper or not, tend to embody.

At this point three major qualifications are necessary. First, my claim about diverse kinds of valuation is first and foremost descriptive—a claim about widespread current attitudes. Probably we cannot make sense of our experience without reference to qualitatively diverse goods. But it is plain that social norms change, and prevailing kinds of valuation change as well. Some of the shifts occur within single people; respect, for example, can turn into love. Often more than one kind operates at the same time in different proportions; respect and love may or may not accompany one another. Within societies and law, kinds of valuation also change over time. Marriage may once have involved more use, and less love, companionship, and affection, than it now does. Of course, the abolition of slavery was designed to signal a shift from use to (a certain measure of) respect.

The second qualification is that the existence of diverse kinds of valuation does not by itself have any clear implications for appropriate law, policy, or even social attitudes. It would be foolish to claim that because people now value relationships, events, objects, or each other in different ways, it follows that law should reflect those diverse kinds of valuation. Judgments about the law require a substantive moral or political argument, not a simple resort to convention. If a particular kind of valuation were really superior (with respect to what is appropriately valued) in public or private life, that kind of valuation might well be used notwithstanding its inconsistency with prevailing social norms. If we are to draw conclusions about appropriate law, policy, and norms, it is because there is an account of the good or the right that supports a particular constellation of valuations. In this chapter, I will generally avoid that complex issue.

The third qualification is that those who believe that goods are valued in different ways need not reject the possibility of reason giving, rational choice, or even trade-offs among those goods. On the contrary, believers in diverse kinds of valuation might be happy to say that choices can occur for reasons and that those choices might well be judged rational or not. These claims about rationality and reason giving need to be explained in some detail, but they should be sufficient to show that there may indeed be a point to deliberating hard about cases that involve goods that are valued in different ways.

II. Incommensurability

A. A Working Definition

The subject of incommensurability raises many complexities, and I want to bracket at least some of the philosophical debate here, concentrating instead on what is particularly relevant to law. Begin with a rough working definition, designed especially for the legal context: *Incommensurability occurs when the relevant goods cannot be aligned along a single metric without doing violence to our considered judgments about how these goods are best characterized.* By our considered judgments, I mean our reflective assessments of how certain relationships and events should be understood, evaluated, and experienced. The notion of a single metric should be understood quite literally. By this I mean a standard of valuation that (1) operates at a workable level of specificity and detail, (2) effaces qualitative distinctions among the goods that it measures, and (3) allows comparison along the same dimension. One example of a real-world metric—indeed the most important for my purposes—is dollars. Ten dollars and $100 can be confidently placed on a single metric, so that $10 is simply a small quantity of the same thing of which $100 is a substantial amount. If two goods are fungible, they are also commensurable. Other metrics are feet, yards, pounds, and of course meters. There are no qualitative distinctions between 10 yards and 100 yards, or between 1,000 pounds and 400 pounds (understood for purposes of currency or weight). By contrast, the notion "more valuable than," or "more conducive to human flourishing," does not qualify as a metric as I am understanding that idea here; such notions allow for qualitative distinctions.

I use the term "metric" in this way partly because of the special importance of the metric of dollars to law, and partly because of the large influence, within law, of approaches that attempt to compare diverse goods along a single dimension. Under this general definition of metric, many possible standards—excellence, well-being, affective allegiance—count as criteria, but not as metrics. Some kinds of valuation—love, respect, wonder, worship—embody no metrics at all as I understand that term.

By "doing violence to our considered judgments," I mean disrupting our reflective assessments of how certain relationships and events should be understood, evaluated, and experienced. To see dating, for example, as "participation in the marriage market" may be to characterize the relevant behavior in a way that is inconsistent with prevailing judgments about what is actually happening. It would also be to alter, for the worse, our conceptions about what dating entails. It follows that I mean to suggest—though I cannot justify the claims here—that incommensurability, thus understood, is an essential part of our social experience and also constitutive of an appropriately discerning and differentiated and (to that extent) good life.

Incommensurability in this relatively thin or weak sense—far thinner and weaker than that found, for example, in the work of Joseph Raz, discussed below—is a familiar phenomenon. It may be, for example, that some people do not believe that any unitary metric can capture their diverse valuations of music, friendship, and work. It may even be that different forms of music, or different kinds of work and friendship, cannot be made commensurable in this way. The point is emphatically not that choices are not made among these things, nor is it that choices of this kind are not based on reasons. Certainly we can have comparability (and hence reason-guided choice) without commensurability. The point is only that it is experientially false to describe the diverse goods as if they were valued along a single metric. Perhaps we could imagine a life or a world in which valuation along such a metric would not be experientially false. But a life or world of that kind would be the stuff of science fiction. An argument on its behalf would call for a large-scale revision of current experience.

Notably, this understanding of incommensurability does not deny the possibility of ordinal rankings, and it need not be inconsistent with anything in decision theory. Many uses of neoclassical economics are fully compatible with incommensurability, thus defined. On the other hand, some utilitarians (operating from the framework set by Sidgwick) do appear to insist on a single metric, and some important aspects of economic analysis of law, including cost-benefit analysis and the Coase theorem, are endangered even by this weak understanding of incommensurability. Even if modern economists rarely deny incommensurability as I have understood it here, an insistence on the unavailability of a single metric will have some important consequences.

B. *Incommensurability, Incomparability, Reasons for Choice*

As I understand the notion here, incommensurability does not entail incomparability.[4] This understanding is different from that offered by many others. In an especially influential discussion, for example, Joseph Raz identifies the two ideas.[5] On his view, two options *A* and *B* are incommensurable when *A* is not better than *B,* not worse than *B,* and not equal in value to *B. A* and *B* thus are incomparable, for there is no quality in virtue of which they may be compared. Something of this sort might be said about the choice whether to listen to Mozart or to read Dickens, or to go swimming or to continue eating, or to visit England or ride horses in Kentucky. Raz thinks that "in the choice between incommensurate options reason is unable to provide any guidance," and that cases of incommensurability "mark the inability of reason to guide our choice."[6]

Some of this seems convincing. Sometimes there is no point to ranking the goods or options at stake, and in such cases claims of comparability are silly; this is true, for example, with the question whether, in terms of overall intrinsic worth, going to England is better than riding horses, or swimming is better than eating. But sometimes people are put in situations of choice, and reasons generally do help in the decision among incommensurable options or goods. If this is true, options may be incommensurable, in the sense that they cannot be aligned along a single metric, or assessed along a single, low-level dimension, without being incomparable, in the sense that we cannot choose among them for good reasons.[7] Indeed, choices among incommensurable options are the stuff not merely of law but of everyday life. Raz argues that such choices tend to turn not on reason, but on whims or on "what we feel like doing."[8] I do not deny that this is sometimes the case, but I think that it is rare.

Sometimes the grounds for choice are extrinsic; they count as reasons but do not depend on any judgment of overall intrinsic worth. I might decide to go swimming rather than have lunch, not because one is intrinsically better, but because I need to exercise, or because I have gained weight, or because I am not very hungry, or because the people I like best are at the pool. Judgments of this sort are based on reasons. The same is true in law and policy. A society may fund recreational activities, rather than subsidize more production of potatoes, because people in the relevant community are now working too hard and vacationing too little, and because they have more than enough potatoes.

Sometimes choices among incommensurable options are based on expressive considerations, that is, considerations not of overall intrinsic worth but of appropriate ways of valuing social goods and bads.[9] Suppose that you are deciding whether to stay home to care for a quite sick child, or instead to hire a nurse and to go to work, where important business must be transacted, involving, let us say, the completion of a merger that would benefit your client and the economy as a whole. To think through this problem, one needs to know a lot of details. But it would be reasonable to think that your relationship to your child, and your love as a parent, require you to stay at home. When your child is very sick, to go to work for certain job-related reasons might well be inconsistent with the way that you feel about your child. There is a public analogue here too. The protection of endangered species, or the allocation of medical care to ailing children, might well be based on judgments of duty that grow out of expressive considerations, pointing to the way that certain options are valued, and ruling off-limits certain grounds for compromising the relevant duty. To say this is to say much too little. But I hope that it is enough to suggest the possibility of reasons for choosing among goods that are incommensurable in Raz's sense.

Even if extrinsic reasons are not decisive, and even if expressive considerations leave much doubt, sometimes judgments can be made, on the basis of reasons, about overall intrinsic worth even in the face of incommensurability. Suppose that I am deciding whether to listen to Mozart or instead to read something by the horror novelist Stephen King. There is no metric along which to rank Mozart and Stephen King, but in terms of aesthetic value, Mozart ranks higher in overall worth, for reasons that involve what is appropriately valued in art, including appeal to human capacities, imagination, freshness, capacity to expand rather than to contract one's field of vision, and so forth. It would be obtuse to say that we have a metric on which Mozart scores higher than King, but we do have reasons by which to assess them. The same may also be true in legal disputes, as, for example, when the preservation of many large beaches would "cost" a specified number of jobs.

This raises an obvious question: Does the fact of choice show that options are commensurable after all? I do not think that it does. We should not identify the actuality of choice with the claim of commensurability. It is odd and unnecessary to say that a unitary metric necessarily "lies behind" or "justifies" all (rational or irrational) choices.[10] We choose whether to take an exciting job in a new city when the move would unsettle our family; we decide hard tort cases; we choose between work and leisure; we decide how much to spend to promote worker safety or energy conservation. These choices are based on reasons and evaluated by reference to them, whether intrinsic or extrinsic. Commensurability is not required for choice.

C. Incommensurability, Freedom, Comparison

Some of the most intriguing instances of incommensurability arise when the relevant kind of valuation not only prevents use of a single metric, but also excludes certain reasons for action altogether.[11] Someone may, for example, value loyalty to a spouse in a way that absolutely precludes the acceptance of favors, or cash, as a reason for infidelity. This is a pervasive aspect of practical reason in law, where the governing rule often rules certain reasons out of bounds.

It might be tempting to think that incommensurability works mostly as a barrier to certain forms of freedom—to the use of a single metric, to certain kinds of exchange, to certain reasons for action. But it is equally plausible to see incommensurability as constitutive of some forms of freedom, and these forms are not easily dispensable. The presence of incommensurability helps make possible certain relationships, attachments, and attitudes that otherwise would be unavailable.[12] If friendship and cash were commensurable, or if a park and $100,000 were valued along a single metric, we could not have certain attitudes toward friendship and toward parks. Indeed, friendship and parks could not be what they now are.

It might also be tempting to suggest that in many cases, we do not have any special problem of incommensurability, but instead a relationship in which some goods are just a lot better than others. Thus Donald Regan says that with respect to social disapproval of the purchase of children, "It is closer to the truth to say that we regard the value of parenthood as incomparably greater than the value of money, than to say that we regard these values as incommensurable."[13] I think that Regan's challenge is unsuccessful, and that often people who refuse trades do so not because of a sharp quantitative difference in value, but because to consider the trade is to do violence to the way that they value the good (a child, a vote, a body part) in question. This point also provides reason to question Ruth Chang's subtle discussion suggesting that some apparent incommensurabilities might be better described as "emphatic comparabilities," as in a refusal to trade based on the judgment that the good one has is emphatically better than the good that is offered.[14] When one refuses to trade $1 million for $75, there is a problem of emphatic comparability; something different is at work when one refuses to trade a child or a friendship for cash.

It might also be tempting to think that insistence on different metrics is an idle linguistic exercise, unconnected to anything of real importance. Perhaps people who disagree about kinds of valuation, and about commensurability, are just disagreeing about how to talk. But redescriptions of human endeavors that assume or insist on commensurability are important. They can also have important constitutive dimensions; that is, they may help transform how (not necessarily how much) various events and relationships are valued and even experienced. Consider some familiar economic descriptions of human endeavors. If someone really thought about dating and romance as participation in a "marriage market," he would be a strange creature indeed (and unlikely, perhaps, to fare well in the relevant practice). If a parent thought that through the provision of love and education, he was simply "investing" in his children, he would have a barely recognizable understanding of the parental role. It is difficult even to imagine the self-conception entailed by this view if it was authentic.

None of this proves that we cannot make sense of our experience without believing in incommensurability as I have understood it here. But perhaps we have enough background with which to begin the project of seeing how the concept bears on law.

III. Law

A. Preliminaries

We cannot say that because people value different events in different ways, it follows that law should have a particular content. Nor can we draw lessons for law from the fact that human values cannot be aligned along a single metric. This is so for three reasons.

First, it is necessary to explain which kinds of valuation are appropriate in order to make recommendations for law. Second, a judgment about the right kind of valuation—even if it can be reached and persuasively defended—need not entail a particular conclusion for law. For example, it might be shown that prostitution entails an improper valuation of human sexuality, but this does not necessarily mean that prostitution should be outlawed. We might think that people do not reflect the right evaluative attitude toward cows if they eat them, without thinking that law should forbid people from eating cows. Third, the legal system has crude remedial tools. Usually it must work with monetary remedies. In view of this limitation, the fact that these remedies are not commensurable with some harms may be at most an interesting theoretical point. What can be said about personal valuations cannot be said about legal institutions. It may follow that often the legal system must put problems of incommensurability to one side, leaving those problems for ethics.

Despite these disclaimers, the existence of incommensurable goods and diverse kinds of valuation does help illuminate many disputes about the substance of law, legal institutions, and legal reasoning. I offer a number of examples here, going very briskly over a wide range of otherwise diverse areas. My goal is emphatically not to resolve these debates. To do this I would have to say a great deal more than I will be able to do here. I intend only to suggest that an understanding of questions of commensurability and appropriate kinds of valuation helps explain what participants in these debates are arguing about.

B. *The Expressive Function of Law*

A unifying theme for the discussion is the expressive function of law.[15] When evaluating a legal norm, we might ask whether the norm expresses an appropriate valuation of an event, person, group, or practice. The point matters for two reasons. The first and more important is, broadly speaking, based on a prediction about the facts: An incorrect valuation by law may influence social norms and experiences and push them in the wrong direction. If the law wrongly treats something as a commodity, for example, the social valuation may be adversely affected. It is appropriate to criticize the law on this ground. Consider debates over capital punishment, abortion, and homosexuality.

This objection is based on a controversial empirical judgment to the effect that the kinds of valuation that are reflected in laws will have effects on social valuations in general. Sometimes this is probably right, but sometimes it is not. Society is filled, for example, with market exchange of goods (like pets and babysitting) that are valued for reasons other than use. The question therefore remains whether the claimed effect on social norms will occur. It is fully plausible, for example, to say that although a law that permits prostitution reflects an inappropriate valuation of sexuality, the effect of the law on social norms is an implausible basis for objection.

But there is a second ground for endorsing the expressive function of law, and this ground is not about social effects in the same sense. The ground is connected with the individual interest in integrity. Following the suggestive discussion by Bernard Williams, we might say that personal behavior is not concerned solely with states of affairs, and that if it were, we would have a hard time in making sense of important aspects of our lives.[16] There are issues as well involving personal integrity, commitment, and the narrative continuity of a life. In Williams's example, someone might refuse to kill an innocent person at the request of a terrorist, even if the consequence of the refusal is that many more people will be killed. Our responses to this case are not adequately captured in purely consequentialist terms.

There may be an analogue at the social and legal level. A society might identify the kind of valuation to which it is committed and insist on that kind, even if the consequences of the insistence are obscure or unknown. A society might (for example) insist on an antidiscrimination law for expressive reasons even if it is unclear whether the law actually helps members of minority groups. A society might protect endangered species partly because it believes that the protection makes best sense of its self-understanding, by expressing an appropriate valuation of what it means for one species to eliminate another.

I do not claim that this point is decisive or that it cannot be countered by a demonstration of (more conventional) bad consequences. But I do suggest that the expressive function of law is an actual and proper part of public debate. Without understanding the expressive function of law, we will have a hard time getting an adequate handle on public views with respect to (for example) civil rights, prostitution, the environment, endangered species, capital punishment, abortion, and much more.

C. Examples

In this section, I discuss a number of areas of law in which kinds of valuation are at stake. In some of these areas, issues of commensurability are also prominent. I emphasize that the brisk and wide-ranging discussion is intended to be exploratory and hardly definitive of the complex matters at stake.

1. Social Differentiation.   In carrying out its expressive function, the law of a liberal society encourages a high degree of social differentiation. It includes the political sphere; the family; markets; intermediate organizations, especially religious organizations; and much more. Michael Walzer's influential book offers an instructive discussion of these different "spheres."[17] It would be especially valuable to be able to understand the social function or purpose of this kind of differentiation. Why might it be a good thing to carve life up in this way? What is the point?

The liberal commitment to social differentiation is best understood as making spaces for different kinds of valuation. Without indulging naive conceptions of the public-private distinction, we can see the family as the characteristic liberal sphere for the expression of love. At its best, politics embodies the forms of respect entailed by processes of reason giving. In religious organizations, the appropriate kind of valuation is usually one of worship and reverence. The market is typically the sphere for use. Things that are bought and sold on markets are typically valued in the way associated with pure commodities—although it is important and also true that many things sold on markets (music, vacations in beautiful places, art, child care) are intrinsic goods and valued for multiple reasons.

Law plays a critical and much-overlooked role in the construction and maintenance of these various spheres, which are anything but natural. We know far too little to say that in the state of nature, there is any such division (though there may well be antecedents). Markets are, of course, a function of the law of property, contract, and tort, without which voluntary agreements would not be possible. It is law that decides what can be traded on markets and how trades can occur. Undoubtedly families of various sorts would arise in the state of nature, but the particular families we have are emphatically a function of law. The law helps to create an independent familial sphere; it also says who may be entitled to its protections and disabilities.

To be sure, institutional practice often deviates from institutional aspiration. Politics is often a realm for use; it has important market-like features. The family is not simply a place for the expression of love. Women and children have often been used, and without their consent. In light of these deviations from social aspirations—aspirations that can be defended with reasons—it is important to conceive of prevailing institutions in quite different ways. Indeed, familiar social criticism consists of a claim that an existing sphere of social differentiation embodies an inadequate kind of valuation. Thus, for example, the family has often been a place for hierarchy and deference, and here it is suggested that processes of mutual respect and reason giving should displace injustice.[18] Many claims for social reform are really arguments for revision of the kinds of valuation prevailing in different social institutions.

2. The Religion Clauses, Civic Equality, and Political Liberalism. A major goal of a liberal republic is to exclude certain kinds of valuation from public life on the ground that they are too sectarian. Such a society thus bans particular "inputs" into politics. It does so because a liberal society is committed to ensuring that some kinds of valuation do not play a public role, either because they express a kind of valuation that is suited only to private life or because they deny the essential premise of political equality. Certain constitutional puzzles tend to dissolve in this light.

Political liberalism is constituted in part by the idea that certain kinds of valuation are too contentious to be a legitimate part of politics. Under the American Constitution, the establishment clause is the key example of the ban on certain kinds of valuation. For example, a law making Easter a national holiday may not be supported on the ground that it reflects the sanctity of Jesus Christ, even if that is the kind of valuation held by the majority. Through this route, we can begin to understand much of the operation of the establishment clause.

An understanding of the expressive function of law may also make sense of the apparent anomaly that a law may be valid if produced by a neutral justification but invalid, even if it is the same law, when produced by a discriminatory justification. A literacy test is an example. Such a test may not be motivated by racial animus, but it is acceptable if supported, in fact, by neutral justifications.

The reason for the asymmetry is that by hypothesis, the first law reflects an appropriate kind of valuation, whereas the second does not. This simple idea underlies the prevailing conception of equality under the Fourteenth Amendment, a conception that is based on a ban on certain kinds of valuation. In the same vein, Holmes famously wrote that "even a dog knows the difference between being tripped over and being kicked."[19]

3. Broadcasting and Free Speech. Many of the sharpest debates in the theory of free speech raise the question whether government may legitimately regulate the broadcasting media in the interest of promoting democratic goals. Issues of appropriate kinds of valuation underlie these debates. Of special importance is the question whether speech should be treated as an ordinary commodity and thus be valued in the same way as other commodities. The claim that it should be so treated often works as a claim of commensurability. On this view, dollars, audience pleasure, and speech ought all to be placed on the same metric, and market outcomes, reflecting that placement, deserve respect.

In the United States, many of the recent debates have been spurred by substantial government deregulation of the airwaves. Some people think that in terms of actual programming, this phenomenon has promoted a kind of accelerating race to the bottom in terms of the quality and quantity of attention required, rather than furthering the democratic goals of attention to public issues and diversity of view. The result has been a sharp split between the democratic conception of free speech and the belief in satisfying consumption choices. If we satisfy consumer desires, we may not promote democratic goals.

Vigorous challenges to deregulated markets in expression are grounded in the idea that speech ought not to be valued in the same way or for the same purposes as ordinary consumer products. From this claim it may follow that a system of free markets is not necessarily compatible with a well-functioning system of free expression. Free speech, in short, is not a (simple) commodity. If the speech market promotes democratic goals, it is because the forces of supply and demand work out that way, rather than a conceptual truth. And it may well turn out that market forces disserve democratic ideals, by deterring substantial coverage of issues and sufficient diversity of view. If this is so, democratic correctives may promote the purposes of the free speech guarantee.

Those who think of speech as a commodity, to be valued in the same way as other things that people desire, are often unable to understand the complaints of people who urge a democratic conception. Thus the former chairman of the U.S. Federal Communications Commission, Mark Fowler, said that "television is jut another appliance . . . It's a toaster with pictures."[20] This is a conspicuous statement of the market conception of free speech. It is jarring because it reveals an unusually stark view of the appropriate kind of valuation of what is produced by the broadcast media.

4. Environmental Protection.   The examples thus far involve the function of law in maintaining appropriate valuation of diverse social goods. Issues of commensurability—of the availability of a unitary metric for making social assessments—also lie in the background, though their application is more complex. In the law of environmental protection, the problem of commensurability often emerges as the prime area of contestation. Many theories of government regulation assess environmental issues by reference to people's "preferences" for environmental quality viewed abstractly, through a unitary scale, along the same metric—that of private willingness to pay. But there are some apparent anomalies in individual behavior here. In particular, ordinary people appear to resist the use of a unitary scale. Consider a few examples:

a. Some people feel insulted when asked how much they would accept for a specified level of environmental deterioration, treating the question as outrageous or a form of bribery, rather as if they had been asked to sell a child or a part of their body. "Studies using WTA (willingness to accept) questions have consistently received a large number of protest answers, such as 'I refuse to sell' or 'I want an extremely large or infinite amount of compensation for agreeing to this,' and have frequently experienced protest rates of 50 percent or more."[21]

b. Some people say that environmental goods have infinite value or that the effort to achieve a clean environment should not be "traded off" against other important values. In opinion polls, people sometimes say that we should achieve a clean environment "regardless of cost."

c. Some apparently popular statutes reflect a kind of environmental absolutism. The controversial Endangered Species Act forbids balancing except in the rarest of circumstances.

d. There are extraordinary disparities in federal expenditures per life saved. In some environmental programs, risks are prevented at enormous cost; the government is willing to spend relatively little to stop other risks. All current efforts to produce uniformity in expenditures have failed.

Phenomena of these sorts reflect irrationality, confusion, interest-group power, or sheer chance. But it would be useful to explore whether there might not be some other kind of explanation. When people are thinking in these various ways, exactly what are they doing?

Some important features of people's valuation of environmental goods come from an insistence that diverse social goods should not be assessed according to the same metric. With this hypothesis, apparent anomalies dissolve or become more readily explicable. Some people, for example, insistently rebel against the idea that we should see all of the following environmentally related consequences as "costs": unemployment, higher prices, greater poverty, dirtier air, more cancer, respiratory problems, the loss of species. If we understand all these things as "costs," to be assessed by the same metric, we will disable ourselves from making important qualitative distinctions.

Through this route, we might help come to terms with phenomena a through d above. For example, the risk charts might at least in part reflect qualitative distinctions among different sorts of hazards. People might not be interested only in cost per life saved, but also in whether the risk was voluntarily assumed, whether the exposing entity knows the facts, whether the underlying activity produces valuable goods, whether the hazard is common, whether the exposure is essential, whether the risk is encountered occupationally or elsewhere, whether the people subjected to risk were able to participate in relevant decisions. They might also be interested in the nature of the risk, thinking, for example, that certain deaths are worse than others. Different kinds of valuation will operate in different settings. Uniformity in expenditures per life saved would be obtuse.

Similarly, the protest answers to certain questions might reflect not sentimentality or simple confusion but a judgment that people value some part of the environment *in a way that forecloses acceptance of even high amounts of money in return for degradation.* Here too there is an analogue to the extreme cases of incommensurability, discussed above, in which people value a certain relationship or good through a kind that disqualifies certain conventional reasons for action, especially acceptance of money as a basis for compromising or eliminating it.

Some of the answers may also have a good deal to do with diverse kinds of valuation. In particular, people may believe that a species or a pristine area has intrinsic rather than instrumental value. When this is so, they do not want to assume the kind of responsibility that is entailed by allowing its elimination for cash.[22] If something of this kind is right, it may be that people think that the loss through one's deliberate action of a pristine area or an endangered species is incommensurably bad, and that this thought should be expressed through regulatory proscriptions. The well-known disparity between willingness to pay and willingness to accept—found by Tversky, Kahneman, Thaler, and others—may well be attributable in part to ideas of this kind, finding different expressive judgments in the two contexts, and distinguishing between the moral status of those judgments. To say the least, this view raises many complexities. It is by no means clear that the relevant judgments about responsibility can be defended. All I mean to suggest is that it is a common idea, and an intelligible one.

5. Cost-Benefit Analysis.   One of the most sharply disputed issues in law and policy involves the role of cost-benefit analysis (CBA). In the most dramatic victory for CBA, the Reagan administration adopted two important executive orders calling for the application of CBA to all regulatory decisions. President Clinton endorsed this approach too, at least in significant part.

There is much to be said in favor of CBA. In the United States, federal regulation is notoriously and pervasively chaotic and irrational. Who could object to the idea that we should systematize costs and benefits and compare them? The question seems especially powerful when it is combined with the plausible claim that the opponents of CBA are confused about their real objection. In fact, it is sometimes said, their real complaint is that some of the relevant variables have not been highly valued. Would it not be a sufficient response to say, to the critics of this form of analysis, that perhaps we should place a higher premium on (for example) human health or the environment, and then proceed with CBA?

At least for some purposes, I do not think that this would be a sufficient response. The real problem with conventional CBA is that it is obtuse. It is obtuse because it tries to measure diverse social goods along the same metric. Suppose, for example, that we are told that the cost of a certain occupational safety regulation is $1 million and that the benefit is $1.2 million. To make a sensible evaluation, we need to know a great deal more. To what do these numbers refer? Do they include greater unemployment, higher inflation, and the scaled-back production of important goods? Do they mean more poverty? At least in principle, it would be much better to have a highly disaggregated system for assessing the qualitatively different effects of regulatory impositions. People should be allowed to see those diverse effects for themselves and to make judgments based on an understanding of the qualitative differences. If all of the relevant goods are aligned along a single metric, they become less visible, or perhaps invisible.

6. Specific Performance and Its Consequences for Private Law Remedies.   A pervasive issue in the law of contract is whether courts should award a damages remedy or instead insist on specific performance. It is typically said that specific performance will be awarded when damages are "inadequate." But if damages seem inadequate, then we might think that they have been set too low and that the right solution is to require the seller to pay more. Surely there is some level at which the court will set the proper amount. To this, the conventional answer is that damages remedies are inadequate when the good at issue is unique. But the notion of uniqueness is a new puzzle. All goods have substitutes of some sort; this is part of the usual understanding of choice amid scarcity.

In explaining the notion of uniqueness, we might note that a damages remedy could be inaccurate for certain goods. Subjective value is peculiarly hard to ascertain in some cases, and there are high search costs for such goods—costs that are also difficult to determine. The existence of a specific performance remedy can be seen as a natural product of information costs faced by the legal system in ascertaining the appropriate damages remedy.

There is undoubtedly a good deal of truth to this. But I suggest that another factor is at work. Specific performance might be awarded because the good in question is not commensurable with cash. This is not to say that it is more valuable than cash. Indeed, it is less valuable, often, than a great deal of cash. The claim is instead that the good is valued in a way that is inconsistent with cash valuation. *What the plaintiff wants, and what she is entitled to get, is a good that she values in the way that she values the object for which she has contracted.* A good that she values in some sense equally—perhaps in terms of "aggregate" valuation—is not a perfect substitute.

If this point is correct, it suggests the need to supplement Calabresi and Melamed's well-known discussion of the choice between liability and property rules.[23] In their terminology, a right is protected by a liability rule if it can be taken upon a payment of compensation. A right is protected by a property rule if it can be taken only through voluntary exchange, and if compensation is therefore an inadequate justification for the taking. Calabresi and Melamed's important discussion rightly emphasizes the relevance of transactions costs, including information costs, to the choice between the two. But this is only part of the picture. It is also the case that property rules will tend to be used in cases in which the relevant right or good is valued in a different way from money. In such cases, courts are reluctant to use liability rules, not because the relevant amount will be set too low, but because it will reflect the wrong kind of valuation of the good at issue. The litigant is entitled to the good and its existing kind of valuation, rather than to a substitute valued in a different way, even if in some sense "equally."

The same ideas underlie an important debate in environmental law, having to do with the appropriate measure of damages for injury to natural resources. There may be a large difference between "restoration cost" for, say, a portion of the Alaska seashore, and "use value," understood as aggregated private willingness to pay for the area in question. Through an important regulation, the Department of the Interior indicated its preference for use value if it was lower than restoration cost. The court of appeals invalidated the regulation.[24] The decision stemmed from an understanding that those who injure natural resources should be required to restore the status quo ante, not because that is more valuable, but because people are entitled to have a good that they value in the way that they value natural resources, rather than the so-called cash equivalent.

7. Blocked Exchanges. Even in a system that respects freedom of contract, there are many possible reasons to block exchanges. A party may lack relevant information; there may be a collective action problem; third parties may be affected; a party may be myopic. But perhaps a pervasive reason is that an exchange ensures that the relevant good will be valued in the wrong way. A society may block exchanges because it wants to fortify existing norms against exchanging certain goods or because it wants to "make a statement" about appropriate valuation.

Judge Posner's argument on behalf of a form of "baby selling" does not quite address this concern; it ignores the expressive function of law.[25] Judge Posner contends that a market for babies would serve most of the relevant policies better than does the current system. In some ways his argument is persuasive. Certainly the desire of infertile couples for children would be better satisfied through a market system. But part of the objection to free markets in babies is expressive in character. The objection is that a system of purchase and sale would value children in the wrong way, possibly with corrosive effects on existing norms. This system would see human beings as commodities, itself, a wrong, and a practice with imaginable harmful consequences for social valuation in general. This is at most a summary of a complex argument, based partly on uncertain empirical judgments, and it is hardly by itself decisive. But we cannot get an adequate grasp of the problem without seeing the point, which arises in debates over prostitution, surrogacy, and pornography. Barriers to the purchase and sale of voting rights, and to waivers of certain legal safeguards, also reflect an understanding of this kind.

8. Legal Reasoning. A belief in diverse kinds of valuation, and in incommensurability, has consequences for current debates about the actual and appropriate nature of legal reasoning. If it can be shown that a well-functioning system of law is alert to these ideas, theories of legal reasoning may change accordingly.

Consider, for example, economic analysis of law. It is clear that this form of analysis has produced enormous gains in the positive and normative study of law. The approach has, of course, been criticized on many grounds, most familiarly that it is insufficiently attuned to distributive arguments. But I think that some questions about economic analysis stem from something quite different and less noticed. In its normative form, economic analysis depends on too thin, flat, and sectarian a conception of value, captured in the notion that legal rules should be designed so as to maximize wealth. The problem with this idea is that the word "wealth" elides qualitative distinctions among the different goods typically at stake in legal disputes. Instead of maximizing wealth, it is necessary to have a highly disaggregated picture of the consequences of legal rules, a picture that enables the judge to see the various goods at stake, and the qualitative differences among them.

If this is correct, we might begin to mount a defense of a form of thinking that has fallen into ill repute: analogical reasoning. A special advantage of analogical reasoning over economic analysis is that the former, unlike the latter, need not insist that plural and diverse social goods should be assessed according to the same metric. The analogical thinker is alert to the manifold dimensions of social situations and to the many relevant similarities and differences. Unequipped with (or unburdened by) a unitary theory of the good or the right, she is in a position to see clearly and for herself the diverse and plural goods that are involved and to make choices among them. In the face of value pluralism, and in a world without metrics by which to make decisions, analogical reasoning is appropriately attuned to qualitative differences among social goods.

There is a related point. Sometimes courts engaged in analogical thinking can create an *incompletely theorized agreement* on particular legal outcomes.[26] Sometimes the incompletely theorized agreement can come from people who are without large-scale theories of the good or the right, or who begin from very different views on those topics. People may know that political speech cannot be regulated without a clear and present danger, without knowing whether they are Kantians or utilitarians, and without knowing what theory lies behind the protection of freedom of speech. In this way, common law adjudication, ungoverned by anything like a unitary general theory, can avoid the charge of sectarianism that is properly leveled at legal judgments that embody a general theory that is not widely shared.[27]

IV. Conclusion

The existence of diverse kinds of valuation, and of incommensurable goods, has not yet played a major role in legal theory. But these issues underlie a surprisingly wide range of legal disputes. An especially large task for legal theory involves an adequate description of how choices are and should be made among incommensurable goods and an adequate account of appropriate kinds of valuation. I have not undertaken that task here; a close inspection of particular contexts would be indispensable to this endeavor. But I conclude with two suggestions. An insistence on diverse kinds of valuation is one of the most important conclusions emerging from the study of Anglo-American legal practice, and an appreciation of those diverse kinds will yield major gains to those seeking to understand and evaluate both public and private law.

Notes

1. Introduction

I am grateful to many people for discussion on the topics of this Introduction. They include Rogers Albritton, Richard Craswell, Barbara Herman, Frances Kamm, David Kaplan, Herbert Morris, Martha Nussbaum, Seana Shiffrin, and Cass Sunstein. I owe a special debt to Kit Fine and Derek Parfit, whose penetrating criticisms and helpful suggestions have made the Introduction better than it was with respect to every relevant covering value. Many of the points made here are discussed in greater detail in forthcoming work.

1. This is not an example of incommensurability by modern lights; unlike the Greeks who had not recognized irrational numbers as such, we can represent the ratios in terms of the reals. There is some disagreement among scholars as to when and with what mathematical object incommensurability was first discovered. There is no doubt, however, that the discovery was of profound importance to the Pythagoreans because, as one commentator put it, "[the discovery] destroyed with one stroke the belief that everything could be expressed in integers, on which the whole Pythagorean philosophy up to then had been based." Kurt von Fritz, "The Discovery of Incommensurability by Hippasus of Metapontum," in David Furley and R. E. Allen, eds., *Studies in Presocratic Philosophy* (London: Routledge & Kegan Paul, 1970), 1:407. Legend has it that Hippasus of Metapontum, thought by many to have discovered the existence of incommensurables, was drowned at sea by the gods for making public his discovery. See also Thomas Heath, *A History of Greek Mathematics* (Oxford: Clarendon Press, 1921), 1:65, 154–157.

2. Joseph Raz, *The Morality of Freedom,* (Oxford: Clarendon Press, 1986). ch. 13. Compare his "Incommensurability and Agency" (this volume) especially n. 1 and accompanying text.

3. See, e.g., H. L. A. Hart, *The Concept of Law* (Oxford: Clarendon Press, 1961), p. 167: "When a choice has been made between such competing alternatives it may be defended as proper on the ground that it was for the 'public good' or the 'common good'. It is not clear what these phrases mean, since there seems to be no scale by which contributions of the various alternatives to the common good can be measured and the greater identified." For a good summary of the line of reasoning leading to this conclusion (which he does not endorse), see Bernard Williams, "Conflicts of Values," in his *Moral Luck* (Cambridge: Cambridge University Press, 1981), pp. 76–77.

4. I say 'precisely' measured because there are those who think that cardinality can be imprecise. See Parfit, Griffin, and Laird as cited in n. 10. Commensurability assumes that cardinality is precise. My characterization of cardinality and ordinality is intended to be intuitive. For a technical account of the notions in accessible terms, see John Broome, *Weighing Goods* (Oxford: Blackwell, 1991), pp. 70–75.

5. Cass Sunstein, "Incommensurability and Valuation in Law," *Michigan Law Review* 79 (1994): 779–861. See also Elizabeth Anderson, *Value in Ethics and Economics* (Cambridge: Harvard University Press, 1993); and Anderson and Richard H. Pildes, "Slinging Arrows at Democracy: Social Choice Theory, Value Pluralism, and Democratic Politics," *Columbia Law Review* 90 (1990): 2121–2214. Anderson and Pildes are concerned with incomparability, not incommensurability, but for reasons that will become clear in my discussion of Anderson in part III, this difference may not be significant.

6. John Finnis, *Natural Law and Natural Rights* (Oxford: Clarendon Press, 1980), ch. 5, sec. 6.

7. Ibid.; David Wiggins, "Deliberation and Practical Reason," *Proceedings of the Aristotelian Society* 76 (1975–1976): 29–51, reprinted in Amelie Rorty, ed., *Essays on Aristotle's Ethics* (Berkeley: University of California Press, 1980), pp. 221–240, and in his *Needs, Values, Truth* (Oxford: Blackwell, 1987), pp. 215–238; and Martha Nussbaum, *The Fragility of Goodness* (Cambridge: Cambridge University Press, 1986), pp. 106–121.

8. David Wiggins, "Weakness of Will, Commensurability, and the Objects of Deliberation and Desire," *Proceedings of the Aristotelian Society* 79 (1978–1979): 251–277, reprinted in Rorty, ed., *Essays on Aristotle's Ethics*, pp. 241–266, and in his *Needs, Values, Truth*, pp. 239–267. See also Nussbaum, *The Fragility of Goodness*, pp. 113–117. Compare Michael Stocker, *Plural and Conflicting Values* (Oxford: Oxford University Press, 1990), ch. 7.

9. See, e.g., Stocker, *Plural and Conflicting Values*.

10. Derek Parfit, *Reasons and Persons* (Oxford: Oxford University Press, 1986), p. 431, and *Practical Realism*, forthcoming; James Griffin, *Well-Being: Its Meaning and Measurement* (Oxford: Oxford University Press, 1986), pp. 81, 96–98, 104; and Thomas Hurka, *Perfectionism* (Oxford: Oxford University Press, 1993), p. 87. See also John Laird, *An Enquiry into Moral Notions* (London: George Allen & Unwin, 1935), ch. 16.

11. The indeterminacy could arise from the 'vagueness' of the values themselves. See Griffin, *Well-Being*, p. 81.

12. This notion of value is broader than usual; 'fulfillment of one's obligation', for example, is not a value in the narrow sense, and 'cruelty' is sometimes thought a *disvalue*, but insofar as we can evaluatively compare things with respect to fulfillment of one's obligations or cruelty, these are values on my definition. I employ this broad notion of value because the arguments I make about comparability apply to all evaluative comparisons, and not just to those with respect to 'values' as that term is usually, more narrowly, understood.

13. Whether the covering value requirement implies that there is no such thing as *good-*

ness—as opposed to betterness—simpliciter is a question I leave unexplored. For interesting discussion on this point, see Judith Jarvis Thomson, "Evaluatives and Directives" in Gilbert Harman and Judith Jarvis Thomson, *Moral Relativism and Moral Objectivity* (Oxford: Blackwell, 1996), pp. 128–129. Thomson thinks that the fact that things can only be good-in-a-way, as opposed to good simpliciter, "results in" the fact that all things can only be better-in-a-way. The five ways in which something can be better than something else (being useful, skillful, enjoyable, beneficial, or morally good) she mentions might provide useful classes into which covering values can be grouped.

14. I am grateful to Anderson for clarifying this point. See her "Practical Reason and Incommensurable Goods" (this volume, n. 14). As editor of this volume, I am shamelessly exploiting my opportunity to have the last word on this matter—at least between these covers. Her claim is more fully discussed in the final part.

15. A few explanatory notes here. First, my concern is with what justifies choice, not with how justification is to be reached, though the two might be linked in obvious ways. Second, the justification of a choice is *conclusive,* that is, not one that can be overruled or outweighed. Third, it is *specific,* that is, relevant to the particularities of a given choice situation and not directed at what is true in all situations (though, as we will see, general claims about justification might emerge from consideration of particular cases). Finally, my discussion should not be taken to restrict attention to actions, objects, events, or states of affair. Anything which can be chosen—certain feelings, attitudes, intentions, for example—can be 'alternatives' for choice.

16. For a rather different view of norms of rationality that may justify choice among incomparables, see Adam Morton's five 'dilemma management strategies', in ch. 2 of his *Disasters and Dilemmas* (Oxford: Blackwell, 1991).

17. See also James Griffin, *Value Judgment: Improving Ethical Beliefs* (Oxford: Clarendon Press, 1996).

18. Specificationist approaches, like Wiggins', are often presented as accounts of the process of rational deliberation rather than accounts of practical justification. For a recent development of the view, see Henry Richardson, *Practical Reasoning About Final Ends* (Cambridge: Cambridge University Press, 1994). See also Wiggins, "Deliberation and Practical Reason", and Aurel Kolnai, *Ethics, Value and Reality* (Indianapolis: Hackett, 1978).

19. See also Elijah Millgram, *Practical Induction* (Cambridge: Harvard University Press, 1997).

20. Note that Raz's quasi-existentialist view does not distinguish between proper deliberation in the case where alternatives are incomparable from that in the case where they are equally good. For a related view, see Isaac Levi, *Hard Choices: Decision Making Under Unresolved Conflict* (Cambridge: Cambridge University Press, 1986), who thinks that choice can be justified if the chosen alternative is "admissible." John Finnis holds a view similar to Raz's about justification in the face of incommensurables: reasons determine eligibility and leave room for "feelings" in individual choice and "fair procedures" in collective choice to guide choice among incommen-

surable, eligible options. See John Finnis, "Commensuration and Public Reason" (this volume).

21. Some of the views considered above may have the resources to deal with this problem. For example, Millgram's view ties justification to past choices and thus may be able to avoid the merit-pump problem. Other views need to show how the problem is to be avoided. One possible response can be extracted from discussion of a closely related problem by Edward McClennen, *Rationality and Dynamic Choice* (Cambridge: Cambridge University Press, 1990), especially ch. 2, 10, and by Warren Quinn, "The Puzzle of the Self-Torturer," *Philosophical Studies* 59 (1990): 79–90, reprinted in Quinn, *Morality and Action* (Cambridge: Cambridge University Press, 1993), pp. 198–209.

22. Thomas Nagel, *The Possibility of Altruism* (Princeton: Princeton University Press, 1970), ch. 5.

23. Compare Henry Richardson's defense of specificationism against the claim that specificationist reasons are ultimately comparisons with respect to some supreme criterion—whether it be practical coherence, the unity of agency, or whatnot. Richardson rightly points out that this claim misunderstands specificationism. The argument I offer does not, however, make this mistake. It claims only that in order for any specificationist reason to justify, there must be a comparison of the alternatives with respect to satisfying or expressing that ground. See Richardson, *Practical Reasoning*, pp. 179–183.

24. My claim that the justifying force of any justifying reason is a comparison of the alternatives with respect to an appropriate covering value is substantive and should not be mistaken for a conceptual claim about the structure of practical justification. It follows trivially from the fact that something is practically justified that it is at least as good with respect to justifiability as the available alternatives. My claim, however, is not that this comparison provides the justifying force to every justifying reason but rather that a comparison with respect to the value that is specific to that choice situation does. Put another way, my concern is with the normativity of justification *specific* to a choice situation, although a general claim about the normativity of justifying reasons emerges from consideration of the specific cases. See also n. 15.

25. Samuel Guttenplan, "Moral Realism and Moral Dilemmas," *Proceedings of the Aristotelian Society* 80 (1979–1980): 61–80.

26. Thomas Nagel, "The Fragmentation of Value," in his *Mortal Questions* (Cambridge: Cambridge University Press, 1979).

27. Joseph Raz, "Mixing Values," *Proceedings of the Aristotelian Society* 65 (suppl.) (1991): 83–100. Compare James Griffin, "Mixing Values," *Proceedings of the Aristotelian Society* 65 (suppl.) (1991): 101–118.

28. Ronald de Sousa, "The Good and the True," *Mind* 84 (1974): 547–548; Walter Sinnott-Armstrong, *Moral Dilemmas* (Oxford: Blackwell, 1988), pp. 66–68.

29. Sinnott-Armstrong, for example, maintains that "the multiplicity of scales" is a source of incomparability among some, but not all, items that are rankable only by

different scales, but he does not explain why only those items and not others are thereby incomparable. See his *Moral Dilemmas,* p. 69. Charles Taylor suggests that it is the diversity of goods that gives rise to incomparability between certain instances of different goods. But it is difficult to see how the mere fact of diversity can explain incomparability among only some instances of the diverse goods when it is compatible with comparability among other instances. See his "Leading a Life" (this volume).

30. That the argument is put in terms of a continuum should not be taken to entail that the difference in creativity between contiguous items on the continuum is purely quantitative. I defend this argument in some detail elsewhere. Compare John Broome's "Is Incommensurability Vagueness?" (this volume), in which a continuum argument is used to argue for the indeterminacy of comparison.

31. See also Charles Taylor, "The Diversity of Goods," in Amartya Sen and Bernard Williams, eds., *Utilitarianism and Beyond* (Cambridge: Cambridge University Press, 1982); Stocker, *Plural and Conflicting Values;* and Anderson, *Value in Ethics and Economics.* Thomas Hurka has argued that a single value can differ in ways that allow for rational regret over a forgone, less valuable alternative. See his "Monism, Pluralism, and Rational Regret," *Ethics* 106 (1996): 555–575. On the question of whether the recognition of different aspects of a value lands us with pluralism, compare Hurka, and Michael Stocker, "Abstract and Concrete Value: Plurality, Conflict and Maximization," (this volume) especially nn. 7–10.

32. Compare Amartya Sen, "Plural Utility," *Proceedings of the Aristotelian Society* 81 (1980–1981): 193–215. Also, indirect forms of utilitarianism can allow for incomparability among the values that reduce to the supervalue.

33. The text accompanying this footnote is puzzling: "Trade-off suggests that we compute the value of the alternative goods on whatever scale is at hand, whether cardinal or *ordinal,* precise or rough-and-ready" (emphasis added). See Steven Lukes' "Comparing the Incomparable: Trade-offs and Sacrifices" (this volume). But an ordinal scale need not involve calculation. Ordinal comparisons can be quantitative without being cardinal, that is, committed to the existence of some unit of value by which the items can be measured. We have already seen that comparison need not be a matter of quantities of some value.

34. The curiousness may be no fault of Raz. I find it unclear whether Raz is simply stating a position—that it is conceptually impossible for friends to judge friendships and money comparable—or attempting to provide a ground for the conclusion that friendships and money are incomparable, at least for friends. I will take as my target the latter claim since given our purposes it is of greater interest and because others have endorsed it (see Lukes' volume essay). At any rate, the first of my objections to the view applies also to the bare claim of conceptual impossibility. See Raz, *The Morality of Freedom,* pp. 346–352. A similar view about incommensurability is held by Cass Sunstein. See his volume essay and "Incommensurability and Valuation in Law."

35. Anderson's claim that items are incomparable if there is no good practical reason to

compare them does not strictly depend on her quantitative view of comparison. The degree of cogency of the claim does, however; it is more plausible to think that there is no good reason to compare a friendship and money if comparison requires cardinal units measuring their merits. At any rate, we can interpret her view without the quantitative assumption, and I have accordingly discussed it as an example under both the third and fourth types of incomparabilist argument.

36. See also Donald Regan, "Authority and Value: Reflections on Raz's *Morality of Freedom*," *Southern California Law Review* 62 (1989): 995–1095. Of course, whether the intrinsic good *is* more valuable turns on what the instrumental good is instrumental to. The thought embodied in norms governing attitudes appropriate toward intrinsic goods may be that the intrinsic good, as such, has a special status vis-à-vis instrumental goods, as such, though perhaps not all friendships are better than all amounts of cash.

37. There is another class of examples Anderson cites to support her pragmatist principle, 'If no good practical reason to compare, then incomparable'. Sometimes there is no good reason to compare items because it is "boring" or "silly" or "pointless" to do so. It is boring, silly, and pointless to compare, for example, the intrinsic aesthetic merits of all the world's limericks. But can such a categorical claim be sustained? We surely can imagine some point to making comparisons that generally would be inane. As editor of *The World's Greatest Limericks,* one might see a great deal of point in comparing limericks with respect to intrinsic aesthetic merit. I suspect that with enough imagination, a practical point for making seemingly inane comparisons can always be found.

38. If the 'rational resolution' of conflict is understood in terms that do not entail determination of the comparative religion that holds between the alternatives, such arguments become significantly weaker. Considerations against such arguments are given by Michael Stocker, "Abstract and Concrete Value" (this volume).

39. For related positions, see, e.g., Lewis Kornhauser, "The Hunting of the Snag: Incommensurability in Ethics and Economics," unpublished ms, who thinks that plausible conditions on orderings of alternatives may underdetermine a single correct ranking; Sinnott-Armstrong, *Moral Dilemmas,* pp. 66–68, who thinks that moral requirements are incomparable if their strengths are not exact; and T. K. Seung and Daniel Bonevac, "Plural Values and Indeterminate Rankings," *Ethics* 102 (1992): 799–813, who think that two items are incomparable if one is better than the other, worse than it, *and* just as good. A powerful, detailed treatment of the possibility of multiple rankings can be found in Isaac Levi, *Hard Choices.*

40. Compare Hurka, *Perfectionism,* p. 87.

41. See Raz, *The Morality of Freedom,* ch. 13; Sinnott-Armstrong, *Moral Dilemmas,* pp. 65–66, also his "Moral Dilemmas and Incomparability," *American Philosophical Quarterly* 22 (1985): 321–329, 327; de Sousa, "The Good and the True," pp. 544–546.

42. Raz's and de Sousa's argument proceed by appeal to rational attitudes of indifference and not by direct appeal to rational judgments we might make. But the argu-

ment is stronger if understood in terms of rational judgments. The strong version I consider is given by Sinnott-Armstrong in the context of moral requirements.

43. See Regan, "Authority and Value."

44. Susan Hurley makes a similar point against Mackie's error theory of moral judgments. See her *Natural Reasons* (Oxford: Oxford University Press, 1988), pp. 278–279. Of course, the strict trichotomist is always free to deny the phenomenology of judgment as I have described it. But a denial without at least a debunking explanation amounts to mere dogmatism.

45. I owe this large point to Derek Parfit, who first pointed out to me that small improvement arguments need not entail incomparability. Parfit uses a small improvement argument to suggest that there is "rough" comparability, that is, imprecise cardinal comparability. See Parfit, *Reasons and Persons*, pp. 430–431.

46. I make a slight modification of Morton's model. See Adam Morton, *Disasters and Dilemmas* (Oxford: Blackwell, 1991), pp. 34–35. Note that since I take Morton's 'diamond pattern' to be a model of biased and unbiased differences, we should not expect to find room for incomparable items, which have no evaluative differences.

47. Note that even if the one option bore only moral value and the other only prudential value, this would probably not be a case of noncomparability with respect to either moral or prudential value; acts that are moral are typically the kinds of things that belong to the domain of 'prudential', and vice versa.

48. See Bernard Williams, *Ethics and the Limits of Philosophy* (Cambridge: Harvard University Press, 1985).

49. For exemplary work of this kind with respect to the value of (objective) morality, see Frances Kamm, *Morality, Mortality*, Vol. II, (New York: Oxford University Press, 1996), ch. 12. Kamm's discussion can be understood as an attempt to illuminate a murky part of the notion of morality through an investigation of the comparative relations holding between its "rights and duties" contributory values and its "well-being/pursuit of conceptions of the good" contributory values.

50. Note that if intrinsic literary value and intrinsic sartorial value are not parts of any other value, then there is no nameless supervalue that has all values as parts.

2. Incommensurability: What's the Problem?

1. This is my fourth attempt at this subject; the previous three are "Are There Incommensurable Values?" *Philosophy and Public Affairs* 7 (1977): 39–59; *Well-Being* (Oxford: Clarendon Press, 1986), ch. 5; and "Mixing Values," *Proceedings of the Aristotelian Society* (suppl.) 65 (1991): 101–118. This fourth attempt inevitably repeats some of the content of the earlier attempts, especially the third one. But the third attempt was too condensed. I try to fill out the story here and make it more convincing, but it remains very sketchy. This attempt is a survey of the whole subject— all kinds of values. And because the issue of commensurability turns, as I say in the text, on the nature of practical rationality over the entire ethical domain, it is bound to be too big a subject for more than the groping exploration I present here.

2. For a fuller development of this case, see Ruth Chang, "Introduction" (this volume).

3. These are Isaiah Berlin's examples; see his *Four Essays on Liberty* (Oxford: Oxford University Press, 1969), pp. xlix–1, liii–liv.

4. Martha Craven Nussbaum's illustration in *Love's Knowledge* (New York: Oxford University Press, 1990), p. 37.

5. This interpretation of incommensurability can be found in, e.g., Bernard Williams, "Conflict of Values," in his *Moral Luck* (Cambridge: Cambridge University Press, 1981), pp. 79–80; John Finnis, *Fundamentals of Ethics* (Oxford: Clarendon Press, 1983), p. 89; Thomas Nagel, "The Fragmentation of Value," in his *Mortal Questions* (Cambridge: Cambridge University Press, 1979), pp. 131–132; Berlin, *Four Essays on Liberty*, pp. lv–lvi.

6. These judgments are "basic" only in that they do not depend on any other judgments about amount of value. This is not to say that they have no backing at all, that they are arbitrary—say, an expression of brute preference. On the contrary, they rest on rich considerations—rich enough to yield standards of correctness. To understand the judgment that such and such is valuable (which has its standards of correctness) is to understand why it is valuable, and so how valuable it is, and so how valuable it is compared to so and so. I discuss this in "Mixing Values."

7. I discuss this more fully in *Well-Being*, ch. 5, sec. 7.

8. This interpretation of incommensurability can be found in, e.g., John Laird, *An Enquiry into Moral Notions* (London: Allen & Unwin, 1935), p. 255. I call such cases "discontinuities" in *Well-Being*, ch. 5, sec. 6.

9. See my *Well-Being*, p. 80.

10. This is Martha Craven Nussbaum's example of incommensurability in her "Plato on Commensurability and Desire," *Proceedings of the Aristotelian Society* (suppl.) 58 (1984): 55–80, reprinted in her *Love's Knowledge*.

11. On "rough equality" see my *Well-Being*, pp. 80–81, 96–98; for a contrary view of it, see Joseph Raz, *The Morality of Freedom* (Oxford: Clarendon Press, 1986), ch. 13, sec. 2.

12. This is Joseph Raz's example and the sort of incommensurability of values that he proposes; see his *The Morality of Freedom*, ch. 13, esp. p. 332. Raz, rightly to my mind, focuses on the question of comparability, defined as I have done, but adopts what seems to me a strange test for its presence: "Two valuable options are incommensurable if (1) neither is better than the other, and (2) there is (or could be) another option which is better than one but is not better than the other" (p. 325). Raz's first clause satisfies one part of the definition of incomparability (neither better than the other), and the second clause is meant to, but I think does not, satisfy the remainder (nor are they equal). Satisfaction of the second clause would show that two items were not *precisely* equal. But it does not show that they are not roughly equal, and rough equality is a form of comparability. Rough equality seems to allow just the sort of relation Raz mentions. Authors A and B may be very different in kind but in the same (high) class, that is, roughly equal; yet one can imagine an author C who is very like A in kind and slightly better, though the most

that one can say is that C is roughly equal to B. For more on the complex notion of "rough equality," see the references in n. 8.

13. I have in mind such philosophers as Charles Taylor ("The Diversity of Goods," in A. K. Sen and B. Williams, eds., *Utilitarianism and Beyond* [Cambridge: Cambridge University Press, 1982], sec. 2) and Alasdair MacIntyre (*After Virtue* [London: Duckworth, 1981], p. 68), who speak of incommensurable values arising from different worldviews or different traditions.

14. T. S. Kuhn, *The Structure of Scientific Revolutions,* 2d ed. (Chicago: Chicago University Press, 1970).

15. This is John Rawls's example of "incommensurable" conceptions of the good; see his "Social Utility and Primary Goods," in Sen and Williams, *Utilitarianism and Beyond.*

16. One does not need different metaphysics or different cultures to get clashing conceptions of life; a very different value theory might on its own be sufficient—say, a conception of a good human life that might emerge from "deep ecology." One would have to see how different a conception from mine emerged, and whether it could still serve to bring comparability to the prudential domain as mine does. Also there is the important question of whether the conception that emerged was superior to mine.

17. It is too large a question for anything but a sketch of an answer here. I develop this section and the next in my *Value Judgement: Improving Our Ethical Beliefs* (Oxford: Clarendon Press, 1996).

18. This is Shelly Kagan's view in *The Limits of Morality* (Oxford: Clarendon Press, 1989), ch. 8.

19. Let me quickly mention two further possible moves. One move (it is Iris Murdoch's in a profile of her in the *Independent,* London, April 29, 1989) is to say that if we had a sufficiently inspiring conception of morality, we should be able to rise to its demands. Inspiration and capacities are causally connected. Inspired enough, we could meet even the demanding injunction, "Be ye therefore perfect." Still, the conceptions of morality that might revolutionize the will I see no reason to adopt, and the conceptions I see reason to adopt do not revolutionize it.

Another move is toward compromise and goes something like this: "It is true that, for the most part, we don't and won't act impartially, but not that, *strictly speaking,* we can't. Maybe, strictly speaking, we can't at certain times of life—say, in the midst of child rearing—but there are other times—say, in youth and old age, without entanglements—when we can. And then we should." But this compromise position still underestimates the problem. Even thoroughly decent, conscientious, well-informed people, even when young or old, do not and will not. "Ought" implies "can." Ethics is a set of rules, attitudes, and dispositions for the guidance of flesh-and-blood people. If full impartiality is not actually forthcoming in their behavior, that counts as its not being available. That is the way commonsense morality sets the limits of its demands, and it is right to do so.

20. The words are from a speech made by Chai Ling, which became the manifesto of

the hunger strikers. Quoted by Li Lu, *Moving the Mountain: My Life in China, from the Cultural Revolution to Tiananmen Square* (London: Macmillan, 1990), pp. 131–132.

21. What I suggest here might be called a "psychological" solution to the problem that ethics is extremely demanding: "ought" implies "can," and we can do only so much. Some think that psychological solutions are unnecessary because morality itself provides the solution. For example, morality stands for justice, and so morality itself requires us to do only our fair share. It would ask us to give only that amount of money to save the starving that, if everyone else were to do the same (whether or not they actually will), would be enough. But moral requirements do not seem to be like that. If you and I are crossing a bridge over a pond and to the left one child was drowning and to the right another one was, and if I panic and run off, then you cannot say, having waded in and saved one, that you can go on your way because you have done your fair share. There are other sorts of moral solutions than this, but I do not know of any satisfactory one. See also n. 22.

22. There is an obvious objection to my explanation. Grant that we need to conduct our moral life with norms (the objection goes) and that they must command a psychologically deep respect, and that the norm, Do not deliberately kill the innocent, is one of them. Nearly everyone accepts that. What is contentious, though, is how exceptions to the norm arise. It is not impossible that, by some fluke, the surgeons *did* know that no one would ever discover that they had killed the recluse. The recluse, let us say, is ill already and on the surgeons' operating table for a high-risk operation, and they could finish him off without arousing the least suspicion. True, their justification for killing the recluse could not stop there. Their justification is the promotion of most value, so the surgeons would need to know the values in prospect well into the possible futures of each of the six people involved. But that, though increasing the fluke, is not quite impossible either; the surgeons might know something about the quality of life of the six; they are, after all, their patients. And, anyway, our knowledge in airplane cases is far from complete. The house in town on which the plane would crash might contain five notorious mafia hit men and the house in the suburbs might contain Mother Teresa. It is, nonetheless, right for you to direct the plane to the suburb, because the probabilities of your successfully limiting the damage are so high. But in this fluke version of the transplant case, the surgeons' knowledge is even more reliable. So, it cannot be limitations on knowledge that make the difference between the two cases.

Now, this objection directs our attention to a fluke: the surgeons' happening to know the costs and benefits. But the nature of our moral life is not determined by flukes. Hard cases make bad law; they also make bad moral norms. The norm, Do not deliberately kill the innocent, arises initially from the great value that we attach to life. But there is the further question how values such as life can enter human thought and action. Given the nature of agents, the role for these values to play in our lives is for us generally to respect them, by not taking innocent life ourselves, and not to promote them, utilitarian fashion. We typically cannot know, even to a reliable degree of probability, what will most promote life. Such Godlike disposal of the affairs of the world is not our role. Ours is the more modest one of respecting life. That must be our general approach, and once we make it that, then we cannot enter into and exit from such respect at will. Moral life, in certain ways, is bound to be deeply conservative. It will be conservative because of the centrality of deep feelings and attitudes. And it will be conservative because of the limitations of knowledge. In fluke circumstances in which we think we can determine the costs and benefits, we still only *think* that we know them. We are held back by both deep feelings and deep skepticism. We therefore demand that any exceptions to an important norm have an especially clear justification. We do not have to pitch the standards of justification so high that only something as thoroughly obvious as the airplane case will do. We might be prepared to accept euthanasia in certain circumstances or obstetricians' sometimes killing the baby to save the mother. But these cases are still a long way from justifying the surgeons' killing the recluse in the transplant case.

23. I say that in general our capacities (e.g., the limitations of our knowledge) impose constraints on the content of moral norms. This would be flatly denied by the sort of objectivists who would maintain that moral norms are independent of human capacities, that they are simply to be discovered by us, that we can hope that their demands will not outstrip our powers, but that this can only be a hope. But these objectivists would have to be able to justify their strong sort of objectivism, and they would still have to answer the main question of ethics, How are we to conduct our lives?, when, according to them, it may turn out that the standards for its conduct are hidden or irrelevant.

24. There is the large question of rational strategies in the face of great ignorance. Might not indirect utilitarianism reappear? Is my point about the transplant case simply that, given how little we know about the costs and benefits at stake, the best policy is, "Better the devil you know"? That looks like indirect utilitarianism because it looks like the plausible thought that our policy until now of applying the norm, Do not deliberately kill the innocent, to transplant cases has at least stood the test of time. If that is simply the thought that we have to abandon maximization in these cases, then it is well short of indirect utilitarianism. If it is the thought that our abandoning maximization is ultimately the maximizing thing to do, then I doubt that we can tell.

I speak here about "utilitarianism" rather than "consequentialism" in order to avoid the further complication that the latter, broader, class brings. But what I say here about the former applies too, I think, to the latter. And if the latter is taken, as it sometimes is, to broaden the category of the "good" to include more than human interests, then consequentialism just raises further doubts about the conception of agency that it must assume. On the difference between utilitarianism and consequentialism, see my "The Human Good and the Ambitions of Consequentialism," *Social Philosophy and Policy* 9 (1992): 118–132.

25. There may still be forms of utilitarianism, or of consequentialism, that fit better. It may be that, in pushing the promotion of value into the background by making it

the criterion of right and wrong, we have not pushed it back quite far enough or back to quite the right place. The most interesting forms of consequentialism in the future, I think, will be those that give it a different background place without having to push it so far into the background that nothing worth calling "utilitarianism" or "consequentialism" remains.

3. Incommensurability: Four Proposals

This paper makes explicit the view about rationality, reasonableness, commensurability, and incommensurability presented in my *Needs, Values, Truth,* 2d ed. (Oxford: Blackwell, 1991). I am grateful, now that I have done it, to Ruth Chang for persuading me to attempt this and to Martin Hollis, John Broome, Peter Hammond, Samuel Guttenplan, Michael Hechter, Ronald Dworkin, and Ruth Chang for their friendly encouragement and advice.

1. Whether fears or expectations are in question depends on the question of whether it is feared that consequentialism will prevail or expected that it will, or what. On these matters, see below, sec. 6.
2. "Such" is an adjective here—as it is everywhere and always in the dialect of this writer. It stands in construction here with "measure" and "property."
3. Of course, if nothing important is left over, then it is not worth insisting that *A* and *B* make claims that are incommensurable. I suppose that one who wishes to explain the idea of incommensurability along these lines and by reference to the choice between the particularized options available in particular cases had better take steps to make incommensurability require the importance of this residue.
4. I use the word *ranking* throughout in the ordinary sense that is fixed by the language, not in a technical sense. It is the genus of which all more recondite or special sorts of ranking are species.
5. Samuel Scheffler, editor's introduction to *Consequentialism and Its Critics* (Oxford: Oxford University Press, 1988), para. 2.
6. This lack is well exposed, albeit in bygone idiom, by W. D. Ross, *The Right and the Good* (Oxford: Clarendon Press, 1930), ch. 2.
7. "Unranked" here, which is simply my response to a technical term used by commensurabilists, is intended to leave room for a distinctive moral *emphasis* among a rational agent's attachments.
8. In Nelson Goodman's sense of "projectible." See his *Fact, Fiction and Forecast* (London: Athlone Press, 1954).
9. See B. A. W. Russell, "The Idea of Cause," in his *Mysticism and Logic,* London, 1917. (In the Penguin edition, see p. 148.) See also Nelson Goodman's account in *Fact, Fiction and Forecast* of what we should require of any satisfactory account of a predicate's being projectible.
10. As always, some may respond by emptying "maximize" of all distinctive content.

The claim that it would show nothing to determine a subject's utilities and his ratio of substitution in a manner that is essentially after the event and simply recapitulatory of it may provoke the response that it is a nontrivial exercise to determine such things as this after the event if the postulates of rational choice theory are to be found to be in force. My claim is not so much, however, that it is *easy* to find the utility schedule and the ratio of substitution after the event, or that curve fitting is by its nature an *easy* exercise, as it is this: If curve fitting is *all* that is attempted, if neither phenomenology is advanced nor any projectible characterization of springs of action is achieved, then nothing of explanatory interest is accomplished. Still less is the ordinary knowledge upstaged that ordinary agents have of themselves and one another. "He ɸ-ed in order to maximize his utility" tells us no more than "there was a reason of some sort why he did what he did."

The incommensurabilists' negative claim does not (I should add) commit them to the denial of physical determinism. If a determinism stated in strictly physical terms were true—I use the subjunctive conditional advisedly here—then that would in no way guarantee the truth of any determinism statable in terms proprietary to economics, psychology, or rational choice theory.

11. Where it has lived on in juristic principles that animate English and American systems of case law and in jurisprudential outlooks that grow out of these systems. See Ronald Dworkin, *Law's Empire* (Cambridge: Harvard University Press, 1986), pp. 257–258.

12. The received misinterpretations of *Nicomachean Ethics* rest on the mistranslation of the Greek words *ta pros to telos*. See my "Deliberation and Practical Reason," *Proceedings of the Aristotelian Society* 76 (1975–1976): 29–51, reprinted in Amelie Rorty, ed., *Essays on Aristotle's Ethics* (Berkeley: University of California Press, 1980), pp. 221–240, and in my *Needs, Values, Truth*.

13. The difficulty is not that weakness makes counterexamples to the thesis. That could be taken care of by saying of the agent that "there is something that he or she is seeking, in so far as he or she is rational, to maximize." The difficulty is that proper or reflective weakness of will is so hard to understand in these terms. If everything trades off against everything else at some predeterminable (however contextually variable) rate and the trading rate reflects everything that matters about it, what reason could anyone have (and what reason could there be for him or her) to think twice about whether to do the act that scored highest or to backslide from the demonstrably optimific act (unless, of course, he or she wanted to go back on the calculation)? It will be harder than it ought to be to understand weakness of will *as having reasons* (of a sort) *of its own*.

14. Nobody deploys anything that is *proprietary* to these theories, I mean. Real empirical inquiries can, of course, dress up their results or even their questions in the garb of rational choice theory, thus enhancing the credentials of the inquirers' professional mystery. This does not mean that their actual results have to go to the credit of rational choice theory.

15. There is one kind of case where one might anticipate that theories of individual choice which see agents as would-be maximizers could have real application, namely the case where the activities to be forecast are by their essential, professed, and explicit nature maximizing activities, e.g., activities in the market place or the bourse. Here one might indeed expect that there could be some impressive predictions to be had and illuminating explanations of outcomes. The same will apply wherever the field to be studied has been non-arbitrarily narrowed down to a specific class of activities that are shown in due course to be candidates to be seen as maximizing of this or that specific end. Nevertheless, successes of this sort would leave it perfectly open how seriously we should take the idea of a theory that will make sense not of a specific class of activities, but of every act of some particular agent, as an act of utility maximizing. They would leave it open how seriously we should take either the idea of an all-embracing theory for all individual agents or the idea of a set of particular and specific theories, one for each agent or even the bare claim to the effect that for each agent *some* such all-embracing theory is possible.

4. Is Incommensurability Vagueness?

This paper was written while I was a Visiting Fellow at the Australian National University in 1993. I owe a large debt to Adam Morton; a pre-publication version of his paper "Hypercomparatives," *Synthese* 111 (1997): 97–114, was the source of many of my arguments. I was also greatly helped by Linda Claire Burns's book, *Vagueness: An Investigation into Natural Languages and the Sorites Paradox* (Dordrecht: Kluwer Academic Publishers, 1991), but unfortunately this paper is handicapped by having been written before Timothy Williamson's *Vagueness* (London: Routledge, 1994) was published. I have received many valuable comments from the audiences to which I have presented the paper, and from many other people too. They include Luc Bovens, Ruth Chang, Dorothy Edgington, Sven Danielsson, James Griffin, Frank Jackson, Douglas MacLean, Philip Pettit, Joseph Raz, John Skorupski, Susan Wolf, and Crispin Wright.

1. This corresponds to condition C2 in Adam Morton, "Hypercomparatives," p. 104.
2. See Adam Morton, "Comparatives and Degrees," *Analysis* 44 (1984): 16–20.
3. Morton, "Hypercomparatives." Morton himself deals with the degrees to which predicates are satisfied, but not with degrees of *truth*.
4. Morton assumes that we shall eventually reach a level where the indeterminacy is hard, but I am not convinced by his arguments. I think we may reach a level where there is no indeterminacy, however.
5. See Michael Dummett, "Wang's Paradox," *Synthese* 30 (1975): 301–324, and Kit Fine, "Vagueness, Truth and Logic," *Synthese* 30 (1975): 265–300.
6. See Fine, "Vagueness, Truth and Logic," pp. 284–285.
7. But see Williamson, *Vagueness,* pp. 154–156, and the references there.

8. Christopher Peacocke, "Are Vague Predicates Incoherent?" *Synthese* 44 (1981): 121–141.

9. Joseph Raz, "Value Incommensurability: Some Preliminaries," *Proceedings of the Aristotelian Society* 86 (1985–1986): 117–134.

10. John Broome, *Weighing Goods* (Oxford: Blackwell, 1991), pp. 136–137.

11. Another example is Charles Blackorby, "Degrees of Cardinality and Aggregate Partial Orderings," *Econometrica* 43 (1975): 845–852.

12. Amartya Sen, *On Economic Inequality* (Oxford: Clarendon Press, 1973), ch. 3.

13. Amartya Sen, *Collective Choice and Social Welfare* (San Francisco: Holden-Day, 1970), chs. 7, 7*.

14. Ibid.

5. Practical Reason and Incommensurable Goods

I thank Ruth Chang, James Griffin, Serge-Christophe Kolm, Elijah Millgram, Joseph Raz, and Cass Sunstein for helpful comments and suggestions.

1. Joseph Raz, *The Morality of Freedom* (Oxford: Clarendon Press, 1986), p. 322.

2. Christine Korsgaard, "Two Distinctions in Goodness," *Philosophical Review* 92 (1983): 169–195; Barbara Herman, *The Practice of Moral Judgment* (Cambridge: Harvard University Press, 1993), pp. 213–214.

3. Immanuel Kant, *Grounding for the Metaphysics of Morals,* trans. James Ellington (Indianapolis: Hackett, 1981), p. 393. Page references to Kant's works in this chapter refer to the standard *Akademie* pagination.

4. Following Korsgaard, "Two Distinctions in Goodness."

5. Immanuel Kant, *Critique of Judgement,* trans. James Meredith (Oxford: Oxford University Press, 1952), pp. 204–205.

6. Immanuel Kant, *Critique of Practical Reason,* trans. Lewis White Beck (Indianapolis: Bobbs-Merrill, 1956), pp. 124–126.

7. Ibid., pp. 229, 236.

8. Elizabeth Anderson, *Value in Ethics and Economics* (Cambridge: Harvard University Press, 1993).

9. Ibid., pp. 19, 224 n. 1.

10. James Griffin has challenged my claim that states of affairs generally have only extrinsic value. He points out that we usually take "φ-ing would cause him pain" as a reason not to φ, without deriving the normative force of this reason from any other consideration. Justification comes to an end with claims about pain, so painless states have intrinsic value. I believe that justification ends here only because we take it for granted that we should treat people decently and that inflicting pain on them is usually incompatible with this. The value of painless states is still derived from the intrinsic value of persons. Two cases demonstrate this. In the first, our favorable regard for an individual, combined with her favorable regard for a cer-

tain sort of pain, prevent "ɸ-ing would cause her pain" from counting as a reason against ɸ-ing. Thus, if James if fond of Sharon, and Sharon relishes the fiery taste of habañero peppers (precisely because of their exquisitely distressing flavor), then the fact that serving her habañeros would cause her pain gives James no reason not to do it. In the second case, our unfavorable regard for an individual gives us reason to inflict pain on him. Our condemnation of a criminal, duly convicted of a heinous crime, gives us a reason to punish him, where punishment, to express our condemnation, must cause distress.

11. But surely the numbers of deaths involved in a choice *sometimes* count! Well, not in virtue of a principle that says that the world is, other things equal, always better for containing more people. This principle is false, and intrinsic value therefore not aggregative, if there are *any* asymmetries between requirements to bring more people into the world and to prevent their deaths, or if there are *any* valid "agent-centered restrictions" that prohibit someone from killing (or committing a lesser wrong) to prevent larger numbers of deaths. When the numbers count, they do so in virtue of a principle that tells us to *respect* human life, not to maximize it.

12. It is no objection to these claims about parental love to argue that parents properly do things that trade off the *welfare* of one child for the welfare of the other. Since parents' time and material resources are finite, such trade-offs inevitably happen. Trade-offs of resources are not the same as trade-offs of love. Furthermore, although love directs parents to promote the welfare of each of their children, it does not generally tell them to maximize the total welfare enjoyed by all their children. For love also directs parents to promote their children's autonomy and moral responsibility even at some cost to their welfare. Even when considerations of welfare alone are at stake, the principle to maximize total child welfare is not generally valid, for it requires parents to neglect children whose needs are hard to satisfy in favor of more easily satisfied children. It is children who have intrinsic value, not their welfare. This means that the role that relative amounts of different children's welfare properly play in parental decision making is governed not by an aggregative principle to maximize child welfare, but by a distributive principle to love each child adequately.

13. Ruth Chang, "Emphatic Comparability and Constitutive Incommensurability, or, Buying and Selling Friends" (unpublished ms.), p. 5.

14. In her Introduction to this volume, Ruth Chang points out that such goods can be compared with respect to their instrumental values for various ends, such as economic development. This does not show that their intrinsic values are comparable.

15. I do not claim that *all* cross-modal comparative aesthetic evaluations are pointless. Some cross-modal comparisons are fascinating—for instance, whether a given story is better rendered on film, stage, or in a novel. However, it is noteworthy that although we have many contests within an artistic form—for best film, best dramatic play, best novel, best song—we have none that ranks the best artwork overall. There is no point to such a contest, for there are no general criteria of aesthetic

worth applicable to all the modes of artistic expression that can sum up everything of aesthetic value about each. The various art forms appeal to too many different aesthetic interests and pleasures—performative virtuosity, insightful exploration of human character, the ingenious play of language, evocative melody, and so forth—that are neither shared by all forms nor sensibly subject to ranking in themselves. A comparison with athletic contests is instructive. We have no contest for best athlete (the decathlon, at best, tells us who the best track-and-field athlete is). The many dimensions of athletic excellence—speed, power, strength, endurance, grace, balance, flexibility, coordination, teamwork, strategic intelligence, team leadership—are too various, not shared by all sports, and often require the development of incompatible skills and body types. A contest that attempted to pit gymnasts, weightlifters, marathon runners, and baseball players against one another in an attempt to judge the best athlete would be injurious to the athletes (imagine a weightlifter's competing on the balance beam or a gymnast's pitching fastballs). It would select for athletes who, modestly accomplished across the entire range of athletic virtues, are truly outstanding in none. And the decision of the winner would more likely be an artifact of the arbitrary weightings assigned to different athletic virtues (perhaps sheer strength plays a bigger role in deciding victory in the contest than endurance) than contingent on the actual performances in the contest (we would know ahead of time that the weightlifter would beat the distance runner). The very attempt to rank athletes comprehensively in different sports makes a mockery of the excellences it is supposed to honor.

16. Ruth Chang, "Against Incomparability" (unpublished ms., 1992).

17. This is compatible with the claim that for any two artworks, one could imagine a context in which we had to choose between them *for one purpose or another.* For example, one might have to choose between displaying a painting and a sculpture in one's home, depending on which would best cover a dent in the wall. But such choices do not require ranking the works on *aesthetic* grounds (with respect to their *intrinsic* value). One might have to decide which of two utterly different artworks to discuss in a short encyclopedia of art. Here again, the decision hardly depends on being able to compare vastly different works on their overall aesthetic merits. One may choose on the basis of distributive rather than ranking criteria—for instance, to satisfy an interest in covering a sufficiently wide range of art forms, eras, genres, and styles—or on extrinsic grounds such as historical importance, fame, or typicality for the genre. I claim that certain intrinsic goodness-of-a-kind judgments (such as aesthetic judgments) fail to support complete rankings, not that no goodness-for-a-purpose judgments can rank items that are incommensurable in intrinsic goodness-of-their-kind.

18. Michael Stocker, *Plural and Conflicting Values* (Oxford: Clarendon Press, 1990).

19. Raz, *The Morality of Freedom,* p. 334.

20. Chang, "Against Incomparability," p. 28.

21. I owe this thought to Joseph Raz.

22. Chang, "Emphatic Comparability and Constitutive Incommensurability," p. 3.

23. One might think that "intrinsic value" names a covering value. This thought errs twice. First, to call a good intrinsically valuable is not to specify a respect in which it is valuable, but to give it an independent status in justification: It generates claims on our actions and attitudes, independent of the value of any other particular. Second, the *states* of mother's continued existence, and the continuation of the friendship, are not intrinsically good. What is intrinsically valuable are *persons:* mother herself, and one's friend. The values of the states are dependent on the values of the persons and determined by the ways we should value the persons, so they are only extrinsically valuable.

24. I explore other sorts of reasons for choice among incommensurables in Anderson, *Value in Ethics and Economics,* pp. 59–63. Chang claims also to reject the view that rational choice in the above case depends on regarding their values as scalar.

25. The step marks the difference between goods that are important only because one cares about them and goods that remain important even when one's caring wanes. Harry Frankfurt, "The Importance of What We Care About," in his *The Importance of What We Care About* (Cambridge: Cambridge University Press, 1988), pp. 80–94. That is why sometimes we feel the intrinsic goods from which obligations flow as binding or tugging us rather than as attracting us: We feel their claims on us even when the desire to satisfy them flags. But feeling a tug is still a way of acknowledging the claims of value, not a way of countermanding them, as traditional deontology holds. My discussion is indebted to Herman's compelling account of how obligations flow from intrinsic value (*Practice of Moral Judgment,* ch. 10).

26. The problem here is not that a person is sacrificed—some circumstances give us no choice but to sacrifice one person or another—but that the *grounds* for the sacrifice are based not on how the person herself should be valued, but on how that person's existence figures in valuable states of affairs. States of the world rather than persons are here taken to be what is intrinsically valuable.

27. Ronald Dworkin, *Taking Rights Seriously* (Cambridge: Harvard University Press, 1977), p. xi; John Rawls, *A Theory of Justice* (Cambridge: Harvard University Press, 1971), p. 61; Robert Nozick, *Anarchy, State, and Utopia* (New York: Basic Books, 1974), pp. 29–33.

28. Milton Russell, "The Making of Cruel Choices," in P. Brett Hammond and Rob Coppock, eds., *Valuing Health Risks, Costs, and Benefits for Environmental Decision Making* (Washington, D.C.: National Academy Press, 1990), pp. 17, 21.

29. Samuel Scheffler, *The Rejection of Consequentialism* (Oxford: Clarendon Press, 1982), p. 20.

30. Chang, "Emphatic Comparability and Constitutive Incommensurability," pp. 17–18.

31. Derek Parfit, *Reasons and Persons* (Oxford: Clarendon Press, 1984).

32. Chang, "Emphatic Comparability and Constructive Incommensurability," p. 22–23.
33. Anderson, *Value in Ethics and Economics,* ch. 5.

6. Incommensurability and Agency

I am grateful to Jonathan Dancy for very helpful comments on an early draft of this essay. The final version of this essay was completed in the spring of 1994.

1. I will use "incommensurable" and "incommensurate" as stylistic variants, and if needed to alleviate monotony I will also use "incomparable" as meaning incommensurable. Strictly speaking, of course, incommensurability does not imply incomparability. Items whose values have no common measure may be comparable in a variety of ways: Of two paintings whose value is incommensurate, one may be more colorful than the other, or older, etc. Besides, the most common use of "incomparable" is to indicate great superiority of one of the items, that is, it entails their commensurability. "How can you compare," one may say, "Mozart and Salieri? Clearly Mozart is incomparably the better composer." Which he is. Hence, incommensurability is not to be confused with incomparability.

2. I use "option" to refer to an action that an agent is both able to perform and has an opportunity to perform. For example, going to Lincoln Plaza cinema for the late show next Sunday is an option for me today. The specificity of options does not entail that all their aspects are specified or decided upon. How to get there may be left undecided. Nor need a specific option be for a simple action like opening a window. It could be a complex course of action such as going on a skiing holiday next January.

3. This essentially Aristotelian conception has been powerfully revived in recent times by G. E. M. Anscombe, *Intention* (Oxford: Blackwell, 1957), a book that influenced many further constructive writings on the subject.

4. This is true of deontic reasons as well, for while what is deontically required may not be one's best option, it is invariably an action that is good in some way or avoids some bad consequences.

5. The primary context in which we refer to reasons is when debating what to do. Secondarily we refer to them to explain what we or others think or thought they have reason to do. Reasons, in short, are considerations that bear on the desirability or otherwise on the case for or against options. Or, in the secondary usage, they are considerations believed by the people under discussion to bear on the case for or against options.

6. Choices made by institutions form a special case. It is hardly ever appropriate to refer to the institution choosing to do what it wants. See "On the Autonomy of Legal Reasoning" in my *Ethics in the Public Domain* (Oxford: Oxford University Press, 1994).

7. What is to be done, either by the person deliberating or by someone else, and either

now or at a later time, or if the opportunity arises—and one need not expect that it will, nor that it may arise—or at a time past, as when one examines one's youth, or someone else's past action.

8. Without thereby implying that they can be neatly divided. The distinction is meant as a rough and ready working distinction, not one capable of bearing much theoretical weight.

9. Note, however, that the discussion will concern only the belief/desire account of *reasons for action,* and not belief/desire accounts of intention or of the explanation of action.

10. I will not discuss the most common charge against the belief/desire account: that it cannot explain the fact that we can reason about what goals we should have in a way that is not entirely dependent on the goals we already have. That is, people ask themselves what they should do and what they should desire in an unconditional way. They ask not, What should I desire to do now given that I already have the following desires? but, What should I desire now, *tout court?* Possibly they ask what I should and what I should not desire in a way that is in principle open to the possibility that all my current desires are misguided or even morally wrong. But whether or not this last question is possible for anyone to entertain seriously, the unconditional question I mentioned is one that we do deliberate about, and its consideration does not presuppose the feasibility of a complete overhaul of all our beliefs and desires. I believe that this charge is justified. But its consideration cannot be undertaken here.

11. I am here repeating and elaborating arguments I have put forward in *The Morality of Freedom* (Oxford: Clarendon Press, 1986), and more specifically in "On the Moral Point of View," in J. B. Schneewind, ed., *Reason, Ethics, and Society: Themes from Kurt Baier, with his Responses* (Chicago: Open Court, 1996), pp. 58–83, in which some of these points are made verbatim.

12. Exceptional cases need not be denied. One may want to want something to prove to oneself that one can want it or to win a bet, etc.

13. It is a mistake to think, as was first suggested by Frankfurt, that endorsement by second-order desires is part of the explanation of the sense in which some desires are ours and some are forces that seize us. Second-order desires may be ours, or be inflicted on us, just like first-order desires. We can have a second-order desire, which is not "ours" in the relevant sense, not to have a first-order desire that is authentically ours. More to the point, we need not have a second-order desire endorsing each of our first-order desires for them to be ours. Since writing this essay, I have explored these matters in "When We are Ourselves: The Active and the Passive," in *Proceedings of the Aristotelian Society* 71 (suppl.) (1997): 211–229.

14. It could have been that I realized, or believed, that the reasons for the action are such that even when the reasons against performing it are taken into account, it would be irrational not to perform it. At the other extreme, I may conceive the desire to perform it because of its good points, even if, given the reasons against it, performing it would be irrational. But most commonly it is neither of these. The

reasons that make me desire to perform an action are simply those reasons for it that I respond to, whereas others leave me relatively cold.

15. Some expressive actions are an interesting borderline case. I kick the table in frustration, or walk up and down. Do I do so to relieve tension (conforming to the pattern I described or satisfying an urge to get rid of it)? Perhaps, but I am also expressing my exasperation, anger, or whatnot, and the fact that an action has expressive meaning is a reason to perform it when such expression is appropriate.

16. The best analysis of such cases is provided by Harry Frankfurt, *The Importance of What We Care About* (Cambridge: Cambridge University Press, 1988).

17. Therefore if I believe that I will have a desire to take up the piano when I retire, I now have reason to prepare for that event.

18. We should, of course, distinguish the anodyne sense in which "I am pleased to meet you"—said as part of a formal introduction to a stranger—indicates pleasure, and pleasure in the sense in which one can take pleasure in wine, dancing, or a good book. Pleasure in the nonanodyne sense is the subject of my remarks.

19. Especially with children. We expect grownups to be in control of their will and emotions, and not to pander to them. But on rare occasions, the disappointment will be so great that it is right to avoid it.

20. I do not mean that it is inappropriate to want to hurt him. I mean that it is inappropriate to consider my wanting to perform an action (when the want is based on an unobjectionable reason) as a consideration for performing it when I know that it will hurt him.

21. Or recedes to become a desire to do the relevant act if an appropriate opportunity arose.

22. See also the discussion of goals and well-being in my *The Morality of Freedom*.

23. See ibid., ch. 12, on the relation between goals and well-being; see also my *Ethics in the Public Domain*, ch. 1.

24. Two popular ideas are: (1) because what we do affects our well-being, the contribution of various options to our well-being provides a basis for commensurating them, and (2) a rational constraint of coherence provides such a basis. I attempted to refute the first in "Facing Up: A Reply," *Southern California Law Review* 62 (1989), and in *Ethics in the Public Domain*, and to refute the second at least partly in "The Relevance of Coherence," *Boston University Law Review* 72:2 (1991): 273–321.

7. Value, Comparability, and Choice

I am grateful to Tom Hurka for helpful discussion of an earlier draft and to Ruth Chang for extremely useful editorial suggestions. I would never have written this paper without the stimulation of the papers and discussion at the conference on incommensurability organized by John Broome, Ruth Chang, and Maurice Salles.

1. In addition to Joseph Raz's "Incommensurability and Agency" (this volume), see his *The Morality of Freedom* (Oxford: Clarendon Press, 1986), ch. 13.

2. James Griffin, *Well-Being* (Oxford: Clarendon Press, 1986), pp. 80–81, 97; Thomas Hurka, *Perfectionism* (New York: Oxford University Press, 1993), p. 87.

3. Griffin, *Well-Being*, p. 97; Hurka, *Perfectionism*, p. 87.

4. In his "Incommensurability: What's the Problem?" (this volume), James Griffin recognizes that denying indifference can be a way of asserting the need for deliberation. And he says that, of course, we should think carefully before we decide two goods are actually roughly equal. But he then reiterates that if we do decide, after all, that they are roughly equal, then deliberation is at an end. "We might in effect, toss a coin" [draft, p. 10]. I agree that finding rough equality would preclude further meaningful deliberation, but I think the point requires further argument.

5. Raz, *The Morality of Freedom*, pp. 332–335.

6. For the record, Raz denies that weighty options so different in kind could be exactly equal in value. Ibid., p. 333.

7. So far as I remember, Moore makes this equation of "good" and "ought to exist" only in the preface to *Principia Ethica* (Cambridge: Cambridge University Press, 1903), which is unfortunate because it is essential to understanding what Moore is about.

8. Aurel Kolnai, "Deliberation Is of Ends," in *Ethics, Value, and Reality: Selected Papers of Aurel Kolnai* (Indianapolis: Hackett, 1978).

9. Griffin, *Well-Being*, p. 80.

10. Griffin, "Incommensurability" [draft, p. 5].

11. Michael Stocker, "Abstract and Concrete Value: Plurality, Conflict and Maximization" (this volume) [draft, pp. 8–9].

12. Ibid. [draft, p. 14].

13. Raz, "Facing Up: A Reply," *Southern California Law Review* 62 (1989): 1221, n. 145.

14. John Broome, "Is Incommensurability Vagueness?" (this volume) [draft, p. 3].

15. Donald Regan, "Authority and Value: Reflections on Raz's *Morality of Freedom*," *Southern California Law Review* 62 (1989): 1058–1059, 1067–1071.

16. Raz, "Incommensurability and Agency" [draft, p. 10, n. 14], speaks of reasons that though apparently known to me, "leave me relatively cold." In the case of Stocker, I am just interpreting, perhaps wrongly, the tone of his descriptions of some cases where I choose a lesser good over a known greater good. For example, Stocker, "Abstract and Concrete Value" [draft, pp. 17–18]. I mean the job case and the classical Greek case, not the wisdom through suffering case.

17. My assertion that we should not doubt the presence of the weaker motives even though they generate no overt behavior may seem inconsistent with my earlier reliance on the argument that we must posit some motivation for Jones's *behavior* of rescuing the baby if we are to view it as the action of a rational agent. I think there is no inconsistency. In order to view Jones as a rational agent, we must posit for him a motivation that explains his behavior. But if the motivation explains the behavior, it cannot be constituted just by the fact of the behavior; it must have an independent existence. If it does, there is no reason not to suppose that even motives that do not generate behavior can exist in the same way. There is indeed no behavior

to show we must posit such weaker motives, but if we have other grounds for positing them, as I have argued we do, the absence of behavior is no impediment.

18. The possible claim that the agent does not respond motivationally to the various reasons severally but merely forms a final intention to act as the totality of reasons requires (if reason provides a definite answer) seems to me of a piece with the idea about second-order reasons discussed and rejected in the text. Notice also that responding to the various reasons severally seems necessary to account for regret.

19. For a subtle and interesting proposal about how an agent's choices might create a scheme of commensuration for her, see Elijah Millgram, "Incommensurability and Practical Reasoning" (this volume).

20. I owe this point to Tom Hurka.

21. Although I have discussed the problematic nature of choice between incomparables elsewhere ("Authority and Value," pp. 1062–1064), I take the present formulation of the problem in terms of the *intelligibility* of choice from Raz's "Incommensurability and Agency." I should therefore emphasize that I am not the "rationalist" Raz imagines raising this problem. I do not believe that wants are reasons any more than Raz does. Indeed, as this section reveals, I believe it slightly less.

22. Raz, "Incommensurability and Agency" [draft, p. 14].

23. Ibid. [draft, p. 17].

24. Ibid. [draft, p. 8].

25. Ibid. [draft, p. 9].

26. Ibid. [draft, p. 12].

8. Incommensurability and Practical Reasoning

I am grateful to Alyssa Bernstein, Hilary Bok, Sarah Buss, Ruth Chang, Alice Crary, Wilfried Hinsch, Geoff Sayre-McCord, Adria Quiñones, Bill Talbott, and Kayley Vernallis for commenting on earlier drafts and, for discussion, to Rebecca Entwisle, Christoph Fehige, David Friedheim, Amy Gutman, and audiences at Williams College, the Hebrew University, and the conference on Incommensurability and Value.

1. There is a terminological point to be cleared up here, however. A number of philosophers have identified forms of reasoning that are directed toward the satisfaction of desires but are not simply finding ways of *causing* the desire to be satisfied; see, for example, the much-discussed list in Bernard Williams, "Internal and External Reasons," in his *Moral Luck* (Cambridge: Cambridge University Press, 1981), p. 104, which adduces, among others, "thinking how the satisfaction [of one's desires] can be combined, e.g., by time-ordering," or "finding constitutive solutions, such as deciding what would make for an entertaining evening, granted that one wants entertainment." Such philosophers may be instrumentalists on my use of the term but not necessarily on their own. For some reason to think that instrumentalism, in my sense, *is* the received view, see Elijah Millgram, "Williams' Argument

Against External Reasons," *Nous* 30:2 (1996): 197–220; for an argument against instrumentalism, see Millgram, "Deciding to Desire," in C. Fehige and U. Wessels, eds. *Preferences* (Berlin: de Gruyter, 1997).

2. See Aurel Kolnai, "Deliberation Is of Ends," in his *Ethics, Value and Reality: Selected Papers of Aurel Kolnai* (Indianapolis: Hackett, 1978), pp. 45, 47f; Williams, "Internal and External Reasons," p. 104.

3. See James Griffin, *Well-Being* (Oxford: Clarendon Press, 1986). ch. 6; John Broome, *Weighing Goods* (Oxford: Blackwell, 1991), ch. 4.

4. The claim needs to be qualified by the now-familiar point, due to Hilary Putnam, that meanings aren't only in the head. I will not pursue the qualification because it does not seem to me to change the course of the current argument.

5. Akrasia is by a philosophers' convention characterized as acting against one's all-things-considered best judgment. If I am right, akratic action is often to be explained by the background awareness that one's all-things-considered best judgment does not have that much to be said for it. For a discussion of the related question of whether incommensurability is *required* in order to make sense of akrasia, see Michael Stocker, *Plural and Conflicting Values* (Oxford: Clarendon Press, 1990).

6. Regret will be most likely in those cases where the satisfactoriness of the chosen option is assessed on the basis of its relative standing vis-à-vis other live options. (If I have not bought the winning lottery ticket, I do not regret it; things are fine as they are now. But if I had *almost* bought the winning lottery ticket, I will probably regret not doing so, and things as they are now may no longer seem fine to me. I am grateful to Ruth Chang for this point.) Incommensurability, by tempting the agent into retrospective reversal of his comparative assessments, will tend to bring the agent—for part of the time, at any rate—to regard his choice as having been regrettable.

7. Barring self-deception, vacillation will rearise when there are alternative ways of viewing the situation corresponding to and perhaps expressive of the competing considerations; here it will take the form of oscillation between the different ways of viewing the choice.

8. The examples are from Joseph Raz, *The Morality of Freedom* (Oxford: Clarendon Press 1986), ch. 13.

9. An interesting variation on this theme concedes that deliberation presupposes commensurability and that ends are incommensurable; commensurability is then advanced as a reform that would make successful deliberation possible across the board. See Martha Craven Nussbaum, *The Fragility of Goodness* (Cambridge: Cambridge University Press, 1986), ch. 4.

10. Kolnai, "Deliberation Is of Ends," pp. 53–54, 57–58.

11. Ibid., p. 58. He has in mind Aristotle's controversial pronouncement at *Nicomachean Ethics* 1112b.

12. These points do not have to be further *ends*, though they might be. Sensual pleasure is not a *further* end, above and beyond eating delicious things.

13. See Henry Jaglom's film *Eating*. Los Angeles: International Rainbow. Produced by Judith Wolinsky.

14. We may stipulate that I am not simply rendering explicit already present but tacit attitudes; the revulsion I feel at the image of myself guiltily reaching into the refrigerator, the focus of my awareness narrowing down to the creamy chocolate icing melting on my palate, allowing me to forget my body . . . all this is a new realization, an attitude I have arrived at in the course of this train of practical reasoning. One way to give force to such a stipulation is to point out that the practical judgments in question depend on conceptual apparatus arrived at in the course of the reasoning: if you do not have the concept *F*, there are attitudes you cannot have toward *F*s. I will not here pursue questions about the normative constraints on the introduction of concepts, and of attitudes involving them, into one's cognitive economy.

    We also need to stipulate that the way in which I now see my desire for the cake is not the upshot of arbitrary choice between two competing ways of seeing the choice situation that are tied to the respective desires. (See n. 7, above.) If I were also to have the realistic option of seeing my desire for a better body as the expression of a degrading and destructive standard of beauty (which would prompt me to celebrate my liberation from the standard by wolfing down the cake), and have no nonarbitrary way of determining which of the two ways of seeing to adopt, my actual choice would be a matter of impulse, self-deception, or something similar to these. I mean to be considering a choice situation in which alternatives of this kind do not pose a problem.

15. There is a number of problems we can bracket here. First, my discovery may be no such thing if, had I chosen the other roommate, I would have ended up thinking the grass greener on *this* side of the fence. But such situations can arise in theoretical reasoning as well, and we do not think they show that one cannot learn from experience; we need merely stipulate that this example is not a case of this kind. Second, one might demand an account of how my experience has supported my conclusion. But there are principled reasons to resist this demand. For one, it is important that one can learn from experience without being able to give an account of how one has done so: often, one *just sees* that *p*, without being able to explain further why one is now justified in asserting *p*.

    Third, philosophers may be inclined to resist my interpretation of the second example. I could not have been learning, from experience, what *matters;* only facts, and not values, can be discovered by observation and experimental reasoning; and so—the objection would run—what we have described must actually have been either the simple acquisition of a new desire, or the discovery that such-and-such circumstances would have the effect of satisfying desires or preferences I already had. I consider these responses elsewhere: Millgram, "Williams' Argument Against External Reasons"; Millgram, "Pleasure in Practical Reasoning," *Monist* 76:3 (1993): 394–415.

16. Although *eudaemonia,* or the well-lived life, is a narrower notion than that of what

matters: one might have the view that what matters does not add up, or even contribute, to a well-lived life.

17. The point here is not that piling up ordinal comparisons is somehow going to produce cardinality (though there are special cases—the well-known von Neumann–Morgenstern construction of utility functions from preferences is one—that could be so described).

18. See Raz, *The Morality of Freedom,* pp. 345–357, for reasons to think that in satisfactory human lives, the perspective grid will remain incomplete.

19. See George Miller, "The Magical Number Seven, Plus or Minus Two: Some Limits on Our Capacity for Processing Information," *Psychological Review* 63 (1956): 81–97.

9. Leading a Life

1. See Amartya Sen and Bernard Williams, eds., *Utilitarianism and Beyond* (Cambridge: Cambridge University Press, 1982).

2. See, for instance, Jürgen Habermas, *Moralbewusstsein und kommunikatives Handeln* (Frankfurt: Suhrkamp, 1983), ch. 4.

3. I am borrowing this term from Bernard Williams's very interesting discussion in *Ethics and the Limits of Philosophy* (London: Fontana, 1985), pp. 182–183.

4. This discussion takes up the terms and the claims laid out in Charles Taylor, *Sources of the Self* (Cambridge: Harvard University Press, 1989), ch. 4.

5. See Immanuel Kant, *Grundlegung zur Metaphysik der Sitten,* in *Kants Werke,* Berlin Academy ed. (Berlin: Walter de Gruyter, 1968), 4:435.

6. See John Rawls, *A Theory of Justice* (Oxford: Oxford University Press, 1971).

7. Richard Wollheim, *The Thread of Life* (Cambridge: Harvard University Press, 1984).

8. I discuss this question further in *Sources of the Self,* chs. 23, 25.

9. See the interesting discussion in Gregory Vlastos, *Socrates* (Cambridge: Cambridge University Press, 1991), which shows how Socrates' supposedly single-minded focus on integrity nevertheless accords a place to other goods.

10. For instance, at 1097a24.

11. One contemporary writer who has very much remembered it, and to whose work I owe a great deal, is Paul Ricoeur. See, in particular, *Soi-Même comme un autre* (Paris: Seuil, 1990), chs. 7–9. My use of the expression "the one and the many" echoes his.

10. Comparing the Incomparable

I am most grateful to Ruth Chang and John Stanton-Ife for their comments on an earlier draft of this paper.

1. James Griffin, *Well-Being* (Oxford: Clarendon Press, 1986), p. 82.

2. Ruth Chang, "Emphatic Comparability and Constitutive Incommensurability, or, Buying and Selling Friends" (unpublished ms.).

3. James Griffin, "Incommensurability: What's the Problem?" (this volume).

4. Joseph Raz, *The Morality of Freedom* (Oxford: Clarendon Press, 1986), p. 322.

5. Chang, "Emphatic Comparability and Constitutive Incommensurability."

6. Elizabeth Anderson, "Practical Reason and Incommensurable Goods" (this volume).

7. Ibid. [draft, p. 21].

8. Raz, *The Morality of Freedom,* pp. 345–357.

9. The example comes from Thomas Schelling, "The Life You Save May Be Your Own," in his *Choice and Consequence: Perspectives of an Errant Economist* (Cambridge: Harvard University Press, 1984), ch. 5.

10. See R. H. Pildes and Elizabeth S. Anderson, "Slinging Arrows at Democracy: Social Choice Theory, Value Pluralism, and Democratic Politics," *Columbia Law Review* 90:8 (1990): 2121–2214.

11. See Anderson, "Practical Reason and Incommensurable Goods." In this paper I shall leave entirely undiscussed the fascinating question of how far our ideals are realized—of how many friendships, for example, match up to our ideal of friendship.

12. See Chang, "Emphatic Comparability and Constitutive Incommensurability." This is not, however, to say that every friendship has an equivalent in money, only that some value relation holds between it and sums of money.

13. Anderson, "Practical Reason and Incommensurable Goods."

14. It may be claimed that comparison need not involve calculation. But I find this claim hard to accept for normal cases. To the extent that it is claimed that if *X* is better than *Y,* there is *some* answer, however imprecise, to the question, "How much better?" I assume that comparison implies calculation.

15. Emile Durkheim, *The Elementary Forms of the Religious Life* (London: Allen and Unwin, 1915), pp. 40–41.

16. I here depart from Durkheim, who defined religion in terms of sacredness, thus speaking (see below) of secular religions. I am using "secular" as the antonym of "religious," not of "sacred."

17. Emile Durkheim, "Individualism and the Intellectuals," trans. S. Lukes and J. Lukes, *Political Studies* 17 (1969): 14–30.

18. Anderson, "Practical Reason and Incommensurable Goods."

19. The most extreme statement of this view I know of is that by Stanley Fish in "Liberalism Does Not Exist," in his *There's No Such Thing as Free Speech and It's a Good Thing Too* (Oxford: Oxford University Press, 1994).

20. For an interesting, and not antiliberal, version of this argument, see Bhikhu Parekh, "Superior People: The Narrowness of Liberalism from Mill to Rawls," *Times Literary Supplement,* February 25, 1994, pp. 11–13.

21. Guido Calabresi and Philip Bobbitt, *Tragic Choices* (New York: Norton, 1978), p. 135.

22. Griffin, *Well-Being,* p. 82.

23. Griffin, "Incommensurability: What's the Problem?" [draft, p. 5].

24. See Schelling, *Choice and Consequence.*

25. That it is a burden is shown in Robert N. Bellah et al., *The Good Society* (New York:

Knopf, 1991), in an interesting interview with a senior regulatory analyst for the U.S. Occupational Safety and Health Administration who "expresses considerable discomfort with the standard economic techniques his agency uses to determine acceptable trade-offs between the often high costs of safe technology and risks to human life" (pp. 27–29).

26. Calabresi and Bobbitt, *Tragic Choices,* p. 180.

27. Ibid., pp. 180–181.

28. Ibid., p. 181.

29. Ibid., p. 178.

30. Ibid., p. 184.

31. Ibid. p. 186. In a footnote, the authors acutely observe that which groups count as "disfavored" is a contingent matter. Why not those who will be killed by collisions with trucks or those who will die of cancer? They suggest that it is arguable that these two groups are the truly least favored in our society. Commenting on Rawls's Difference Principle, they remark that an accurate statement of it "should account for these implicit judgments about which disfavored groups will receive special attention, and how much" (p. 232).

32. Ibid., p. 178.

33. Ibid., p. 184.

34. Ibid., p. 185.

35. Ibid., p. 178.

36. Ibid., pp. 183, 184.

37. Ibid., p. 187.

38. Ibid., pp. 186–189.

39. Ibid., p. 184.

40. For example, "Dealing with small changes in small risks makes the evaluation more casual and takes the pricelessness and pretentiousness out of a potentially awesome choice." Schelling, *Choice and Consequence,* p. 144.

41. See Martin Riesebrodt, *Pious Passion: The Emergence of Modern Fundamentalism in the United States and Iran,* trans. Don Reneau (Berkeley: University of California Press, 1993), in which fundamentalism is described as regulating "all situations and spheres of life": it denies "structural pluralism," and this denial "signifies the united whole fundamentalism sees formed by private life, the family, politics, the economy, justice, and culture through the subordination of all of them to religious law. Society is not differentiated into particular spheres with particular ethics" (pp. 181–182).

11. Abstract and Concrete Value

This work summarizes and extends some of the central claims of my *Plural and Conflicting Values* (Oxford: Oxford University Press, 1990). As well as those thanked there, I want to thank Jonathan Adler and Julia Driver. A version of this paper was presented to the

Incommensurability and Value conference, held in Normandy, France, Spring 1994. My thanks are owed to participants, and especially to the organizers of the conference: John Broome, Ruth Chang, and Maurice Salles.

1. George E. Moore, *Principia Ethica* (Cambridge: Cambridge University Press, 1960).
2. Donald Davidson, "How Is Weakness of the Will Possible?" in Joel Feinberg, ed., *Moral Concepts* (Oxford: Oxford University Press, 1969).
3. R. Jay Wallace, "How to Argue about Practical Reason," *Mind* 99 (1990): 355–385.
4. Bernard Williams, *Problems of the Self* (Cambridge: Cambridge University Press, 1973), p. 179.
5. W. D. Ross, *The Right and the Good* (Oxford: Oxford University Press, 1963), p. 28.
6. See, for example, David Wiggins, "Weakness of the Will, Commensurability, and the Objects of Deliberation and Desire," *Proceedings of the Aristotelian Society* n.s. 79 (1978–1979): 251–277, reprinted in Amelie O. Rorty, ed., *Essays on Aristotle's Ethics* (Berkeley: University of California Press, 1980); Martha Craven Nussbaum, "Plato on Commensurability and Desire," *Proceedings of the Aristotelian Society* (suppl.) 58 (1984): 55–80, and *The Fragility of Goodness* (Cambridge: Cambridge University Press, 1986); Myles Burnyeat, "Aristotle on Learning to be Good," in Rorty, *Essays on Aristotle's Ethics;* Davidson, "How Is Weakness of the Will Possible?" For contrary views, see my "Some Structures for Akrasia," *History of Philosophy Quarterly* 1 (1984): 267–280, "Akrasia and the Object of Desire," in Joel Marks, ed., *The Ways of Desire* (Chicago: Precedent Books, 1986), and *Plural and Conflicting Values;* Frank Jackson, "Davidson on Moral Conflict," in Ernest LePore and Brian McLaughlin, eds., *Truth and Interpretation* (Oxford: Basil Blackwell, 1986).
7. James Fishkin and Thomas Hurka have made this objection. I draw the following arguments from Hurka's "Monism and Rational Regret," *Ethics* 106 (1996): 555–575, a version of which was delivered at the Incommensurability and Value conference. My thanks are owed to Ruth Chang for discussion. Hurka's main explicit target is *Plural and Conflicting Values,* and also Wiggins's and Nussbaum's works, mentioned above; Bernard Williams, "Ethical Consistency," in his *Problems of the Self;* Ronald DeSousa, "The Good and the True," *Mind* 83 (1974): 534–551; Susan Hurley, *Natural Reasons* (New York: Oxford University Press, 1990); John Kekes, *The Morality of Pluralism* (Princeton: Princeton University Press, 1993); and Jonathan Dancy, *Moral Reasons* (Oxford: Blackwell, 1993).
8. Stocker, *Plural and Conflicting Values,* for example, pp. 181–185.
9. Hurka claims that *Plural and Conflicting Values* invokes spurious pluralisms and simply assumes that ontological differences make for evaluative pluralism, and that this is the only "reason" it offers to think that there are plural values. But that work does not argue from ontological plurality to evaluative pluralism: that, quite generally, no two ontologically distinct items—that is, no two items—can have all their evaluative features be of the very same evaluative sort(s). It argues at length and in many different ways against both spurious pluralism and spurious monism (see especially

ch. 7, secs. 4–5) and also for cases and sorts of genuine evaluative pluralism and monism.

10. Hurka often seems to advance this evaluative argument. For example, he claims (p. 563 and sec. 3) both that there is no evaluative difference between benefiting one person and benefiting another—the difference in beneficiary does not make for an evaluative difference—and also that nonetheless it can be rational to regret that the person not benefited was, in fact, not benefited. As I understand this case, however, these different beneficiaries do make for pluralism. On my view, this is why rational regret is possible here. My arguments are found in *Plural and Conflicting Values,* in this work (for example, in the immediately following discussion of the two similar theories), and in my "Review of Thomas Hurka, 'Monism, Pluralism, and Regret',," in James Dreier and David Estlund, eds., *Brown Electronic Review Series,* World Wide Web (www.Brown.edu/Departments/Philosophy/Bears/ homepage.html), posted 9.3.96. I found many claims, but no arguments, to the contrary in Hurka's piece. Taken as making an evaluative claim, I read his article simply as claiming that rational regret does not require plural goods.

This, I think, is standard: two philosophers each think the other simply begs the question. The decision may have to rest with others. If they are inclined to this evaluative reading of Hurka, however, they will see from the outset that it is the evaluative issue, not the ontological one, that must be judged.

11. Joseph Raz, *The Morality of Freedom* (Oxford: Oxford University Press, 1986).

12. See, for example, Frances Kamm, "Non-Consequentialism, the Person as an End-in-Itself, and the Significance of Status," *Philosophy and Public Affairs* 21 (1992): 354–389.

13. On such cases and on the general issue of moderation, see Michael Slote, "Moderation, Rationality, and Virtue," in *The Tanner Lectures on Human Values* (Salt Lake City: University of Utah Press, 1986) vol. 7. My thanks are owed to Slote for our discussion of these matters. See also Richard Routley, *Maximizing, Satisficing, Satisizing: The Difference in Real and Rational Behaviour Under Rival Paradigms,* Discussion Papers in Environmental Philosophy, no. 10 (Canberra, Australia: Philosophy Department, Australian National University, 1984). My thanks are also owed to Laurence Thomas for discussion of this issue.

14. This seems the gravamen of Philip Pettit's criticism of Michael Slote's argument against maximization. See Philip Pettit, "Satisficing Consequentialism," *Proceedings of the Aristotelian Society* (suppl.) 58 (1984): 165–176, and Michael Slote, "Satisficing Consequentialism," *Proceedings of the Aristotelian Society* (suppl.) 58 (1984): 139–164.

15. Aristotle, *Nicomachean Ethics,* translated by W. D. Ross and J. O. Urmson, in Jonathan Barnes, ed., *The Complete Works of Aristotle* (Princeton: Princeton University Press, 1984).

16. Susan Wolf, "Moral Saints," *Journal of Philosophy* 79 (1982): 419–439, and Robert Adams, "Saints," *Journal of Philosophy* 81 (1984): 391–401.

17. My thanks are owed to Russell Hardin for this objection and for discussion of much else in this paper.

18. See my *Plural and Conflicting Values,* ch. 9, esp. sec. 2.

12. Commensuration and Public Reason

1. St. Thomas Aquinas, *Summa Theologiae* I–II q. 90 a.lc (the account concludes, in a.4c, in the definition: "a kind of ordination of reason, directed to the common good, promulgated by the person or body that has responsibility for the community"). The phrase *regula et mensura* translates the phrase *kânon kai metron* used by Aristotle in *Nicomachean Ethics* [hereafter *Nic. Eth.*] III.4: 1114a33, where, however, Aristotle is giving expression to his pervasive thesis that the standard and measure of what is truly noble and pleasant is not so much a proposition (rule) or set of propositions as a person, the good person (the *spoudaios,* the man of maturity and substance), as distinct from the mass of humankind. And see text at n. 31 below.

2. Bentham did envisage that the unit for utilitarian commensurating might have to be money. See the quotations and citations (and helpful discussion of commensuration and incommensurability in general) in Germain Grisez, "Against Consequentialism," *American Journal of Jurisprudence* 23 (1978): 35–36; see also p. 30 for Bentham's confession that "the addibility of happiness of different subjects" is a fiction.

3. See Joseph Boyle, Germain Grisez, and John Finnis, "Incoherence and Consequentialism (or Proportionalism)—A Rejoinder," *American Catholic Philosophical Quarterly* 64 (1990): 271–277. In their surrejoinder, Peter Simpson and Robert McKim, "On the Alleged Incoherence of Consequentialism," *American Catholic Philosophical Quarterly* 66 (1992): 93–98, continue to beg the question by assuming that someone following a merely emotional motive such as selfishness acts for a "rational motive" even though not acting for a good such as might be included in the "calculation of the goods offered by the several alternatives."

4. Richard Posner, *The Problems of Jurisprudence* (Cambridge: Harvard University Press, 1990), pp. 373, 377, finally compromises by arbitrary deference to moral standards that "we," on unexplained grounds, happen to hold.

5. Richard H. Pildes, "Conceptions of Value in Legal Thought," *Michigan Law Review* 90 (1992): 1529; see also Richard H. Pildes and Elizabeth S. Anderson, "Slinging Arrows at Democracy: Social Choice Theory, Value Pluralism, and Democratic Politics," *Columbia Law Review* 90 (1990): 2162–2165.

6. See Immanuel Kant, *Grundlegung zur Metaphysik der Sitten,* p. 442. Page references to Kant's works refer to the standard *Akademie* pagination.

7. See Immanuel Kant, *Die Metaphysik der Sitten: Tugendlehre,* pp. 377, 382.

8. Ibid., p. 377.

9. See the footnote to the title of section III of the general information to the Metaphysics of Morals in Immanuel Kant, *Die Metaphysik der Sitten: Rechtslehre,* p. 218 n.

10. Ibid., pp. 215–216; Kant, *Grundlegung,* pp. 441–444.

11. Kant, *Grundlegung,* pp. 421–423.

12. Kant, *Rechtslehre,* pp. 234–235, 245–246, 250, 317, 348, 365.

13. Kant, *Tugendlehre,* pp. 424, 426, where Kant opines that in human sexual activity, nature's end is procreation.

14. For example, having suggested (against the mainstream of Western philosophical and theological ethics) that sexual intercourse between a sterile couple is contrary to reason ("nature's end"), Kant envisages a countervailing "permissive law of morally practical reason, which in the collision of its determining grounds makes permitted something that is in itself not permitted (indulgently, as it were), in order to prevent a still greater violation." Kant, *Tugendlehre,* p. 426 (in Immanuel Kant, *The Metaphysics of Morals,* trans. Mary Gregor [Cambridge: Cambridge University Press, 1991], pp. 221–222).

15. Joseph Boyle, Germain Grisez, and Olaf Tollefsen, *Free Choice: A Self-Referential Argument* (Notre Dame; University of Notre Dame Press, 1976); Joseph Boyle, John Finnis, and Germain Grisez, *Nuclear Deterrence, Morality and Realism* (Oxford: Oxford University Press, 1987), pp. 256–257.

16. See *Nic. Eth.* VI.4:1140a7.

17. See, e.g., *Nic. Eth.* VI.4:1140a2–23, which also (like I.1:1094a4–6) assimilates *poiêsis* with *technê;* VI.5:1140b3–4; also see *Politics* I.4:1254a8 (*bios praxis, ou poiêsis:* life is doing things, not making things, action not production).

18. In *Metaphysics* IX.6:1048b18–35, Aristotle perhaps gives some clues to the rationale of his famous but difficult teaching (e.g., *Nic. Eth.* VI.2:1139b4) that *praxis* (quite unlike *poiêsis*) is its own end; the point he there makes is that in actions *(praxis)* properly speaking there is no inherent limit, since they have no end beyond themselves the attainment of which would provide for them their terminus. In other words it is the *open-endedness* of action (and thus of life, and of *euzen* [living uprightly and well], and of flourishing) that Aristotle counts as its most decisively characteristic feature.

19. Plato, *Apology,* 32c–d; John Finnis, *Fundamentals of Ethics* (Oxford: Oxford University Press, 1983), pp. 112–120.

20. Plato, *Apology,* 32d. In fact the government of the Thirty was overthrown shortly afterward, and so Socrates was, on that occasion, spared.

21. E.g., Plato, *Crito,* 49c–d.

22. On the "ripples in the pond" problem, and the want of any objective theory of probability, see Finnis, *Fundamentals of Ethics,* pp. 88–89; on the incommensurability of risk with gravity, see Finnis, Boyle, and Grisez, *Nuclear Deterrence, Morality and Realism,* pp. 243–244.

23. See John Finnis, *Natural Law and Natural Rights* (Oxford: Clarendon Press, 1980), pp. 36–42.

24. St. Thomas Aquinas, *Expositio in Libros Aristotelis Ethicorum,* proem.; John Finnis, "Natural Law and Legal Reasoning," in Robert P. George, ed., *Natural Law Theory: Contemporary Essays* (Oxford: Clarendon Press, 1992), pp. 139–140.

25. See Finnis, *Natural Law and Natural Rights,* chs. 3–4; Germain Grisez, James Boyle,

and John Finnis, "First Principles, Moral Truth, and Ultimate Ends," *American Journal of Jurisprudence* 32 (1987): 104–115. A list: (1) *knowledge* (including aesthetic appreciation) of reality; (2) *skillful performance,* in work and play, for its own sake; (3) *bodily life* and the components of its fullness, viz. health, vigor, and safety; (4) *friendship* or harmony and association between persons in its various forms and strengths; (5) the sexual association of a man and a woman which, though it essentially involves both friendship between the partners and the procreation and education of children by them, seems to have a point and shared benefit that is irreducible either to friendship or to life-in-its-transmission and therefore (as comparative anthropology confirms and Aristotle came particularly close to articulating [e.g., *Nic. Eth.* VIII.12: 1162a15–29] not to mention the "third founder" of Stoicism, Musonius Rufus) should be acknowledged to be a distinct basic human good, call it *marriage;* (6) the good of harmony between one's feelings and one's judgments (inner integrity), and between one's judgments and one's behavior (authenticity), which we can call *practical reasonableness;* (7) *harmony with* the widest reaches and most *ultimate source* of all reality, including meaning and value.

26. See also Finnis, Boyle, and Grisez, *Nuclear Deterrence, Morality and Realism,* pp. 281–284; Grisez, Boyle, and Finnis, "Practical Principles, Moral Truth, and Ultimate Ends," pp. 121–129.

27. Kant, *Grundlegung,* pp. 433–434.

28. On the incoherence involved in attempting to maximize, simultaneously, two non-independent variables, see James Griffin, *Well-Being* (Oxford: Oxford University Press, 1986), pp. 151–154. Griffin (p. 151) thinks the formula is "typically" used by utilitarianism's enemies, but the sources he cites (pp. 357–358) scarcely support this, and his own commentary belies it by his final reflection (p. 359) that "many persons . . . will still think that the formula is all right and that our job is to find words to express what we have always really had in mind in using it"—these "many persons" are not enemies of utilitarianism. Griffin's own theory of morality (see, e.g., pp. 155–162, 201–206, 251), though purportedly in the utilitarian tradition, moves a long way toward the open-endedness of integral human fulfillment and the first principle of morality, which I defend. But he sees rational commensurability between forms of good where I would deny it, because the *decisions* whereby we "form" the "basic preferences" with which we "*construct*" a "scale of measurement of well-being" are treated by him (p. 103) as if those decisions were rational *judgments.* I would say: creating a measure is not to be equated with identifying a measure.

29. Why only of *innocent* persons? On the relevance of innocence and the question whether this restriction is justified, see Finnis, Boyle, and Grisez, *Nuclear Deterrence, Morality and Realism,* pp. 309–319.

30. Kant's second/third formulation of his categorical imperative ("treat humanity in oneself and others always as an end and never as a means only": *Grundlegung* p. 429) is another formulation of this specification of morality's master principle. Kant's own interpretation of it is unsatisfactory because his conception of "human-

ity" is too thin, and this because he fails to acknowledge the basic human goods and reasons for action. See Finnis, *Fundamentals of Ethics,* pp. 120–124.

31. See, e.g., Guido Calabresi and A. Douglas Melamed, "Property Rules, Liability Rules, and Inalienability: One View of the Cathedral," *Harvard Law Review* 85 (1972): 1126, n. 71; John Finnis, "Allocating Risks and Suffering: Some Hidden Traps," *Cleveland State Law Review* 38 (1990): 200–206.

32. Aristotle, *Nic. Eth.* III.4:1114a33 (see n. 1 above); Finnis, *Natural Law and Natural Rights,* pp. 102, 129.

33. Of course, this does not seem that it was "indeterminate" in the strong sense of the word which the Critical Legal Studies Movement uses so vaguely and uncritically, that is, indeterminate in the sense of being wholly unguided by reason. See John Finnis, "On 'The Critical Legal Studies Movement,'" *American Journal of Jurisprudence* 30 (1985): 21–42, also in John Eekelaar and John Bell, eds., *Oxford Essays in Jurisprudence: Third Series* (Oxford: Oxford University Press, 1987), pp. 147, 157–161. The good of bodily life and integrity is a genuine reason always practically relevant; and some further rational criteria for decision are provided by facts about human reaction times and susceptibility to impact, and by the rational demand for consistency with our individual and communal tolerance or intolerance of *other—* nontraffic—threats to that good. And though rationally underdetermined, the decision to permit fast-moving traffic, *once made,* provides an often fully determinate rational standard for treating those accused of wrongful conduct of wrongfully inflicting injury. Likewise with trusts, in bankruptcy, and so forth.

34. This commensurability is asserted, in effect, in writings such as Louis Kaplow, "An Economic Analysis of Legal Transitions," *Harvard Law Review* 99 (1986): 509–617; see the discussion in Pildes, "Conceptions of Value in Legal Thought," pp. 1534–1537.

35. *Olmstead* v. *United States* 277 U.S. 438 (1928), at 470 *per* Holmes J. (dissenting), emphases added.

36. John Finnis, "On Reason and Authority in *Law's Empire,*" *Law and Philosophy* 6 (1987): 372–375.

37. See Ronald Dworkin, *Law's Empire* (Cambridge: Belknap Press of Harvard University Press, 1986), pp. 404–407.

38. Pildes and Anderson, "Slinging Arrows at Democracy," pp. 2147–2158.

39. Unlike Dworkin's trumping rights, which are not inviolable but can be overridden in "emergency": *Taking Rights Seriously* (Cambridge: Harvard University Press, 1978), p. 354.

40. The obligations of friendship, speaking generally, are not very strong; the relation one has with friends is really a kind of instance of the relations one ought to have with every "neighbor" and is subject to virtually all one's other responsibilities. It is different if the friendship is specified to *marriage;* here there are unconditional rights and obligation.

41. See John Finnis, "The Authority of Law in the Predicament of Contemporary Social Theory," *Journal of Law, Ethics and Public Policy* 1 (1984): 115–137; John Finnis,

"On Positivism and the Foundations of Legal Authority," in Ruth Gavison, ed., *Issues in Contemporary Legal Philosophy: The Influence of H. L. A. Hart* (Oxford: Oxford University Press, 1986), pp. 62–75; John Finnis, "Law as Coordination," *Ratio Iuris* 2 (1989): 97–104.

42. For the spectacular misunderstandings that occur when game theory's "rational choice" jargon is transferred to ethical or other third-order discussions, see John Finnis, "Concluding Reflections," *Cleveland State Law Review* 38 (1990): pp. 235–237.

13. Incommensurability and Kinds of Valuation

Some of the issues discussed here are dealt with in much more detail in Cass R. Sunstein, "Incommensurability and Valuation in Law," *Michigan Law Review* 92:4 (1994): 779–861.

1. I owe much help in the discussion here to Elizabeth Anderson, *Value in Ethics and Economics* (Cambridge: Harvard University Press, 1993); Anderson uses the term "modes of valuation" to express the same idea.
2. See ibid.
3. The point is interestingly missed in an astonishing article, J. Waldfogel, "The Deadweight Loss of Christmas," *American Economic Review* 83:5 (1993): 1328–1336, which finds four billion dollars in annual deadweight losses from noncash gifts and assumes that cash gifts are more efficient and therefore preferable.
4. The two are distinguished in Michael Stocker, *Plural and Conflicting Values* (Oxford: Oxford University Press, 1990), pp. 175–178; Charles Larmore, "Pluralism and Reasonable Disagreement," *Social Philosophy and Policy* 11:1 (1994): 67–69.
5. Joseph Raz, *The Morality of Freedom* (Oxford: Clarendon Press, 1986), ch. 13.
6. Ibid., pp. 334, n. 1.
7. See the instructive discussion in T. K. Seung and Daniel Bonevac, "Plural Values and Indeterminate Rankings," *Ethics* 102:4 (1992): 799–813; see also James Griffin, *Well-Being* (Oxford: Clarendon Press, 1986).
8. See Joseph Raz, "Incommensurability and Agency" (this volume).
9. See Anderson, *Value in Ethics and Economics;* Elizabeth Anderson, "Practical Reason and Incommensurable Goods" (this volume); Cass R. Sunstein, "On the Expressive Function of Law," *University of Pennsylvania Law Review* 144:5 (1996): 2021–2053.
10. See Raz, *The Morality of Freedom*, p. 327.
11. This is the understanding in Richard Warner, "Incommensurability as a Jurisprudential Puzzle," *Chicago-Kent Law Review* 68 (1992): 147–170. See also the discussion of constitutive incommensurabilities in Raz, *The Morality of Freedom*, pp. 345–353, and of exclusionary reasons in Joseph Raz, *Practical Reason and Norms*, 2d ed. (Princeton: Princeton University Press, 1990).
12. See Raz, *The Morality of Freedom*, p. 354.
13. Donald Regan, "Authority and Value," *Southern California Law Review* 62 (1989): 1058.

14. Ruth Chang, "Emphatic Comparability and Constitutive Incommensurability, or, Buying and Selling Friends" (unpublished ms.).

15. See generally Sunstein, "Incommensurability and Valuation in Law." I am indebted here to Anderson, *Value in Ethics and Economics,* and Richard H. Pildes and Elizabeth Anderson, "Slinging Arrows at Democracy: Social Choice Theory, Value Pluralism, and Democratic Politics," *Columbia University Law Review* 90 (1990): 2121–2214.

16. Bernard Williams, "A Critique of Utilitarianism," in J. J. C. Smart and Bernard Williams, *Utilitarianism: For and Against* (London: Cambridge University Press, 1973).

17. Michael Walzer, *Spheres of Justice* (New York: Basic Books, 1983).

18. See Susan Moller Okin, *Justice, Gender and the Family* (New York: Basic Books, 1989); Jean Hampton, "Feminist Contractarianism," in Louise M. Antony and Charlotte Witt, eds., *A Mind of One's Own* (Boulder, Colo.: Westview, 1993), pp. 227–255.

19. Oliver Wendell Holmes, *The Common Law* (Boston: Little, Brown, 1881), p. 3.

20. Quoted in Bernard Nossiter, "The FCC's Big Giveaway Show," *The Nation,* October 26, 1985.

21. Robert Cameron Mitchell and Richard T. Carson, *Using Surveys to Value Public Goods* (Washington, D.C.: Resources for the Future, 1989), p. 34. "These extreme responses reflect the feelings of outrage often seen when communities are faced with the prospect of accepting a new risk such as a nuclear power plant or waste disposal facility." Daniel Kahneman, Jack Knetsch, and Richard Thaler, "Anomalies—The Endowment Effect, *Perspectives* 5:1 (1991): 203.

22. See Rebecca Boyce et al., "An Experimental Examination of Intrinsic Values as a Source of the WTA-WTP Disparity," *American Economic Review* 82:5 (1992): 1366–1373.

23. Guido Calabresi and A. Douglas Melamed, "Property Rules, Liability Rules and Inalienability: One View of the Cathedral," *Harvard Law Review* 85 (1972): 1089–1128.

24. *Ohio v. DOI,* 880 F.2d 432 (D.C. Cir. 1989).

25. See Richard Posner, *Sex and Reason* (Cambridge: Harvard University Press, 1992).

26. See Cass R. Sunstein, "Incompletely Theorized Agreements," *Harvard Law Review* 108 (1995): 1733–1772, and *Legal Reasoning and Political Conflict* (New York: Oxford University Press, 1996).

27. This is a challenge to the Hercules metaphor; see Ronald Dworkin, *Law's Empire* (Cambridge: Belknap Press of Harvard University Press, 1985), on the ground that Hercules is too sectarian; but it is not a challenge to the claim that there are right answers in law. For discussion, see Cass R. Sunstein, "On Analogical Reasoning," *Harvard Law Review* 106 (1993): 741–791, and *Legal Reasoning and Political Conflict.* Of course, there are nonanalogical approaches that insist on the plurality of goods.

Contributors

Elizabeth Anderson is Associate Professor and Arthur F. Thurnau Professor of Philosophy and Women's Studies at the University of Michigan, Ann Arbor.

John Broome is Professor of Philosophy at the University of St. Andrews.

Ruth Chang is Assistant Professor of Philosophy and Law at Rutgers University.

John Finnis is Professor of Law and Legal Philosophy at the University of Oxford, Fellow and Praelector of University College, Oxford, and Biolchini Professor of Law at the University of Notre Dame.

James Griffin is White's Professor of Moral Philosophy at the University of Oxford and Fellow of Corpus Christi College, Oxford.

Steven Lukes is Professor of Moral Philosophy at the University of Siena, Italy.

Elijah Millgram is Associate Professor of Philosophy at Vanderbilt University.

Joseph Raz is Professor of the Philosophy of Law at the University of Oxford, Fellow of Balliol College, Oxford, and Visiting Professor of Law at Columbia University.

Donald Regan is William W. Bishop, Jr., Collegiate Professor of Law and Professor of Philosophy at the University of Michigan, Ann Arbor.

Michael Stocker is Guttag Professor of Ethics and Political Philosophy at Syracuse University.

Cass R. Sunstein is Karl N. Llewellyn Distinguished Service Professor of Jurisprudence of the Law School and the Department of Political Science at the University of Chicago.

Charles Taylor is Professor of Philosophy at McGill University.

David Wiggins is Wykeham Professor of Logic and Metaphysics at the University of Oxford and Fellow of New College, Oxford.

Index

This index follows the use of the terms "incommensurability" and "incomparability" as outlined in the editor's Introduction. Page references to material relating to incomparability where the author uses the term "incommensurability" are given in italics.

Hart, H. L. A., 255n3
Herman, Barbara, 269n2, 272n25
Holmes, Oliver Wendell, 229, 247
Hume, David, 216, 223
Hurka, Thomas, 4–5, 130, 259n31,
  260n39, 276n3, 277n20, 283n7,
  283–284n9, 284n10
Hurley, Susan, 261n43, 283n7

Importance, 174–175, 183; different notions of, 173; utilitarian notion of,
  174; Kantian notion of, 174;
  Nietzschean notion of, 175; articulation of judgments of, 178–181, 182–
  183. *See also* Goods
Imprecise equality, 4–5. *See also* Equality;
  Fourth relation; Parity; Rough equality
Incommensurability: defined, 1, 35–36,
  52–53, 54–55, 58–60, 63–64,
  238–239; mathematical, 1, 52–53,
  203, 255n1; Kuhnian, 1, 39;
  distinguished from incomparability,
  1–2, 35, 37, 203, 240; significance
  of, 2, 3, 53–54; weakness of, 2–3,
  239; relevance to law, 216–217, 234,
  243–244, 248–254; as due to
  openendedness, 221–222; of fit and
  soundness, 230–231; constitutive,
  232; hierarchical, 232
Incommensurateness, 273n1. *See also*
  Incommensurability; Incomparability
Incomparabilist arguments, 2–3, 13–28,
  136–138; from vagueness, 5–6,
  22–23, 88–89, 136–137; as
  arguments for fourth relation, 13–15,
  21–22, 22–24, 25–26, 261n44; from
  diversity of values, 14–17; from
  bidirectionality, 16–18; from
  noncalculative deliberation, 17–20;
  from constitution or norms, 19–21;
  from rational irresolvability of
  conflict, 20–22; from multiplicity of

rankings, 21–24; from relevance of
  small improvements, 23–26, 261n44
Incomparability: defined, 1, 3–4, 6, *90,
  98, 151, 159, 184, 185;* distinguished
  from incommensurability, 1–2, 8–9,
  35, 37, 203, 240; importance of, 2–3,
  8–10; and practical reason, 2–3,
  7–10, 13–14, 36, *90–91,* 138–139,
  151–152, *164;* relation of to
  Trichotomy Thesis, 4–5, 6, *91,* 110,
  151, 223; determinate versus
  indeterminate, 5; necessarily relative to
  values, 6–7, 14–15, 27–28, *98;* with
  respect to intrinsic merits, 7; and value
  pluralism, 14–16, 203–204; as
  absence of evaluative differences,
  26–27; diamond model of, 26–28;
  distinguished from noncomparability,
  27–28, 29–30; noncomparability
  neutral as to, 29; and indifference,
  38–39, 130–131; prudential, *40;*
  source of, 49; and indeterminateness,
  88–89; pragmatic theories of value
  on, *98–103;* "no good reasons"
  principle for, *99, 100,* 260n37;
  hierarchical, *104–105, 186;*
  presupposed by agency, *110–111;* and
  conceptions of agency, *111–113, 127;*
  and intelligibility of choice, *113,*
  130–131, 144–150; whether easy to
  identify, 137–138, 138–139;
  instrumentalist model of practical
  reasoning on, 154–155, *156–157,
  157–158;* cross-cultural, 170; as
  meaninglessness of comparison, *185;*
  as pointlessness of comparison, *185;*
  as inappropriateness of comparison,
  185, 195. See also Incomparabilist
  arguments
Incompatibility, 35–36, 37–38, 39–40,
  184
Indeterminacy: of truth value, 28–29,